Contributions To Global Historical Archaeology

Series Editor:

Charles E. Orser Jr.
The University of Western Ontario
London, ON, Canada

Vanderbilt University
Nashville, TN, USA

More information about this series at http://www.springer.com/series/5734

Tim Murray • Penny Crook

Exploring the Archaeology of the Modern City in Nineteenth-century Australia

 Springer

Tim Murray
College of Arts, Social Sciences and
Commerce
La Trobe University
Melbourne, VIC, Australia

Penny Crook
Department of Archaeology and History
La Trobe University
Melbourne, VIC, Australia

ISSN 1574-0439
Contributions To Global Historical Archaeology
ISBN 978-3-030-27168-8   ISBN 978-3-030-27169-5   (eBook)
https://doi.org/10.1007/978-3-030-27169-5

This Springer imprint is published by the registered company Springer Nature Switzerland AG
The registered company address is: Gewerbestrasse 11, 6330 Cham, Switzerland

To all the extraordinary people who lived on The Rocks and the Commonwealth Block and left behind their stuff. May we continue to tell their stories for the years to come.

Contents

1 Preface and Introduction 1
  The Structure of the Book 2
  Acknowledgements 3
  References 4

**2 Exploring the Archaeology of the Modern City:
Melbourne and Sydney Compared** 7
  Managing Data to Promote Comparison 11
    The EAMC Archaeology Database 12
    People + Place 13
  Transnational Comparisons 14
  Back to the Modern City 16
  References 16

3 Transnational Archaeologies: Colonial and Postcolonial 21
  Transnational Archaeologies 24
  Archaeologies of the Modern City 25
  References 27

4 Immigration to Australia: 1820–1900 31
  Coming to Australia 35
  The Hyde Park Barracks 39
  References 43

5 Archaeology at First Government House, Sydney 47
  The Excavation 48
  The EAMC Approach at First Government House 49
  The First Government House 51
    Who Made the Archaeological Record at FGH? 53
  Building First Government House: 1788 54

Living Ruins: Decay, Extension and Repair of the First
Government House   56
  Supersession: The Demolition of First Government House,
  1845–1846.   57
  At the Governor's Table   60
Governor King's Spode.   61
The Tendril Pattern: Fine Dining and the Macquaries   66
The Governor's Guardhouse.   68
The Establishment of the Governor's Guard.   69
Inside the Guard House.   72
A Passage Through the Guard House: Truncation, 1838   73
Discussion.   76
References.   77

6   **Global Material Culture in the Modern City**   81
    Human-Made, Machine-Made   82
    Retail Empires: Supplying the Colonial Markets   85
    Travelling Light: Sea Chests and Essential Chattels.   87
    Implications for Historical Archaeology.   89
    Concluding Remarks.   90
    References.   91

7   **Sanitary Reform and Comparative Assemblage**
    Analysis: Methodology   95
    Introduction.   95
    Sydney: A Young Colonial City   96
      The 1857 Sewerage Scheme   98
    Melbourne.   101
    Cesspit Fill as an Archaeological Resource   102
    Household Links.   102
    Comparative Assemblage Analysis: Contrasting Households   104
    The EAMC Approach.   105
    References.   107

8   **The Cumberland and Gloucester Streets Site,**
    The Rocks, Sydney   111
    Introduction.   111
    The 'Big Dig': The Cumberland and Gloucester Streets Site.   111
      The Excavation   114
    Introduction to the Study Group.   114
    1 Carahers Lane (c. 1848–1902).   116
      The Cesspit Fill (MC B197)   117
      The Occupants   118
    3 Carahers Lane (c. 1848–1902).   121
      The Cesspit Fill (MC B077)   122
      The Occupants   123

5 Carahers Lane (c. 1856–1902).   125
 The Cesspit Fill (MC B294)   125
 The Occupants   126
122 Cumberland Street (c. 1833–1891)   128
 The Cesspit Fill (MC A138)   128
 The Occupants   130
124 Cumberland Street (c. 1833–c. 1907)   133
 The Cesspit Fill (MC A310)   134
 The Occupants   138
126 Cumberland Street (c. 1833–c. 1907)   140
 The Cesspit Fill (MC A140)   141
 The Occupants   142
93 Gloucester Street (c. 1822–1891)   143
 The Cistern–Cesspit Fill (MC F044)   144
 The Occupants   145
97 Gloucester Street (c. 1817–c. 1907).   147
 The Cesspit Fills (MCs C056 and C220)   149
 First Cesspit: Southwest Yard (MC C220)   149
 Second Cesspit: Northwest Yard (MC C056)   150
 The Occupants   151
101 Gloucester Street (1822–c. 1907)   154
 The Cesspit Fill (MC C130)   154
 The Occupants   155
References.   157

9   The Commonwealth Block in Melbourne.   161
A Brief History of Excavation   162
 Little Lon (1998).   163
 Black Eagle and Oddfellows Hotels (1990)   164
 17 Casselden Place (1995)   164
 Casselden Place Phase 3 Testing (2001).   164
 Casselden Place (2002–2003).   164
 271 Spring Street (2017).   166
A Brief History of Analysis   166
Commonwealth Block Stories   169
Introduction to the Study Group.   170
 Lot 25C, Leichhardt Street (1851–1920)   171
 143 Lonsdale Street (1847–1918) (Lot 30).   173
 147 Lonsdale Street (1849–1950) (Lot 33B)   176
 Lot 36A, Little Leichardt Street (1851–1898)   179
 147 Spring Street (1849–1918) (Lot 55A)   181
 255 Spring Street (1849–1918) (Lots 57A and B)   181
 7 Casselden Place (1851–1909) (Lot 69)   185
 128 Little Lonsdale Street (1850–1910) (Lot 84A)   186
 Off 73 Little Lonsdale Street (1847–1918) (Lots 90A and B)   189

Concluding Remarks.   191
   Madam Diana De Beaumont aka Madame Diane
   de Beaumont-Beaumbac: Owner of Lots 26 and 27,
   Leichardt Street.   192
   Mary and George Williams: Tenants of Lot 26,
   Leichhardt Street (1871–1876)   193
   William Hinds: Owner of Lot 84A, Little Lonsdale
   (1853–1895)   193
References.   194

10 Domestic Consumption: Patterns and Comparisons.   197
   Overview of the Selected Deposits: A Basis for Comparison   197
      Integrity.   204
      Dating   204
      Deposition Events.   209
   Overview of the Residents   210
      Sydney.   218
      Melbourne.   218
   Comparative Analysis   219
      Tablewares.   219
      Teawares   235
      Moralizing and Educational China.   240
      Home Décor   241
      Drinking, Alcohol and Soda Bottles   245
   Life After Bankruptcy: The Doyle Family – A Case Study   249
   References.   254

11 Local and Global Lessons from 20 Cesspits from Australia   257
   Comparison and Comparability: Some Challenges
   for Further Research   259
   In Search of Integration: Sorting Signals from Noise.   262
   Concluding Remarks.   263
   References.   266

Appendix 1: List of Matching Sets   269

Index.   285

About the Authors

Tim Murray is Charles La Trobe Professor of Archaeology at La Trobe University. As a practicing archaeologist with an interest in history and epistemology, his research and publication have focused on the history and philosophy of archaeology, the archaeology of the modern world and heritage archaeology. His most recent books include *World Antiquarianism: Comparative Perspectives* (co-edited with Alain Schnapp, Lothar von Falkenhausen and Peter Miller, Getty Research Institute, 2013), *An Archaeology of Institutional Confinement: The Hyde Park Barracks, 1848–1886* (co-authored with Peter Davies and Penny Crook, Sydney University Press, 2013), *From Antiquarian to Archaeologist: The History and Philosophy of Archaeology* (Pen and Sword Press, 2014) and *The Commonwealth Block, Melbourne: A Historical Archaeology* (co-authored with Kristal Buckley, Sarah Hayes, Geoff Hewitt, Justin McCarthy, Richard Mackay, Barbara Minchinton, Charlotte Smith, Jeremy Smith and Bronwyn Woff, Sydney University Press 2019). His current projects are based around the general theme of transnational archaeologies in the long nineteenth century, with particular focus on 'contact' archaeology, urban archaeology and technology transfer, demonstrating the importance of the history of archaeology for building more robust archaeological theory.

Penny Crook is a Research Fellow at La Trobe University. She is a historical archaeologist and specialist in the analysis of nineteenth-century material culture in Australia and the United Kingdom. Her most recent book is *An Archaeology of Institutional Confinement: The Hyde Park Barracks, 1848–1886* (co-authored with Peter Davies and Tim Murray, Sydney University Press, 2013).

Chapter 1
Preface and Introduction

This book draws together a selection of findings of nearly 20 years of research by the authors into the historical archaeologies of early Sydney and Melbourne, Australia (see Murray 2013). Specifically it reports research from two major projects. The first is the Sydney-based *Exploring the Archaeology of the Modern City* project (EAMC) which was established in 2001 by Murray and several industry partners, to analyse and interpret the large assemblages excavated from historical archaeological sites which are held in storehouses across Sydney. Funding for the project was provided by the Australian Research Council (ARC) through its SPIRT (Strategic Partnerships Industry – Research and Training Scheme [C00002438]), from the then Historic Houses Trust of NSW, and the ARC grant under its Linkage Scheme (an industry programme that succeeded SPIRT) to support follow-up work at the Hyde Park Barracks (LP 08822081). The second is the Melbourne-based research into the archaeology of the Casselden Place site (popularly known as 'Little Lon' but also the Commonwealth Block) which began before the Sydney project and continues. Unlike the EAMC, our work in Melbourne has received significant support from private developer funding alongside a series of grants from the Australian Research Council (DP 1093001, LP 098224) and has involved the input of a significant group of historians, heritage archaeologists and managers, museum staff, undergraduate and postgraduate students, research assistants as well as a post-doctoral fellow.

The core of this book – and the end game of these efforts – is the analysis of a sample of the large archaeological collections from the Cumberland and Gloucester Streets site, in The Rocks area of Sydney, and from the Commonwealth Block in Melbourne. Given the scale of the artefact assemblages and the complexities of the sites involved, we can only briefly explore a sample of the archaeological collections from both sites as a basis for addressing the potential of comparison with the assemblages from similar sites to contribute to the goals of the overall project. Both sites have been (and will continue to be) reported separately (see, e.g. Crook et al. 2005; Godden Mackay Heritage Consultants 1999; Murray 2005, 2006; Murray and Mayne 2001, 2002, 2003; Murray et al. 2019).

© Springer Nature Switzerland AG 2019
T. Murray, P. Crook, *Exploring the Archaeology of the Modern City
in Nineteenth-century Australia*, Contributions To Global Historical
Archaeology, https://doi.org/10.1007/978-3-030-27169-5_1

In this new work, we build on these original reports by drawing together, updating and contextualising work published elsewhere to materially advance our agendum of global comparison among urban sites from the nineteenth century. In essence this book is another step on a long journey that reflects some of what we have learned over the past 20 years and much more about what remains to be done. In doing this we have revised (and indeed changed and corrected) some of our original conclusions and the theoretical precepts and empirical information they derived from. Our thinking about these matters has benefitted greatly from urban archaeologies produced in North America, Northern Europe and elsewhere in Australia (see, e.g. Birmingham 1990; Brighton 2009; Casey and Lowe 2000; Frost and O'Hanlon 2009; Jeffries et al. 2009; Karskens 1999; Mehler 2013a, b; Mullins and Warner 2008; Mullins et al. 2013; Praetzellis and Praetzellis 2004; Owens and Jeffries 2016; Proudfoot et al. 1991; Richard 2011; Rimmer et al. 2011; Rothschild and Wall 2014; Wall 1992; Yamin 2000), but we have also been the beneficiaries of recent research into the archaeologies of diasporas and of migration and ethnogenesis that have become so important to the interpretation of major social processes in the nineteenth and twentieth centuries on a global scale.

As a result we hope that we now more clearly understand the complex business of writing about the archaeology of cities created during the nineteenth century (and the myriad issues this entails) and some of the important causes and consequences of their growth and the even greater complexities of writing about both. Importantly we still have much work to do exploring the myriad connections between artefacts, archaeological contexts and the people who lived in those places.

The Structure of the Book

Given the fact that this book reports work that has evolved over the past 20 years, and which continues, in Chap. 2 we briefly chart that evolution, and in Chap. 3 we give a somewhat fuller account of our current approach to understanding the forces that have created the modern city in Australia (and elsewhere) and the broader social and cultural contexts within which such cities lie. In Chap. 4 we continue this discussion through an account of migration to Australia during the nineteenth century, with a worked example of the Hyde Park Barracks in Sydney focusing on the period when it was a facility for housing migrant women from Britain and Ireland. One of the distinguishing features of our research has been (in Sydney especially) is a sustained engagement with previously excavated assemblages from major sites such as First Government House and the Hyde Park Barracks. In Chap. 5 we present our interpretation of this reanalysis of the assemblage from the First Government House site, the foundation exemplar of colonial government in Australia. This is followed in Chap. 6 by a broad discussion of material culture in the modern city and in Chap. 7 the specifics of comparative assemblage analysis and sanitary reform in Sydney and Melbourne. Chapters 8 and 9 present the background data for the analysis of cesspit deposits from the Cumberland and Gloucester Streets site in Sydney and the

Commonwealth Block in Melbourne which is presented in Chap. 10. Here we compare those data with a focus on reporting insights into domestic lives in Sydney and Melbourne. Chapter 11, which concludes the volume, extends this discussion into a broader consideration of the contribution these new data might make to our understanding of the archaeology of the modern city in Australia and elsewhere. Chapter 12 comprises an appendix reporting data about matching sets among the assemblages.

Acknowledgements

We thank the Australian Research Council for long-term funding and support of our research in Sydney and Melbourne. We also gratefully acknowledge the support of our industry partners the Sydney Harbour Foreshore Authority (now Property NSW), the Council of the City of Sydney, the then Historic Houses Trust of NSW (now Sydney's Living Museums) and GML Pty Ltd. Our association with the last two organisations has been continuing over the entire course of our research, and we are particularly grateful for the insight and enthusiasm of Helen Temple and Richard Mackay in their early support of our work.

Penny Crook acted as Project Archaeologist and Laila Ellmoos as Project Historian for the EAMC. Crook was assisted by Sophie Pullar who catalogued artefacts at the Hyde Park Barracks, along with several volunteers who assisted with photography throughout the project. Peter Davies acted as post-doctoral research fellow on the subsequent work at the Barracks (see Davies et al. 2013). None of this work would have been possible without the aid of hardworking curators and collections managers: Michael Bogle, Samantha Fabry, Bridget Berry, John Peterson, Gary Crocket, Fiona Starr and Wayne Johnson.

Murray gratefully acknowledges the Getty Research Institute for the award of a Fellowship at the Getty Centre, Los Angeles, in the last quarter of 2017. This provided a wonderful environment in which to progress revisions to an earlier version of our manuscript.

Projects as long and as complex as these require the combined efforts of literally hundreds of people from site archaeologists and their staffs through professional staff in museums and heritage agencies. Restrictions of space preclude a complete list of such personnel, but the great contribution of the following is particularly acknowledged.

We have been fortunate to have the collaboration of Professor Alan Mayne particularly at the 'Little Lon'/Casselden Place site but also as a guide through the complexities of urban history, especially the histories of what have been termed slums. Alan's thinking about the issues of making deeper meanings about the histories of such places and the lives of people so frequently lost to history has been inspirational and a major spur to undertaking archaeological research that could come closer to matching the richness of historical research.

Historians Laila Ellmoos, Kasia Zygmuntowicz and Barbara Minchinton provided a wealth of documentary evidence to contextualise our analyses of the assemblages from the Commonwealth Block and The Rocks. This book presents only a small sample of the fantastic wealth of stories about the people who inhabited both locales (often including images of people and places). We anticipate that future publications will make more of this wonderful resource available to a wider audience. Grace Karskens made an important contribution to our understanding of the history of The Rocks and of Sydney more generally.

Archaeologists Christine Williamson, Sarah Hayes, Paul Pepdjonovic and Bronwyn Woff undertook the analysis of the large assemblages that were the core of the Melbourne project. Penny Crook oversaw the development of the database and its frequent consolidation.

Charlotte Smith and her associates at the Museum of Victoria were towers of strength in managing the vast collections from the Commonwealth Block and other key Melbourne sites. Charlotte transformed into a significant collaborator when she provided institutional support to our early work on the management of the large databases we were generating and underscoring the importance of such work for the proper management of archaeological collections.

Wei Ming performed his usual magic in the creation of maps and plans (alongside Penny Crook).

Christine Williamson kindly reviewed an early draft of this manuscript, and we are grateful for her comments and input.

Last, we thank our long-suffering editors at Springer, Chuck Orser, Teresa Kraus, Joseph Quatela, Christi Lue and Sowmya Thodur for their much-tried patience.

References

Unpublished

Casey and Lowe Associates. 2000. *Archaeological Investigation: CSR Site, Pyrmont (Jacksons Landing)*. Unpublished report prepared for Lend Lease Development, 3 vols, December 2000.
Godden Mackay Heritage Consultants. 1999. *The Cumberland/Gloucester Streets Site, The Rocks: Archaeological Investigation Report*, Volumes 1, 3–5, prepared for the Sydney Cove Authority. Sydney: Godden Mackay Logan Pty Ltd.

Published

Birmingham, J. 1990. A Decade of Digging: Deconstructing Urban Archaeology. *Australian Historical Archaeology* 8: 13–22.
Brighton, S.A. 2009. *Historical Archaeology of the Irish Diaspora: A Transnational Approach*. Knoxville: University of Tennessee Press.
Crook, P., L. Ellmoos, and T. Murray. 2005. *Keeping up with the McNamaras: A Historical Archaeological Study of the Cumberland and Gloucester Streets Site, The Rocks, Sydney*. Sydney: Historic Houses Trust of NSW.
Davies, P., P. Crook, and T. Murray. 2013. *Archaeological Research at Hyde Park Barracks, Sydney*. Sydney: Australasian Society of Historical Archaeology.

Frost, L., and S. O'Hanlon. 2009. Urban history and the future of Australian cities. *Australian Economic History Review* 49 (1): 1. https://doi.org/10.1111/j.1467-8446.2008.00246.x.

Karskens, G. 1999. *Inside The Rocks, The Archaeology of a Neighbourhood.* Alexandria, NSW: Hale and Iremonger.

Jeffries, N., A. Owens, D. Hicks, R. Featherby, and K. Wehner. 2009. Rematerialising Metropolitan Histories? People, Places and Things in Modern London. In *Crossing Paths or Sharing Tracks? Future Directions in the Archaeological Study of Post-1550 Britain and Ireland*, ed. A. Horning and M. Palmer, 323–350. Woodbridge: Boydell Press.

Mehler, N. 2013a. Globalization, Immigration, and Transformation: Thoughts from a European Perspective. *Historical Archaeology* 47: 38–49.

———., ed. 2013b. *Historical Archaeology in Central Europe.* Special Publication Series (Society for Historical Archaeology). Rockville, MD: [Columbus, OH]: Society for Historical Archaeology; PAST Foundation.

Mullins, P., and M.S. Warner, eds. 2008. Living in Cities revisited: Trends in Nineteenth and Twentieth Century Urban Archaeology. *Historical Archaeology* 42 (1): 1–137.

Mullins, P., T. Ylimaunu, A. Brooks, T. Kallio-Seppä, M. Kuorilehto, R. Nurmi, T. Oikarinen, V.-P. Herva, and J. Symonds. 2013. British Ceramics on the Northern European Periphery: Creamware Marketing in Nineteenth Century Northern Finland. *International Journal of Historical Archaeology* 17 (4): 632–665.

Murray, T. 2005. Images of 'Little Lon': Making History, Changing Perceptions. In *Object Lessons: Archaeology and Heritage in Australia*, ed. J. Lydon and T. Ireland, 167–185. Melbourne: Australian Scholarly Press.

———. 2006. Integrating Archaeology and History at the 'Commonwealth Block': 'Little Lon' and Casselden Place. *International Journal of Historical Archaeology* 10 (4): 395–413.

———. 2013. Expanding Horizons in the Archaeology of the Modern City: A Tale in Six Projects. *Journal of Urban History* 39 (5): 848–863. https://doi.org/10.1177/0096144213479308.

Murray, T., and A. Mayne. 2001. Imaginary Landscapes: Reading Melbourne's 'Little Lon. In *The Archaeology of Urban Landscapes: Explorations in Slumland*, ed. A. Mayne and T. Murray, 89–105. Cambridge: Cambridge University Press.

———. 2002. *Vanished Communities: Investigating History at 'Little Lon', An ARC Funded CDROM.* Melbourne: La Trobe University and Swish Group.

———. 2003. (Re)Constructing a Lost Community: Little Lon: Melbourne, Australia. *Historical Archaeology* 37 (1): 87–101.

Murray, T., K. Buckley, S. Hayes, G. Hewitt, J. McCarthy, R. Mackay, B. Minchinton, C. Smith, J. Smith, and B. Woff. 2019. *The Commonwealth Block, Melbourne: A Historical Archaeology.* Sydney: Australasian Society for Historical Archaeology and Sydney University Press.

Owens, A., and N. Jeffries. 2016. People and Things on the Move: Domestic Material Culture, Poverty and Mobility in Victorian London. *International Journal of Historical Archaeology* 20: 804–827.

Praetzellis, M., and A. Praetzellis, eds. 2004. *Putting the 'There' There: Historical Archaeologies of West Oakland, 1-880 Cypress Freeway Replacement Project.* California: Anthropological Studies Center, Sonoma State University.

Proudfoot, H., A. Bickford, B. Egloff, and R. Stocks. 1991. *Australia's First Government House.* Sydney: Allen & Unwin and the Department of Planning.

Richard, F.G. 2011. Materializing Poverty: Archaeological Reflections from the Post Colony. *Historical Archaeology* 45 (3): 166–182.

Rimmer, J., P. Connelly, S. Rees Jones, and J. Walker. 2011. Special Collection: Poverty in Depth: New International Perspectives. *International Journal of Historical Archaeology* 15: 533–636.

Rothschild, N., and D. Wall. 2014. *The Archaeology of American Cities.* Gainesville: University of Florida Press.

Wall, D. 1992. Sacred Dinners and Secular Teas: Constructing Domesticity in Mid-19th-Century New York. *Historical Archaeology* 25: 69–81.

Yamin, R., ed. 2000. Tales of Five Points: Working-Class Life in Nineteenth-Century New York. *Reports prepared for Edwards and Kelcey Engineers, Inc. and General Services Administration (Region 2)*, 6 vols. West Chester, Pennsylvania: John Milner Associates.

Chapter 2
Exploring the Archaeology of the Modern City: Melbourne and Sydney Compared

Over 20 years ago, historian Alan Mayne and archaeologist Tim Murray became interested in finding a way in which they could tell the stories that were locked up in the thousands of boxes of artefacts derived from the excavation of a major urban site (Little Lon, also known as the Commonwealth Block and Casselden Place) in Melbourne, Australia. Following the work of archaeologists at The Rocks in Sydney (as well as earlier work in New York City and in San Francisco), they believed that the best way forward was to work towards models integrating archaeological and other historical data in ways that did not sacrifice the integrity of either. It has proved to be a lot more challenging than they thought (Lydon 1995, 1999; Karskens 1994, 1997a, b, 1999, 2000, 2001, 2003, 2006; Karskens and Thorp 1992; Mayne and Murray 1999, 2001; Praetzellis & Praetzellis 2004, 2009; Yamin 1998, 2000, 2001a, b).

In this chapter Murray and Crook explore the evolution of our research into the urban archaeologies of Melbourne and Sydney from the earliest formulations based on a desire to better understand the genesis of urban Australia and the lives of the poorer inhabitants of Melbourne. Over the past 20 years, our vision has broadened to a more encompassing search for an understanding of the context of urbanism in the colonial and imperial worlds of the eighteenth and nineteen centuries, which has involved the development of frameworks of comparison with sites scattered across Europe, the Americas and, of course, Australia. Thus what was originally a focus on one major site in Melbourne has gradually transformed into a focus on the place of the modern city in the transnational archaeology of the modern world.

The first project was the analysis of Little Lon, a site in the centre of Melbourne that was part of a city block generally known as the Commonwealth Block (see Fig. 2.1). Two bedrock goals for research were set here: first, to develop an integrated analytical framework – bridging history and historical archaeology – of urban society and its embedded material culture in nineteenth- and early-twentieth-century Australia and, second, to analyse within this framework material culture recovered from the site. Mayne and Murray believed that because neither goal had

© Springer Nature Switzerland AG 2019
T. Murray, P. Crook, *Exploring the Archaeology of the Modern City in Nineteenth-century Australia*, Contributions To Global Historical Archaeology, https://doi.org/10.1007/978-3-030-27169-5_2

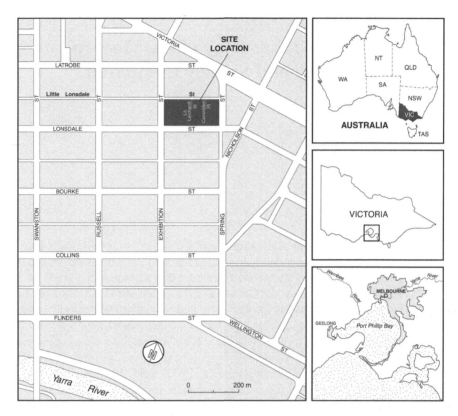

Fig. 2.1 Location of the Commonwealth Block, Melbourne, and the 'Little Lon' and Casselden Place sites

yet been achieved in Australian historical archaeology, a trend had developed that served to dissolve 'the city' as a coherent unit of study or to simply use the artefacts to 'illustrate' narratives, primarily derived from the analysis of written documents. The Little Lon project sets out to 'read' the cityscape as a cultural landscape (see Murray 2013 for a fuller exposition of the genesis of this approach).

Mayne and Murray understood that this very specific historical research required historians to approach the archives – to 'read' them – in a different way, not necessarily to support some highly abstract approach to space and culture but to help answer practical puzzles and problems. They were well aware that this reflexive approach, which is inductive and data driven, occurs against a complex background of historical discourse. The crucial point for them was that neither this background of deductive strategies, perspectives and assumptions nor the conventional narratives of the history of the modern city should dominate. Instead they should be responsive to an active engagement with material culture and archaeological contexts. Of equal importance was an understanding that the job of the historian should not stop with the development of a research design but that it had to continue through all phases of research (before, during and after excavation) sometimes dealing with specific issues raised by the archaeologists and at other times developing interpretive and explanatory options that would propel analysis.

Improving regimes of analysis was obviously one way to promote the difficult business of meaningfully integrating quite disparate datasets, thus using archaeological data to seriously engage with (and possibly revise) conventional readings of social processes or sociocultural categories over the last 200 years. Another way was to expand the disciplinary interpretive repertoire and seek ways to engage with conceptions of the city that moved the field of urban historical archaeology into new areas, extending an engagement with history, sociology and geography beyond the revisionist history of the slum (in large part driven by Mayne's research) that has been so liberating to urban social history in recent years.

Mayne and Murray very soon discovered that significant tensions and oppositions lurked just below that pretty superficial understanding. The initial results from the work at Little Lon have been widely published, and there is no need to discuss them again (see Mayne and Murray 1999, 2001; Murray 2006b; Murray and Mayne 2001, 2003). Important tensions and issues that remain have been a focus of our research for this book (aspects of which are discussed in Chaps. 8, 9, 10 and 11) comprise:

- The role of the particular and the general, the small and large scale, the national and the transnational in problem definition, analysis and integration
- Serious problems related to the archiving of urban archaeological collections
- Building databases that foster assemblage-based analyses of sites
- The pressing need to look, much longer and harder, at research design in urban historical archaeology

Much of this continuing research now occurs under the rubric of 'e-research' or 'digital humanities', but the issues are more than methodological – given that they go to the heart of more abstract inquiries into what we wish to know about the historical archaeology of the modern city. But there are also fascinating and vexing matters related to comprehending the formation processes of urban archaeological records and linking such perceptions to strategies that can help us assess the usefulness or otherwise of the questions we routinely ask, to set the tolerance limits of interpretations and, of course, to describe the kinds of integrations between archaeological and historical data that might occur.

Mayne and Murray reflected on the disjunction between the great precision of historical documentation at Little Lon and the much less precise archaeological data from the houses in the Casselden Place section of the original Little Lon site. This is now understood to be a common enough occurrence in urban historical archaeology. Of course it is important to establish how we can pursue our conventional desire to explore domesticity, community, family life, issues of residence and mobility and still larger issues of how and what people produce and consume in cites, but it is equally important for us to try to understand how data and questions can give rise to different agendas. The different resolving powers of different kinds of data remain a significant issue for research in this field. In this case the richness of documentary data can create an illusion of archaeological riches, where we find that finer scales of chronological resolution (down to the single year) can lead to a pixilation or loss of resolution in archaeological information that does not occur so obviously at chronologically coarser scales of analysis. In essence the integration of what we now understand to be quite disparate datasets has become a focus of research in itself (Murray and Mayne 2001, 2003; Murray 2002, 2006a, b; Murray and Crook 2005).

Murray responded to these broad challenges in a series of five linked research projects with multiple collaborators, beginning with the *Exploring the Archaeology of the Modern City* (EAMC, 2001–2004). Crook's collaboration was fundamental to research on the Sydney sites, but she also has been centrally involved in more recent analyses of the Commonwealth Block assemblages. The core idea was that increasing both temporal and spatial scale could bring new patterns into focus, which might overcome the disparity in resolving powers that Mayne and Murray had noted in the material from the cottages in Casselden Place, Melbourne (the core of the original analysis at Little Lon).

Murray and Crook recognised the need to compare sites located in Sydney and Melbourne (and later in London) to gain a clearer understanding of the genesis and development of urban communities (and, at a more pragmatic level, to see whether it was possible to generalise about the composition of 'working-class' or indeed 'middle-class' assemblages). The structure of these comparisons (which occur in local, national and international settings) is thus described (see Fig. 2.2).

The EAMC project was established in 2001 via significant support from the Australian Research Council and its SPIRT Scheme, which underwrote research links between La Trobe University and the project industry partners: the Historic Houses Trust of NSW, the Sydney Harbour Foreshore Authority, Godden Mackay Logan Pty Ltd, the NSW Heritage Office, Heritage Victoria and the City of Sydney. Our goal was to comprehensively analyse and interpret the large assemblages excavated from historical archaeological sites held in storehouses across Sydney. The primary aim was to develop a clearer and more precise understanding of Sydney's past material, personal and working worlds from its archaeological remains, than had been previously attempted. The archaeological collections from Hyde Park Barracks, First Government House, the Royal Mint, Susannah Place, the Cumberland and Gloucester Streets site, the Paddy's Market site and Lilyvale, in The Rocks were selected as the foundation group for a citywide analysis. Prior to undertaking intra-site research on each assemblage, the records (excavation records and reports, the artefact database and related historical material) of all sites were reviewed for their accuracy and their utility within the research programme (Crook et al. 2003a, b, c, d, e, f, g).

As a result a detailed assemblage analysis was carried out for the Hyde Park Barracks, First Government House and the Cumberland and Gloucester Street sites which have all been reported (Crook et al. 2005; Crook and Murray 2006a, b). Some of the outcomes of that more detailed research are presented in Chaps. 8 and 10. Follow-up projects at the Hyde Park Barracks and further work on the assemblages from the Commonwealth Block in Melbourne were also funded by the Australian Research Council and built on close links with the Historic Houses Trust of NSW

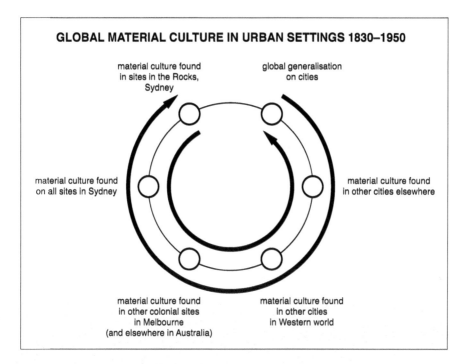

GLOBAL MATERIAL CULTURE IN URBAN SETTINGS 1830–1950

material culture found
in sites in the Rocks,
Sydney

global generalisation
on cities

material culture found
on all sites in Sydney

material culture found
in other cities elsewhere

material culture found
in other colonial sites
in Melbourne
(and elsewhere in Australia)

material culture found
in other cities
in Western world

Fig. 2.2 Schematic of Global Material Culture in Urban Settings 1830–1959. (First published in Murray and Mayne 2001, p. 104)

(later Sydney's Living Museums) at the Barracks and the Museum of Victoria – the repository of the Commonwealth Block collection.

Crook's doctoral dissertation (comparing Cumberland and Gloucester Street assemblages with contemporaneous sites in London) has taken this research still further in search of a clearer archaeological understanding of consumption (Crook 2005, 2008, 2011).

Research by Murray and Crook in Sydney followed both global and local concerns, but we have also been working up our data at the very local level. However you first need quality datasets, and it is the creation and manipulation of these that is providing a firmer foundation for our work in urban archaeology in Australia and internationally.

Managing Data to Promote Comparison

It became clear in the early months of the EAMC project, as database files and spreadsheets started coming in, that we needed to invest a significant portion of our time building a customised database management system. This was to solve two problems: first, the aggregation, review, upgrade and analysis of artefact catalogue records, and accompanying stratigraphic data, from target sites and, second, the capture and analysis of a range of historical records. The two systems were to be created independently but needed to connect at the analysis phase.

The result was two relational databases: the *EAMC Archaeology Database* and the *People + Place* database (Crook et al. 2006a; Crook and Murray 2006c). Both were designed by Crook in Microsoft Access. The *Archaeology Database* comprised an expansion of a database built in 1999 for Crook's honours research at the Cumberland and Gloucester Street site, based on the Godden Mackay Logan artefact catalogue, and it was further enhanced to accommodate Little Lon collections in 2011. *People + Place* was designed from scratch in collaboration with historian Laila Ellmoos who completed all data input. They were shared in full (Crook et al. 2006b), and despite a number of technical limitations, the *Archaeology Database* has been and in some cases remains in use by other researchers.

The databases present a concrete contribution to both of our core themes of integration and of creating and exploring patterns, in the historical and archaeological data. We outline some key features on both systems to illustrate the issues that arise when we seek to integrate documentary and archaeological information.

The EAMC Archaeology Database

The EAMC Archaeology Database is a customised relational database designed to store, display, search and analyse archaeological data. While primarily concerned with artefact data, it is more than an artefact catalogue and contains the following features:

- A detailed catalogue of artefacts
- A register of stratigraphic context data
- A register of type series data
- The capacity to hold multiple images of key artefacts
- In-built data definitions
- A range of tools to make the task of cataloguing assemblages more efficient

The design of the core artefact table was based on the Cumberland and Gloucester Streets site artefact catalogue and extended and modified by the EAMC team to include new fields and features from other catalogues. The core relational structure of the database, integrating artefacts, contexts and type series was developed by Crook (1999) while undertaking honours research at the University of Sydney.

An important feature of the EAMC Archaeology Database is transparency, and ancillary fields were introduced to record useful information about how the record was compiled. For example, notes could be made about the minimum vessel count allocated to a particular record (e.g. 'count based on mouthpieces') so that future users had more than just a final catalogue determination. They could see why a particular sherd was catalogued in the way it was and assess the accuracy of the record for themselves.

With respect to content, the EAMC Archaeology Database drew together, for the first time, artefact data from several of Sydney's major urban excavations: the Cumberland and Gloucester Streets site, the Lilyvale site, the site of First Government House and Paddy's Market. A total of 697,926 sherds, captured in 149,838 records and accompanied by over 5000 images, were collated in the database at the time of its public release.

People + Place

The *People + Place database* was designed to store, display, search and analyse historical data about individuals and buildings or places. Its primary intention is to link archaeological assemblages with the houses, shops and public houses from which they were excavated and the people who lived and worked there. It has three major features:

1. It has the capacity to hold data from many different types of historical sources, encompassing birth certificates, council rates records, newspaper articles and manuscripts that mention a particular building, occupant or landlord.
2. It records both this 'raw' data and summarised biographies about people and places, enabling future users to verify the information presented to them.
3. It tracks filial and other relationships between individuals linked to the study area, including marriages, parents and siblings, business partnerships and friendships.

The two key organising principles of the database are people and place or individuals and structures. By allocating specific historical data to unique identifiers for individuals and structures, the *People + Place database* allows us to weave these elaborate chains of evidence into a holistic account of individuals and the places they were connected to. We established the links at the smaller end of the scale, by linking all artefacts to their unique building number and consequently the individuals known to occupy the places. We developed screens in the database to tally all artefacts recovered from each building (by function groupings) and – for those rare cases – to connect individuals to artefacts found at a particular address. *People + Place* also allows the interrogation of broader patterns of occupation: how long people lived at a particular address and whether they moved around the area or out of it (i.e. were they long-term tenants or transient, were they owner-occupiers or did they live close to family members?). Thus it can reveal trends in the relationships between landlords and tenants or between individuals within households or across family groups.

Transnational Comparisons

The transnational comparative agendum that was first modelled in 2001 (see Fig. 2.2) began to bear fruit in 2004 with the establishment of a collaborative research project with the Museum of London's London Archaeological Archive and Resource Centre (LAARC). While comparisons between the sites in Melbourne and Sydney continued, Crook conducted analyses of archaeological material in London, to compare mid-nineteenth-century patterns of consumption between Sydney and London. The results of Crook's approach to the archaeological vectors of quality, cost and value first appeared in 2005 but was significantly expanded in her doctoral dissertation (Crook 2008).

The core of Crook's dissertation was the comparison of a group of four domestic assemblages from three archaeological sites in Lambeth, London, that were held in the LAARC, with three sites from The Rocks in Sydney. Crook chose to focus on detailed comparisons between sites and artefact classes in order to develop strategies to more effectively deal with methodological limitations she had identified in the course of research in Sydney and Melbourne. A key innovation here was Crook's recognition that manufacturing quality has an important role to play in assemblage analysis, whether the assemblages are from London or Sydney. This was particularly evident in creating accounts of the composition of what have been considered to be working-class assemblages. Crook understood very well that explicit comparative methodologies were vital to achieving analyses that made it possible to undertake the mechanics of large-scale assemblage analysis while, at the same time, making it possible to explore the assumptions that underlie the concepts and categories (such as working class and middle class) that archaeologists and historians routinely deploy. In this sense it is entirely possible that (for archaeologists at least) such categories might be mutually defining but different across the modern world. Characteristically there has been research on archaeologies of the middle class, especially in the United States, but the point at issue is whether the broad patterns of assemblage composition that could be taken as indicative of middle-class consumption would translate to Australia (Cantwell and Wall 2001; Praetzellis 1998; Rothschild and Wall 2014; Wall 1992; Young 2003).

However, apart from the foundational work of a historian of material culture Linda Young, little detailed archaeological research had been done, although of course many of the same shared definitional concerns have been discussed by historians. Crook's argument that in order to gain a more comprehensive understanding of working-class assemblages in Australia we should also seek to define middle-class assemblages, was a call to action that came too late in our current research cycle to directly influence the analyses we present in this book, which does not include quality analyses or indeed data related to comparisons with London assemblages. We mention it here as a key development that will play a central role in shaping the evolution of transnational archaeologies in our research.

Crook's approach to understanding the nexus between quality, cost and value of a class of nineteenth-century material culture has improved our capacity to 'read' consumption from an archaeological perspective. One of the primary reasons for this is the clear potential for a more sophisticated integration of written documentary evidence with assemblages of material culture recovered by archaeologists.

Thus our original goal of seeking ways to tell stories about the literally millions of artefacts locked away in museum basements all over Australia provided the impetus for over 20 years of excavation and analysis and led to both methodological and theoretical developments in Australian historical archaeology. That journey has also involved a change of focus: from deploying the evidence of archaeology to further exploring the content of concepts such as 'the slum' to considering how historical archaeologists might engage more broadly with social histories of the city.

The analysis of assemblages derived from the earlier research at Little Lon and the more recent work on the Cumberland and Gloucester Streets sites and on other sites in Sydney and Melbourne has allowed us to establish whether there were similar patterns of residence, occupancy, ethnicity and community life in two different cities on the edge of the modern world. However, in doing this, we have come to understand the complex and ambiguous nature of urban archaeological deposits from the mid- to late nineteenth century, and to more fully appreciate that the act of comparison between sites, cities and continents is neither straightforward nor innocent. Although we have not felt it possible at this point to draw definitive conclusions about 'life at the social and geographical margins', we have greatly expanded our understanding of the historical archaeology of specific sites within those cities and contributed to the construction of new stories about people and places. At a more general level, we have also clearly identified some of the major questions that will continue to drive our research in Australia and in London and further characterise comparisons between contemporaneous sites in Australia, England and North America. Here are just a few of many examples which have also been outlined in Murray et al. 2019:139–140).

First, the broad question of *how to understand domestic assemblages*. This implies a great many subsidiary questions such as: What are the vectors of assemblage formation in nineteenth-century cities? How did people acquire goods, what did they cost, and what was the nature of consumer demand? Was social emulation a dominant force in the creation of demand? Is there such a thing as a typical poor, working-class, middle-class or artisan domestic assemblage?

Second, the broad question of *what roles cities have played in the movement of goods from centre to periphery and vice versa* and then in the distribution of those goods to other population centres. In this reading centre and periphery exist at regional, national and global scales. The operation of Sydney, Melbourne (or indeed London), in terms of their hinterlands is one matter, but the interaction of cities within countries, and between cities, on a global scale, is really only now appearing on the agenda of urban historical archaeology.

Third, the broad question of *what roles cities have played in the movements of people*, either from the metropolitan to the periphery or from the countryside into cites. This last question has itself become the inspiration for new research into the consequences of immigration, both in Australia and in source countries such as England and Ireland. This is not only about exploring conventional issues of how colonies become nations and English people, for example, become Australians, but also about considering the consequences of immigration for sundered families and sundered communities, through an investigation of memory, through written and oral documentary sources and, of course, through material culture at both ends of the immigration process.

To develop the kinds of methodologies necessary to exploit this broader comparative agenda, we must acknowledge and respond to the complexity of the landscapes we are trying to interpret. The integration of history and archaeology occurs at many levels, and in some cases, rigorous analytical comparison is best teamed with individual stories – speculative though they may be – to fully explore the archaeology of the modern city. Conversely, analyses of historical data (such as the mean value of building stock in a given area) and individual artefacts may be a more appropriate level at which to integrate archaeologically derived information – be it at the household, site or larger scale. We must employ all the armoury of archaeological inquiry – both deductive and inductive reasoning, attention to the detail of *both* documentary and archaeological datasets and a commitment to their effective integration – to make a significant contribution to the histories of modern cities. It is that capacity to simultaneously capture complexity and simplicity that provides us with an interpretive landscape where we can pursue the tangled web of local and transnational variables that create both the specificity of place and their generalisation through comparison and contrast.

Back to the Modern City

The research trajectories we have pursued across multiple projects since the EAMC began in 2001 – working together, independently and collaborating with others – have brought us back to this common endeavour: exploring the archaeology of the modern city. Our work remains limited by access to data – particularly in the transnational sphere, the quality of accessible data and the stubbornness of the datasets that we have, and have created, in revealing their patterns to us. While we are not yet ready for direct transnational comparisons and the detailed indexation of quality rankings in the assemblages we explore in this book, we can offer a direct comparison between assemblages from two great Antipodean cities and ponder the implications of this for our understanding of the historical archaeology of the modern city.

References

Cantwell, A.-M., and D. Wall. 2001. *Unearthing Gotham: The Archaeology of New York City.* London: Yale University Press.

Crook, P. 1999. The Meaningless Public Smile? Housing, Mass Consumption and Material Ambiguity in the Rocks, Sydney (c1833–c1931). BA honours thesis. University of Sydney.

———. 2005. Quality, Cost and Value: Key concepts for an interpretive assemblage analysis. *Australasian Historical Archaeology* 23: 15–24.

———. 2008. 'Superior Quality': Exploring the nature of cost, quality and value in historical archaeology. PhD Thesis, La Trobe University Archaeology Program School of Historical & European Studies Faculty of Humanities & Social Sciences.

———. 2011. Rethinking Assemblage Analysis: New Approaches to the Archaeology of Working-Class Neighborhoods. *International Journal of Historical Archaeology* 15: 582–593. https://doi.org/10.1007/s10761-011-0158-6.

Crook, P., L. Ellmoos, and T. Murray. 2005. Keeping up with the McNamaras: A historical archaeological study of the Cumberland and Gloucester Streets site, The Rocks, Sydney. In *Archaeology of the Modern City Series 8*. Sydney: Historic Houses Trust of New South Wales.

———. 2006a. *People+Place: A Guide to Using the Database. Archaeology of the Modern City Series*, 9. Sydney: Historic Houses Trust of New South Wales.

———. 2006b. EAMC Databases, Version 1.0. In *Exploring the Archaeology of the Modern City Project Databases*, ed. P. Crook, L. Ellmoos, and T. Murray. Sydney: Historic Houses Trust of NSW.

Crook, P., and T. Murray. 2006a. *The Historical Archaeology of the First Government House Site, Sydney: Further Research*, Archaeology of the Modern City Series. Sydney: Historic Houses Trust of NSW.

———. 2006b. *An Archaeology of Institutional Refuge: The Material Culture of the Hyde Park Barracks, Sydney, 1848–1886. Archaeology of the Modern City 1788–1900*. Sydney: Historic Houses Trust of NSW.

———. 2006c. *Guide to the EAMC Archaeology Database. Archaeology of the Modern City Series 10*. Sydney: Historic Houses Trust of New South Wales.

Crook, P., T. Murray, and L. Ellmoos. 2003a. Assessment of Historical and Archaeological Resources of the Lilyvale Site, The Rocks, Sydney. In *Archaeology of the Modern City 1788–1900*, 2nd rev ed. Sydney: Historic Houses Trust of New South Wales.

———. 2003b. Assessment of Historical and Archaeological Resources of Susannah Place, The Rocks, Sydney. In *Archaeology of the Modern City 1788–1900*, 2nd rev ed. Glebe: Historic Houses Trust of New South Wales.

———. 2003c. Assessment of Historical and Archaeological Resources of the Paddy's Market Site, Darling Harbour, Sydney. In *Archaeology of the Modern City 1788–1900*, 2nd rev ed. Sydney: Historic Houses Trust of New South Wales.

———. 2003d. Assessment of Historical and Archaeological Resources of the Cumberland and Gloucester Streets Site, The Rocks, Sydney. In *Archaeology of the Modern City 1788–1900*, 2nd rev ed. Sydney: Historic Houses Trust of New South Wales.

———. 2003e. Assessment of Historical and Archaeological Resources of the Royal Mint Site, Sydney. In *Archaeology of the Modern City 1788–1900 6*, 2nd rev ed. Sydney: Historic Houses Trust of New South Wales.

———. 2003f. Assessment of Historical and Archaeological Resources of the First Government House Site, Sydney. In *Archaeology of the Modern City 1788–1900*, 2nd rev ed. Sydney: Historic Houses Trust of New South Wales.

———. 2003g. Assessment of Historical and Archaeological Resources at the Hyde Park Barracks. In *Archaeology of the Modern City 1788–1900*, 2nd rev ed. Sydney: Historic Houses Trust of New South Wales.

Karskens, G. 1994. The Cumberland/Gloucester Streets Site, The Rocks: An Historical Discourse. Report prepared for Godden Mackay Logan and the Sydney Cove Authority.

———. 1997a. *The Rocks: Life in Early Sydney*. Melbourne: Melbourne University Press.

———. 1997b. Crossing Over: Archaeology and History at the Cumberland/Gloucester Street Site, The Rocks, 1994–1996. *Public History Review* 5/6 (1996–1997): 30–48.

———. 1999. *Inside The Rocks: The Archaeology of a Neighbourhood*. Sydney: Hale and Iremonger.

———. 2000. Engaging Artefacts: Urban Archaeology, Museums and the Origins of Sydney. *Tasmanian Historical Studies* 4 (1): 39–64.

————. 2001. Small Things, Big Pictures: New Perspectives from the Archaeological of Sydney's Rocks Neighbourhood. In *The Archaeology of Urban Landscapes: Explorations in Slumland*, ed. A. Mayne and T. Murray. Cambridge: Cambridge University Press.

————. 2003. Revisiting the World View: The Archaeology of Convict Households in Sydney's Rocks Neighbourhood. *Historical Archaeology* 37 (1): 34–55.

————. 2006. Making City Lives: Urban Archaeology and Australian Social, Cultural and Urban History. In *Cities in the World, 1500–2000*, ed. A. Green and R. Leech. Leeds: Maney Publishing.

Karskens, G., and W. Thorp. 1992. History and Archaeology in Sydney: Towards Integration and Interpretation. *Royal Australian Historical Society Journal* 78: 52–75.

Lydon, J. 1995. Boarding Houses in The Rocks: Mrs Ann Lewis' privy, 1865. Public History Review 4: 73–88.

————. 1999. 'Many inventions': the Chinese in the Rocks, Sydney 1890–1930. Monash University, Clayton, Vic.

Mayne, A., and T. Murray. 1999. In-Little-Lon-Wiv-Ginger-Mick': Telling the Forgotten History of a Vanished Community. *Journal of Popular Culture* 33 (1): 49–60.

————. 2001. The Archaeology of Urban Landscapes: Explorations in Slumland. In *The Archaeology of Urban Landscapes: Explorations in Slumland*, ed. A. Mayne and T. Murray. Cambridge: Cambridge University Press.

Murray, T. 2002. But that was Long Ago: Theory in Australian Historical Archaeology 2002. *Australasian Historical Archaeology* 20: 8–14.

————. 2006a. Introduction. *International Journal of Historical Archaeology* 10 (4): 291–298.

————. 2006b. Integrating Archaeology and History at the Commonwealth Block: 'Little Lon' and Casselden Place. *International Journal of Historical Archaeology* 10 (4): 385–403.

————. 2013. Expanding Horizons in the Archaeology of the Modern City: A Tale in Six Projects. *Journal of Urban History*, first published on March 6, 2013 as https://doi. org/10.1177/0096144213479308.

Murray, T., K. Buckley, S. Hayes, G. Hewitt, J. McCarthy, R. Mackay, B. Minchinton, C. Smith, J. Smith, and Bronwyn Woff. 2019. *The Commonwealth Block, Melbourne: A Historical Archaeology*. Sydney: Australasian Society for Historical Archaeology.

Murray, T., and P. Crook. 2005. Exploring the Archaeology of the Modern City: Issues of Scale, Integration and Complexity. *International Journal of Historical Archaeology* 9 (2): 89–109.

Murray, T., and A. Mayne. 2001. Imaginary Landscapes: Reading Melbourne's 'Little Lon'. In *The Archaeology of Urban Landscapes: Explorations in Slumland*, ed. A. Mayne and T. Murray. Cambridge: Cambridge University Press.

————. 2003. (Re) Constructing a Lost Community: 'Little Lon', Melbourne, Australia. *Historical Archaeology* 37 (1): 87–101.

Praetzellis, A. 1998. Introduction: Why Every Archaeologist Should Tell Stories Once in a While. Historical Archaeology 32 (1): 1–3.

Praetzellis, M., and A. Praetzellis, eds. 2004. *Putting the 'There' There: Historical Archaeologies of West Oakland, 1-880 Cypress Freeway Replacement Project. Report Prepared by Anthropological Studies Center*. Rohnert Park: Sonoma State University.

————, eds. 2009. *South of Market: Historical Archaeology of 3 San Francisco Neighborhoods. The San Francisco – Oakland Bay Bridge West Approach Project. Report Prepared by Anthropological Studies Center*. Rohnert Park: Sonoma State University.

Rothschild, N., and D. Wall. 2014. *The Archaeology of American Cities*. Gainesville: University of Florida Press.

Wall, D. 1992. Sacred Dinners and Secular Teas: Constructing Domesticity in Mid-19th Century New York. *Historical Archaeology* 25: 69–81.

Yamin, R. 1998. Lurid Tales and Homely Stories of New York's Notorious Five Points. *Historical Archaeology* 31 (1): 74–85.

————. 2001a. Becoming New York: The Five Points Neighbourhood. *Historical Archaeology* 35 (3): 1–5.

————. 2001b. Alternative Narratives: Respectability at New York's Five Points. In *The Archaeology of Urban Landscapes: Explorations in Slumland*, ed. A. Mayne and T. Murray. Cambridge: Cambridge University Press.

Yamin, R.ed. 2000. *Tales of Five Points: Working-class Life in Nineteenth Century New York. Reports Prepared for Edwards and Kelcey Engineers, Inc. and General Services Administration (Region 2)*. Vol. 6. West Chester: John Milner Associates.

Young, L. 2003. *Middle Class Culture in the Nineteenth Century: America, Australia and Britain*. New York: Palgrave Macmillan.

Chapter 3
Transnational Archaeologies: Colonial and Postcolonial

Whenever the historian's sources go 'beyond words', and this is the case when you adopt a transnational perspective, archaeology is a card to be counted on. (Saunier 2013, 128)

In Chap. 2 we discussed the evolution of our approach to the archaeology of the modern city in Australia. We remarked that our original goals owed much to a concern by urban historians, particularly Alan Mayne, that previous accounts of life in the poorer parts of Melbourne (which very much included what later became known as Little Lon) were heavily influenced by notions of slum life that owed much to the ideology of social reform in the late nineteenth and early twentieth centuries. While our early work was unashamedly focused on seeking a more nuanced integration of documentary and archaeological records in inner Melbourne, from the start it was strongly influenced by an international discourse about urban poverty and 'slum life' in the nineteenth centuries. Early influences from the history of London and from the archaeology of Five Points (e.g. Yamin 2000), Boot Mills (e.g. Beaudry and Mrzowski 2001) and San Francisco (e.g. Praetzellis and Praetzellis 2004) were strong and during the early phases of the project were matched by studies from the United States, Britain, South Africa and Canada, which were subsequently collected as a single volume (Mayne and Murray 2001). In this sense understanding the specifics of small places such as Little Lon required us to adopt a multiscalar approach to identifying and interpreting the archaeological signatures of life in the modern city, which was exemplified in Fig. 2.2. At its roots the archaeology of the modern city in Australia was also an archaeology of the transnational forces that shaped the modern world before, during and after Australia was settled by the British in 1788.

In this chapter we develop these arguments to outline the basis of a broader transnational approach that links the crucial vectors of social and cultural change in nineteenth- and early-twentieth-century Australia, which also have wider global sources and influences. Our particular concerns in this book flow from the need to document the historical archaeological elements of change and variation that resulted from large-scale migration to Australia (from Europe and elsewhere) and the creation of new societies on the far side of the world. Although our major focus in this book is on free migration (as distinct from convictism) and life in the two major urban centres of Melbourne and Sydney, we are very much aware that other

© Springer Nature Switzerland AG 2019
T. Murray, P. Crook, *Exploring the Archaeology of the Modern City in Nineteenth-century Australia*, Contributions To Global Historical Archaeology, https://doi.org/10.1007/978-3-030-27169-5_3

significant vectors – such as convictism, the dispossession of the indigenous inhabitants of the continent, the development of the pastoral economy of Australia and the transfer of technologies from around the globe to Australia – play a considerable role here. Research into these vectors (both in Australia and elsewhere) is a developing challenge for the future.

Contemporary historical archaeology is much concerned with understanding capitalism, colonialism and modernity (e.g. Orser Jr 1996, Orser 2000; Paynter 2000). Analyses of material culture recovered from archaeological contexts have tended to focus on what material things have to tell us about class (e.g. Leone and Potter Jr 1999; Wurst and Fitts 1999), ethnicity and race (e.g. Franklin and Fesler 1999; Singleton 1999), gender (e.g. Wall 1994) and the consequences of colonialism (e.g. Hall 2000; Murray 2004). While there has been a strong tradition of exploring the archaeology of rural settlements, it has long been understood that the city provides the crucial context for investigating the archaeology of capitalism and modernity. But urban archaeological assemblages (especially those created over the last 250 years) tend to be very large and complex, requiring considerable time and knowledge to allow material culture to be transformed into primary historical and archaeological data, which can then support analysis and interpretation. It is also now more widely understood that approaching the archaeology of the modern world requires a framework of methods and theories that will successfully integrate material evidence drawn from sites around the world, with dense local historical documentation. The sheer *amount* of evidence is a major challenge to historical archaeologists but then so is the creation of viable strategies for integrating the various types of evidence we routinely deal with (e.g. oral history, photographs, written documents, plant and animal remains and material culture).

The modern world of the nineteenth century was the outcome of processes that had their roots in the first 300 years of European expansion, as well as forces such as industrialisation, large-scale migration and heightened forms of colonialism that came to the fore after those years. Thus an overarching aim of our research has been to link the historical archaeology of the earlier Atlantic world (e.g. Elliot 2006) with the archaeologies of the Indian Ocean (e.g. Parthasarathi and Riello 2014) and Pacific worlds by tracing historical continuities and discontinuities over the past 500 years. Our research is founded on an interdisciplinary collaboration with economic, social and cultural history and explicitly acknowledges that previous historical research into urbanisation, migration, convictism, pastoralism and technology transfer in Australia and elsewhere is fundamental to the conduct of archaeological research and the analysis of material culture in these contexts (Blainey 1966; Butlin 1994; Davidson 1994; Frost 2014; Jupp 2007; Linge 1979; Robin 2009; Ville 2000).

We aspire for our research to make a useful contribution to more general understanding of the movements of people (critically, including convicts), the growth of cities, the development of the Australian economy (particularly that based on pastoralism) as a subset of a general inquiry into archaeologies of global commodities, the archaeology of indigenous–settler interactions and technology transfer across the globe in the 'long nineteenth century'. These inquiries reach far past the scope of our book, but they do provide a clear indication of the general context of our research.

In the United States, historical archaeology has always been concerned with transnational matters, particularly the great flows of people, material culture, technology and, of course, capital, all of which left Europe for the peripheries in the late sixteenth century and have been washing back and forth ever since (e.g. Brighton 2009; Hall 2000; Leone and Potter Jr 1999; Orser Jr 1996; Williams and Voss 2008). Over the past three centuries, people around the globe have been participating in what has been called the modern world system – comprising not only flows of people, capital and trade but ideas, aspirations and, perhaps more concretely, material culture as various as locomotives and teacups.

It is a commonplace observation that the pace and intensity of interaction between people scattered all over the globe rapidly increased during this time and that the pace and intensity of social and cultural change has matched this. These are the centuries of mass production and consumption and of the increasing industrialization of all aspects of life – changes that have been understood, especially in recent times, as having the potential to create a global social and cultural uniformity (e.g. Appadurai 1996; Berger and Huntingdon 2002; Glick Schiller et al. 1992). This uniformity might have crushed the identities of those societies and cultures that, for whatever reason, have lost the capacity to generate and sustain distinctive identities. In the past decade or so, these have become highly sensitive matters, since people have been forced to contemplate the consequences of global markets and their local impacts. Equally sensitive are the challenges societies face from the movements of people – no matter whether they are referred to as economic refugees, asylum seekers or illegals – and from flows of culture, both to and from the countries of the West and within the West itself.

This global perspective has powered fundamental research into the archaeology of the 'Atlantic world' since European exploration of the New World and West Africa and has gained particular force in the archaeology of slavery (Hall 2000; Orser Jr 1996, 2010), capitalism (Croucher and Weiss 2011; Leone and Potter Jr 1999) and, since the mid-1990s, the archaeology of indigenous–settler interactions in North and South America (Silliman 2005).

Notwithstanding this overarching context of practice, much historical archaeology still rests on small-scale, single-site research that presents challenges for global comparisons between sites of a similar antiquity and broadly similar historical contexts. This is especially the case in Australia: here, with the exception of recent work in the archaeology of the modern city and explorations in maritime archaeology (Stanniforth and Nash 2006), practitioners have tended to dispense with the original broad comparative vision of the founders of historical archaeology (Birmingham and Jeans 1983; Connah 1988; Jeans 1988). This arises in part from the predominance of archaeological research in applied development contexts, with notable exceptions such as Casey (2004) and Mackay and Karskens (1999); here the vast bulk of research explores the excavation and recording of single sites and remains published only in the grey literature.

Transnational Archaeologies

Given its genesis as the archaeology of the European colonisation of North America, historical archaeology at its core has sought to address two major issues. The first is the need to build concepts that demonstrate the importance of archaeological data (and the material culture that lies at its core) to the writing of social and economic history. The second is the need to articulate local, regional, national and global scales in interpretation and analysis. Historical archaeology has the demonstrated capacity to track material culture in circulation from the point of production to the many points of consumption, revealing the connections and different sense of duration that have frequently gone unremarked by document-based historians. This circulation of material culture in archaeological contexts has long encouraged an understanding that multiscalar approach to problem selection and analysis should be a major goal for the discipline (e.g. Orser Jr. 2010). The interplay of global and local frames of reference and the challenges faced when both archaeologists and historians seek to integrate archaeological and written documentary information have driven historical archaeologist to look much more closely at core processes such as migration, colonisation and ethnogenesis (particularly in societies where 'hybrid', creole or 'subaltern' societies have been created through colonialism) (Beaudry and Parno 2013; Burmeister 2000; Butler 2001; Dawdy 2000; Lilley 2006; Praetzellis and Praetzellis 2004; Voss 2015). Contemporary historical and archaeological research has targeted key issues and contexts for modern scholars and readers: indigenous–settler relations; the transfer of agricultural, manufacturing and managerial technologies; the movements of people and material culture; and the development of cities in the modern world.

Over the past 40 years, historical archaeologists have sought to contribute to a broader understanding of how new societies were created from old (either emigrant or indigenous) and of how class, ethnicity and gender have played out in the nations created out of imperialism and colonialism. However, while these are to an extent local and unique phenomena, they have taken place within the broader context of global modernity. Significant flows of capital, technology, consumer goods and people were encouraged both within and outside the British Empire, especially into the United States. Between 1815 and 1914, 22.6 million people left Britain for settlements, and colonies spread out across the world, as did hundreds of millions of pounds worth of capital investment in railways, ports, cities, ships and agricultural and pastoral enterprises and the building of modern infrastructure such as courts, schools and universities.

This was a century of astounding global mobility. Archaeologists have begun to explore some of the *archaeological* contexts within which settler colonies, such as those in Australia, became established and then transformed into nations, during a period of intensifying globalisation. However, as Murray remarked in the editorial introduction to *The Archaeology of Contact in Settler Societies* (Murray 2004), exploring the archaeology of nation-building during this period, in the early twenty-first century, largely subverts the pre-eminence of the narratives that have told the national story by uncovering the 'hidden histories' of the marginalised and oppressed. These historical archaeologies of transformation, diaspora and globalisation are also about frontiers, blurred boundaries, the refashioning of ethnicities and identities and the survival of core elements of indigenous ethnicities (e.g. Croucher and Weiss 2011; Parker and Rodseth 2005). The political context of transnational historical archaeologies is undeniable and pervasive, since postcolonial societies simultaneously celebrate diversity and cultural and social possibilities from an extraordinarily eclectic sampling of global cultural capital while seeking to retain identities that have created the cohesion of nations.

Archaeologies of the Modern City

The most recent evolution of our research programme links the analysis of archaeological data, material culture and historical documents to a close examination of life in nineteenth-century cities – and by extension as a contrast to life in rural areas. In the future our programme will continue to explore issues of scale, particularly the interaction of the local and the global that have guided us thus far (Mullins and Warner 2008; Murray and Crook 2005; Orser Jr. 2010). Migration continues to be one of the most deeply contested aspects of the archaeology of the modern world, both in sixteenth- to eighteenth-century contexts and those of the nineteenth and twentieth centuries. Indeed, significant re-examinations of the already highly disputed role of migration as an explanation for culture change in archaeology have reignited debates about archaeological characterisations of the processes of social and cultural change resulting from the mobility of people and material culture and the creation of the colonial and postcolonial worlds. These debates centre on how an increasingly globalised and homogenous material culture could be interpreted by its consumers in culturally heterogeneous ways across the world. This has led to a focus on the complexities of material culture as a marker of relationships and identities (some linked to ethnicities and others not) (Beaudry and Parno 2013; Dawdy 2000; Lawrence 2003; Mullins and Warner 2008; Praetzellis and Praetzellis 2004; Richard 2011; Ross 2012; Voss 2015).

Yet scale can be approached as a way of gaining a clearer picture of archaeological phenomena as they appear at the level of the household, the community, the city or even the globe, and the comparison of urban sites at all levels across the world (and the analysis of patterns that are revealed) continues to be a major challenge. Our goal is to build on the research presented in this volume to gain a clearer *archaeological* understanding of the genesis and development of urban communities in the United Kingdom, the United States, and Australia and to extend research into the archaeological origins of the urban middle class in Australia. Murray has described the structure of these comparisons (which flow from the small scale to the large and back again) as a reflexive process of multiscalar comparison and contrast (see Figure 2.2). Our continuing research into these complex historical processes will stress test that conception and lead to the building of new archaeological theories accounting for the identity of the modern city. While we currently have not been able to convincingly integrate data and perspectives from these different scales into new and richer stories about people and places, we have developed a clearer understanding of the challenges that will have to be met before we can do so.

A renewed interest in urban historical archaeology focusing on the analysis of large and complex artefact assemblages and detailed research into relevant written documents has created new opportunities for interpretation (see the contributors to Mayne and Murray 2001, but see especially Praetzellis and Praetzellis 2004; Yamin 2000) and builds on fundamental research into artefacts and systems of interpretation that have guided urban historical archaeology since the late 1980s (e.g. Miller 1991; Shackel 1994). We now know that inner-city communities during the nineteenth and early twentieth centuries are more socially and culturally diverse than the previous stereotypes have allowed, and new histories of cities are beginning to reflect this (e.g. Cantwell and Wall 2001). These will be histories of dynamism and people, of material culture, of how people live in cities and of the role of cities in the modern world as crucibles of social and cultural change. Modern cities are places of residence, employment, manufacture, trade, education, innovation and creativity and political and social action. They are also places where poverty, inequality, wealth, privilege and enterprise underwrite the further evolution of culture and society. For while we might argue about the chronology of the modern city, there is no argument that cities continue to be one of the most significant theatres of human action. Structured comparisons between domestic assemblages (and related documentary information) in Melbourne and Sydney will make it possible to further explore (from an archaeological perspective) the issues of cultural homogeneity and heterogeneity outlined above, but they currently lie beyond the scope of this book.

Over the past 40 years, historical archaeologists have sought to contribute to a broader understanding of how new societies were created from old (either emigrant or indigenous) and how class, ethnicity and gender have played themselves out in the nations created out of imperialism and colonialism. However while these are, to an extent, local and unique phenomena, they have taken place within the broader context of global modernity. This broader context acknowledges that, especially over the past two centuries, people around the globe have been participating in the modern world system – not only comprising flows of capital and trade but also ideas, aspirations and, perhaps more concretely, material culture as various as locomotives and teacups. These have been the centuries of mass production and mass consumption, of the increasing industrialization of all aspects of life which have been understood, especially in recent times, as having the potential to create a global, social and cultural uniformity that might crush the identities of those societies and cultures which (for whatever reason) lose the capacity to generate and sustain distinctive identities. 'Transnational archaeologies' explore the consequences of mobility, transformation, diaspora and globalisation, but they are also about frontiers, blurred boundaries and the refashioning of ethnicities and identities (e.g. Beaudry 2003; Cohen 1997).

In Chap. 4 we apply these understandings to a discussion of migration to Australia in the nineteenth century. This will be a story about motivations for and mechanisms of migration to Australia, the development of government and private institutions to manage the mass of people seeking new lives in Australia and the impacts of migration on the cities of Melbourne and Sydney.

References

Appadurai, A. 1996. *Modernity at Large: Cultural Dimensions of Globalization*. Minneapolis: University of Minnesota Press.

Beaudry, M. 2003. Concluding Remarks: Disruptive Narratives? Mulitdimensional Perspectives on 'Britishness'. In *Archaeologies of the British: Explorations of Identity in Great Britain and Its Colonies*, ed. S. Lawerence, *1600–1945*. London: Routledge.

Beaudry, M., and S. Mrzowski. 2001. Cultural Space and Worker Identity in the Company City: Nineteenth-Century Lowell, Massachusetts. In *The Archaeology of Urban Landscapes. Explorations in Slumland*, ed. A. Mayne and T. Murray, 118–131. Cambridge: Cambridge University Press.

Beaudry, M.C., and T.G. Parno. 2013. Introduction: Mobilities in Contemporary Historical Archaeology. In *Archaeologies of Mobility and Movement*, ed. M.C. Beaudry and T.G. Parno, 1–16. New York: Springer.

Berger, P.L., and S.P. Huntingdon. 2002. *Many Globalizations: Cultural Diversity in the Contemporary World*. Oxford: Oxford University Press.

Birmingham, J., and D. Jeans. 1983. The Swiss Family Robinson and the Archaeology of Colonisation. *Australian Journal of Historical Archaeology* 1: 3–14.

Blainey, G. 1966. *The Tyranny of Distance. How Distance Shaped Australia's History*. Melbourne: Sun Books.

Brighton, S.A. 2009. *Historical Archaeology of the Irish Diaspora: A Transnational Approach*. Knoxville: University of Tennessee Press.

Burmeister, S. 2000. Archaeology and Migration. Approaches to an Archaeological Proof of Migration. *Current Anthropology* 41 (4): 549–567.

Butler, K.D. 2001. Defining Diasporas: Refining a Discourse. *Diaspora* 10 (2): 189–219.

Butlin, N.G. 1994. *Forming a Colonial Economy, Australia 1810–1850*. Melbourne: Cambridge University Press.

Cantwell, A.-M., and D. Wall. 2001. *Unearthing Gotham: The Archaeology of New York City*. London: Yale.

Casey, M. 2004. Falling Through the Cracks: Method and Practice at the CSR Site, Pyrmont. *Australasian Historical Archaeology* 22: 27–43.

Cohen, R. 1997. *Global Diasporas: An Introduction*. London: UCL Press.

Connah, G. 1988. *'Of the Hut I Builded': The Archaeology of Australia's History*. Melbourne: Cambridge University Press.

Croucher, S., and L. Weiss, eds. 2011. *The Archaeology of Capitalism in Colonial Contexts*. New York: Springer.

Davidson, B.R. 1994. The Development of the Pastoral Industry in Australia During the 19th Century. In *Pastoralists at the Periphery. Herders in a Capitalist World*, 79–102. Tucson: University of Arizona Press.

Dawdy, S.L., ed. 2000. Creolization. *Historical Archaeology* 34 (3): 1–133.

Elliot, J.H. 2006. *Empires of the Atlantic World: Britain and Spain in America 1492–1830*. New Haven: Yale University Press.

Franklin, M., and G. Fesler, eds. 1999. *Historical Archaeology, Identity Formation, and the Interpretation of Ethnicity*. Williamsburg, VA: Colonial Williamsburg Foundation.

Frost, L. 2014. Urbanisation. In *2015. The Cambridge Economic History of Australia*, ed. S. Ville and G. Withers. Melbourne: Cambridge University Press.

Glick Schiller, N., L. Basch, and C. Blanc-Szanton, eds. 1992. *Towards a Transnational Perspective on Migration: Race, Class, Ethnicity, and Nationalism Considered.* New York: New York Academy of Sciences.

Hall, M. 2000. *Archaeology and the Modern World: Colonial Transcripts from South Africa and the Chesapeake.* New York: Routledge.

Jeans, D. 1988. World Systems Theory: A Theoretical Context for Australian Historical Archaeology. In *Archaeology and Colonisation: Australia in the World Context,* ed. J. Birmingham, D. Bairstow, and A. Wilson, 62–69. Sydney: Australian Society for Historical Archaeology.

Jupp, J. 2007. *From White Australia to Woomera: The Story of Australian Immigration.* 2nd ed. New York: Cambridge University Press.

Lawrence, S. 2003. At Home in the Bush: Material Culture and Australian Nationalism. In *Archaeologies of the British: Explorations of Identity in Great Britain and Its Colonies 1600–1945,* ed. S. Lawrence, 211–223. London: Routledge.

Leone, M.P., and P.B. Potter Jr., eds. 1999. *Historical Archaeologies of Capitalism.* New York: Plenum.

Lilley, I. 2006. Archaeology, Diaspora and Decolonization. *Journal of Social Archaeology* 6 (1): 28–47.

Linge, G.J.R. 1979. *Industrial Awakening: A Geography of Australian Manufacturing 1788–1890.* Canberra: ANU Press.

Mackay, R., and G. Karskens. 1999. Historical Archaeology in Australia: Historical or Hysterical? Crisis or Creative Awakening? *Australasian Historical Archaeology* 17: 110–115.

Mayne, A., and T. Murray, eds. 2001. *The Archaeology of Urban Landscapes: Explorations in Slumland.* Cambridge: Cambridge University Press.

Miller, G.L. 1991. A Revised Set of CC Index Value for Classification and Economic Scaling of English Ceramics from 1787 to 1880. *Historical Archaeology* 25 (1): 1–25.

Mullins, P., and M.S. Warner, eds. 2008. Living in Cities Revisited: Trends in Nineteenth and Twentieth Century Urban Archaeology. *Historical Archaeology* 42 (1): 1–137.

Murray, T., ed. 2004. *The Archaeology of Contact in Settler Societies.* Cambridge: Cambridge University Press.

Murray, T., and P. Crook. 2005. Exploring the Archaeology of the Modern City: Melbourne, Sydney and London in the 19thth Century. *International Journal of Historical Archaeology* 9 (2): 89–109.

Orser, C.E., ed. 2000. Contemporary Issues Forum: American Historical Archaeology. *American Anthropologist* 103: 621–704.

Orser, C., Jr. 1996. *A Historical Archaeology of the Modern World.* New York: Plenum.

———. 2010. Twenty-First-Century Historical Archaeology. *Journal of Archaeological Research* 18: 111–150.

Parker, B.J., and L. Rodseth. 2005. *Untaming the Frontier in Anthropology, Archaeology and History.* Tucson: University of Arizona Press.

Parthasarathi, P., and G. Riello. 2014. The Indian Ocean in the Long Eighteenth Century. *Eighteenth Century Studies* 48 (1).

Paynter, R. 2000. Historical Archaeology and the Post-Columbian world of North America. *Journal of Archaeological Research* 8: 169–217.

Praetzellis, A., and M. Praetzellis. 2004. Becoming Jewish Americans. In *Putting the "There" there: Historical Archaeologies of West Oakland,* ed. A. Prezellis and M. Praetzellis, 68–71. Rohnert Park: Anthropological Studies Centre, Sonoma State University.

Richard, F.G. 2011. Materializing Poverty: Archaeological Reflections from the Post Colony. *Historical Archaeology* 45 (3): 166–182.

Robin, L. 2009. Fleecing the Nation. *Journal of Australian Studies.* 23: 150–158.

Ross, D.E. 2012. Transnational Artefacts: Grappling with Fluid Material Origins and Identities in Archaeological Interpretations of Culture Change. *Journal of Anthropological Archaeology* 31 (1): 38–48.

Saunier, P.-Y. 2013. *Transnational History*. New York: Palgrave.

Shackel, P.A. 1994. *Personal Discipline and Material Culture: An Archaeology of Annapolis, Maryland, 1695–1870*. Knoxville: University of Tennessee Press.

Silliman, S. 2005. Culture Contact or Colonialism? Changes in the Archaeology of Native North America. *American Antiquity* 70 (1): 55–74.

Singleton, T.A., ed. 1999. *"I, Too, Am America": Archaeological Studies of African-American Life*. Charlottesville, VA: University Virginia Press.

Stanniforth, M., and M. Nash, eds. 2006. *Maritime Archaeology: Australian Approaches*. New York: Springer.

Ville, S. 2000. *The Rural Entrepreneurs: A History of the Stock and Station Agent Industry in Australia and New Zealand*. Melbourne: Cambridge University Press.

Voss, B. 2015. What's New? Rethinking Ethnogenesis in the Archaeology of Colonialism. *American Antiquity* 80 (4): 655–670.

Wall, D. 1994. *The Archaeology of Gender: Separating the Spheres in Urban America*. New York: Plenum.

Williams, B., and B. Voss. 2008. The Archaeology of Chinese Immigrant and Chinese American Communities. *Historical Archaeology* 42 (3): 1–4.

Wurst, L., and R.K. Fitts, eds. 1999. Confronting Class. *Historical Archaeology* 33 (1): 1–195.

Yamin, Rebecca, ed. 2000. *Tales of the Five Points: Working-Class Life in Nineteenth Century New York*. West Chester: John Milner and Associates 6 Volumes.

Chapter 4
Immigration to Australia: 1820–1900

One of the great themes of modern history is the movement of poor people across the face of the earth. For individuals and families the economic and psychological cost of these transoceanic migrations was severe. But they did not prevent millions of agriculturalists and proletarians from Europe reaching the new worlds in both the Atlantic and Pacific basins in the nineteenth century. These people, in their myriad voyages, shifted the demographic balance of the continents and created new economies and societies wherever they went. (Richards 1993, 250)

In this chapter we briefly review the context and nature of nineteenth-century immigration to the British colonies of what was to become Australia, and present a case study drawn from the historical archaeology of the Hyde Park Barracks in Sydney. Of course immigration from the British Isles (and elsewhere) to Sydney had occurred *before* 1820, and most certainly occurred *after* 1901, to what had become the federated nation of Australia. Indeed, from the first settlement in 1788 as a convict station established in Sydney, populations both free and convict entered the continent continuously. However, in the context of this book, with its focus on the consequences on the development of nineteenth-century Sydney and Melbourne, our scope is necessarily more limited. Here our primary interest lies in the mass movement of populations from the British Isles (and to a lesser extent also from the rest of Europe, the United States, China and Western Asia) to two new cities on the edge of the world. As such the nature of our inquiry shares many of the fundamental concerns of historical archaeologists of nineteenth-century North America into the mass movements of people from Europe and the creation of new societies in new worlds.

Nonetheless there are very real differences in the context and consequences of immigration in both continents. Although Australia was much influenced by the Irish diaspora, as was the United States (see, e.g. Brighton 2011), the impact of migration to the continent by other nationalities or ethnicities (Spanish, French, African, Jewish and Europeans outside the British Isles such as Germans, Swedes and Poles) was much less until, in the case of Greeks, Italians and populations from Eastern Europe, after the end of the Second World War. The great exception to that generalisation is the immigration of Chinese where significant numbers entered

© Springer Nature Switzerland AG 2019
T. Murray, P. Crook, *Exploring the Archaeology of the Modern City in Nineteenth-century Australia*, Contributions To Global Historical Archaeology, https://doi.org/10.1007/978-3-030-27169-5_4

Australia (as they had in the United States) in search of gold (see, e.g. Mountford and Tufnell 2018; Voss 2005).

The greatest difference between the North American and Australian cases lies in the social and cultural impact of settlement and immigration. Archaeologists in North America have long focused on the creation of new cultural forms and ethnicities through the dispossession of indigenous peoples, the introduction of slaves from Africa (see, e.g. Card 2013; Cusick 1998; Dawdy 2000; Lightfoot 1995; Mrozowski 2010; Schneider and Panich 2014; Stein 2005; Voss 2008) and the settlement of discrete parts of the continent by Spanish, French, Dutch and English populations (see, e.g. Crews et al. 2017; Thomas 1989; Waselkov 1997). This was not the case in Australia where the continent was settled as part of an expanding network of British colonies after the loss of its colonies in what became the United States. While not quite an immigrant monoculture (there were significant differences within the Anglo–Celtic populations related to religion and the consequences of internal colonialism within the British Isles), there were regions such as South Australia that attracted significant settlement by Germans and miners from Cornwall; during this period there was no alternative force to seriously challenge the sway of British culture and institutions. Of course this is not to say that cultural alternatives did not exist among indigenous communities or indeed among ethnic groups such as the Germans, the Scots or the Chinese; it is just that in the nineteenth century, they were effectively dominated and to a large extent hidden or simply unrecognised. The reversal of this monocultural society is one of the most important consequences of immigration to Australia after 1945 as a result of great pulses of migration from Europe, Asia and Africa. It remains a powerful social and political force to this day.

Thus from the very first years of colonial settlement, Australia was an immigrant society, no matter whether the population was predominantly either convict or free. It is therefore hardly surprising that immigration, especially the numbers and origins of migrants, has proved to be a subject of intense political interest throughout the history of Australia. There have been many vectors for divergent opinions, but the most notable relate to the influence of British government policy with respect to the migration of its subjects and the racial composition of the colonies of Australia as a destination for non-British populations. Since the Federation in 1901, the influence of British government policy in this area has waned, but it has been replaced by an intensifying local interest as debates have raged about the need to either open or close Australia to peoples from outside the British Isles. Immigration and the notion of a 'big' or 'small' Australia, of a multicultural versus and monocultural society and of social and cultural cohesion versus diversity all remain incendiary political topics (see, e.g. Jupp 2018).

Notwithstanding the importance of the political context of immigration to Australia, our task as historical archaeologists is to comprehend migration as a process that had an intense social, cultural and economic impacts. Our interest focuses on a time when the British Empire was at its height, when flows of capital, technology, consumer goods and people were encouraged both within the Empire and outside it, especially into the United States. Between 1815 and 1914, 22.6 million people left Britain for settlements and colonies spread out across the world, as did hundreds of millions of pounds worth of capital investment in railways, ports, cities, ships, agricultural and pastoral enterprises and the building of institutions as various as courts, schools and universities (Baines 1985; Bayly 2004; Harper and Constantine 2010; Murdoch 2004). For the vast bulk of that century, settler colonies were not yet nations, and non-settler colonies, especially in Asia and Africa, were decades away from gaining their independence. Indeed much of the visual (as well as conventional) rhetoric of Empire was of the 'mother' (Britannia) and her 'daughter' colonies.

This was a century of quite astounding global mobility, exemplified on the large scale by the considerable populations that 'rushed' the sites of gold strikes first in California and then for almost a century in various parts of Australia, then to the Yukon, Siberia and South Africa (see, e.g. Mountford and Tufnell 2018). But this mobility also happened at a very personal scale with soldiers and administrators and their families on colonial or imperial service or economic refugees from the west of Ireland moving to England and then on to the United States and often to Australia (Broome 1984; Haines 1997; Richards 1985).

This sets us the great challenge of exploring some of the contexts within which settler colonies, such as those in Australia, became established and then transformed into nations, during a period of intensifying globalisation. But as Murray remarked in *The Archaeology of Contact in Settler Societies* (2004), exploring the archaeology of nation-building during this period is, in the early twenty-first century, to a large extent subverting the pre-eminence of the narratives that have often told the national story. These historical archaeologies of transformation, diaspora and globalisation are also about frontiers, blurred boundaries and the refashioning of ethnicities and identities. The political context of transnational historical archaeologies is undeniable and pervasive, as postcolonial societies at once celebrate diversity and cultural and social possibilities deriving from an extraordinarily eclectic sampling of global capital while also seeking to retain identities that have created the cohesion of nations.

But immigration on the scale we discuss had significant and lasting impacts on Britain and the other European nations that lost population during the nineteenth and twentieth centuries. Most obviously this was at the level of dislocated communities and fundamentally altered landscapes that were already significantly under pressure due to enclosure and industrialization. These changes were well understood at the time, and the physical marks of immigration are enduring and continuing, especially in the case of what were effectively European landscapes abandoned by people who had left for new worlds.

Social dislocation in source countries such as Britain was also understood and widely discussed. Parting was always difficult, but as the century unfolded and sea travel became faster, more reliable and above all cheaper, contact by post at least kept the first generation of contacts strong. Indeed many migrants utilised this chain of contacts to manage their own migration. But when did English, Irish or Scottish immigrants become Australian and how did this come about? (see, e.g. Eddy and Schreuder 1988). The politics of connection and affiliation were deemed by some to be essential and celebrated in icons of Englishness. For others forced to leave their homes through eviction (as was the case for many Highland Scots) or starvation, thoughts of home were perhaps not so rosy. Throughout the century opinions changed in Britain, as well as in Australia, about the consequences of immigration for both societies. At times British commentators lamented that the best of England were leaving for Australia – to the long-term detriment of Britain. At others the emphasis was placed on ridding England of the poor and destitute. Naturally it was never that simple. Colonial governments most certainly did not want people who were incapable of making their way in the periphery, but there was a strong sense that provided with opportunity, people of whatever class could thrive, especially women. Again there were many who earnestly believed that in places such as Australia, it was possible to both shed the light of Anglo–Saxon civilization in places where the darkness of 'savagery' and 'barbarism' had up to then flourished unchecked, as well as to create better societies, not just for those at the bottom of the class ladder but for all. But for this to occur, the political and cultural connectedness of Empire was paramount, and technology was to be the agent for making this happen. Certainly there were many who believed that the flow of history favoured the periphery over the metropolitan. Consider the thoughts of William Charles Wentworth, a chief agitator for self-government in the colony of NSW and a truly awful amateur poet. His *Australasia* concludes:

> And, O Britannia! shouldst thou cease to ride
> Despotic Empress of old Ocean's tide; –
> Should thy tamed Lion – spent his former might, –
> No longer roar the terror of the fight; –
> Should e'er arrive that dark disastrous hour,
> When bow'd by luxury, thou yield'st to pow'r; –
> When thou, no longer freest of the free,
> To some proud victor bend'st the vanquish'd knee; –
> May all thy glories in another sphere
> Relume, and shine more brightly still than here;
> May this, thy last-born infant, then arise,
> To glad thy heart and greet thy parent eyes;
> And Australasia float, with flag unfurl'd,
> A new Britannia in another world.

But of course the job of maintaining racial and cultural destiny through the politics of imperial cohesion was always going to be difficult. Notwithstanding great flows of population, capital and technology and despite the transference of political and cultural institutions, class structures, ideologies of domesticity and social aspiration, underwritten by the mass consumption of mass-produced consumer goods, newspapers and magazines, the point of colonisation was also the beginning of a journey of separation and differentiation. There are many reasons why this happened. All settler societies generated internal tensions from a variety of sources, among them are labour and capital, gender, cultural diversity among immigrants and of course relations with indigenes. Resolving these required local solutions, sometimes at odds with the wishes of the metropolitan. The political and social evolution of settler colony into independent nation is thus understandable, even if its causes, precise histories or consequences can be debated.

Much less attention has been paid to the role played by material culture in this differentiation and separation from Britain. A recurring question in this book relates to the issue of how an increasingly globalised and homogenous material culture could be 'read' by its consumers in culturally heterogenous ways. Histories of settler societies such as Australia have long stressed the importance of technological innovation spurred on by isolation or as Geoffrey Blainey (1966) aptly put it: 'the tyranny of distance'. But such histories have also understood the overwhelming significance of the development of the global market. As Cain (2015) has observed, between 1800 and 1850, the volume of world trade grew by two and a half times. Over the next 60 years, it was to increase tenfold. It is widely understood that the discovery of enormous reserves of gold first in California and then in Australia was an important impetus for growth, but it is also true that the application of steam technology to transport (on land and at sea) made it all possible.

This discussion has very broadly sketched some of the issues raised by a historical archaeology of migration to Australia. We now turn to a consideration of specifics which will enhance our understanding of the migrant experience.

Coming to Australia

EVERYTHING was ready—boxes packed, tinned, and corded; farewells taken, and ourselves whirling down by rail to Gravesend—too much excited—too full of the future to experience that sickening of the heart, that desolation of the feelings, which usually accompanies an expatriation, however voluntary, from the dearly loved shores of one's native land. (Clacy 1853, 5)

In the nineteenth century, some 1.6 million people arrived from Europe, North America and Asia to the British colonies dotted around the continent of Australia. As a result the societies of the indigenous occupants were fundamentally transformed through the consequences of conquest, occupation and dispossession. Some indigenous societies, for example, in the island of Tasmania, were literally brought to the edge of extinction. Populations declined severely, and traditional ways of life were in many cases supplanted (or at the very least hidden from view) by a new colonial order that paid scant heed to indigenous ways or sensibilities. Rather, these people frequently became a 'problem' in their own country, one that might be resolved by the historical inevitability of their passing into extinction or 'ameliorated' by setting them to work in the new pastoral economies. From 1788 right through the nineteenth century, the British colonies of what in 1901 was to become Australia created a new settler society based on wealth derived from land taken from its original inhabitants and transformed by people who were free, indentured, convicted or themselves dispossessed. There is no single story of arrival and survival, rather a multitude of pathways through the trauma of dispossession and the somewhat different trauma of people journeying to a new life half a world away. Our work in The Rocks and on the Commonwealth Block has brought to light many of these experiences – the good and the bad – that are inextricably linked with the foundation of two major Australian cities.

Australia is the product of global migration, and it should therefore come as no surprise that such foundational matters have spawned a very large literature reflecting the complexity of the process – no matter whether it is occurring in the nineteenth, twentieth or the twenty-first centuries. Historians have used the lens of migration to explore the creation of new societies from old and their impacts on the societies that were the source of the migrant populations. A great deal has been written about the migrant experiences of the Irish, Scottish and English who came to Australia and the translation of fundamental elements of the law and cultural practices of the British Empire to new lands. Sectarian enmities (particularly those between Catholics and Protestants) remained important for many years, as did the possibility that old conflicts between the Irish and the English could be refought on the far side of the world. Similarly, historians have focused on issues flowing from a consideration of gender and the ambiguities that fostered the oppression of women at the same time as creating societies where women were among the first in the world to gain suffrage. Given the turbulent history of race in Australia – beginning with the indigenous inhabitants and spiking with Anglo–Celtic responses to what was perceived as the invasion of white Australia by Asian (particularly Chinese) migrants – race and racism, especially within the context of the British Empire, have been a core interest among social historians. Much the same intensity of focus has been applied to the history of labour in Australia, reflecting its representation as a worker's arcadia with the very early introduction of the 8-hour work day and numerous innovations in social policy. Of course much has changed since the nineteenth century, but it is important to remember that for free migrants, the prospect of high wages and good working conditions, as well as the freedom from the social and cultural constrictions of Britain, was an important 'pull' factor at the time.

These are significant matters of context that allow us to explore both the 'push' and 'pull' factors that convinced so many free people that the long, costly and dangerous journey to Australia was worth undertaking. Why go to Australia when North America (and even South Africa) was so much closer? Naturally for convicts there was no element of choice! It is well understood that there were significant 'push' factors for free migrants leaving Britain and Ireland. Chief among these, especially for the urban and rural populations, was poverty linked to the massive social changes wrought by industrialisation and the transformation of British agriculture that led to significant 'surplus' populations in both the city and the country. Governments certainly saw this as a problem that could be rectified by supporting immigration, given that very few of these people had sufficient resources to meet the high costs of coming to Australia. There was also highly significant migration from Ireland to Australia (and elsewhere) as a result of the starvation and dispossession caused by the Great Famine. We shall have more to say about those journeys later in this chapter. However not all free migrants to Australia were drawn from the ranks of the urban and rural poor. Significant migration from what would be understood as 'middle-class' groups also occurred, especially in the wake of the gold rushes of the 1850s and the economic boom that followed until the 1880s. Nonetheless it is a valid generalisation that most of the people whose lives we explore in this book are drawn from those who only had their labour (skilled or unskilled) to sell. For them the 'pull' of significant subsidies for the costs of their journeys and the attractions of a place with relatively high wages and a wealth of opportunity, as well as cheap land, were sufficient incentives.

But of course the vast bulk of the first migrants were not free. Australia was occupied by the British in the wake of its loss of the American colonies in the late eighteenth century. The need to find a replacement territory to dump excess criminals from British gaols (as well as the pressing demands of vying with the French for global domination) made locating a new convict station in Australia a logical move. The First Fleet of 11 ships (made up of convict transports and accompanying naval vessels) set sail in 1787, landing at Sydney on early 1788. The 1350 people who had endured the journey found themselves witnesses to the proclamation of a new British colony, the survival of which for the first 40 years depended on the forced labour of convicts. Naturally there were free people on board the First Fleet and more steadily came out with other fleets. Migration was a hot-button issue even then; with the British government openly supporting free migration only after 1820 and as a result of agitation by the free settlers in Sydney, transportation of convicts to the colony of New South Wales ended in 1840. Transportation continued to the colonies of Van Diemen's Land (1803, later named Tasmania), Moreton Bay (1824, later named Queensland) and Perth (1829 originally only by free settlers but it soon moved to a mix of free and convict settlers) to ensure the survival of the settlement. Transportation to Australia finally ceased in 1868, by which time approximately 165,000 convicts had made the journey, representing some 10% of the total migrant population in the nineteenth century.

For the greater part of the first 70 years of British settlement, the colonial economies were firmly linked to the exploitation of terrestrial and marine resources. The pastoral economy of eastern Australia was built around sheep, and the export of wool derived from extensive open range grazing was made possible by the use of shepherds, both convict and free. It is well understood that relatively cheap and easy access to land was a major 'pull' factor attracting impoverished agriculturalists from Britain and Ireland. Though we are also now fully aware of the devastating impact of the introduction of hard-hoofed animals on the ecological sustainability of the rangelands of Australia, this took until about the 1880s to manifest itself in the more densely settled southeast of the continent (see, e.g. Murray 2018). But what led to a massive spike in migration to Australia was the discovery of significant gold deposits in New South Wales and Victoria from 1851 (Mountford and Tufnell 2018).

The discovery of gold, first in New South Wales and then in the newly formed colony of Victoria, transformed Australia absolutely. In 1851 the Australian population was 437,655, of which 77,345, or just under 18%, were Victorians. A decade later the Australian population had grown to 1,151,947, and the Victorian population had increased to 538,628. This rapid growth was almost entirely due to gold and caused significant strains to the local economies and challenges to governments. Where were these new people to be housed? How were they to be managed? (Pescod 2003). Clashes between governments and miners were not infrequent, as were more race-based conflicts between miners and Chinese immigrants who endured active discrimination, sometimes leading to riots and deaths.

Notwithstanding these large flows of population to the colonies of New South Wales and Victoria (often from other Australian colonies), governments clearly understood that there was still a significant shortage of labour, and the most direct way of dealing with this was to fund the migration of skilled immigrants from Europe. Assisted migrants received passage assistance from colonial government funds (drawn from the sale of land in Australia). The British government paid for the passage of the poor, and of course there was an important contribution made by private groups (such as that established by Caroline Chisholm) and by the migrants themselves.

Immigration on this scale provided fertile ground for contention. On the one hand, in Britain there could be great approval as the country could be rid of those who had failed in the struggle for existence and represented an economic, social and indeed moral drag on Victorian society. But there were others who lamented the loss to Britain of stout agriculturalists and labourers who still had so much to offer the mother country. This sentiment was most memorably expressed in *The Last of England* (1855) painted by Ford Maddox Brown, where our migrants to Australia brave the tumult of the oceans to make their way to a better world. Back in the colonies, opinion was equally divided. While all governments were quite clear that they were not keen to receive the 'sweepings of England', most believed that well-articulated 'pull' factors would attract the right sort of migrant.

Indeed the were a multiplicity of ways people came to Australia, whether it was through local or British private philanthropy, the activities of governments (British and colonial), local associations in Ireland and Britain or (perhaps most important of all) members of extended families that relied heavily on the experience of others to first guide their choice of Australia as a destination and then to light the pathway. The importance of private letters and public discussions where migrants wrote of their experiences in Australia cannot be underplayed, especially in the common case of chain migration, as well as in the popular response to the blandishments of local recruiting agents.

The best example of a British government body devoted to the encouragement and support of migration was the Colonial Land and Emigration Commission. The Commission was created in 1840 to undertake the duties of two earlier and overlapping authorities which were both under the supervision of the Secretary of State (see Hitchins 1931; Pescod 2001). These were the Colonisation Commissioners for South Australia, established under a parliamentary Act of 1834, and the Agent General for Emigration, appointed in 1837. The new commission dealt with grants of land, the outward movement of settlers, the administration of the Passenger Acts of 1855 and 1863 and, from 1846 to 1859, the scrutiny of colonial legislation. In 1855 it became the Emigration Commission. In 1873 the administration of the

Passenger Acts was transferred to the Board of Trade. The commission's powers were gradually given up to the larger colonies as they obtained self-government.

The Colonial Land and Emigration Commissioners were responsible for the management of land sales in Australia, using some of the proceeds to promote and regulate emigration to its constituent colonies. This included the selection and conveyance of migrants through the use of emigration officers based at London, Liverpool, Bristol, Greenock, Leith, Dublin, Cork, Belfast, Limerick, Sligo and Londonderry. The Commissioners were to prepare plans of emigration, select persons for free passages, charter ships, regulate conditions on board British passenger vessels, safeguard the health and comfort of the emigrants by appointing surgeons and matrons and protect emigrants against fraud. This was to be achieved through a series of Passenger Acts. One of the most important duties of the Commissioners was the general supervision and administration of the working of the many Passenger Acts. Although there were large numbers of migrants from England and Scotland during this period, the agents based in Ireland did a particularly brisk trade during the years of the Great Famine. In the next section, we discuss aspects of this episode in migration to the city of Sydney.

The Hyde Park Barracks

The Hyde Park Barracks (see Fig. 4.1) was built under instruction from Governor Lachlan Macquarie between 1817 and 1819 to provide secure accommodation for male government-assigned convicts who, until that time, roamed Sydney's streets after their day's work and were responsible for their own lodgings. The Barracks' complex was constructed by skilled convict labour to a design specified by the convict architect, Francis Greenway. In Greenway's original Georgian design, the compound comprised a central dormitory building, enclosed by perimeter walls with corner pavilions that contained both cells and guard houses. Two ranges flanked the northern and southern perimeter walls and included a kitchen, bakery and mess, in addition to residential quarters for the Deputy Superintendent and his family. The Barracks was intended to house 600 convicts, but up to 1400 were known to have been accommodated there at any one time (see Davies et al. 2013).

Following the cessation of convict transportation to NSW in 1840, the number of convicts in government service was in decline, and new uses for the old Greenway building were soon found. In 1848, the few convicts still living at the Hyde Park Barracks were moved to Cockatoo Island, and the main Barracks' building was refitted to accommodate orphans and a new kind of mobile workforce: the single, female migrant:

> The building known as Hyde Park Barracks having survived the system of supplying this colony with Labour, to which it so long ministered, has been appropriated as a place in which the Orphan Immigrants will be lodged until provided their places. Situated at the corner of Hyde Park [it] is an open place, which, though in immediate proximity to the busi-

Fig. 4.1 The Hyde Park Barracks, Sydney (Photographer: Murray)

ness thoroughfares of Sydney, is not one itself, with the Government Domain behind it stretching to the Waters of Harbour, and an uninterrupted view to the Heads of Port Jackson, surrounded by a spacious yard enclosed by high walls, and close to the principal Church of England and Roman Catholic churches, and to the residences of the clergymen who officiate there, this building appears to possess every advantage that could be desired, with reference to the health, the seclusion and the moral and religious instruction of the inmates, and the convenience of persons coming to hire them. It consists of three stories, divided into large airy wards, and affords convenient accommodation for about 300 persons. The females are under the immediate superintendence of an experienced resident matron, who was appointed by the Colonial Land and Emigration Commissioners to the charge of the children who arrived last year in the '*Sir Edward Parry*', and where efficiency in that situation caused her appointment to the office which she now fills.

(*Annual Report of Immigration in NSW* 1848, page 5, SRNSW 4/4708 in HPB Research folder: 'AONSW Immigration and Government Asylum Records')

The emigration of women to Australia, both convict and free, began with the First Fleet, with 568 male and 191 female convicts on board. By the time transportation ended, in 1853 for New South Wales, Tasmania, Norfolk Island and Moreton Bay and in 1868 for Western Australia, approximately 158,702 male and female convicts had reached Australia. Approximately 72,500 men and 11,500 women came to the colony of New South Wales, with a further 12,000 female convicts sent to Van Diemen's Land and Norfolk Island. Women represented about 15% of all convicts. The situation with respect to the relative proportions of male and female free (unassisted) migrants was somewhat different, being some two to one. Unassisted female emigrants arrived as wives, daughters and mothers, mostly within a family group. These free settlers paid their own passage.

Mrs Charles Clacy in her *A Lady's Visit to the Gold Diggings of Australia 1852–53* remarked:

> If you can go under suitable protection, possess good health, are not fastidious or 'fine-ladylike', can milk cows, churn butter, cook a good damper, and mix a pudding, the worst risk you run is that of getting married, and finding yourself treated with twenty times the respect and consideration you may meet with in England. (1853, 127)

The Female Immigration Depot housed at Hyde Park Barracks from 1848 to 1886 was the primary reception and hiring depot in Sydney for 'unprotected' females. During its 38 years of operation, the depot received some 40,000 working-class Irish, English, Scottish and Welsh female immigrants. Caroline Chisholm, known as 'the emigrant's friend', earned this title for her work with poor migrants to Australia in the nineteenth century and was sufficiently famous in England to have been the basis of Dickens' Mrs Jellyby in *Bleak House*. In 1841 Chisholm established her Female Immigrant Home in Sydney to care for migrant women who were without refuge or support which in key ways was a precursor to the government-run Immigration Depot at the Barracks. Chisholm is credited with being particularly influential in reviving a British family reunion scheme, which organised government-assisted or free passage to the colony for many families of ex-convicts between 1847 and 1852.

British campaigns to assist women to emigrate to Australian colonies had begun in the 1830s. In the 1840s, the final cessation of convict transportation sparked renewed interest in securing migrant labour, and hundreds of thousands refugees were fleeing the Great Famine in Ireland. Under a new scheme, orphans from Irish poorhouses and industrious single women were brought to Australia under free passage, and from 1848 they were received at the Hyde Park Barracks. During the 38 years of its operation as an Immigration Depot (1848–1868), some 40,000 women took refuge within its walls. A display at the Barracks tells their stories and utilises artefacts drawn from the excavation of the site (https://sydneylivingmuseums.com.au/exhibitions/female-immigration-depot-1848-1886).

In the years 1848–1850, a total of 4114 orphan girls, some no more than 14 years old, were shipped on government-funded immigrant vessels from Ireland to the Australian colonies. These girls had been handpicked by government officials and removed from county workhouses that had become seriously overcrowded especially after 1845 when the potato crop (the staple food and income source for Irish tenant farmers) continued to fail. There were grievous consequences – famine and deaths from starvation and widespread eviction of tenants by owners. Families and community lives were seriously disrupted, and by 1848, the death toll had reached 1 million, with approximately 20% of deaths occurring in a workhouse. This appalling state of affairs prompted Earl Grey, then Secretary of State for the Colonies (1846–1852), to develop an immigration scheme to relieve the pressure on the workhouses by removing orphans to the Australian colonies. The costs of the scheme were to be borne by the British government.

Fig. 4.2 Irish Famine Memorial in the grounds of Hyde Park Barracks (Photographer: Whiteghost. ink · Date: 2013-07-07 16:06:15 License: Creative Commons Attribution-Share Alike 3.0)

The impoverished families of Irish emancipists were the major source of migrants at this time, and the grounds of the Barracks contain a powerful memorial to their journey (see Fig. 4.2). Over 4000 orphaned young women were encouraged to emigrate from Britain and offered the opportunity of employment in the growing colony. In the early 1850s, the Immigration Depot also housed the wives and children of convicts brought to the colony at government expense to be reunited with their husbands and fathers. An ex-convict of good conduct and sufficient means could apply to the governor for their family to be given free passage to the colony.

The offices of the Agent for Immigration and the hiring rooms of the Female Immigration Depot were located on the ground floor of the Barracks building, with temporary accommodation for new arrivals transferred from the Quarantine Station on the second and third floors. The immigrant women were supervised by a matron and resided in the Barracks for a short period until 'hiring day' when colonists engaged them as domestic servants. Of the thousands of women who passed through the depot, some stayed for a week or more and others less than a day. Until such engagements were arranged, the women were confined for their own protection and ministered to by clergy. In addition to the Female Immigration Depot, the Hyde Park Barracks first accommodated some 2253 Irish orphan girls (until 1852), the Immigration Office and many other government agencies in the northern and southern ranges of the complex. In 1862, the top floor of the central dormitory building was given over for the use of the Government Asylum for Infirm and Destitute Women, following the colonial government's assumption of responsibility for the care of the aged and infirm.

The matron played a dual role as superintendent to both the Depot and the Destitute Asylum. The asylum inmates experienced a very different kind of life within the Barracks walls, some staying for a month-long spell when their rheumatism affected their ability to work, others lying bedridden on the top floor, hidden away for years and sometimes decades from the young immigrant girls and office workers below. The able-bodied inmates were subject to a strict regimen of domestic duties, and all women of the asylum had their share of religious instruction and comfort from volunteer, evangelical organisations who brought flowers, small gifts and religious tracts to read to the old women.

The archaeology of the Hyde Park Barracks has the capacity to tell us much about the experience of female immigration (and the operation of institutions such as Destitute Asylum (and their English cousins, the workhouses)) in the nineteenth century. The bulk of the collection was excavated between 1980 and 1981, with the remainder recovered during monitoring works of the museum grounds from 1982 to 1997 (see Davies et al. 2013 for a full discussion focused on the women of the Destitute Asylum).

As our analysis of the collection proceeds, we have had to constantly tack between the individual and the institutional, between the worlds outside and inside the Barracks and of course between material culture and written documents. There is tremendous richness here. There are many things to emphasise, but the most important of all is the sheer untapped potential of sites like the Barracks which existed all over the western world in the nineteenth century. Detailed assemblage-based analyses of the material culture found at the Barracks constitute a great resource for understanding the history of migration as a vital element of the history of the modern world.

References

Baines, D. 1985. *Migration in a Mature Economy: Emigrations and Internal Migration in England and Wales, 1861–1900*. Cambridge: Cambridge University Press.

Bayly, C. 2004. *The Birth of the Modern World, 1780–1914: Global Connections and Comparisons*. Malden: Blackwell.

Blainey, G. 1966. *The Tyranny of Distance: How Distance Shaped Australian History*. Melbourne: Sun.

Brighton, S. 2011. Middle-Class Ideologies and American Respectability: Archaeology and the Irish Immigrant Experience. *International Journal of Historical Archaeology* 15: 30–50.

Broome, R. 1984. *Arriving*. Sydney: Fairfax, Syme and Weldon.

Cain, P. 2015. *British Imperialism 1688–2000*. 3rd ed. London: Taylor and Francis.

Card, J., ed. 2013. *The Archaeology of Hybrid Material Culture*. Carbondale: Southern Illinois University Press.

Clacy, E. 1853 (1997). *A Lady's Visit to the Gold Diggings of Australia in 1852–1853*. London: Schultze & Company. Reprinted University of Sydney Library.

Crews, K., M. Warner, and M. Purser. 2017. *Historical Archaeology Through Western Eyes*. Lincoln: UNP.

Cusick, J., ed. 1998. *Studies in Culture Contact: Interaction, Culture Change, and Archaeology, Occasional Paper No. 25*. Carbondale: Center for Archaeological Investigations, University of Southern Illinois.

Davies, P., P. Crook, and T. Murray. 2013. *Archaeological Research at Hyde Park Barracks, Sydney*. Sydney: Australasian Society of Historical Archaeology.

Dawdy, S. 2000. Understanding Cultural Change Through the Vernacular: Creolization in Louisiana. *Historical Archaeology* 34 (3): 107–123.

Eddy, J., and D. Schreuder, eds. 1988. *The Rise of Colonial Nationalism: Australia, New Zealand, Canada and South Africa First Assert Their Nationalities 1880–1914*. St. Leonards: Allen and Unwin.

Haines, R. 1997. *Emigration and the Labouring Poor. Australian Recruitment in Britain and Ireland, 1831–60*. Houndsmills: Macmillan.

Harper, M., and S. Constantine. 2010. *Migration and Empire*. Oxford/New York: Oxford University Press.

Hitchins, F. 1931. *The Colonial Land and Emigration Commission*. Philadelphia: University of Pennsylvania Press.

Jupp, J. 2018. *An Immigrant Nation Seeks Cohesion: Australia from 1788*. London: Anthem Press.

Lightfoot, K. 1995. Culture Contact Studies: Redefining the Relationship Between Prehistoric and Historical Archaeology. *American Antiquity* 60 (2): 199–217.

Mountford, B., and S. Tufnell, eds. 2018. *A Global History of Gold Rushes*. Berkeley: University of California Press.

Mrozowski, S. 2010. Creole Materialities: Archaeological Explorations of Hybridized Realities on a North American Plantation. *Journal of Historical Sociology* 23 (1): 16–39.

Murdoch, A. 2004. *British Emigration, 1630–1914*. Houndsmills: Macmillan.

Murray, T. 2004. The Archaeology of Contact in Settler Societies. In *The Archaeology of Contact in Settler Societies*, ed. T. Murray, 1–16. Cambridge/New York: Cambridge University Press.

———. 2018. Towards an Archaeology of Extensive Pastoralism in the Great Artesian Basin in Australia. In *Historical Archaeology and Environment*, ed. Marcos André Torres de Souza and Diogo Menezes Costa, 109–127. New York: Springer.

Pescod, K. 2001. *Good Food, Bright Fires and Civility: Immigrant Depots of the Nineteenth Century*. Kew: Australian Scholarly Publishing.

———. 2003. *A Space to Lay My Head: Immigrant Shelters of Nineteenth Century Victoria*. Kew: Australian Scholarly Publishing.

Richards, E. 1985. *A History of the Highland Clearances, vol. 2: Emigration, Protest, Reasons*. London: Croom Helm.

———. 1993. How Did Poor People Emigrate from the British Isles to Australia in the Nineteenth Century? *Journal of British Studies* 32 (3): 250–279.

Schneider, T., and L. Panich, eds. 2014. *Indigenous Landscapes and Spanish Missions: New Perspectives from Archaeology and Ethnohistory*. Tucson: University of Arizona Press.

Stein, G., ed. 2005. *The Archaeology of Colonial Encounters: Comparative Perspective*. Santa Fe: School of American Research.

Thomas, D., ed. 1989. *Columbian Consequences, 3 vols*. Washington, DC: Smithsonian Institution Press.
Voss, B. 2005. The Archaeology of Overseas Chinese Communities. *World Archaeology* 37 (3): 424–439.
———. 2008. *The Archaeology of Ethnogenesis: Race and Sexuality in Colonial San Francisco*. Berkeley: University of California Press.
Waselkov, C. 1997. *The Archaeology of French Colonial North America*. Tucson: Society for Historical Archaeology.

Chapter 5
Archaeology at First Government House, Sydney

The surviving subsurface footings of the First Government House (FGH) complex are the earliest archaeological remains of British occupation in Australia, dating to 1788 the year of invasion and first settlement. Excavated between 1983 and 1992, these architectural features and associated artefacts, alongside those of the adjacent guard house, have sparked over 35 years of historical–archaeological investigations into colonial architecture, government printing, dining, the lives of the governors who occupied the House from 1788 to 1845, and the urban dynamic of the city which moved in to claim this extraordinary site for commercial development (see Fig. 5.1).

The assemblage from the First Government House site was selected for inclusion in the EAMC project. Given the comprehensive nature of the published accounts of the archaeology recovered from the FGH prior to 1987, we concentrated our efforts on the archaeological features recovered during the 1990–1991 excavations of the guard house and revisiting some components of the 1983–1987 assemblage in light of the extensive historical research conducted for the excavations (Proudfoot 1983; Annable 1992) and gathered by the Historic Houses Trust of NSW (now Sydney Living Museums) in preparation for the Museum of Sydney on the Site of First Government House which opened in 1995. This work was published in a Trust monograph (Crook and Murray 2006c).

In this chapter we begin with a review of previous research and an outline of our methodology. Following a discussion of the formation processes and sequence of construction at FGH, we provide two studies of different aspects of its archaeology: first, the tablewares and dining equipage of Governors King and Macquarie, and, second, the unusual architectural history of the guard house, built c. 1812 and partially demolished in 1838.

© Springer Nature Switzerland AG 2019
T. Murray, P. Crook, *Exploring the Archaeology of the Modern City in Nineteenth-century Australia*, Contributions To Global Historical Archaeology, https://doi.org/10.1007/978-3-030-27169-5_5

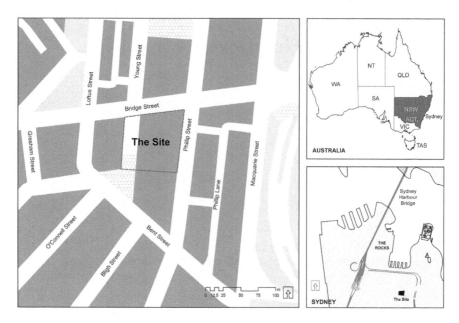

Fig. 5.1 Location of the First Government House site, Sydney. (P. Crook)

The Excavation

Archaeological investigation of FGH began under the direction of Anne Bickford in February 1983 in preparation for building a multi-storey office tower. Following the discovery of remains of the First Government House in February 1983, the future of the site was fiercely contested, but development work proceeded nonetheless. Following the decision to significantly alter the proposed development to conserve the archaeological remains, the site was backfilled, and a drainage system was installed to conserve the subsurface remains in 1984 and 1985, respectively. From 1990 to 1992, in preparation for the Museum of Sydney and building the Governor Phillip and Governor Macquarie Towers, new excavations were undertaken in Young Street and Raphael Place – also directed by Anne Bickford – and other trenches on the main site (in the 'Commemorative Area', now the Museum fore-court) were reopened (Bickford 1993a, b; Bickford and Petrie 1993). In 1996, when road works were undertaken on the corner of Bridge and Phillip Streets, Godden Mackay Logan monitored the excavations. (For a detailed summaries of the excavations, see Crook and Murray 2006c, 13–18; Stocks 1988a, 2–8; Bickford 1993b, 10–49) (See Figs. 5.2 and 5.3).

Anne Bickford and other archaeologists who have written about the site, have stressed that the first four stages of excavation were run as rescue or salvage operations – directed by and limited to meeting the the needs of the development (Stocks 1988a, 8).

The remains underlying the main site have been preserved for posterity and one day may be reopened and excavated to complete the archaeological picture of

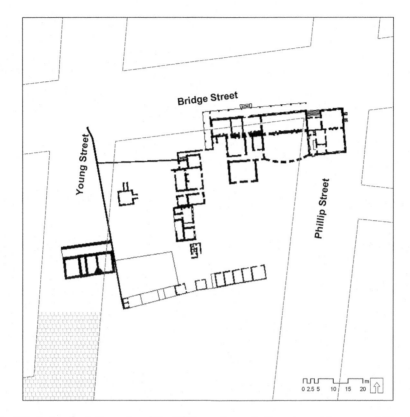

Fig. 5.2 Archaeological remains of the FGH complex and adjacent guard house overlaid on the current street grid (approximate locations only). (P. Crook after M. Lewis 1845, Proudfoot et al. 1991, 5 and Bickford 1993a: Fig. 5)

FGH. It is regrettable but necessary to accept that after 35 years, all archaeological work to date (including this publication) is a work-in-progress. While considerable time was invested in the excavation of the main site, the excavation strategy is best described as test trenching for key structural features, and many artefact-rich deposits still lie below the surface (Proudfoot et al. 1991, 65).

Much more of the archaeological record in Young Street and Raphael Place was completely excavated, but only some remains were conserved in situ owing to the pressure and constraints of the development schedule (Bickford 1993b, 12, 16, 25, 31, 44).

The EAMC Approach at First Government House

The structural remains of First Government House and its outbuildings provide unique physical evidence of the first permanent official dwelling built in the fledgling colony of New South Wales. Intrinsically these remains reveal details about the

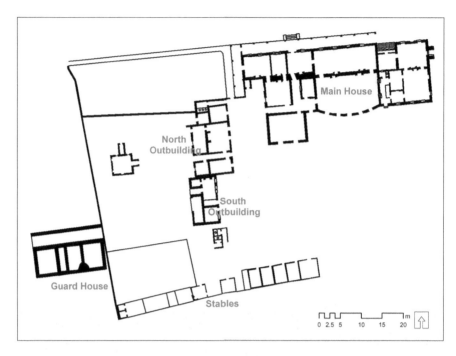

Fig. 5.3 Outline of key architectural features from the First Government House site, known from historical and archaeological sources. (P. Crook after Lewis 1845, Proudfoot et al. 1991, 20 and Bickford 1993a: Fig. 1)

solutions found to overcome the difficulties faced by the colonists in the new and untested environment and, at a broader level, have sparked inquiries into other aspects of life in the colony at the time – Aboriginal contact, social distinction and the nature of governance. While these and greater levels of cultural significance are widely agreed, the contribution of the artefact assemblages to an understanding of the site, and the colony is more difficult to determine.

The level of site disturbance and time constraints placed on the excavation created a relatively small and incomplete assemblage that hampered the interpretative efforts of the archaeologists and artefact specialists working on all phases of the excavation (e.g. see Stocks 1988b, 81; Thorp 1987, 4). With few intact domestic or work-related deposits and only a small portion of the house revealed during excavation, most of the research questions to be asked of the site concern building techniques and structural foundations.

The most compelling avenues of inquiring regarding the First Government House site have been discussed in Australia's First Government House (Proudfoot et al. 1991). The book provides a historical overview of the site from 1788 to the late 1980s, focusing on its use as Australia's First Government House from 1788 to 1845, and its subsequent demolition in 1845–1846. The authors sought to integrate history and archaeology by providing a detailed account of the archaeological excavations carried out on the site from 1982 to 1989, as well as showing how artefacts revealed aspects of the history of the site in conjunction with written and other archival sources. While it is limited to the earliest phases of excavation and was prepared before the first full catalogue of assemblage was undertaken, it remains the most comprehensive synthesis of the archaeology of FGH to date.

Given this resource and factors of site disturbance and a restricted approach to excavation, the strategies for utilising the assemblage for large-scale analysis within the EAMC project were more limited than those at the Cumberland and Gloucester Streets site (Crook et al. 2005), and the Hyde Park Barracks (Crook and Murray 2006a; Davies et al. 2013). However, the exceptional cultural significance of the First Government House site dictates that even small contributions to the understanding of the site are considered to be important and worthy of further investigation.

Our approach concentrated on developing aspects of the second phases of excavation excluded from the 1991 publication and pursuing issues or topics common to both excavations.

In preparation for the analysis, the two databases of the FGH and YRP excavations were combined into one (see Crook et al. 2003; Crook and Murray 2006b). This basic dataset was enhanced by entering context data from most stratigraphic units in both phases of excavation and artefact box numbers, and undertaking some basic data management maintenance. This allowed us to examine for the first time the total number of artefacts from each phase of occupation on the First Government House site. A small number of records were upgraded with weights, measures and additional descriptive information. However, the majority of the data used in this chapter is derived directly from the original catalogues.

The First Government House

First Government House was one of the first[1] permanent European buildings constructed in the colony of New South Wales, and was the primary seat of Government in New South Wales from 1788 to 1846. The House and its outbuildings served as a residence and office for the Governor and his family. It was both a public and private place. Many 'domestic' activities, such as eating and drinking, were regularly conducted as public affairs. Banquets and dinners catering for dozens of individuals were a regular occurrence on special occasions, such as the King's birthday. The guest list grew over the years from nearly 100 guests in 1811 to 500 in 1835 (Gillespie 1975, 45, 96). Such events would not have been possible without the staff of servants housed at Government House.

The House was also an administrative centre. Government orders were read, reports were received, musters were held, and from 1795 to at least 1800, the

---

[1] The first stone-hewn house was built by Lieutenant Governor Ross; work commenced 1 month before the foundation stone of First Government House was laid (Broadbent 1997, 21).

government printer was housed there. At times the administrative affairs of the colony became too chaotic. In 1810, Governor Macquarie established a schedule to deal with such matters, and in June 1811, he announced that 'petitions, memorials etc. mostly of a frivolous and unimportant nature would only be received on Mondays' (HRA 7, 267, 542 in Hughes and HHT n.d.).

Governor Macquarie and his predecessor, Governor Bligh, both went to great lengths to reclaim the privacy of Government House and the Governor's Domain. Bligh had 'ditched in' the southern boundary of the Domain which had hitherto been freely accessed by the public, and he soon set about demolishing houses cluttering the rear of Government House. His Government Order of 23 July 1807 was uncompromising, stating that:

> *the present occupiers are required and directed to quit possession of their said houses, taking away or disposing of their materials, the said grounds being wanted for Government purposes.* (Sydney Gazette, 26 July 1807)

Governor Macquarie constructed a stone wall around the whole of the domain (8 foot or 2.13 m high is some sections), blocked off the carriageway to the west of Government House with a new guard house, and tirelessly pursued the eviction of the remaining lessees in the vicinity of the government domain, those of Mr. Palmer with his windmill and Mr. Riley with his bakery. Macquarie also issued a strict Government Order in October 1812 prohibiting all access to Government Domain land, including the grazing of stray animals, the cutting of wood or shrubs, quarrying stone or digging loam (Proudfoot et al. 1991, 103).

Complete privacy was not achieved until the Governor relinquished the prominent position on the crest of Bridge Street, and the house was rebuilt deeper into the Domain in 1845. Of course the new Government House was required for other reasons. First Government House had never been in a state of good repair for any length of time. Until Governor Bourke's term, prior to the final approval to rebuild Government House in 1837, all governors made substantial alterations or repairs to the house or grounds or both. The exception was Governor Brisbane who made the Parramatta residence the official Government House during his term.

Of course, it is important to recall that maintaining the Government House at Port Jackson was not the only residence of the Governor and his staff. The Government House at Parramatta was built in c. 1799, providing summer accommodation for the governors[2] (with the aforementioned exception of Governor Brisbane) and alternative accommodation when extensive repairs were being undertaken in Sydney. The Parramatta house stands today and has its own history of renovation and extension. Governor Macquarie's ambitious extension of First Government House was matched by his remodelling of Government House, Parramatta. In addition to these two, the public works department maintained several other government houses in important towns across New South Wales, including those at Windsor (built in 1796) and Port Macquarie (built in 1821).

---

[2] According to Broadbent (1992, 12), Governor Macquarie used the Parramatta residence during the winter months.

Who Made the Archaeological Record at FGH?

The First Government House was built for the Governor by convicts. While the Governor, and at certain periods his family, may be considered the primary residents, there was an extensive staff that also occupied the house and its outbuildings to cook, clean and assist with clerical duties. Then there were the regular visitors and occasional guests.

The archaeological record does not always reflect the lives of important persons or notable events. While First Government House was a place of many significant events and occurrences – declarations, the confinement of a despised Governor Bligh by a 'Rebel government', the 're-education' of a young Aboriginal man (McBryde 1989) – these events tend not to leave identifiable traces in the archaeological record of the place. The individuals most important to the process of the development and depletion (creation and destruction) of the archaeological record were often those who spent the least time on site, namely, the builders or maintenance workers. While they may not have been aware of it, a relatively small crew of men laying services for a temporary office building in 1912 could, and in the case of First Government House did, wipe out a large part of an archaeological record accumulated over 130 years by hundreds of individuals who lived in, operated, serviced or mended the Governor's residence.

Indeed, the continuing use of the main part of site in the late nineteenth century and the ongoing maintenance of roads and drainage channels on the outer margins of the site as it survives today have had a significant impact on the archaeological resources that remain. More than 1481 (approximately 50%) contexts and 76,000 artefacts were brought in, or turned over, by construction workers in the 136 years following the demolition of the First Government House. A number of early sites were notably disturbed by these processes.

The archaeological record which did survive was complex enough to begin with. While there are more than 1200 contexts and 60,500 artefacts that can be attributed to the First Government House period with confidence, few of these were uniquely associated with individual structures (see Fig. 5.5), and only approximately 80 contexts can be considered occupation deposits, arising from activities other than construction or maintenance, and some of these were only tentatively attributed.

While construction activities often leave behind substantial archaeological remains – namely the footings – which may be closely dated to a known historical event, often the material used during building works is brought in from other sites. While many artefacts may be trapped in foundation trenches, or mixed with builder's deposits then sealed by further construction, it is rarely possible to attribute those pieces to the people occupying the site.

The material caught up in the First Government House drainage system is perhaps a different matter, because the entry points for each channel were on the grounds of First Government House itself. After 1812 when Macquarie secured the boundaries of the First Government House complex and walled in the entire Domain, gaining occasional access to Government House would have been quite difficult, and the likelihood of external refuse deposition can be ruled out – unless deliberately brought on site for in-filling purposes. Furthermore, even though material may have been discarded within the Governor's residential complex, it was not necessarily used by the Governor. The fragments of local, European and Asian crockery, alcohol bottles, clay pipes and meat cuts that are most likely to have been used and discarded on site may well have been used, and potentially even owned, by servants and assistants.

Building First Government House: 1788

The first residence was a prefabricated oilcloth 'portable house' erected on 29 January 1788 for Governor Phillip immediately after the arrival of the British fleet in Sydney Cove. In the ensuing months, makeshift accommodation across the east and west sides of the cove was provided for the roughly 1000 new settlers along with barracks for marines, huts for convicts and, more importantly, wharfage and storehouses for the supplies brought with the fleet. Progress was slow. The structures were all timber, varying in stability from the rough post-wattle-and-daub[3] examples to the more substantial timber buildings such as the barracks, hospital and storehouses. Phillip intended these to stand for 'some years' and they were encased with brick and stone when such materials became available (HRA I 1, 74 and HRNSW I, 124 in Bridges 1995, 12–13; Proudfoot et al. 1991, 41). While the timber at hand was described by David Collins as 'flaky and rotten' (Proudfoot et al. 1991, 41), timber huts had to be used until a local source of lime was discovered and brickmaking was begun.

With the most urgent building projects completed or underway, Governor Phillip turned his attention to erecting a permanent structure to serve as his residence and an administrative centre of the colony. It was not the first design for a masonry structure in Sydney Cove – the first government storehouse was probably built of brick (Proudfoot et al. 1991, 38), and Lieutenant Governor Major Roger Ross had begun his stone-built cottage a month before (Broadbent 1997, 1), nonetheless it was the first permanent official residence in the colony.

On the 15 May 1788, Governor Phillip laid the first foundation stone along with an engraved copper foundation plate (recovered by workmen laying a telegraph cable tunnel in 1899, now held in the Mitchell Library, Sydney), bearing the following transcript:

> *His Excellency*
> *ARTHUR PHILLIP Esq.*
> *Governor in Chief and*

---

[3] Posts were spaced out and infilled with a weave of twigs which would then be daubed over with clay, a technique known as 'wattling' (Bridges 1995, 13).

> *Captain General*
> *in and over the Territory of New South Wales, &c, &c, &c*
> *landed in this Cove,*
> *with the first Settlers of this Country, the 24th Day of January; 1788 and on the 15th*
> *Day of May,*
> *in the same Year, being the 28th of the Reign of His present Majesty*
> *GEORGE the THIRD,*
> *the first of these stones was laid.*

The house was nestled into the bedrock of the slope leading down to the east side of Sydney Cove. It was in an excellent position, overlooking the settlement and being visible from all vantage points around the cove.

The simple Georgian design – initially single-storey but soon expanded to include six rooms over two floors – was probably the work of convicts Henry Brewer and James Bloodworth (Proudfoot et al. 1991, 40, 55–56; Bridges 1995, 14–15) (see Fig. 5.4). The stone foundations of the structure were carried up in brick and mortar made from imported lime, shellfish from nearby Darling Harbour, mud and clay. The majority of bricks recovered from the excavation are local examples, made in Brickfield Hill (near present-day Chinatown) – one even bearing the impression of a eucalyptus leaf (Proudfoot et al. 1991, 45). They are described as fragile.

Fig. 5.4 Detail from 'A direct North general View of Sydney Cove the chief British Settlement in New South Wales as it appeared in 1794 being the 7th Year from its Establishment. Painted immediatly [sic] from Nature by T. Watling'. (Dixson Galleries DG60, courtesy of the Dixson Galleries, State Library of NSW)

Living Ruins: Decay, Extension and Repair of the First Government House

Between 1789 and 1845, nine successive governors of the colony of New South Wales lived at First Government House. Four of the governors substantially modified the building and surrounding structures, while they lived there: Governor Hunter in 1794, Governor King in 1801, Governor Macquarie in 1811 and again in 1818 under the direction of Francis Greenway and, finally, Governor Ralph Darling in the period from 1827 to 1828 (for details see Proudfoot et al. 1991, 71–124, 126). While the majority of these renovations reflected the need to expand and improve the facilities, they were also often in response to the poor condition of the residence which in 1790 Governor Phillip expected to stand for 'a great many years' (HRNSW 1 [2]: 330 in Proudfoot et al. 1991, 44).

By 1798, David Collins reported that the floor had given way (Proudfoot et al. 1991, 74). When the Governor King and his family arrived in the colony in 1799, they found that the shingle roof was decayed and indoor timber work had warped and split, declaring it 'not habitable until new roofed, and the rotten door and window frames replaced' (Proudfoot et al. 1991, 84).

It is possible that these repairs were not undertaken or were perhaps only initiated as temporary measures, because in 1806, Governor Bligh wrote that:

> *Government House and Offices wants new doors, windows, window shutters, lining and frames, shingling, flooring, whitewashing and plastering. All in so rotten a state, [it all] wants to be new....* (Proudfoot et al. 1991, 89)

In 1809, more repairs were needed to accommodate the next governor, Lachlan Macquarie, who assumed office on 1 January 1810. However the new coat of paint did little to satisfy the Lieutenant Colonel and his wife, Elizabeth. By October 1810 the government bricklayers had started work on a suite of rooms at the back of the house 'to answer the purposes of a Drawing Room, an Office and a Family Bed Room' (Broadbent 1997, 31). The new dining room or 'Great Saloon' (built behind Governor King's large drawing room) was ready enough by June 1811 to accommodate the whole of the civil and military officers and 'principal gentlemen of the colony' at dinner when 72 persons were seated. The room was not fully completed until October 1812. In December the Macquaries 'took possession of and Slept for the first time in their New Bed Room' (Broadbent 1997, 31).

Meanwhile, the unimproved offices and outbuildings of the remainder of the complex continued to age and deteriorate. In 1816, Governor Macquarie complained bitterly about the small, poorly planned offices which 'now Exhibit a Most ruinous Mean Shabby Appearance' (Proudfoot et al. 1991, 99) and proposed erecting an entirely new building on a different site within the Domain, which he and Elizabeth had set about improving following their arrival in 1810. Despite the disapproval of the plan by Lord Bathurst, Macquarie proceeded with one element of the overall design: stable sleeping quarters designed by Francis Greenway (now the Conservatorium of Music). The foundation stone was laid in December 1817, but Macquarie was forced to abandon the idea of building a new Government House.

In 1818, he commissioned another small extension to the First Government House which was completed by 1820. Remarkably, a carved sandstone lunette bearing a sunburst design from Macquarie's east wing extension was recovered from the excavation (Proudfoot et al. 1991, 101–102). It is very similar to the one that appears in an 1836 view of the House by Charles Rodius (Proudfoot et al. 1991, 96–97):

> *The final phase of major modification to the house was undertaken by Governor Darling who chose to extend the existing dwelling rather than act on the permission granted to him to construct a new house—a major endeavour which would divert labour and materials from more urgent public works throughout the colony. The additional rooms, stair case and passageways were built between June and November 1827, and First Government House took its final form.*

Five years later, in 1832, the succeeding Governor, Richard Bourke, disregarded Darling's 'improvements' and re-established the campaign to build a new Government House:

> *...the present Government House in Sydney is a collection of Rooms built at different times by Successive Governors, and is in consequence not only extremely inconvenient and unsightly but in Such a bad state of repair, as to demand the immediate expenditure of a large Sum of Money to render it habitable and decent. The Roof and flooring are in many parts decayed and the bad Smells, which prevail in the principal Sitting Room, are not only Unpleasant but unwholesome. So bad indeed was the condition of this house Considered to be upon the close of Sir Thomas Brisbane's Government, that Lord Bathurst authorized General Darling to commence building a New one immediately on his arrive here in 1826. This permission, as Your Lordship is aware, was not acted upon; and, Since that period, nothing has been done for the improvement, and but little towards the repair of the old house, and it has now reached that state of deterioration, in which it would be a waste of Money to expend any large Sum for its preservation.* (State of Government House, Sydney, November 1832, HRA 16, 785)

Designs were drawn up by the celebrated English architect, Edward Blore, but final approval was not awarded by the British Government until 1837, and the new house was not ready until 1845. In the meantime, only essential repairs were made to the original Government House. The most substantial of these were the construction of new privies in 1837, and the replacement of an outbuilding roof damaged by fire (Proudfoot et al. 1991, 123). Despite some appreciation of the picturesque elements of the overgrown cottage and grounds (Proudfoot et al. 1991, 125), there was little sentimental attachment to the complex that so inconveniently disrupted the carriage of the city street grid to the wharves along what was soon to become Circular Quay.

Supersession: The Demolition of First Government House, 1845–1846

While the first plans to demolish First Government House were implied by street extensions proposed in the 1830s, the final approval for demolition was not given until 1845. Its fate was largely determined by the proclamation of street extensions

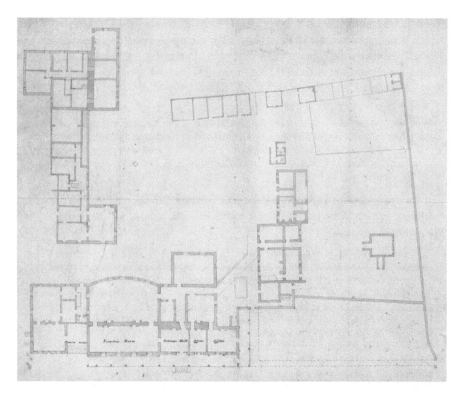

Fig. 5.5 Plan accompanying the 'Report on the Present state of the Old Government House' prepared by M. Lewis on 15 September 1845 for a Board of Survey. (SR NSW: Colonial Secretary,
NRS 905 [4/2727.2], courtesy of State Records NSW)

down to Circular Quay on 6 January 1845 (Proudfoot et al. 1991, 124), but it was
not condemned until Governor Gipps moved to the new Government House in June
1845[4] and options for the repair and use of the old house for public offices were
considered by an appointed Board, including the Colonial Architect, Mortimer
Lewis (see Fig. 5.5). Their findings, reported in September 1845, were clear:

> *To attempt repair to this building generally with a view to upholding it, would I am of opin-*
> *ion, cost as much as or more than the expense of rebuilding, and as it stands immediately in*
> *the way of the project new Streets and upon Land that will readily sell, it appears more*
> *advantageous to remove the whole, than attempt to hold up any portion of it. (Lewis 1845;*
> *in Proudfoot et al. 1991, 129–131)*

Demolition began shortly after August 1845, but there are some conflicting
reports regarding the length of time taken to demolish the whole complex. On 30
December 1845, the *Sydney Morning Herald* reported that 'The Old Demesne' had

---

[4] It was reported that, during the move to the new Government House, 'Hyde Park men' (convict
labourers) employed to carry Governor Gipps' goods and chattels stole money and jewellery from
him (Gillespie 1975, 130).

been dismantled (*Sydney Morning Herald*, 30 December 1845, quoted in Gillespie 1975, 129). This was only partly true as Mortimer Lewis reported in March 1846 that only the original house and newer extensions 'that stood in way and interfered with the prolongation of Bridge Street, has been cleared away' (12 Mar 1846, letter to the Colonial Secretary, SR NSW 4/2717.2 in Proudfoot 1983, 79).

In May 1846 Lewis reported 'that the Wing at the end nearest Macquarie Street has been since removed, and that Workmen are still engaged in taking down the remaining portion of the Building' (8 May 1846, letter to the Colonial Secretary, SR NSW 4/2717.2 in Proudfoot 1983, 81). In July, George Paton wrote to the Colonial Secretary offering to purchase bricks from the house at a rate of 5/–per thousand; and tenders were called for their sale in August. The cost of 'pulling down Old Government House' for the year of 1846 amounted to £307 (Proudfoot 1983, 81).

So, while we cannot be certain in which month the last brick was tumbled and the last stone upturned, it was probably around mid-1846, 8–9 months after demolition commenced.[5] The length of time taken to demolish the complex is telling. There was after all 57 years of construction, expansion and maintenance to unravel. As Lewis's letters to the Colonial Secretary indicate, the complex was demolished wing by wing, focusing on those elements that stood in the way of the development of the surrounding urban plan. It is unknown when the outbuildings were demolished, where the stock piles were or which structure or wing – within the complex – was demolished last.

It is known that the guard house, outside the walled First Government House complex, was not demolished until December 1847, 2 months after the move to the new guard house, completed in October (Annable 1992, 5).

Interestingly, the two stages of demolition left different archaeological signatures. More artefacts were recovered from the guard house demolition layers than were found overlying the outbuildings and those parts of the main house revealed during excavation. The proportion of this assemblage that has been identified as building material is also greater than that for all the excavated First Government House compound buildings put together: 64.3% vs 27.5%.[6] It is possible that the Public Works demolition team, working over the 8 or 9 months, was more thorough than contractors who had just a month to clear away the guard house and so left proportionately more behind. The period of time over which each site was left dismantled and abandoned may also account for the difference, as individuals may have made use of remnant bricks and stones left behind. It may also be a result of the fact that other major projects in the vicinity needed the rubble in 1845–1846 when First Government House was dismantled, but not in December 1847 when the guard house was demolished.

---

[5] Proudfoot has argued that the demolition took over a year to complete on the basis of a claim on 10 August 1846 for 'Female Servants cleaning and taking care of Govt House after Gipps' departure' (AO 4/7217.2 in Proudfoot 1983, 79).

[6] This relationship is not likely to be a product of the different collecting and cataloguing strategies of both excavation phases and artefact identification projects.

Speculations aside, the demolition layers across the site played a significant role in defining the overall stratigraphy. In many areas, the demolition rubble sealed the remains of First Government House below. Above this, in the vicinity of the main site, silty layers had washed in after the site was abandoned and left open to the elements. As development proceeded, bit by bit with the municipal council storage shed (built by 1865), the Phillip Street terraces (1867), and the Young Street terraces (1874), demolition rubble was levelled, additional fill was brought in and other pockets of rubble fill were dug through to lay services and foundations.

At the Governor's Table

Dining was an important aspect of life in First Government House. Here, governors entertained visiting dignitaries, foreign explorers, select members of their core staff and their native friends: Arabanoo, Colbee and Bennelong, or the whole force of the colony's elite on the most special occasions. The guest list for the King's Birthday ball and supper in 1835 comprised nearly 500 individuals, and a temporary supper room was erected to stage the event (*The Herald*, 1 June 1835 in Gillespie 1975, 96). In this context of viceregal responsibility, the selection, range and size of a durable and presentable dinner and glassware service demanded far more attention than an ordinary domestic acquisition.

While we might suppose that the serviceability of dinnerwares was an important symbol of the development of the colony as a whole, the first governors had more pressing concerns: supplying, hunting and growing the food to put on the plates. The provision of tablewares was the responsibility of each individual governor, rather than the colonial administration. It is widely known that military men in the late eighteenth and early nineteenth centuries travelled from station to station with their own services (Sussman 2000, 46), and it is probable that naval officers – and the first four governors before Governor Macquarie were experienced naval officers – were accustomed to this practice.

We know little about the wares Governor Phillip brought with him on the First Fleet, and the archaeological record of those first 5 years is too fragmentary to enable us to determine the services of each governor. From the few drainage deposits thought to predate 1800,[7] there are just 24 sherds of creamware (banded and plain), 4 sherds of oriental porcelain, 1 sherd of blue transfer-printed earthenware and 1 sherd of blue shell edgeware. Whether these represent the goods and chattels of governors Phillip (1788–1792), Hunter (1795–1800) or the interim governors Grose (1792–1794) and Paterson (1794–1795), we simply do not know. Little can

---

[7] 16R4: 03, 24R6: 11, 38R16: 08, 38R16: 08, 10a, 20, 38R16: 14, 38R16: 20, 38R16: 21, 38R5–38R6: 09, 38R6–38R9: 25a, 40R12: 11, 40R14: 17, 40R16: 15, 40R8: 06, Y-N: 1084, Y-N: 1092, Y-N: 1096. See artefacts: FGH09417, FGH09419, FGH10364, FGH10385, FGH10386, FGH10387, FGH10389, FGH10391, FGH10407, FGH10410, FGH10411, FGH10497, YRP5764, FGH10628, FGH10646, FGH11023 and FGH12110.

be said of Governor Bligh's (1806–1808) service owing to a lack of deposits that may be securely dated to his occupation. We know a great deal more about Governor King (1800–1806) who brought to the colony nearly 1000 vessels of table- and glassware ordered from Josiah Spode, one of the most prominent potters and supply houses in England. Sherds of Spode ware were found across the First Government House site, and it is likely that at least of these belong to Governor King's service.

Governor King's Spode

Tucked away in the research files in the Resource Centre of the Museum of Sydney is a three-page order for crockery, glassware, kitchen wares and bedroom sets placed by Governor King with Josiah Spode of London in August 1798. The document was discovered by Joy Hughes among King's private papers in the lead-up to the opening of the museum on the site of First Goverment House.

The order had been placed 3 months after King had been awarded a dormant commission for the position of Governor of New South Wales and almost 2 years since King and his family had left the small colony on Norfolk Island.

King had been a captain of the First Fleet and commander of the first settlement at Norfolk Island. After a brief visit to London in the winter of 1790–1791, during which he married Anna Josepha Coombes, he returned to the island in November 1791 to assume the position of Lieutenant Governor. He returned home to England in 1796 owing to a debilitating spell of gout. While his health recovered, his financial situation worsened. Having had only a small salary and personal capital worth no more than £1500, King considered retiring to a farm in the West Country (Shaw 1967) (see Fig. 5.6).

On 1 May 1798, he was awarded the commission to succeed Governor Hunter in the event of the latter's death or absence from the colony, and the King family made preparations to the return to Sydney Cove. Difficulties with HMS Porpoise delayed the journey, and they did not reach the colony until April 1800, but by this time, King was carrying a dispatch to recall Governor Hunter. Most of their goods, packed on another ship, arrived in November of that year (Copeland 1999, 29–30). The delay in the arrival of their household effects was of little consequence given that the family were unable to move into Government House until September, as Hunter was reluctant to relinquish his position to King.

The Spode order was large. King ordered two dinner services of 'Blue Line', a service of 'Best Queens Ware', sprigged and other tea vessels and numerous additional vessels, such as teacups and teapots, chamber pots, wash basins and jugs, garden pots, egg stands, mustard pots and the list goes on.

The range of wares would have allowed Governor King to hold parties for dinner, tea or breakfast. Together the 3 full services comprised 18 dozen dinner plates (the 'flat plates'), 6 dozen soup plates and 6 dozen entrée plates (the small plates). The order of 6 dozen plain wine glasses suggests that King was planning to cater for no more than 72 individuals, and probably more commonly in settings of 48, requiring

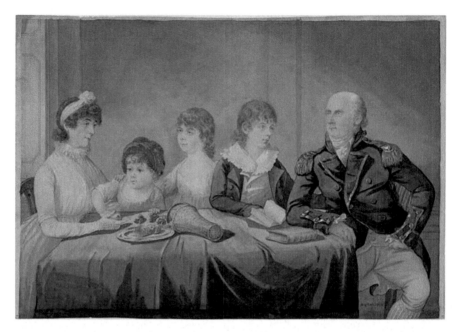

Fig. 5.6 Philip Gidley and Anna Josepha King, and their children Elizabeth, Anna Maria and Philip Parker. (Robert Dighton, 1799; ML 1244, courtesy of the Mitchell Library, State Library of NSW)

only the Blue Line service.[8] To serve the courses were 78 platters, 6 soup tureens, 12 sauce tureens, 6 salad dishes, 6 fish drainers, 6 vegetable dishes and 12 covered dished (8 square, 4 oval). The 46 bowls 'and stands' in 4 sizes were probably also intended for table service.[9] There was also a dessert service in Blue Line with 8 compotiers and 18 'open work edge' plates.

Four dozen cup and saucer sets were ordered: 12 presumably in Queensware (cost: 1 s 9d); 1 dozen 'breakfast cups' (also known as 'Irish'-sized cups) in blue sprig (7 s 6d); another blue-sprig dozen, possibly the smaller, 'London' size (6 s 6d); and another dozen, 'standard' sized, in 'Basket work decoration' (8 s). There were three teapots of different size, two sugar boxes and four milk jugs in the sought-after black basalt fabric, along with four slop bowls 'to match Cups & Sauc[e]rs' (into which the dregs of tea leaves from cups was poured) and four sugar basins.

---

[8] It is unclear why 216 dinner plates – 3 per person when catering for 72 – were required. Two per person may have been required for each course following entrée, but three cannot be so easily accounted for. It is possible that part of the order was to be used at other residences of the Governor and/or that a portion of them was set aside in case of breakage.

[9] These 'stands' for bowls were probably oversized saucers, rather than raised platforms that often accompanied tureens or other more elaborate serving wares (Alasdair Brooks pers. comm.). Alternately, the 'bowls and stands' may represent oversized teabowl and saucers (see Miller 1991, 15), or perhaps hygiene-related articles, given their placement just above wash-hand bowls, water ewers and chamber pots, in the invoice.

Altogether, the invoice lists an extraordinary 934 individual items of ceramic and glass serving wares and other household items. The size of service is large compared with other, published invoices from the English potteries of the period (e.g. see Whiter 1978, Appendix III; Coysh and Henrywood 1997, 107–8; Godden 1969, 93–95, 151–53). However, those available make for a limited comparison, as they appear to be smaller invoices, embellishing existing services in smaller increments given the ongoing access to the market – a luxury King certainly did not have once he set sail for New South Wales. While the service was certainly far more extensive than that acquired by an average middle-class English gentleman, the order may best be described as a modest one, befitting a colonial governor in a distant outpost, responsible for large-scale, viceregal entertaining.

It is important to note that the selected fabrics – a minimally decorated creamware service, with some more expensive black-basalt teawares – were inexpensive compared to highly decorated continental porcelains. It was not bone china, the latest ceramic innovation to please the middle-class market, perfected by Josiah Spode I in 1796, nor was it transfer-printed, a technique first used on earthenware in 1784, again by Spode, and quite popular, in the chinoiserie fashion, by the turn of the century (Copeland 1999, 7). Further, while the range of vessels is extensive, there were other more-specialised vessels available, such as cress dishes and asparagus servers, spoon trays, bottle holders and ice pails (see Godden 1969, 93–95). King may well have already owned some of these vessels, perhaps in porcelain, silver or pewter; they may have been outside his financial reach; or he may have determined that colonial Sydney was not quite ready for such extravagance. King's salary was to be £1000 per annum, but as noted he had not been receiving a full and regular income since leaving Norfolk Island, and £36 was an appropriately modest outlay (Fig. 5.7).

So what of the ordered service has survived to the present? Creamware is certainly one of the few wares that survived on site in a wide range of service vessels. There were about 1400 fragments of creamware recovered from First Government House-period contexts, the largest concentration (39%, 581 sherds) being in the levelling fills laid down prior to the construction of the guard house in c. 1812. Another 169 were attributed to the occupation of the guard house. All told, the 1400 fragments represent a conservative minimum number of 49 vessels.

While it cannot be assumed, all 49 vessels belonged to Governor King or were derived from the 1798 order; it is very likely that some of the archaeological examples represent a portion of the 270 items of Queensware purchased in London.

Six of these vessels are stamped 'SPODE'.[10] While this number seems small, not all pieces would have been stamped (in the year 1798, Josiah Spode II had only just taken over from his father and was beginning to implement a policy of more consistent stamping), and many small stamped fragments may not have survived in the archaeological record.

Several of the vessel forms identified in the creamware assemblage recovered from First Government House deposits (excluding demolition) correspond with

---

[10] There were two stamped 'WEDGWOOD' from post-FGH periods of occupation (YRP6084 and YRP6085).

Fig. 5.7 One of the two black basalt sherds recovered from the site (YRP6211). This was probably the base of a tea-serving vessel, probably a teapot or sugar basin. It was recovered from a thick layer of yellow clay above a barrel drain, near the guard house and predates 1810

items in the order. Most of the key elements of a regular dinner service are represented: plates, tureens, serving dishes and strainers. In fact, the creamware assemblage represents more functions than any other ceramic type recovered on site.

What is quite curious about the dominance of creamware on the site is the lack of 'Blue Line' which King had ordered in duplicate, along with a dessert service, comprising 350 vessels altogether. While other items listed in the order, such as the black basalt tea vessels (see Fig. 5.8), have been recovered from the site, no blue-banded creamwares have been identified in the assemblage.

'Blue Line', Pattern 103, is not listed in the Spode pattern book, but Robert Copeland surmises that it was probably similar to another known creamware service with simple bands around the rim and marly (see Copeland 1999, 31, 33). If this is correct, Blue Line is probably similar to an olive–brown-banded creamware service that was found in the construction trench fill for, and later inspection pits into, the box drain attributed to the Hunter period (FGH09417, FGH09419, FGH09413–4, FGH09538) and the demolition or robbing of the perimeter wall (see Fig. 5.9). A minimum number of 13 vessels of olive–brown-banded creamware were recovered, all from the main First Government House site.

Two very small fragments of olive–brown-banded creamware show signs of blue glaze and staining and otherwise vary in shades from olive to brown. The earliest experiments in underglaze colouring at Spode have been noted to be 'somewhat brown' owing to the Staffordshire potters' yet-to-be-perfected knowledge of the impact in underglaze colours submitted to great heat (Hayden 1909, 273). Thus, there is a small possibility – speculative, of course – that the brown-banded creamware was intended to be, or once was, blue (see Fig. 5.10).

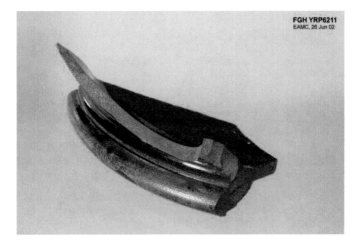

Fig. 5.8 Oval sauce tureen in creamware, impressed '3' (YRP6089)

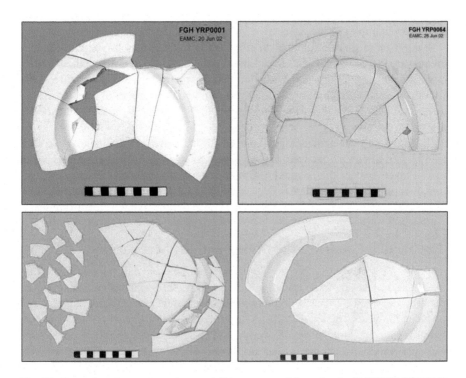

Fig. 5.9 Examples of creamware plates and dishes recovered from the site (YRP0001, YRP0064, YRP0456 and YRP6087). Some of these may have formed part of King's extensive 'Best Queens Ware' dinner service

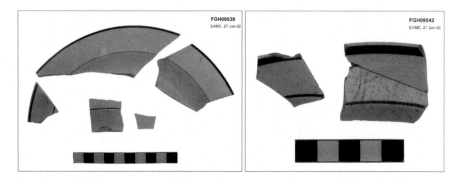

Fig. 5.10 Olive-brown-banded creamware. Based on available comparisons, it is likely that 'Blue Line', ordered by Governor King from Spode, was quite similar in appearance

That the sherds appear in a drain that has been dated to the Hunter period is not greatly problematic. While of course it is possible that Governor Hunter had a similar service, the presence of sherds in the construction trench fill for the drain might be better explained by the disturbance enacted from later inspection pits which also contained examples of the ware.

Even if these small fragments do represent Blue Line, they are outnumbered by creamware (49 to 13). Was the Blue Line service well-kept and maintained, and the creamware used for daily use? Was it left behind when King returned home in 1808, for other governors to break and discard over a longer time period? Did successive governors also bring their own creamware, possibly Spode, and it's not King's after all?

Unfortunately the archaeological record at First Government House is not sufficiently stratified to answer these questions conclusively. However, when linked together with the detailed historical record of the Governor's material culture, it is possible to speculate.

The Tendril Pattern: Fine Dining and the Macquaries

Another dominant pattern surviving in multiple vessel forms was a distinct tendril pattern, identified by the cataloguers as being manufactured by Benjamin Adams between the years 1809 and 1820, as described by A. W. Coysh (1972). The fragments recovered from the First Government House site differ slightly from Coysh's example which was footless and impressed 'B. ADAMS'. None of the First Government House examples have the impressed 'ADAMS' mark although one was printed 'H' (YRP6155); another three were printed '3' (YRP5925, YRP6154, YRP6156). At least one example in the collection has a vestigial foot (YRP6133) rather than being footless, and the pattern here is slightly different. The central, stylised flower recovered from First Government House was not contained within a circular band and contains less detail. The border on all examples in the First Government House collection is also different, with an additional narrow tendril border within the dark blue band.

It may well be that this plate is a later derivation of the original Benjamin Adams plate and is, therefore, closer to 1820 than 1809 in date. Alternatively, this particular set may have been made by another manufacturer. Only two small fragments were found in contexts predating 1811, but in both cases, there are concerns of later disturbance.

If it is accepted that these vessels were made by Adams, their manufacture coincides with the administration of Governor Macquarie (1810–1821), and it is most likely that the set belonged to him, or to his successor, Thomas Brisbane (1821–1825). It also coincides with the expansion of the small colony, and it is tempting to see this shift in the selection of the Governor's tablewares from the austere and plain to the fashionable and ornamental blue transfer print, as a reflection of the growing sophistication of colonial dining practices and New South Wales society in general. To what extent such comparisons may be extended to the conscious intentions of either governor is debatable. The trend fits neatly with Governor Macquarie's and his wife Elizabeth's personal ambitions for the colony, and if they were purchased by the Macquaries following his commission, as the Kings had done, they represent an interesting and very contemporary choice in the latest style (see Figs. 5.11 and 5.12).

Fig. 5.11 Tendril-pattern plate (YRP5925).
(P. Crook et al. 2003)

Fig. 5.12 Tendril-pattern
teacup (YRP6142).
(P. Crook et al. 2003)

The Governor's Guardhouse

The Governor's guard house was an ancillary building located adjacent to the Government House complex and was excavated in 1991 as part of the Young Street and Raphael Place excavations. In comparison with First Government House, little historical information survives about the adjoining guard house. It was rarely the subject of detailed description, sketching or measured drawing, so the excavators had few historical resources to work with when investigating the remains of the structure underlying present-day Young Street. The excavation was reported in a brief document which focussed on the archaeological evidence (Bickford 1993a). Our review of this report during the EAMC project and closer examination of Rosemary Annable's historical research (1992) revealed a significant alteration made to the structure in 1838 (Crook and Murray 2006c, 50–63). We present an overview reanalysis of the guard house, which is ostensibly a story of an unremarkable building eclipsed by an expanding street grid, as a reminder of the many stories of ordinary people, places and things that make up the modern city. When the archaeological evidence calls for scrutiny and explanation, we go back to the historical evidence and interrogate it from a new perspective.

The Establishment of the Governor's Guard

The 'Governor's Body Guard' was established by Governor King in 1802 to accompany him while travelling and when in Sydney to deal with 'other emergencies where horsemen [were] required'. Controversially, King used 'conditionally and provisionally' pardoned convicts, rather than military men, to serve as his Guard. When formed, the Guard comprised Lieutenant George Beale (a 'gentleman convict' who killed his opponent in a duel) and five other convicts (HRA 5, 22–23, 25, 26 in Hughes and HHT n.d.).

Over the next 8 years, two other troopers were added to the Guard, and in 1807, a 'guard house' was situated to the northwest of the First Government House complex, in what was to become Macquarie Place. It is unknown whether this was a facility specifically for the Governor's Guard, or one shared with the General Guard.

The Governor's Huard House underlying Young Street is listed among public works carried out by Governor Macquarie from 1810 to 1821, along with a 'Commodious Main Guard House' (on the corner of George Street and Charlotte Place on the western side of the cove) and a barrack with stable and garden for the Governor's Guard of Light Horse (on the site of the Mitchell Library, later the School of Industry; Macquarie to Bathurst, 27 July 1822 in HRA 10: 684–5).

In April 1810, 3 months into his term as Governor, Macquarie wrote to Secretary Castlereagh, requesting permission to expand the eight-trooper guard to comprise one sergeant, 1 corporal and 12 private troopers – all men 'borne on the strength of the 73rd regiment', not convicts (HRA 7, 350 in Hughes and HHT n.d.). Castlereagh was surprised to learn that the Guard existed at all and instructed Macquarie to disband it (HRA 7, 365 in Hughes and HHT n.d.). Macquarie replied in protest that the Guard performed vital duties and had done so for 8 years, reinstated his request to expand the Guard, insisted that the cost of expansion would be negligible and advised that he would maintain the Guard as is, until he received a response (HRA 7, 612–613 in Hughes and HHT n.d.). In November 1811, Macquarie was still arguing with the Home Office, this time to the Earl of Liverpool; and as late as June 1813, Macquarie was attempting to justify to Earl Bathurst the quarterly charge of £25 for the Governor's Body Guard in the Public Accounts (HRA 7, 495–6, 712 in Hughes and HHT n.d.).

The prolonged difference of opinion, from 1810 to 1813, is curious given that pictorial evidence dated to 1812 confirms that Macquarie had already built a guard house for the very troopers he had been directed to disband. This new structure replaced the c. 1807 guard house that stood in way of the planned Macquarie Place triangle and was built across the carriageway that led to the wharf and stores on Farm Cove. The obstruction of this carriageway was part of an overall strategy of securing a buffer around Government House and formalising its western and southern boundaries (see Fig. 5.13).

Bickford (1993b, 54) has argued that the guard house may have been built in 1810 when several buildings in the vicinity of Government House were moved to make way for Macquarie Place.

Fig. 5.13 The first known depiction of the guard house adjacent to the main Government House complex. Detail from a 'View of Part of Sydney, the Capital of New South Wales, taken from Dawes Point', drawn by J Eyers, engraved by W Preston and published by Absalom West on 30 November 1812, from *Views in New South Wales, 1813–1814 [and] Historical account of the colony of New South Wales, 1820–1821.* (PX∗D 65 [IE10526294] FL10526481, courtesy of the Mitchell Library, State Library of NSW)

No official documentation of the design and construction of the building, the payment of labourers or purchase of supplies has been identified (Annable 1992, 4). Like the later c. 1818 extensions to Government House, the stables (begun 1817) and so many other Macquarie public buildings, design and construction began before approval had been granted, and sometimes before it was sought. In the case of the guard house, while Macquarie probably had the authority to construct what was a fairly small structure without recourse to the Home Office, the outlay for a facility required by a troop that should have been disbanded suggests a deliberate strategy to conceal the construction of the building among other public projects.

In the first depictions of the guard house by Absalom West in 1812 and 1813, you can just make out some of the form and architectural details of the building – a six-column verandah and a large arched doorway, flanked by three windows a side. Similar details can also be made out in later townscapes drawn from the east cove, including one by Captain James Wallis, of the 46th Regiment, c. 1815–1817 (Fig. 5.14), and others dating to the 1820s depict troopers marching up and down the approach (see c. 1820 view from Bunkers Hill, Fig. 5.15). Closer-range views of the guard house have not survived. By the time the guard house was built, the trees along the northwestern boundary of First Government House had matured. In the 1810s and 1820s, views of Government House within its setting favoured vantage points in the Domain or Farm Cove, obscuring the view of the guard house and outbuildings (e.g. see McCormick 1987, plates 111 and 112) (see Figs. 5.15).

Other primary documents provide more detailed information about the guard house. An 1828 plan of Macquarie Place provides the first reliable outline of the building's floor plan. It was then a long, thin building facing Bridge Street, on the

Fig. 5.14 Details from 'A view of the Cove & Part of Sydney New South Wales. Taken from Dawes Battery', engraved by W. Preston from an original drawing by Captain Wallis, 46th Regiment, 1815–1817. (James Wallis, *Historical Account of the Colony of NSW*, London 1821, Dixson Library F82/28, courtesy of the Dixson Library, State Library of NSW)

Fig. 5.15 Details from c. 1820 view from Bunkers Hill showing uniformed guards in the approach to guard house. ('View of Government domain & part of Sydney taken from Bunker's Hill N. S. Wales', unsigned watercolour by Richard Read, senior. NLA PIC R6369 LOC 2308; by permission of the National Library of Australia)

same alignment as Government House, positioned at an angle, rather than perpendicular to the First Government House perimeter wall, and importantly stretching from the perimeter wall to the boundary of the Colonial Secretary's Office.

John Carmichael's view of *Sydney from the Domain Near Government House*, published in 1829, provides the only detailed depiction of the guard house, in the foreground of the official residences down Bridge Street. While only part of the structure is depicted, the engraving provides several important details, particularly the height of the verandah, built about 1 m above the approach (using the guards as a human scale) which itself rises fairly steeply from Bridge Street. While it is difficult to confirm, it also appears that there is a doorway behind the guards sitting on the verandah, not another window, so it may be that there was a central doorway, plus two others leading off the verandah. The gabled roof appears to be shingled, and it generally has the appearance of the other c. 1812 Macquarie guard house on the western side of the cove.

By 1833, the Guard again came under financial attack from the Home Office again. With salaries and clothing for the Guard nearing £400 per annum, Governor Bourke was instructed to disband the troop on 28 March 1833 (HRA 17, 61–62 in Hughes and HHT n.d.). On 28 October 1834, having received no confirmation of its abolition, the Home Office again instructed Bourke to disband the Guard (HRA 17, 563 in Hughes and HHT n.d.). Bourke was rebuked again on 10 March 1835 when it was discovered that he had simply renamed the Guard the 'Mounted Orderlies' and proceeded to spend even more on their maintenance (HRA 17, 696 in Hughes and HHT n.d.). By 1835, the Home Office 'regretted' that their instructions had not been carried out and requested that if the guard must continue, they must be placed 'in every respect on the same footing as the Mounted Police' (HRA 18, 186 in Hughes and HHT n.d.). In the mid-1840s, the 'Mounted Orderlies' were amalgamated with the Mounted Police and were disbanded in 1860 (Stanley 1986, 58).

Inside the Guard House

The excavation report prepared by Anne Bickford in 1993 discussed each component of the guard house, as it was recovered in each trench. The front room and approach were in Trench YA, the rear rooms in YB and the yard in YC. The discussion of the guard house focused on its construction and occupation, with some reference to the substantial disturbance in the area. The structure is described as having a long, narrow front room, three rear rooms divided by a long thin room, 'probably a corridor' (Bickford 1993a, 14).

During excavation, several features in the rear rooms of the guard house were described as an 'extension' to the long, narrow front room (see, e.g. Context Sheets for YA: 0511) – probably owing to the sequence of wall construction. The southernmost wall (YA 816) forming the external east–west back wall was built first, and the western north–south interior walls (YA 827 and YA 877) were butted onto it. The fireplaces (YA 830) in the eastern and middle rooms were keyed into wall YA 816. Unfortunately, most other corner points in the foundations were destroyed by a drain installed in Young Street in the 1850s and later services, so it is not possible to identify how the walls of the front room fitted into the sequence of construction, which would provide more conclusive evidence of possible extension.

All things considered, it is unlikely that these foundation courses represent an extended structure. Rather the long narrow 'front room' is more likely the verandah with it visible stone face rising above the slope (see Crook and Murray 2006c, 55–58 for detailed discussion). Of the remaining three rear rooms, separated by a 'corridor', it is unlikely that this was the original layout. Given the historical evidence for truncation in 1838, it is more likely that the eastern foundation wall of the 'corridor' – butted to the southern wall – actually represents the rebuilt external wall of the newly shaped structure as described below. Thus, the original layout comprised three rooms, the central room – into which the arched doorway would have opened – being slightly larger than the other two. While this reinterpreted layout cannot be confirmed without the excavation of the foundations under the western kerb of Young Street, it is a better fit with the available historical evidence (Crook and Murray 2006c, 57).

A Passage Through the Guard House: Truncation, 1838

In 1838 when repairs were being made to the Colonial Secretary's Office, the Colonial Architect wrote to the Secretary requesting permission to allow 'a passage to be conducted through the present guard house' (Annable 1992, 4). Using the side wall of the Colonial Secretary's outbuilding to form a new street, they planned to reinstate part of the passageway to the jetty on Farm Cove that had been blocked off by Macquarie in c. 1812. The Colonial Architect promised 'that the alteration which will become necessary in the guard house, can be easily effected without occasioning any material inconvenience' (SR NSW 4/2391.9 Colonial Secretary from Colonial Architect 1838 in Annable 1992, 4). For 1838, £24.13.3 is allocated to repairs of the 'Guard House, near Government House' (SR NSW Blue books for 1838 4/270 Public Works p. 65 in Annable 1992, 6) indicating that the alterations necessary for this passageway were carried out.

Returning to the Macquarie Place plan dated to 1828, we can derive rough measurements for the guard house by comparing it with the adjacent buildings. The guard house is depicted as being approximately the same length as, but half the width of, the adjacent Colonial Secretary's Office, which was 50 by 24 feet, or around 15 by 8 m. This suggests that the guard house was around 15 by 4 m. While the width may be exaggeratedly narrow, the length is probably correct.

Because the structure continued under the western kerb of Young Street, the full length could not be determined during excavation, but the surviving remains confirm that the guard house was *at least* 12 m long.

In all other plans of the guard house, it is depicted as a long narrow structure, in alignment with First Government House and always stretching from the boundary of First Government House in the east, to the boundary of the Colonial Secretary's Office to the west (see Fig. 5.16).

However, in the two detailed drawings of the guard house, made by government surveyors in the 1840s, we see a structure approximately half the length of the Colonial Secretary's Office and showing a passageway alongside the guard house.

The structure depicted in Gordon's 1842 and Townsend's 1845 surveys is squarish, roughly 7.5 by 8 m (again based on the known measurements of adjacent buildings), not the long, thin 15 by 4 m plan depicted in 1828.[11] While there are some inconsistencies between each surveyor's depiction of First Government House,

---

[11] Note that Townsend draws the verandah separately; Gordon does not seem to depict the guard house verandah at all (although the First Government House verandah is represented as a series of columns).

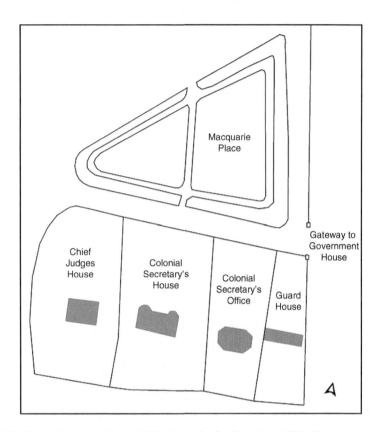

Fig. 5.16 Plan of Macquarie Place, 1828. (P. Crook after Broadbent 1997, 45)

particularly when compared with Mortimer Lewis's detailed 1845 plan,[12] they both concur on the size and squat shape of the now truncated guard house. But how does this compare with the archaeological evidence?

Having established that the guard house was significantly altered in 1838, a better explanation for the archaeological foundations becomes apparent.

While, as previously discussed, the surviving foundations revealed evidence of a structure more than 12 m long, they also included a questionable internal wall

---

[12] The two plans differ in their representation of the layout of Government House and its outbuildings. The primary reason being that both surveys were for the purpose of planning the new street grid rather than preparing a detailed architectural plan of First Government House and its associated structures. Gordon's 1842 plan is far less detailed, each structure being represented in block form to present the approximate location of each structure. Townsend, on the other hand, recorded details of bevelling and the portico of the Colonial Secretary's Office and Macquarie's saloon. Aside from these minor distinctions, Gordon depicts the First Government House outbuilding complex and three separate structures, Townsend depicts them as part of one range of buildings, much more alike to Mortimer Lewis's detailed plan prepared in 1845, prior to demolition. Unfortunately, the guard house was not included in Lewis's detailed drawing of the First Government House complex.

(YB 877), deeper than the other internal wall YB 827 and butted rather than keyed into the southern wall YB 816. Its position – approximately through the centre of the guard house – also does not fit the pictorial evidence for a wide, arched doorway in the northern elevation.

It is far more likely that this stone foundation was the base for a new external wall, rather than an (original or modified) internal wall.

Our revised interpretation of the floor plan of the original guard house proposes that the original layout comprised three rooms – the central room (into which the arched doorway would have opened) being slightly larger than the other two. When the building was truncated, the central room was narrowed, and the western room lost altogether. Consequently, the wall that appeared to be an internal division marking the corridor is reinterpreted as the new, external wall foundation laid in 1838.

It is probable that the remaining foundations to the west of this wall were simply covered over after the brick wall (and possibly upper levels of the foundation course) were removed to make way for the passageway.[13] If the long, front 'room' is indeed a verandah, it may be that no additional foundation wall was constructed to support the verandah wall and the columns were simply relocated. Either way, any evidence left behind after the complete demolition of the structure was significantly disturbed in this area by the Young Street drain (a large, rubble backfilled pit covers the area where foundation walls or postholes for the columns would have been aligned).

In addition, there are several unusual nonstructural deposits that are better explained by the semi-demolition of the guard house. In journals and context sheets, the trench supervisors in this area made reference to building debris found in under-floor spaces of the guard house that could not be identified and conclusively attributed to construction or demolition. Deposits clearly identified as 'guard house occupation' were recorded as overlying, not abutting, foundation courses.

The primary group of deposits associated with the guard house, recovered from the northern approach (including YA: 194, the 'major' deposit 'almost certainly derived from the guard house, cleaning, repairing'; see context sheet), were inter-changeably described as household refuse and building debris (in contrast to the rear of the guard house which was 'kept fairly clean', see Bickford 1993a, 11). One deposit, YA: 220, was associated with reroofing the guard house, owing to the triangular-sectioned mortar pointing recovered from it, and it was noted that the probable base for the building's steps (YA: 159) was found amidst these construction–refuse deposits. During excavation, the deposits were clearly associated with demolition of the guard house, but it was noted that it could not be 'the final demolition of the guard house', perhaps associated with an extension.

In the rear yard, a surface was made of broken tiles. Re-examination of the historical plans suggests that the yard may have been created when the passageway was put through the guard house, the broken tile yard surface, created from the dismantled half-roof or more probably the whole roof makes much more sense: the

---

[13] No road surface was revealed, probably owing to significant disturbance of the Young Street drain, and the fact that much of the area that would be road was concealed under the Young Street west kerb.

broken roof tile was used to create the surface of the new yard, and the bricks from
the building were probably also used in the new boundary wall.

Either the entire building was reroofed in shingles rather than tiles or the whole
roof was removed at once.

Discussion

As with all previous phases of investigation at the First Government House site, the
studies of tablewares and of the guard house, rely heavily on documentary evidence.
Historical milestones shaped the phasing of the construction sequences revealed
during the 1983–1992 excavations, and even the artefacts which are unmistakably
associated with First Government House (such as the sandstone lunette of Governor
Macquarie's c. 1818 extensions) were dependent on historical records to tease out
their significance. Given that Governor Phillip's 1788 foundation plate – the primary physical evidence with which to identify this important place – was removed
from the site in 1899, were it not for the paintings, engravings, correspondence and
surveyor's plans, the archaeological remains on the corner of Bridge and Phillip
Streets would be little more than another complex of colonial building foundations
in want of mortar.

The dominance of historical narrative in interpretations of the site of the First
Government House site has drawn criticism in the past. Birmingham (1990, 13–14)
found fault with the publication *Australia's First Government House* for its failure
to integrate history and archaeology in a meaningful way, using the physical remains
as mere illustrations of textual or graphic sources traced to the occupation of each
governor. Birmingham presented this criticism as an example of the generally inad-
equate methodology of urban Australian historical–archaeological projects in which
archaeological data is overwhelmed by historical data.

However, at the site of First Government House site, the datasets are unevenly
matched. Here we have much more than the intermittent occupant's name in a postal
directory and a coloured outline on a city services map. Not only is there a scaled
drawing of the complex in its final years, and earlier sketches indicating room usage,
the House appears in dozens of images, its occupants and families are well known
from published biographies, and their views and opinions of the House itself are
preserved in the official records of the government of New South Wales. On the
other hand, there is an archaeological record complicated by decades of extension
and renovation, heavily disturbed by late nineteenth- and twentieth-century development, and investigated under the limitations of a rescue excavation.

Despite these hindrances, the available historical and archaeological evidence
has been utilised to make genuine contributions to the history of the site. The over-
lap between history and archaeology was insufficient and, for example, could only
tentatively contribute to our understanding of the personal possessions of the governors. Even with independent historical records of purchases made and specific

styles of tableware with manufacturer's marks, the archaeological data were rarely precise enough to link to a particular governor to an assemblage of tableware with a high degree of confidence. While the available evidence allows for plenty of discussion, in the end, we can legitimately only speculate about the unrecorded histories of the site: the visionary, ambitious and spendthrift Governor and Mrs. Macquarie embracing the fashionable and ornamental over the plain reliable services of the less-affluent Kings.

In other cases, finding the intersection between history and archaeology, such as the cost of the alterations to the guard house and the demolition–occupation fills found during excavation, forces us to pursue new lines of inquiry and shift the focus onto subjects that otherwise may never be recognised as elements of the greater pattern of the development of the city of Sydney.

The First Government House site is a place of exceptional cultural significance. The discovery of the archaeological remains of this troublesome viceregal complex was the catalyst for several advances in the urban evolution of the Sydney CBD: it was a boon to the heritage protection movement, it sparked a resurgent interest in the foundations of colonial government, and it gave the city of Sydney a new museum.

Since the excavation, historical–archaeological investigations have contributed to our understanding of the House, the governors who lived there and the colony they shaped. It is remarkable that after two decades, it still is possible to learn more about this important site, despite the difficulties posed by site disturbance and a high-pressure excavation. While, on their own, the analyses presented in this chapter comprise only a small component of the total story of the site, they demonstrate the importance of both preserving and returning to the archives of Sydney's archaeological heritage.

References

Unpublished

Hughes, J., and Historic Houses Trust of NSW. n.d. 'Workforce', Research Folder Held in the Resource Centre, Museum of Sydney.

Proudfoot, H. 1983. 'The First Government House, Sydney and the Subsequent History of the Site after 1845: Historical Study'. Unpublished Report. Premier's Department and the Department of Environment and Planning.

Stocks, R. 1988a. 'First Government House Site, Sydney: Stratigraphic Analysis Report'. Unpublished report. Canberra: NSW Department of Planning, Heritage Resource Services, Anutech.

———. 1988b. First Government House Site: Phillip Street Terraces Watching Brief, for the Department of Environment and Planning, and Alcova Holdings Pty. Ltd.

Thorp, W. 1987. The First Government House Site Ceramics Assemblage: Analysis of Selected Levels, 1788–1969 unpublished report for NSW Department of Planning, Heritage Resource Services, Anutech, Canberra.

Published

Annable, R. 1992. 'First Government House Young Street Guard House'. Unpublished Report. Museum of Sydney Resource Centre.

Bickford, A. 1993a. 'FGH Site Young Street and Raphael Street Excavation Final Report: Catalogue Reports'. Unpublished Report 3. State Authorities Superannuation Board.

———. 1993b. 'FGH Site Young Street and Raphael Street Excavation Final Report: Excavation Report'. Unpublished Report 1. State Authorities Superannuation Board.

Bickford, A., and L. Petrie. 1993. 'FGH Site Young Street and Raphael Street Excavation Final Report: FGH-AB Catalogue Report'. Unpublished Report 2. State Authorities Superannuation Board.

Birmingham, J. 1990. A Decade of Digging: Deconstructing Urban Archaeology. *Australian Historical Archaeology* 8: 13–22.

Bridges, P. 1995. *Foundations of Identity: Building Early Sydney 1788–1822*. Sydney: Hale & Iremonger. https://trove.nla.gov.au/work/21123062.

Broadbent, J. 1992. Macquarie's Domain. In *The Age of Macquarie*, ed. James Broadbent and Joy Hughes, 3–18. Carlton, VIC: Melbourne University Press in association with Historic Houses Trust of NSW.

———. 1997. *The Australian Colonial House: Architecture and Society in New South Wales, 1788–1842*. Potts Point, NSW: Hordern House in association with the Historic Houses Trust of NSW.

Copeland, R. 1999. Spode and Australia: Two Interesting Pieces of Documentary Evidence. *English Ceramic Circle* 17 (1): 29–33.

Coysh, A.W. 1972. *Blue-Printed Earthenware 1800–1850*. Devon, England: David & Charles.

Coysh, A.W., and R.K. Henrywood. 1997. *The Dictionary of Blue and White Printed Pottery, 1780–1880*. Suffolk, England: Antique Collectors' Club.

Crook, P., L. Ellmoos, and T. Murray. 2005. *Keeping up with the McNamaras: A Historical Archaeological Study of the Cumberland and Gloucester Streets Site, The Rocks, Sydney*. Archaeology of the Modern City Series 8.Sydney: Historic Houses Trust of New South Wales. http://www.latrobe.edu.au/amc/assets/downloads/KeepingUpWithTheMcNamaras.pdf.

Crook, P., and T. Murray. 2006a. *An Archaeology of Institutional Refuge: The Material Culture of the Hyde Park Barracks, Sydney, 1848–1886*. Archaeology of the Modern City 1788–1900. Sydney: Historic Houses Trust of NSW. http://www.latrobe.edu.au/amc/assets/downloads/12-HPB.pdf.

———. 2006b. *Guide to the EAMC Archaeology Database*. Archaeology of the Modern City Series 10. Sydney: Historic Houses Trust of New South Wales. www.latrobe.edu.au/amc/downloads/10-ArchDB.pdf.

———. 2006c. *The Historical Archaeology of the First Government House Site, Sydney: Further Research*. Archaeology of the Modern City Series. Sydney: Historic Houses Trust of NSW.

Crook, P., T. Murray, and L. Ellmoos. 2003. *Assessment of Historical and Archaeological Resources of the First Government House Site, Sydney*. 2nd rev. Archaeology of the Modern City 1788–1900. Sydney: Historic Houses Trust of New South Wales. http://www.latrobe.edu.au/amc/assets/downloads/5_FGHAssessReport.pdf.

Davies, P., P. Crook, and T. Murray. 2013. *An Archaeology of Institutional Confinement: The Hyde Park Barracks, 1848-1886*. Sydney: Sydney University Press.

Gillespie, R. 1975. *Viceregal Quarters: An Account of the Various Residences of the Governors of New South Wales from 1788 Until the Present Day*. London: Angus & Robertson.

Godden, G. 1969. *Caughley and Worcester Porcelains, 1775–1800*. London: Herbert Jenkins.

Hayden, A. 1909. *Chats on English Earthenware: A Practical Guide for the Collector*. London: T. Fisher Unwin.

Lewis, M. 1845. 'Report on the Present State of the Old Government House Prepared by M Lewis for the Board of Survey'. Colonial Secretary, Letters received. SR NSW.

McBryde, I. 1989. *Guests of the Governor: Aboriginal Residents of the First Government House.* Sydney: Friends of First Government House Site.

McCormick, T. 1987. *First Views of Australia, 1788–1825: A History of Early Sydney.* Sydney: David Ell Press.

Miller, G. 1991. A Revised Set of CC Index Value for Classification and Economic Scaling of English Ceramics from 1787 to 1880. *Historical Archaeology* 25 (1): 1–25.

Proudfoot, H., A. Bickford, B. Egloff, and R. Stocks. 1991. *Australia's First Government House.* Sydney: Allen & Unwin and the Department of Planning.

Shaw, A.G.L. 1967. King, Philip Gidley (1758–1808). In *Australian Dictionary of Biography*, vol. 2, 55–61. Melbourne: Melbourne University Press.

Stanley, P. 1986. *The Remote Garrison: The British Army in Australia 1788–1870.* Kenthurst, N.S.W.: Kangaroo Press.

Sussman, L. 2000. British Military Tableware, 1760–1830. In *Approaches to Material Culture Research for Historical Archaeologists*, ed. D.R. Brauner, 44–55. Pennsylvania: The Society for Historical Archaeology.

Whiter, L. 1978. *Spode: A History of the Family, Factory and Wares from 1733 to 1833.* London: Barrie & Jenkins.

Chapter 6
Global Material Culture in the Modern City

In this chapter we examine the manufacture and movement of goods. Just as people migrated about the globe in the nineteenth century in response to a wide variety of historical circumstances, goods were made, transported and discarded within the parameters of changing cultural, technological and economic processes. In order to understand how patterns of material culture might reflect patterns of migration or the cultural norms and challenges of migration (i.e. the archaeology of migration), we must first understand the goods themselves.

Here we introduce the concept of 'global material culture', a phrase which we use to describe the core range of domestic goods consumed throughout the world in the nineteenth century. These products of modern industries were packed in the holds of immigrant ships and exported by enterprising merchants to the farthest ends of the earth to service the needs of widely dispersed populations of migrants and indigenous communities. International trade and colonial provisioning were not, of course, unique to the Victorian period. Large, extra-colonial export markets existed long before. The export of European delftwares, oriental porcelain and stonewares of the seventeenth and eighteenth centuries are excellent examples. However, trade of this kind did not result in the movement of such vast quantities of goods, nor creating the unmistakable archaeological signature of printed earthenware, pressed glass and vulcanite which washed up along the shorelines of the postcolonial world. Movements of material culture on this scale are best explained by a combination of global trade and the consequences of large-scale migration and the expansion of colonialism which we explored in Chap. 3.

While we recognise this as a global movement of goods, we avoid the term 'globalisation' on account of its fluid definition (Horning and Schweickart 2016, 39) and its more popularly understood identification with the activities of multinational corporations in the twentieth and twenty-first centuries. The precedents of this more recent global trade were clearly apparent in the nineteenth century, and, as we discuss below, some firms took pride in their international connections. Nonetheless, the scale and uniformity of global trade were significantly different pre- and post-World War 1.

© Springer Nature Switzerland AG 2019
T. Murray, P. Crook, *Exploring the Archaeology of the Modern City in Nineteenth-century Australia*, Contributions To Global Historical Archaeology, https://doi.org/10.1007/978-3-030-27169-5_6

In the Australian colonies, the economic reach of the British Empire also affected participation in 'global' networks, and, until Federation in 1901, trade with 'Home' was both ostensibly protected and preferred. This narrows our focus to the material culture of the Anglophone world, and we do so acknowledging the arguments of Mehler (2013) and others who have called on a broader scope for historical archaeology.

This is a necessarily brief account of the processes underlying the global distribution of this class of material culture. We begin with the manufacture of domestic goods, their transport, sale and use within nineteenth-century cities, specifically British colonial cities, and then consider the general approaches employed in historical archaeology to analyse and interpret the archaeological signatures of this material. (For other and more detailed accounts of material culture and consumption in the nineteenth century, see McKendrick, Brewer and Plumb 1982; Weatherill 1988; Shammas 1990; Young 2003; McCracken 1988; Brewer and Porter 1993; Blaszczyk 2000). For archaeological accounts, see Spencer-Wood (1987), Gibb (1996), Wurst and McGuire (1999), Mullins (2011a, b) and Crook (2008, in press-a, in press-b).

Human-Made, Machine-Made

The period of Georgian and Victorian migration across the British colonial network coincided with one of the most expansive and rapid transformations of the material world experienced in human history. We know this great epoch as the 'industrial revolution', and it is a subject of great debate among social, industrial and economic historians (e.g. Mokyr 1999; Allen 2009). Here we focus on the material impact of these changes, particularly, three key discussion points concerning manufactured goods of this period: increased output, the concentration of production in regions and product regularisation.

The introduction of large-scale, steam-powered machinery in late eighteenth-century manufactories gave rise to production quotas unheard of in the preindustrial world. While one craftsman working in a team of 10 could produce 5000 pins per day using hand-tools (A. Smith 1776, 21), a single pin-making machine could output 125,000 pins per day (Hill 1921, 319). Spinning jennies, power looms, a plethora of steam-powered and foot-operated presses to stamp Birmingham brass goods, ceramic plates and glass vessels all allowed manufacturers' production output levels to multiply by 10- and 20-fold.

Combined with reduced labour costs and product innovation, this improved efficiency lowered the cost of goods and opened new markets. Demand soared as the price of former luxuries fell within the reach of a considerable proportion of lower-income families. The 'cheapening' of domestic goods is often interpreted as a decline of quality craftsmanship (e.g. Erskine 2003, 9; for discussion see Berg 2005, 99). The founders of the Arts and Crafts movement in the late nineteenth century certainly held this view. While there may have been a reduced commitment to innovation in ornamentation, mechanisation was welcomed in many industries as improving production quality (see Crook 2008, 147 ff. for more detailed discussion). For example, in 1878, an automated cup-making machine at the factory of Pinder, Bourne & Co. was praised not just for its ability to make 500–600 articles per hour but the fact that they were 'made sounder and more uniform than those made by hand' (*The Pottery & Glass Trades' Journal* 1878, vol. 9 [1]: 135).

As mechanisation advanced, capital investment increased. A potter, carpenter, weaver or glass blower with modest capital could establish a small workshop and hire one or two hands. The most innovative and best-engineered machines required a major capital investment – not merely in the equipment but also in factory accommodation, fuel, materials and skilled and auxiliary labour (including management and administration). Access to transport infrastructure, natural resources and sources of skilled labour led to clustering of many major industries in regional centres in the United Kingdom (Popp 2001), Europe and later in the United States.

These regional hubs had a significant impact on the distribution of goods and fed a new kind of global material culture. The latest patterns and shapes of Staffordshire chinaware, Sheffield plate, Bohemian crystal and French porcelain – all produced in their tens of thousands in regularised forms – could be recognised in the far-flung outposts of the colonies as well as the large cities of Europe. Notwithstanding the custom designs made for individual markets (e.g. the American Cities series), sherds of the 'usual suspects' of the Anglophone dinner table – transfer-printed Willow, Asiatic Pheasant and Rhine patterns – appear by the sieve load in archaeological sites in cities and towns in Australia, the United Kingdom, South Africa, Canada and the United States. They are also found in other parts of the globe reached by global trade.

This overarching homogeneity belies a more complex variability of domestic goods in the nineteenth century. Hand in hand with the increased mechanisation, the concentration of industry and mass distribution of goods over vast distances, there was a greater *range* of domestic goods on offer to nineteenth-century consumers than ever before (Berg 2005, 23–25). While to some extent, there was an increased similarity in product lines, it would be many decades before industrial output could qualify as 'mass production' as defined by the twentieth-century model of production-line processing and the integration of interchangeable parts. Many trades remained labour-intensive, and manufacturers excelled in product rather than process innovation (Popp 2001; Crook 2008, 176–178). Large factories operated alongside small specialised workshops and the market were flooded with thousands of choices. Willow-pattern prints were chopped up and rearranged to fit onto plates, teacups, soup ladles, pepper shakers, asparagus stands and a raft of other purpose-made Victorian crockery. These were shaped in classical forms with rococo scrolls, plain rims or geometric patterns. Some were made from creamware, some stoneware and some bone china. They may or may not have been embellished with gilding, and there was considerable variation in 'traditional' patterns (see Copeland 1980 for examples).

Amidst this great variety in material forms, we need to ask: what was the *significance* of all of this variety in daily life? Was the structure of social interaction which used this material culture more variable and more complex than it had been in previous generations? This at least seems likely, but we cannot be entirely sure. It is certainly well-accepted that the development of new imitative materials to create a range of products with new functions (or forms previously restricted to manufacturer of more precious materials) was an integral part of the formation and maintenance of the burgeoning middle classes (McKendrick et al. 1982; Weatherill 1988; Shammas 1990; Berg and Clifford 1999; Young 2003; Berg 2005). This cultural development is often referred to as the 'consumer revolution', and most social scientists acknowledge the 'active' role of goods in changing social and domestic relations. The distinctive attributes of seasonal fashions in clothing, tablewares and furnishings (as well as the house itself) allowed members of the middling classes to quickly distinguish their fellows from people who pretended to be. It was the not the physical cues alone which guided these subtle judgements, it was how the goods were *used*. The latest and most expensive dress would reveal the owner a 'wannabe' if she did not know how to walk with modesty and grace. The most fashionable porcelain dinner service could not conceal the less genteel origins of its owners if they did not know how to lay out the meal (or direct their servants to do it for them).

While the operation of material culture in the rich social life of the nineteenth-century middle classes has been well explored (Young 2003; Cohen 2006), there are challenges in applying these lessons to archaeological material culture and to the material lives of the working classes. The kinds of documentary evidence which have shed light on socio-material operations of the nineteenth-century bourgeoisie (letters, journals, novels and newspaper serials) were rarely created by members of the working classes. Other sources, such as insolvency and probate records, do provide useful information about the (economically) valuable goods and chattels of working-class people, but these do not articulate the finer categorical distinctions that comprise the standard artefact catalogue and give hope to connecting archaeological signatures with significant social practices.[1]

Much of this discussion concerning the significance of material variability concerns the use of goods for external display, communication and the maintenance of social groupings. Typically such goods were purchased at the higher end of the consumer scale. The majority of goods recovered from urban archaeological sites, however, tend to represent a lower class of goods, including kitchenwares and utilitarian items. Some of these wares may have had little more significance to their owners than they might have attributed to a mixing bowl or scrap pan. Not all domestic goods were manufactured or purchased for the milieu of *conspicuous consumption*, and some of those which were may have been utilised for socially unambitious and unsentimental purposes. See Crook (in press-a) for further discussion on the range of approaches to assessing value in the modern world archaeology and Appadurai (1986) and Smith (2007).

---

[1] See Crook 2008 for exploration of these matters using store and mail-order catalogues of the second half of the nineteenth century.

Ornamental and other durable goods had a high resale value in the nineteenth-century marketplace and were used as financial security and relatively liquid assets. English landlords had the right to seize and sell the goods of a tenant who failed to meet their rental dues (Beeton 1861, 566; Philp 1883, 223). Goods and chattels, family keepsakes, clothing and even footwear were left with pawnbrokers as guarantees of short-term loans. In peripheral (colonial) markets, the durable goods retained a higher value. Even the humble clay pipe could be on-sold:

> The colonists prize clay pipes before all others; they are choice in their selection and highly prize the old much-used ones; a pipe which originally cost but a halfpenny, after being dyed black as a coal by constant smoking, will sell for as much as ten shillings. (Lancelott 1852, 87)

We will return to subject of colonial markets later in this chapter, in the context of advice to emigrants, but for now we turn to the transport and distribution of goods.

Retail Empires: Supplying the Colonial Markets

The emergence of the modern economic system, industrialisation, colonial expansion and population growth led to major changes in retail practices in the eighteenth and nineteenth centuries. The once direct relationship between consumers and local farmers, smithies or drapers was intercepted by 'middle men', i.e. shopkeepers and agents. The sale of goods became a commercial endeavour independent of their production, and the act of selecting them became a pastime in its own right. The verb to shop was coined in the eighteenth century (Kingston 1994, 1), and the market place itself became more permanent and gentrified in undercover arcades and bazaars.

Urban bazaars comprised a collective of small specialist dealers, who agreed to work to set a governing rules and principles, including the determination of fixed prices (Adburgham 1964, 138). By the 1860s the first department stores and co-operative societies were formed to consolidate and centralise multiple specialist trades under the one financial entity. With sufficient market share to bargain with the big manufacturers, vast capital derived from cash-only payments and innovations such as aggressive advertising and mail-order shipments, these hallmark institutions revolutionised the retail sphere and forced down the price of many domestic goods in the late nineteenth century. (For a more detailed account of the history of shopping, see Jefferys 1954; Adburgham 1964; Davis 1966; D. Alexander 1970; Winstanley 1983; N. Alexander and Akehurst 1999; Rappaport 2000. For Australian histories, see Kingston 1994; Pollon 1989; Webber et al. 2003. For discussion in the context of historical archaeology, see Crook 2000, 2008; Cook et al. 1996; Wurst and McGuire 1999).

In the colonial context, markets were too small to support complex industries, and all but some low-quality, utilitarian domestic goods were imported from Britain or Europe. The great wholesale and retail institutions played an important role in the distribution of global material culture. Where people moved, markets followed. Many English wholesale agents and co-operative and department stores were keen to look after Britons abroad (particularly those servicing employers of the crown deployed across the empire) as much as those at home. The Civil Service Supply Association, for example, printed a special export price list and had a special notice about 'Goods for India and Colonial Markets', including 'punkahs for table, wall, or suspension lamps' (Association 1880, 172). Some wholesale traders specialised in the colonial market. Henry S. King & Co., for example, had local agents in Sydney, Melbourne, Brisbane and Adelaide, and they also arranged passenger fares on various liners (King and Co 1880, 4).

The shipping rates were surprisingly reasonable. In 1895, the postal charge for 2 lbs of goods sent from Harrods in London to New South Wales was for 1s. 6d. (18d.). Getting the same weight of goods from Anthony Hordern & Sons. stores in Sydney to the outer townships of New South Wales, however, costs almost half that amount (8d). Harrod's advised customers buying from their 'Export List' to add roughly 20% to the cost of the goods to cover packaging (in cases or casks), shipping, freight and insurance, but the customer then had to pay any import duties and tariffs once they landed (and this varied between the Australian colonies). Import duties and tariffs were greater impediments to trade outside of the empire and were a source of bitter complaint by English manufacturers exporting to the United States:

> ...whilst the Americans are allowed to import into England free of duty such glass as they are able to manufacture cheaper than we can, and to compete with English manufacturers at home, we are not allowed to send a single glass or china article into the United States without being mulcted [sic] to the extent of 40 per cent. of its value. (The Pottery & Glass Trades' Journal 1 [1], Jan. 1878, 9)

The role of wholesale traders and their agents in Australian colonies in the nineteenth century is poorly understood. It is clear that local agents would have received and forwarded orders directly placed by colonial customers with large London firms, such as King & Co., but it is unclear if these same agents also supplied shopkeepers at wholesale rates throughout the colony. Large Australian stores, for their part, sought to consolidate their ties with the hub of intercontinental trade – Anthony Hordern & Sons. and the Mutual Stores both had London offices, and A. Hall & Co. even claimed to have a furniture manufactory in London (G. Smith 1994, vi). These local enterprises were able to establish a strong foothold in the supply chain while maintaining a greater command of local demand than the London-based traders (see Ewins 1997, 15, 105 ff. for examples of the American trade). Independent shopkeepers kept apace with developments at 'home' via trade literature, and those with the means were encouraged to visit (*The Australian Storekeeper's Journal*: February 1895:m 11–12). Colonial exhibitions provided an opportunity to examine some of the latest wares, without the arduous travel, and for manufacturers to examine their market:

> We are glad to hear that several firms propose sending to the Exhibitions at Sydney this year and at Melbourne next year. The Australian and New Zealand markets are certainly deserving of attn. (The Pottery & Glass Trades' Journal: no.4, vol 2, Apr 1879, 51)

The success of colonial merchants depended on their ability to order the right goods in the right quantities, and it is in this context that we can begin to understand how and why there might be such variation between stores when arguably the same goods were being shipped to storekeepers in Norfolk, England, as well as The Rocks, Sydney, in the colony of New South Wales.

Travelling Light: Sea Chests and Essential Chattels

The journey to the New World would have been a daunting expedition for most migrants. However the emigrant experience was far from homogenous. Families and individuals left their homelands for different reasons, in response to different pressures and with variable access to capital. The preparations for young, single government-assisted migrants, or those fleeing starvation in Ireland, were quite different to those of established, self-funded entrepreneurial settlers. Those in the poorest circumstances may have had to sell valuable possessions to raise the fare of the passage or meet expenses while waylaid in London awaiting their ship.

The many published guide books on immigration to various receiving colonies,[2] along with surviving merchants' 'lists of necessaries', reveal something of the process of selecting the goods and chattels necessary to start a new life in a new land. Their advice was to bring as little luggage as possible, but each author had a different idea about the definition of travelling light – the only consensus being *no furniture*. There were of course the essentials for the shipboard journey (which could take between 5 and 12 months):

> *...a well supplied medicine chest, with all the uses and doses of the medicines legibly labelled upon the bottles, and one or, two medical books to accompany it; also a dozen spoons or so, and a large tea-pot, all of British plate; a dozen knives and forks, and two or three table-cloths; a good cot, with hair mattress, and four blankets.* (Baker 1845, 203)

Many emigrants cooked for themselves aboard the ships to reduce the cost of their fare and avoid the reputedly poor-quality provisions supplied on passenger ships. In addition to basic cooking utensils, they needed supplies which would last at least 5 months, which:

> *...ought to consist of biscuit and flour in casks, salt pork, corned beef, fresh preserved provisions, pickled eggs and tongues, potatoes, carrots, split peas, rice, plums, raisins, salt suet, butter in earthenware pans, three or four bottles of soda powders, a few bottles of spirits, (no duty is paid for them,) and porter; also tea, coffee, and sugar, two or three cakes of gingerbread, and a pound or two of tobacco.*[3] (Parker 1833, 223–24)

---

[2] For example, Parker 1833 (Van Diemen's Land [Tasmania]), James 1838 (South Australia and Port Phillip [Victoria]), Baker 1845 (Sydney & Melbourne), Wiley and Putnam 1845 (American colonies), Maconochie 1848 (all Australian colonies), Lancelott 1852 (all Australian colonies) and Earp 1852 (Australian goldfields).

[3] Parker (1833: 223) notes that 'There is no general rule as to the quantity of luggage and freight' for steerage passengers – i.e. it would vary from ship to ship.

While these items were in ready-use, many items packed for use on arrival in the colony were stored on board in sea chests for months and in many cases not opened until the immigrants were settled in their new homes. Goods had to be packed carefully to survive the journey, and clothing and leather goods were stowed with tin or zinc to prevent mildew.

Some immigrants sacrificed some of their stowage capacity for items purchased for the purpose of selling for profit, in lieu of ready money, once in the colony. Maconochie (1848, 22–23) commented upon, and advised against, this practice.

As early as the 1830s, emigrants were reassured that they could buy essential tools and agricultural implements at reasonable prices in the colony provided they were careful not to fall prey to inflated prices (Parker 1833, 222, 240–241). Nonetheless domestic goods were more economical to bring from Home. Cooking utensils, saucepans, stoves, 'ironmongery, hardware, tools, and in fact, all imported metal goods in demand in the colony' (Lancelott 1852, 87, 105) were up to 200 per cent dearer in 1850s Melbourne than in England. Baker advised his readers that:

*Crockery is an article which is generally dear in the colony [of New South Wales], and therefore the emigrant should take out such of his **old stock** as he may think he will require.* (Baker 1845, 204 emphasis added)

Lancelott (1852) prepared his readers for the likelihood of going without crockery and other furnishings until they were well settled in the colony. Many new migrants, he observed, made-do having their:

…sea-chests and packing-cases serve as chairs, tables, and bedsteads; some even lay the bed on the floor. It is also usual, as crockery and glass-ware are scarce and dear, for the young colonists to content themselves, for a period, with the tin plates, mugs, &c., which they brought with them to use on the voyage. This, semi-barbarous as it may appear, is the mode of life pursued by nearly all the stead, respectable young settles; and it certainly is the best, most convenient, and economical procedure for all who go out without a government of other certain engagement…Besides, appearances there are nothing; the sea voyage has prepared folk for roughing it, and for three parts of the year the weather is so warm and fine, that no one requires the numerous home comforts so indispensible in Britain. (Lancelott 1852, 81–2)

Twenty years earlier, Parker had warned:

Never forget that you are in a country, where, for a few years at least, prudence requires that the veil of oblivion should be drawn over many of the comforts, and still more of the luxuries of life, to which perhaps you have been accustomed for many years. Whatever may be your circumstances, things of this sort cannot be indulged in for a time, without departing from those maxims of prudence, which have been already inculcated. (Parker 1833, 240)

In addition to these pragmatic considerations, many emigrants carried in their sea chests small mementoes and keepsakes, family heirlooms and jewellery, perhaps special plated wares or crockery, photographs (in later decades), letters, cards and papers – sentimental reminders of home and loved ones. Such precious things were probably valued well above the domestic chattels necessary to make their new life. They would have been sorely missed in the new colony.

Implications for Historical Archaeology

What can we learn from the mechanics of transporting people and goods around the globe in the nineteenth century? Before assessing the archaeological lessons derived from the published advice to emigrants, we must consider it in the context of their publication. The reduced costs of printing technology in the late eighteenth and early nineteenth centuries, along with change in marketing structures, led to a bloom in pamphlets and penny journals to satisfy a wide variety of tastes (Rummonds 2004). Small publishing houses engaged their local networks of writers (and often their wives) to publish short articles directing the ranks of the middle classes on how to cook, arrange their furniture, manage their staff, treat their family's ailments and conduct their legal affairs. Pending their popularity, these short articles were often compiled into published manuals or books, such as *Hints on Household Taste, in Furniture, Upholstery and Other Details* by Charles Eastlake ([1868] 1969, 186) or the legendary *Mrs Beeton's Book of Household Management* by Isabella Beeton (1861). Notwithstanding Mrs Beeton's great contribution to the management of households across the Anglophone world, her words and advice were highly subjective, based on her own personal experiences.

This is true also of the printed advice offered to prospective migrants. Of the few emigrant-advice authors discussed here, each experienced very different aspects of colonial life. Charles John Baker, for example, was a failed migrant whose short 'residence in the colony was…clouded by domestic misfortune' (Baker 1845, v), and he returned to London to take up a career as a solicitor. The great penal reformer Captain Alexander Maconochie (1848) spent over 8 years in colonies, but as private secretary to the Governor of Van Diemen's Land and later Superintendent of Norfolk Island, his émigré experience was atypical of the emigrant 'with small capital', to whom his address was directed. Henry Walter Parker, Esquire, admitted he had never been to Van Diemen's Land, which he argued renders his advice the most objective, having received his 'information from the most authentic and respectable sources' (Parker 1833, iv). Regardless, the reach of these published advice books is unknown, and many prospective emigrants may not followed their advice, perhaps preferring the advice of friends and family who had already made the journey.

When we consider the written accounts of actual emigrants, some of the stories are shared; others are not. From this mix, however, we can establish some general patterns and expectations that influence our interpretation of the archaeological record of migrants in Australia and, to a lesser extent, other British colonies in the nineteenth century. First, for the 2 or 3 years, we should expect there to be little waste and a good deal of making do. We should expect that the *majority* of goods (particularly large furnishings) would have been bought or acquired in the colony. They might have been new, or second-hand, purchased from fellow migrants or local colonists. A smaller assemblage of goods brought from Home probably comprised two distinct parts: a collection of practical and essential items for cooking, medicinal care (a camper's kit, if you like) and daily carriage (a supply of durable clothing) and a collection of smaller, personal and potentially sentimental items, including jewellery, a family bible (or other texts) and perhaps heirloom plate. The prospect of a small quantity of items brought for the specific purpose of resale in the colony (i.e. liquid assets) should not be discounted, nor should it be assumed that they were always on-sold. Poor selection (perhaps based on poor advice given in one the manuals!) or a change in market conditions may have left migrant families with unsaleable goods on their hands. Either way, they are unlikely to have existed in sufficient quantity to significantly influence the archaeological record of immigration.

Looking beyond the source of manufacture or sale of the objects, it is necessary to discuss the element of consumer choice. One of the fascinating elements of the advice literature is the gentle preparation of the prospective emigrant to shift their expectation of standards of consumption and consequently any significance which they might attach to observed behaviours. Baker describes the upper and middling echelons of Melbourne society in the mid-1840s (following the depression) to be less extravagant than their counterparts in London. He claims that money was not lavished on 'useless but tempting trifles' – panoramas, talking canaries, exhibitions or white bait dinners (1845, 27) – and there were fewer balls and large dinner parties:

> ...yet hospitality of the table is not altogether unpractised, but, on the contrary, is often extended with a kind and easy welcome, instead of the ceremony and state which in England so frequently destroy enjoyment. (Baker 1845, 28)

When examining the archaeological record of immigration, we should expect to see patterns of consumption which learned in the old country adapted to local conditions. As new communities were formed and new migrants joined existing communities, social relations – and their material expression – were thrown into sharp relief. This presents the opportunity to capture migrant families at a remarkable stage in their 'modern' lives. They were adapting their tastes to a new market, a new social network, a new set of behaviours so clearly distinguishable from their 'Home' model, all the while managing a significant change in their lifestyle and income.

Of course cultural change is not one way; the presence of large numbers of new migrants in any colonial community must have had some influence of local taste. Bringing new fashions or gadgets in the latest styles, they had the opportunity to set trends as well as assimilate with local practices. It is in this capacity that global material culture both shaped and was shaped by the movement of people across the Anglophone world in the nineteenth century.

Concluding Remarks

The multidimensional nature of the archaeology of immigration provides for the analysis of material culture at the macro- and microscales. We can move from the comparison of the a single waste pit in a migrant's home in Sydney, or their camp on the Melbourne goldfields, with that of a native-born local or to the transnational comparison of assemblages from 'Home' or other colonies across the globe.

The chief requirement, in this respect, is for large-scale assemblage analysis: comparable analytical data (and lots of it) and a commitment to developing suitable methodologies with which to process and interpret that data. These two elements were the chief components of the Exploring the Archaeology of the Modern City (EAMC) project which will be discussed in the next chapter.

References

Adburgham, A. 1964. *Shops and Shopping, 1800–1914: Where, and in What Manner the Well-Dressed Englishwoman Bought Her Clothes*. London: George Allen & Unwin Ltd.

Alexander, D. 1970. *Retailing in England During the Industrial Revolution*. London: Athlone Press.

Alexander, N., and G. Akehurst. 1999. *The Emergence of Modern Retailing, 1750–1950*. London/Portland/Oregon: Frank Cass.

Allen, R. C. 2009. *The British Industrial Revolution in Global Perspective*. New Approaches to Economic and Social History. Cambridge: Cambridge University Press.

Appadurai, A. 1986. Introduction: Commodities and the Politics of Value. In *The Social Life of Things: Commodities in Cultural Perspective*, ed. A. Appadurai, 3–63. Cambridge: Cambridge University Press.

Baker, C.J. 1845. *Sydney and Melbourne: With Remarks on the Present State and Future Prospects of New South Wales, and Practical Advice to Emigrants*. London: Smith, Elder.

Beeton, I.M. 1861. *Beeton's Book of Household Management*. London: S. O. Beeton.

Berg, M. 2005. *Luxury and Pleasure in Eighteenth-Century Britain*. Oxford: Oxford University Press.

Berg, M., and H. Clifford. 1999. *Consumers and Luxury: Consumer Culture in Europe 1650–1850*. Manchester: Manchester University Press.

Blaszczyk, R. L. 2000. *Imagining Consumers: Design and Innovation from Wedgwood to Corning*. Studies in Industry and Society. Baltimore: Johns Hopkins University Press.

Brewer, J., and R. Porter, eds. 1993. *Consumption and the World of Goods*. London/New York: Routledge.

Civil Service Supply Association. 1880. *Export List*. London: The Association.

Cohen, D. 2006. *Household Gods: The British and Their Possessions*. New Haven: Yale University Press.

Cook, L.J., R. Yamin, and J.P. McCarthy. 1996. Shopping as Meaningful Action: Towards a Redefinition of Consumption in Historical Archaeology. *Historical Archaeology* 30 (4): 50–65.

Copeland, R. 1980. *Spode's Willow Pattern and Other Designs after the Chinese*. London: Cassell Ltd.

Crook, P. 2000. Shopping and Historical Archaeology: Exploring the Contexts of Urban Consumption. *Australasian Historical Archaeology* 18: 17–28.

———. 2008. '"Superior Quality": Exploring the Nature of Cost, Quality and Value in Historical Archaeology'. PhD Thesis, La Trobe University Archaeology Program School of Historical & European Studies Faculty of Humanities & Social Sciences.

———. 2019. Approaching the Archaeology of Value in the Modern World. *Post-Medieval Archaeology*. https://doi.org/10.1080/00794236.2019.1601381.

———. in press. Commodities and Consumption. In *Industrial Archaeology Handbook, ch 40*, ed. E.C. Casella and M. Nevell. London: Oxford University Press.

Davis, D. 1966. *A History of Shopping*. London: Routledge & Kegan Paul.

Earp, G. B. 1852. *The gold colonies of Australia, and gold seeker's manual: with illustrations of the implements required in the search for the gold ore, as well as the progress of the gold mining to the latest period, and ample notices of Australian gold geology and mineralogy; with the chemical and metallurgical treating of gold ore*. London: G. Routledge.

Eastlake, C. L. 1969. *Hints on Household Taste in Furniture, Upholstery and Other Details*. Fasc. of 4th ed. 1878. New York: Dover Publications.

Erskine, N. 2003. *Kingston Ceramics: A Dictionary of Ceramic Wares in the Norfolk Island Museum*. Norfolk Island: Norfolk Island Museum.

Ewins, N. 1997. 'Supplying the Present Wants of Our Yankee Cousins…': Staffordshire Ceramics and the American Market 1775–1880. In *Journal of Ceramic History*, vol. 15. Stoke-on-Trent: City Museum & Art Gallery.

Gibb, J.G. 1996. The Archaeology of Wealth: Consumer Behavior in English America. In *Interdisciplinary Contributions to Archaeology*. New York: Plenum Press.

Hill, H.C. 1921. *The Wonder Book Of Knowledge*. New York: J. C. Winston Co.

Horning, A., and E. Schweickart. 2016. Globalization and the Spread of Capitalism: Material Resonances. *Post-Medieval Archaeology* 50 (1): 34–52. https://doi.org/10.1080/00794236.2016.1169490.

James, T. Horton. 1838. *Six months in South Australia with some account of Port Philip and Portland Bay in Australia Felix: with advice to emigrants, to which is added a monthly calendar of gardening and agriculture adapted to the climate and seasons*. Facsimile edition, 1962. Adelaide: Public Library of South Australia.

Jefferys, J.B. 1954. *Retail Trading in Britain 1850–1950: A Study of Trends in Retailing with Special Reference to the Development of Co-Operative, Multiple Shop and Department Store Methods of Trading*. London: Cambridge University Press.

King, Henry S. and Co. 1880. *Cash Price List*. London: The Company.

Kingston, B. 1994. *Basket, Bag and Trolley: A History of Shopping in Australia*. Melbourne: Oxford University Press.

Lancelott, F. 1852. *Australia as It Is: Its Settlements, Farms, and Gold Fields*. London: Colburn and Co.

Maconochie, A. 1848. Emigration: With Advice to Emigrants, Especially Those with Small Capital. In *Addressed to the Society for Promoting Colonization*. London: John Ollivier.

McCracken, G.D. 1988. *Culture and Consumption: New Approaches to the Symbolic Character of Consumer Goods and Activities*. Bloomington: Indiana University Press.

McKendrick, N., J. Brewer, and J.H. Plumb. 1982. *The Birth of a Consumer Society: The Commercialization of Eighteenth-Century England*. Bloomington: Indiana University Press.

Mehler, N. 2013. Globalization, Immigration, and Transformation: Thoughts from a European Perspective. *Historical Archaeology* 47 (1): 38–49.

Mokyr, J. 1999. *The British Industrial Revolution : An Economic Perspective*. 2nd ed. Boulder: Westview Press.

Mullins, P.R. 2011a. *The Archaeology of Consumer Culture*. Gainesville: University Press of Florida.

———. 2011b. The Archaeology of Consumption. *Annual Review of Anthropology* 40: 133–144. https://doi.org/10.1146/annurev-anthro-081309-145746.

Parker, H.W. 1833. *The Rise, Progress, and Present State of Van Diemen's Land with Advice to Emigrants: Also a Chapter on Convicts Showing the Efficacy of Transportation as a Secondary Punishment*. London: J. Cross.

Philp, R. K. 1883. *Enquire within upon Everything*. 67th ed., rev. London: Houlston & Sons.

Pollon, F. 1989. *Shopkeepers and Shoppers: A Social History of Retailing in New South Wales from 1788*. Sydney: The Retail Traders' Association of New South Wales.

Popp, A. 2001. *Business Structure, Business Culture and the Industrial District: The Potteries, c.1850–1914*. Aldershot: Ashgate Publishing Ltd.

Rappaport, E.D. 2000. *Shopping for Pleasure: Women in the Making of London's West End*. Princeton: Princeton University Press.

Rummonds, R.-G. 2004. *Nineteenth-Century Printing Practices and the Iron Handpress: With Selected Readings*. London: British Library.

Shammas, C. 1990. *The Pre-Industrial Consumer in England and America*. New York: Oxford University Press.

Smith, A. 1776. *An Inquiry Into the Nature and Causes of the Wealth of Nations*. Vol. 2. London: W. Strahan and T. Cadell.

Smith, G. 1994. *The Grandest Display of Household Furniture in the Colony, A Catalogue of Furniture by A Hall & Co, George Street, Sydney, 1897*. Taree: Wongoolah Publishing.

Smith, M.L. 2007. Inconspicuous Consumption: Non-Display Goods and Identity Formation. *Journal of Archaeological Method and Theory* 14 (4): 412–438. https://doi.org/10.1007/s10816-007-9040-6.

Spencer-Wood, S.M. 1987. *Consumer Choice in Historical Archaeology*. New York: Plenum Press.

Weatherill, L. 1988. *Consumer Behaviour and Material Culture in Britain, 1660–1760*. London/New York: Routledge.

Webber, K., I. Hoskins, and J. McCann. 2003. *What's in Store? A History of Retailing in Australia*. Sydney: Powerhouse Publishing and the New South Wales Heritage Office.

Wiley, J., and Putnam, G.P. 1845. *Wiley & Putnam's Emigrant's Guide Comprising Advice and Instruction in Every Stage of the Voyage to America; Also, Information which the Emigrant Needs on Arrival*. London: Wiley & Putnam.

Winstanley, M.J. 1983. *The Shopkeeper's World, 1830–1914*. Manchester: Manchester University Press.

Wurst, L.A., and R.H. McGuire. 1999. Immaculate Consumption: A Critique of the "Shop till You Drop" School of Human Behavior. *International Journal of Historical Archaeology* 3 (3): 191–199. https://doi.org/10.1023/A:1021914220703.

Young, L. 2003. *Middle-Class Culture in the Nineteenth-Century: America, Australia and Britain*. Hampshire/New York: Palgrave Macmillan.

Chapter 7
Sanitary Reform and Comparative Assemblage Analysis: Methodology

Introduction

In this chapter we examine the historical context of an urban archaeological phenomenon: the backfilling of decommissioned cesspits and privies with domestic waste. This is a practice known throughout the modern world in metropolitan cities such as London, Sydney, Melbourne, New York, Minneapolis, Washington and many others throughout the Anglophone world (Mayne 1982; Wong 1999; Crane 2000; McCarthy and Ward 2000; Fitts 2001; Halliday 2001; Jeffries 2006; Hayes and Minchinton 2016). Like many aspects of urbanisation, it was one subject to increasing regulation in the Victorian era as population density increased and politicians, councillors, engineers and entrepreneurs worked to solve the many problems linked to the management of services and waste.

The exploration of cesspit fills must be understood in the broader context of the management of domestic waste throughout human history. Since humans have been making and using things, waste has been piling up. The accumulation (and reuse) of shell middens, and the by-products of stone tool manufacture, has a long history in sedimentary and mobile communities (Smith 2012). Deliberate discard of rubbish in excavated pits appears to have commenced in the Neolithic era and has been the subject of archaeological debate for this and later eras (Joyce and Pollard 2010; Jervis 2014). As camps became villages, towns and later cities, industry intensified (creating more by products) and domestic life became more settled, giving rise to more *things* to sit on, cook with, serve with and of course store and maintain all those accoutrements.

Minimisation of waste was a long-standing goal of production, so that all parts of a slaughtered cow had their use – meat for food, hide for leather, tallow for candles

This chapter is an expansion and refinement of an earlier work, *The Analysis of Cesspit Deposits from The Rocks, Sydney* published by the authors in *Australasian Historical Archaeology* 22 (pp. 44–56).

T. Murray, P. Crook, *Exploring the Archaeology of the Modern City in Nineteenth-century Australia*, Contributions To Global Historical Archaeology, https://doi.org/10.1007/978-3-030-27169-5_7

and soap and bones and horns for combs and utensils (Jørgensen 2012: 349) – and worked goods were repaired or in the case of metalcraft, recycled. Nevertheless, waste was still created and had to be dealt with. In the mediaeval era, households collected refuse in barrels and later relocated it (Jørgensen 2012, 350), but not all householders could or did keep their waste on private land. When rubbish was dumped on the street or in waterways, it became a public issue. The first waste disposal regulations appeared in the mediaeval era and were commonplace by the end of the fifteenth century (Jørgensen 2012, 350). As populations increased and cities became larger, waste management became a more complex problem. As we explored in Chap. 6, the industrial revolution gave rise to a significant increase in the number and range of domestic goods putting greater burden on waste management services.

The management of human waste is a closely related matter, but one with greater consequences for the health of communities. Prior to the introduction of modern toilets, human waste was collected in chamber pots and tossed directly into waterways or cesspits. Cesspits are deep pits dug into the ground, positioned below a small 'closet' fitted with a seat or row of seats, to collect human waste until such time as the waste seeps away or can be dug out and relocated off-site (Lewis n.d.: sec. 9.05 [Sanitation]). A cesspit may be used in combination with a mechanised flushing device supplied by reticulated or other water (making it a water closet) and may be used to discard kitchen slops and other waste. Regardless of the waste it collects, the key feature of a cesspit is that waste was not carried away in pipes.

The nineteenth century was a pivotal time in urban sanitation. In the then world's largest city of London – where the population tripled between 1800 and 1850 – the Thames and its local tributaries system failed to disperse household sewage mingled with piped water (Dobraszczyk 2012, 379). Connections between overcrowding and disease were debated in the early part of the nineteenth century but environmental links were attributed to 'miasmas' or foul air surrounding polluted waterways rather than the water itself. It was not until 1855 that a cholera outbreak in Soho was isolated to a single water pump but several years before widespread acceptance of waterborne, rather than airborne, disease (Halliday 2001, 129–30).

Efforts to remove human waste from areas of dense population were enshrined in metropolitan acts, such as the *Nuisances Removal and Diseases Prevention Act* (1846) which encouraged owners to close their cesspits and connect to the sewer. The sewerage infrastructure of London was overhauled, and in the decades that followed, this became a template for other cities across the world (Dobraszczyk 2012, 379) including Sydney and Melbourne.

Sydney: A Young Colonial City

The township of Sydney was established in 1788 when Governor Arthur Phillip laid out the first camp for the 1300-odd convicts and marines of the First Fleet in Sydney Cove. The settlement was clustered around a natural tributary, later known as the Tank Stream, which served as the water supply until pollution forced its abandonment in 1826.

As the population of the city of Sydney and its suburbs grew in the nineteenth century, the inadequacy of basic municipal provisions such as water supply, drainage, and sewage disposal seriously endangered the health and well-being of those living in the city's most overcrowded wards. It was not until 1837 that piped water reached the growing city, but take-up of the new supply was slow, and in 1851, only 1000 houses out of 8000 in the vicinity of the mains were connected. Everyone else relied on public fountains or standpipes or paid for supplies from water carters (Clark 1978, 55–56).

Water supply was only one of the challenges faced by the inhabitants of the growing city of Sydney; the management and disposal of water and other waste was another. In the absence of garbage collection or underground drainage, kitchen slop pails and chamber pots were at times tossed into yards, or emptied directly onto the street (Jones 1984, 11; Dowse 1888 cited by Karskens 1999, 82). On the steep slopes of The Rocks, such activities posed a particular problem, as William Stanley Jevons recorded in 1858:

> As sewers and drains of proper construction are quite unknown here…the drainage of each house or hovel simply trickles down the hill, soon reaching, as the case may be, the front and back of the next lower house. In many places filthy water is actually seen to accumulate against the walls of the dwellings, soaking, of course, beneath the foundations and the floors above which the family live. (Jevons 1929, 13)

While Jevons was probably drawing attention to the most extreme cases of sanitary malfunction, that they happened at all is concerning by modern standards. By Jevons's time, the majority of houses or house rows in The Rocks (and throughout the other city wards) would have had cesspits. However poor construction, improper maintenance and the sharing of single pits for multiple houses often led to overflows – forcing residents to find alternative disposal arrangements.

According to R. Seymour, Inspector of Nuisances, the most 'effective' kind of cesspit was built on sandy soil with unmortared bricks that allowed liquid waste to seep into surrounding soil. Such pits could last 3 or 4 years without being emptied (Sydney City and Suburban Sewage and Health Board [hereafter referred to as the 'Health Board'] Health Board 1875a, 6 [q. 181]). While these required less maintenance in the short term, the seepage contaminated surrounding soil and water supplies if built too close or upslope from a neighbouring well.

On the other hand, impervious cesspits could overflow after heavy rain, or overuse, and in 1875, R. Seymour cited 'instances where closets have had to be cleaned out four times in six weeks' (Health Board 1875a, 6 [q. 179]; c.f. Wong 1999, 60). The key problem was poor construction, in this case the reverse of the ideal 'seepage' cesspit: these pits were contained, but not waterproof. They were built with no supporting drainage or superstructure footings to prevent rain- or groundwater in mixing with the waste.

To counter the odour and 'sanitise' the waste, a variety of additives, such as ash, charcoal, carbolic acid or lime, were tossed into the pit, but these were not in themselves always pleasant. When the Inspector of Nuisances arranged for the deodorisation of an odorous cesspit in Kent Street with carbolic acid, the residents said 'they would sooner have the smell of the closet' (Health Board 1875a, 5 [q. 209]).

The 1857 Sewerage Scheme

In 1851 the City of Sydney Corporation sought out a new source of water from Botany, south of Sydney, and began planning for the introduction of sewer lines. In 1859, the five principal harbour outlets of the new sewerage scheme were completed, and the first water from Botany was pumped into Sydney (Aird 1961, 129; Clark 1978, 61). A trigonometric survey was conducted between 1854 and 1857 to plan the layout of the mains (Select Committee 1854; Williamson 1984, 276). The map was redrawn and annotated as new mains were installed, and a second, final, version of it was completed in 1865 (Figs. 7.1 and 7.2). While the map is invaluable in documenting the boundaries of house lots in the years between 1854 and 1857 and 1858 and 1865, the position of some water mains and sewer lines may only be as *planned* in 1857 and 1865, not as built. Further, the mere presence of a sewer main was not a necessary cause for a landlord or home owner to connect to it. By the end of 1876, only 8126 of Sydney's 16,924 houses in the city wards were connected to the sewer mains (Clark 1877, 843).

Fig. 7.1 Details from the 1857 trigonometric survey showing the nine houses selected for analysis. The black line of the planned sewer along Longs Lane and partially down Carahers Lane (SRNSW: NRS 9929, Trigonometric Survey of the City of Sydney, 1865 [sheet no. B2], courtesy of State Records NSW and GML)

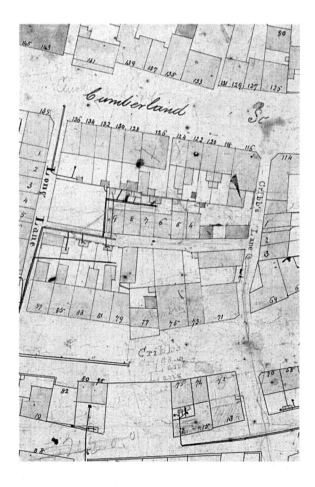

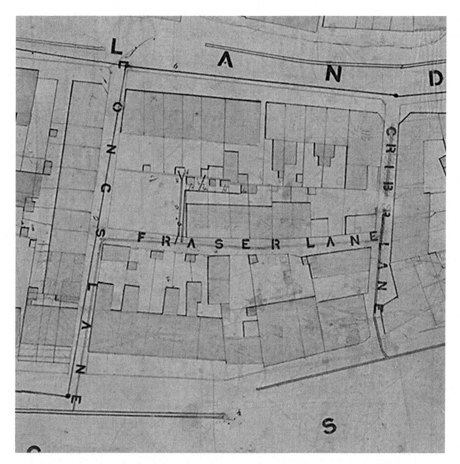

Fig. 7.2 Detail from the 1865 Trigonometrical Survey of Sydney showing the red line of the sewer coming up Longs Lane and all the way down Carahers (then Fraser) Lane. (Source: 'City of Sydney – Trigonometrical Survey, 1855-1865', Block A1, City of Sydney Archives, CRS1042/1 [https://atlas.cityofsydney.nsw.gov.au/maps/city-of-sydney-trigonometrical-survey-1855-1865/city-of-sydney-trigonometrical-survey-1855-1865-block-a1/])

Karskens (1999, 89) has argued that the rollout of sewerage infrastructure was part of a difficult transition for urban people from the customary, private management of ablutions to the public management of waste and refuse that became so necessary in large cities in the nineteenth century. Many tenants and landlords were aghast at paying water rates, connection and maintenance fees for facilities they would rather manage themselves. A more cynical view is that landlords were aghast at *paying* and were untroubled by the substandard infrastructure in the city wards (Fitzgerald 1987, 80).[1]

---

[1] There was a similar response in other cities across the globe, for example, New York; see Geismar 1993: 63.

Inadvertently, the resistance may have worked in their favour, for the 1857 scheme was the source of 'nuisances' more foul than an average cesspit could produce. One of the scandals of the 1875 investigation of the Sydney City and Suburban Sewage Health Board was that of the 5400 closets supplied with water from the Sydney water mains, 4700 were directly connected with the mains (Health Board 1875b, 353 [13]). That is, fresh water was not retained in a separate cistern before being pumped in to the closet's flushing mechanism. When a blockage caused a closet to overflow, it ran back into the main water supply. When one of the members of the Health Board inspected a property with a direct connection, he tested the water in an adjoining yard and found solid faecal matter in just a small glass of water. Some of these connections may have been illegal installations to evade the high rates, others a result of insufficient legislative power to force landlords, unwilling to meet the additional expense, to install cisterns and flap-traps to prevent contamination.

These powers were finally awarded to the city council, under the *Nuisances Prevention Act*, introduced in 1876 following the recommendations of the Health Board. It was now possible to dictate the dimensions, materials and construction of new cesspits and compel alterations to existing substandard pits. Further, the cleansing of pits was regularised and centralised, with the city council charging a set fee (probably higher than that negotiated with individual contractors) and having the authority to force occupants to clean-out their pits. It was recommended that pits be cleaned once every 3 months – which the Health Board acknowledged would 'no doubt tend to increase the expense', but was necessary for the 'health of the inhabitants, and common decency' (Health Board 1875a, 373 [5]). It may well be that these increased and enforceable costs were enough to encourage landlords who had not yet connected their properties to sewer mains to do so. The new powers and additional scrutiny may also explain the installation and repairs of at least two cesspits on the Cumberland and Gloucester Streets site in the 1870s, 1880s and 1890s.

In 1875, Inspector of Nuisances John Doherty gave evidence at the Health Board inquiry that when a cesspit was converted to a water closet, it was 'all cleaned out with sand or soil', before pipes were laid, and it was sealed over (Health Board 1875a, 373 [5]). While this was clearly the case in some parts of Sydney, archaeological evidence from The Rocks suggests that inorganic, household and other refuse were preferred to clean sand and soil.

Cesspit fills from The Rocks are typically described as single-event deposits and often considered to be the result of a household clean-out. Discrete layers are often identified, and recovered as unique strata, but in most cases conjoin analyses reveal them to be derived from a single source. The deposits usually contain some complete, or near-complete, vessels: the percentage ranged from 1.0% to 21.9% of MNV (see Table 10.2).

Melbourne

Melbourne was founded in 1835 by private settlers willing to test the bounds of colonial governance by building outside the declared settlements of New South Wales. The 'village' grew into a town which was incorporated in 1842 and declared a city in 1847. At this time, the town relied on the Yarra River for drinking water but, like metropolitan waterways across the globe, also used it for waste disposal. The discovery of gold in 1851 brought the matter to a head when the population increased fivefold in 7 years.

The Board of Commissioners of Sewers and Water Supply was formed in 1853, and water piped from Yan Yean Reservoir began to flow in 1857. This encouraged residents to run water through their cesspits which in turn caused excessive seepage into surrounding subterranean features and ghastly overflows. In 1861 the Board of Health set out to improve the quality of cesspits with a circular of leakproof designs for a bluestoned-lined pit and a 'cask cesspool' or buried barrel (Hayes and Minchinton 2016, 14). Three years later, the Board began recommending the installation of new 'earth closets', above-ground pans cleared by 'nightmen', and issued 616 notices to remedy leaking cesspits (Hayes and Minchinton 2016, 15–16). It was not until 1867 that they had the legal authority to enforce these orders when the *Public Health Amendment Act 1867* made overflow, leakage and seepage from cesspits illegal (Hayes and Minchinton 2016, 16).

In 1870, the Melbourne City Council introduced a municipal night pan collection service, and the Inspector of Nuisances began issuing closure notices for problematic cesspits (Hayes and Minchinton 2016, 16). In 1876, with the passage of *The Public Health Amendment Act 1876*, the Council could force the closure of all cesspits and banned the construction of new ones altogether (Hayes and Minchinton 2016, 12, 17).[2] Melbourne relied on night soil collection until 1897 – four decades after introduction of piped water – when the first homes were connected to the new metropolitan sewerage scheme.

Melbourne's successive sanitary reforms have had a significant impact on the archaeological record. As Hayes and Minchinton (2016) have demonstrated, compliance with these regulations can be seen in the 39 cesspits recovered from the Little Lon and Casselden Place excavations (see also McCarthy 1989; Godden Mackay Logan et al. 2004). The pits provided material evidence of the succession of sanitary reforms. One bluestone cesspit and four barrel cesspits fitted the specifications of the 1861 circular (Hayes and Minchinton 2016, 14). Two of the barrels had been installed within an existing cesspit suggesting compliance with a works order. Unlined, timber-lined and cement-lined pits were also identified.

---

[2] This is the same year that the *Nuisances Prevention Act* was passed in Sydney which still permitted construction of new cesspits despite the availability of sewerage mains.

Cesspit Fill as an Archaeological Resource

While understanding the progress and the complications of citywide sewerage enhances our understanding of life on archaeological sites, it was the conversion process itself that left us with a rich resource for exploring the daily life of households. Cesspits were to be cleaned out – for the last time – before pipes were laid and the pit sealed over. Practices varied from city to city regarding the nature of the fill, but even when statutes or official reports called for 'clean sand or soil' (e.g. Sydney in 1875; Health Board 1875a, 5), it is clear from archaeological evidence that inorganic, household and other refuse were used.

These backfill assemblages often contain complete or near-complete vessels – that is, vessels likely to be useful but no longer wanted alongside smaller fragments of waste likely to have been moved from a shorter-term rubbish pile. Once sealed, they are less likely to be subject to disturbance other than maintenance of pipes just below ground level. These types of backfills have been described as 'clearance' assemblages:

> 'Clearance groups' may be defined as closed deposits of deliberately discarded, everyday household artefacts, with little evidence for chronological contamination, representing the final fill of a substantial cut feature, such as a cess pit, well or cistern, in which the contents are preserved as a discrete assemblage. Such features would have been regularly cleaned out during their active lifetime and kept free of an excess of accumulated debris and waste. The final fill may represent a large-scale clear-out of selected goods from the property or properties using the feature, coinciding with its use coming to an end. (Pearce 2000, 144–5)

This can sometimes be linked to a change in household ownership or a death in the family (McCarthy and Ward 2000, 121; see Wheeler 2000a, 11–12), but in the case of sanitary reform, the discard was likely to be opportunistic as house after house in the row was connected to the main sewer line or subject to council upgrades. This kind of clearance presents another analytical benefit: the deposits in each house were created within a short timeframe, giving a 'snapshot' of the street or neighbourhood.

Household Links

While the fills usually offer an interesting array of artefacts, can we be confident that they are the possessions, or even refuse, of the occupants of the home adjacent to which they were discarded?

While the occupier (often a tenant) was responsible for the regular clearing of cesspits, the establishment and maintenance of sewer connections were the domain of the owner.[3] It is not unreasonable to expect that if there were opportunities for

---

[3] In at least 1875, the owner formally applied to the City Engineer to connect their property to the sewer mains (Sewage and Health Board – Minutes of Inquiry, 1875, p. 5 in *V&P* 1875, vol. 4, p. 345). Note the occupier was responsible for the regular clearing of cesspits.

free rubbish disposal to be had, and the owner lived nearby, they may have conducted a clean-out of their own. This very possibility raises as many questions regarding the nature of the owner–occupier relationship, as it does about the attitude of owners or tenants towards the less pleasant elements of urban life in the nineteenth century.[4] It is simply unknown, for example, whether the activity of on-site rubbish disposal and void filling was considered an opportunity or chore.

Twentieth-century attitudes towards household refuse are very different to those of the nineteenth century, before reliable garbage collection became commonplace. With regard to Washington municipal garbage collection, Crane (2000, 21, 22) points out that while organic refuse or 'garbage' (food remains and dead animals) was a primary concern throughout the nineteenth century, 'rubbish' (inorganic refuse, bottles, broken teacups, etc.) was not considered a problem until late in that century. It is clear from various Health Board inquiries in Sydney in the mid- to late-nineteenth century that inorganic refuse was a valuable commodity for anyone wanting to 'fill up large holes' on their properties (e.g. see Health Board 1875b, 351 [11]).

In the absence of detailed historical documentation, the archaeological assemblages themselves may be able to suggest the circumstances of the episodic fills – or at least rule out some speculation. For example, if an owner insisted on making use of the opportunity of a rubbish pit in their tenants' yards, the event ought to produce a homogenous deposit in cesspits backfilled in adjacent properties under the ownership of the one individual.

Another alternative is that the engineers and workmen provided the fill. In this case, it is *likely* that they used a supply of 'clean' sand or soil fill, as reported in the 1875 Sydney inquiry. Nonetheless, the possibility that they made use of refuse collected by the city carts to fill in these 'large holes' cannot be ruled out. If the latter were the case, we would expect to see homogenous deposits and numerous conjoins across house lots.

Given the close-knit nature of many nineteenth-century communities and the fact that many residents in both The Rocks and Little Lon were related to each other by birth or marriage, it is also possible that neighbours may have helped each other out, either by offering free garbage disposal or perhaps finding a few unwanted items to fill their neighbours' void.

Numerous properties were also vacant from time to time. In such cases, sewer connections along with other renovations may have been made while no tenant was present. In this case, the backfill may be the goods left behind by the tenants, or be sourced from elsewhere.

Whether it was the result of landlord-, tenant- or council-organised work, the likelihood of cross-house lot discard was probably affected by whether or not neighbouring properties were connected to the sewer mains at the same time. There was one instance of this in our Rocks study group: a cross-property conjoin occurred between 3 and 5 Carahers Lane and the neighbouring properties along Cumberland

---

[4] It is said that some middle-class families were so ashamed to be seen collecting water supplies from public fountains or pumps that they sent their children to do it for them (Clark 1978: 60–61).

Street. It is more likely to be the result of the (absentee) owner arranging for all properties to be connected at one time, rather than of owner deposition.

Unfortunately, archaeological data are often not precise enough to *conclusively* phase the connections of neighbouring properties. Studies suggest that ceramic tablewares have an average lifespan of 15–20 years beyond the date of manufacture and purchase (Adams 2003, 38). Further, ceramic manufacture often ranged across several decades. This means that if the latest minimum date of artefact manufacture for a ceramic vessel is 1860, its deposition date should be 1875–1880. Consequently, it should not be surprising to find coins, clay pipes or single-use containers like aerated-water bottles[5] dating to the early 1880s alongside dinner plates last made in the 1860s. Conversely, in cases where single-use or short-term artefacts date to within 5 years of minimum manufacture dates for ceramic tablewares, there ought to be sufficient evidence to argue for a brief time lag, i.e. a timely (perhaps even fashionable) consumption of new products and styles.

For the Cumberland and Gloucester Streets site (introduced in Chap. 8), we do have a historically informed TPQ for some backfills along Carahers Lane and Gloucester Street: 1866 when the sewer was laid down Carahers Lane (Sewerage and Water Supply, 10th report, 1866 1867: 30–31; Karskens 1999: 89). Even with these dating tools, in neighbourhoods with high tenancy turnover like The Rocks and Little Lon, the prospect of tying fills to families in tenanted dwellings is challenging.[6]

Comparative Assemblage Analysis: Contrasting Households

Numerous comprehensive analyses of nineteenth-century privy backfills have been undertaken in the United States (Wall 1991, 1999; Geismar 1993; Fitts 1999; Carnes-McNaughton and Harper 2000; McCarthy and Ward 2000; Wheeler 2000b; Brighton 2001; Fitts 2001; Yamin 2001; Praetzellis and Praetzellis 2004), with a smaller number in the United Kingdom (Matthews 1999; Pearce 2000; Jeffries 2006; Jeffries et al. 2014; Owens and Jeffries 2016) and Australia (Starr 2001). By comparing the contents from house to house, archaeologists have explored consumer choice, diet, health and other dimensions of daily life.

Fitts (1999) demonstrated the middle-class 'culture of conformity' – the penchant among New York residents to follow the prescriptive literature and stock their sideboards with matching sets of Gothic, ironstone wares. Peña and Denmon (2000) used the backfills of a double-vault privy at a boarding house in Buffalo, New York State, and the private home and shop front next door to understand how the boarding house keepers may have distinguished the material culture of their own family unit from that provided to their boarders.

---

[5] Note, many aerated water and other bottles were reused.

[6] See Groover 2001 for a statistical predictive response to this problem on rural sites occupied by several generations of the same family.

Large-scale comparative assemblage analysis of the kind outlined above is not limited to cesspit backfills. It is the goal of many large archaeological research projects. Comparing and contrasting material cultural from neighbouring or distant dwellings can be achieved with dedicated rubbish pits, underfloor deposits or other deposits which can be linked to individual households with confidence. In certain areas, these can be linked directly to families known through historical records, but this is not always the case. An excellent example is Samford's (2007) study of 103 subfloor pits from 5 slave quarters across excavated from 3 eighteenth-century Virginian plantations. The names of the slaves who occupied these cabins are not known, but Samford was able to identify cultural and spiritual practices through comparative analysis of a large group of pits.

This approach redresses the limitations of archaeology carried out in the Archaeological Heritage Management industry, particularly the necessary focus on individual sites within the boundary of the study site alone. When exploring material culture at the city-scale, more comprehensive data can be ascertained by comparing a greater number of smaller, contained deposits from different households than a handful of very large deposits from one or two households – although these too can be interesting. While large sites with detailed historical records can supply ample source material for interpretation, these sometimes rely on interpreting the presence or absence of individual finds. When the dataset is broadened to comparative assemblages, the relative quantity of finds can be assessed.

This is the benefit of large urban sites, like the Cumberland and Gloucester Streets and Commonwealth Block sites. Covering multiple city blocks, numerous comparable structures, features and assemblages were recovered. Thirty-nine cesspits were identified at the Commonwealth Block, making intra-site analysis complex and rewarding. But why stop there?

The EAMC Approach

The focus of the original Exploring the Modern City project was the city of Sydney, but the framework and methodologies have been employed to conduct detailed analysis of the Commonwealth Block collections. As discussed in Chap. 2, the database was shared among both projects, enabling the comparative analysis of Rocks and Melbourne assemblages that is the core of this book.

In both studies, rather that outlining thematic research goals as had been appropriately done for the original excavation reports,[7] we sought out the most archaeologically reliable datasets, regardless of their association with a particular family or occupation phase, or the kinds of research questions they were likely to address. Datasets were extended by cataloguing previously bulk-bagged material and calculating minimum vessel counts for recorded artefacts.

---

[7] The research design underwriting the Cumberland and Gloucester streets investigation was organised around five main research questions concerning class, gender, standards of living, neighbourhood character and governance (Godden Mackay and Karskens 1994: 72 & 1999).

In the Rocks, we focused on post-1860s cesspit backfills. Ten cesspit fills from nine houses (see Chap. 8) were analysed with minimum vessel counts being prepared and specific cases of matching sets being recorded. The analysis was first published in *Keeping up with the McNamaras* (2005), and details of cataloguing and analysis procedures such as master context groupings, TPQ revisions, minimum vessel counts and matching sets can be found there (Crook et al. 2005, 30–32).

At the Commonwealth Block, most of the fills were analysed, but ten have been selected here (see Chap. 9) on the basis that their size and age were most comparable to the Rocks study.

Our analysis is focused on ceramic and glass vessels. There has been some criticism of the archaeological preoccupation with ceramics at the expense of classes of artefacts, especially 'small finds' (see Cumberpatch and Blinkhorn 1997). We acknowledge such criticisms but observe that a significant part of the problem is the speculative and often simplified association of ceramics of unspecified frequency with socio-economic status: a Spode plate 'does not a middle-class family make' (Davison 2003, 42). As we noted in 2005, ceramic-specific models for classification and analysis developed United States (e.g. Otto 1977; Miller 1980, 1991; Klein 1991), had little traction in Australia, and when used, they were often limited to isolated examples from the one site (e.g. Lydon 1995).

It remains difficult to start the process of teasing out the *meanings* of ceramic vessels, designs and materials in relation to socio-economic or other measures, when very few studies have sought to rigorously characterise multiple assemblages (Fitts 1999 among others; for exceptions, e.g. see Praetzellis and Praetzellis 2004). Our aim for the EAMC was to establish some of these characteristics and to *quantify* rather than speculate about the relative proportion of various vessel styles and, furthermore, the correspondence of those styles to particular vessel forms. Our aim has been to prepare rigorous comparative datasets, each with a long shelf life, to sketch out just how many Spode plates, wine glasses and matching sets you can expect to find in a working-class household.

Our approach to the documentary research shares a similar aim. We developed the People+Place Database so that we could manage and store large volumes of occupancy data, meticulously researched by historian Laila Ellmoos, not just from the Cumberland and Gloucester Streets site but the immediate vicinity of Sections 70, 74 and 75: the blocks bounded by Gloucester, Cumberland, Essex and Argyle Streets (and including Susannah Place, see Ellmoos & Crook 2006 and Crook et al. 2006). While this is still only a small segment of The Rocks, and an even smaller sample of Sydney's urban landscape, it is a rigorous dataset with potentially multiple uses beyond the life of the EAMC project.

The system of recording has also enabled us to integrate documentary and archaeological data at the most basic level: that of creating relational links in the database. Of course, the far more meaningful, challenging and successful levels of integration between historical documents and archaeological material occurred when comparing the *results* and consequent *interpretations* of each suite of data. These were, too, often based on additional, detailed historical data gathered for particular families. Nonetheless, the particular stories we tell here were given added weight when told against the backdrop of more general patterns identified in the material culture and documentary records. While these 'higher-level' examples of integration were developed outside the confines of the database's statistical manipulation, they were made far easier by organising all data based on a common variable: place.

References

Adams, W.H. 2003. Dating Historical Sites: The Importance of Understanding Time Lag in the Acquisition, Curation, Use, and Disposal of Artifacts. *Historical Archaeology*: 38–64.

Aird, W.V. 1961. *The Water Supply, Sewerage, and Drainage of Sydney*. Sydney: Metropolitan Water Sewerage and Drainage Board.

Brighton, S.A. 2001. Prices That Suit the Times: Shopping for Ceramics at the Five Points. *Historical Archaeology* 35: 16–30.

Carnes-McNaughton, L.F., and T.M. Harper. 2000. The Parity of Privies: Summary Research on Privies in North Carolina. *Historical Archaeology* 34: 110–197

Clark, W. 1877. Sydney Water Supply: Report to the Government of New South Wales on Various Projects for Supplying Sydney with Water, 16 May 1877. In *Votes and Proceedings of Legislative Assembly of New South Wales 1876–77*, vol. 3, 789–840. Sydney: Government Printer

Clark, D. 1978. "Worse than Psychic": Sydney's Water Supply 1788–1888. In *Nineteenth-century Sydney: Essays in Urban History*, ed. Max Kelly, 54–65. Sydney: Sydney University Press, in association with the Sydney History Group.

Crane, B.D. 2000. Filth, Garbage, and Rubbish: Refuse Disposal, Sanitary Reform, and Nineteenth-Century Yard Deposits in Washington, D.C. *Historical Archaeology* 34: 20–38.

Crook, P., L. Ellmoos, and T. Murray. 2005. Keeping Up with the McNamaras: A Historical Archaeological Study of the Cumberland and Gloucester Streets site, The Rocks, Sydney. *Archaeology of the Modern City Series 8*. Sydney: Historic Houses Trust of New South Wales.

Crook, P., L. Ellmoos, and T. Murray. 2006. People+Place: A guide to using the database. *Archaeology of the Modern City Series 9*. Sydney: Historic Houses Trust of New South Wales.

Cumberpatch, C.G., and P.W. Blinkhorn. 1997. Introduction. In *Not So Much a Pot, More a Way of Life: Current Approaches to Artefact Analysis in Archaeology*, Oxford Monograph 83, ed. C.G. Cumberpatch and P.W. Blinkhorn, v–vi. Oxford: Oxbow.

Davison, G. 2003. The Archaeology of the Present: "Excavating" Melbourne's Postwar Suburbs. In *Exploring the Modern City: Recent Approaches to Urban History and Archaeology*, ed. T. Murray, 41–63. Sydney: Historic Houses Trust of NSW.

Dobraszczyk, P. 2012. History of Consumption and Waste, World, 1800s. In *Encyclopedia of Consumption and Waste: The Social Science of Garbage*, ed. C.A. Zimring and W.L. Rathje, 378–381. Thousand Oaks: SAGE Publications.

Ellmoos, L., and P. Crook. 2006. People+Place database. In EAMC Databases, Version 1.0, ed. Penny Crook, Laila Ellmoos, and Tim Murray, Compact Disc. Sydney: Historic Houses Trust of NSW.

Fitts, R.K. 1999. The Archaeology of Middle-Class Domesticity and Gentility in Victorian Brooklyn. *Historical Archaeology* 33: 39–62. https://doi.org/10.1007/BF03374279.

———. 2001. The Rhetoric of Reform: The Five Points Missions and the Cult of Domesticity. *Historical Archaeology* 35: 115–132.

Fitzgerald, S. 1987. *Rising Damp: Sydney 1870–90*. Melbourne: Oxford University Press.

Geismar, J.H. 1993. Where is Night Soil? Thoughts on an Urban Privy. *Historical Archaeology* 27: 57–70.

Godden Mackay, and G. Karskens. 1994. The Cumberland/Gloucester Streets Site, The Rocks: Archaeological Assessment and Research Design. Godden Mackay Heritage Consultants for the Sydney Cove Authority and the Heritage Council of NSW.

Godden Mackay Logan, Austral Archaeology & La Trobe University. 2004. *Casselden Place, 50 Lonsdale Street, Melbourne, Archaeological Excavations Research Archive Report – Volume 1: Introduction and Background.* Sydney: Unpublished Report Prepared for ISPT and Heritage Victoria.

Halliday, S. 2001. *The Great Stink of London: Sir Joseph Bazalgette and the Cleansing of the Victorian Metropolis.* Phoenix: Sutton Publishing.

Hayes, S., and B. Minchinton. 2016. Cesspit Formation Processes and Waste Management History in Melbourne: Evidence from Little Lon. *Australian Archaeology* 82: 12–24.

Health Board. 1875a. Sydney City and Suburban Sewage and Health Board Second Progress Report, 25 June 1875. *Votes and Proceedings of the New South Wales Legislative Assembly* 4: 369–418.

———. 1875b. Sydney City and Suburban Sewage and Health Board First Progress Report. *Votes and Proceedings of the New South Wales Legislative Assembly* 4: 335–368.

Jeffries, N. 2006. The Metropolis Local Management Act and the archaeology of sanitary reform in the London Borough of Lambeth 1856–86. *Post-Medieval Archaeology* 40: 272–290.

Jeffries, N., R. Featherby, R. Wroe-Brown, I. Betts, S. Harrington, and B. Richardson. 2014. 'Would I Were in an Alehouse in London!': A Finds Assemblage Sealed by the Great Fire from Rood Lane, City of London. *Post-Medieval Archaeology* 48: 261–284. https://doi.org/10.1179/0079423614Z.00000000057.

Jervis, B. 2014. Middens, Memory and the Effect of Waste. Beyond Symbolic Meaning in Archaeological Deposits. An Early Medieval Case Study. *Archaeological Dialogues; Cambridge* 21: 175–196.

Jevons, W. S. 1929. Remarks Upon the Social Map of Sydney, 1858. Sydney Morning Herald, November 6.

Jones, S. 1984. *Cleanliness Is Next to Godliness: Personal Hygiene in New South Wales 1788–1901.* Sydney: Historic Houses Trust of New South.

Jørgensen, D. 2012. History of Consumption and Waste, Medieval World. In *Encyclopedia of Consumption and Waste: The Social Science of Garbage*, ed. C.A. Zimring and W.L. Rathje, 348–351. Thousand Oaks: SAGE Publications.

Joyce, R.A., and J. Pollard. 2010. Archaeological Assemblages and Practices of Deposition. In *The Oxford Handbook of Material Culture Studies*, ed. D. Hicks and M.C. Beaudry. Oxford: Oxford University Press.

Karskens, G. 1999. *Inside the Rocks: The Archaeology of a Neighbourhood.* Sydney: Hale & Iremonger.

Klein, T.H. 1991. Models for the Study of Consumer Behavior. *Historical Archaeology* 25: 1–2.

Lewis, M. n.d. Australian Building: A Cultural Resource.

Lydon, J. 1995. Boarding Houses in The Rocks: Mrs Ann Lewis' privy, 1865. *Public History Review* 4: 73–88.

Matthews, K. 1999. Familiarity and Contempt: The Archaeology of the "Modern". In *The Familiar Past? Archaeologies of Later Historical Britain*, ed. S. Tarlow and S. West, 155–179. London: Routledge.

Mayne, A.J.C. 1982. *Fever, Squalor and Vice—Sanitation and Social Policy in Victorian Sydney.* St. Lucia: University of Queensland Press.

McCarthy, J. 1989. *Archaeological Investigation: Commonwealth Offices and Telecom Corporate Building Sites, The Commonwealth Block, Melbourne, Victoria, Volume 1: Historical and Archaeological Report.* Unpublished Report. Austral Archaeology for the Department of Administrative Services and Telecom Australia.

McCarthy, J.P., and J.A. Ward. 2000. Sanitation Practices, Depositional Processes, and Interpretive Contexts of Minneapolis Privies. *Historical Archaeology* 34: 111–129.

Miller, G.L. 1980. Classification and Economic Scaling of 19th Century Ceramics. *Historical Archaeology* 14: 1–40.

———. 1991. A Revised Set of CC Index Value for Classification and Economic Scaling of English Ceramics from 1787 to 1880. *Historical Archaeology* 25: 1–25.

Otto, J.S. 1977. Artifacts and Status Differences: A Comparison of Ceramics from Planter, Overseer, and Slave Sites on an Antebellum Plantation. In *Research Strategies in Historical Archeology*, ed. S. South, 91–118. New York: Academic Press.

Owens, A., and N. Jeffries. 2016. People and Things on the Move: Domestic Material Culture, Poverty and Mobility in Victorian London. *International Journal of Historical Archaeology* 20: 804–827. https://doi.org/10.1007/s10761-016-0350-9.

Pearce, J. 2000. A Late 18th-Century Inn Clearance Assemblage from Uxbridge, Middlesex. *Post-Medieval Archaeology* 34: 144–186. https://doi.org/10.1179/pma.2000.004.

Peña, E.S., and J. Denmon. 2000. The Social Organization of a Boardinghouse: Archaeological Evidence from the Buffalo Waterfront. *Historical Archaeology* 34: 79–96.

Praetzellis, M. & A. Praetzellis (eds). 2004. *Putting the "There" There: Historical Archaeologies of West Oakland, 1-880 Cypress Freeway Replacement Project*. California: Report Prepared by Anthropological Studies Center, Sonoma State University.

Samford, P. 2007. *Subfloor Pits and the Archaeology of Slavery in Colonial Virginia*. Tuscaloosa: University of Alabama Press.

Select Committee. 1854. Final Report from the Select Committee on the Sydney Sewerage and Water Appropriation Bill with Minutes of Evidence. In *Votes and Proceedings of the New South Wales Legislative Council*.

Sewerage and Water Supply, 10th report, 1866. 1867. In *Votes and Proceedings of Legislative Assembly of New South Wales 1866*, 4–5:30–31.

Smith, M.L. 2012. History of Consumption and Waste, Ancient World. In *Encyclopedia of Consumption and Waste: The Social Science of Garbage*, ed. C.A. Zimring and W.L. Rathje, 346–348. Thousand Oaks: SAGE Publications.

Starr, F. 2001. Convict Artefacts from the Civil Hospital Privy on Norfolk Island. *Australasian Historical Archaeology* 19: 39–47.

Wall, D. diZerega. 1991. Sacred Dinners and Secular Teas: Constructing Domesticity in Mid–19th-Century New York. *Historical Archaeology* 25: 69–81.

———. 1999. Examining Gender, Class, and Ethnicity in Nineteenth-Century New York City, Historical Archaeology. *Historical Archaeology* 33: 102–117.

Wheeler, K. 2000a. Theoretical and Methodological Considerations for Excavating Privies. *Historical Archaeology* 34: 3–19.

———. 2000b. View from the Outhouse: What we can learn from the excavation of privies. *Historical Archaeology* 34: 1–2.

Williamson, I.P. 1984. Coordination of Cadastral Surveys in New South Wales' The Australian Surveyor. *The Australian Surveyor* 32: 274–292.

Wong, A. 1999. Colonial Sanitation, Urban Planning and Social Reform in Sydney, New South Wales 1788–1857. *Australasian Historical Archaeology* 17: 58–69.

Yamin, R. 2001. Becoming New York: The Five Points Neighbourhood. *Historical Archaeology* 35: 1–5.

Chapter 8
The Cumberland and Gloucester Streets Site, The Rocks, Sydney

Introduction

In this chapter we introduce our study of ten assemblages recovered from cesspit backfills in nine houses on the Cumberland and Gloucester Streets site (CUGL), in Sydney foreshore precinct known as The Rocks. For each assemblage we briefly describe the history and architecture of the house allotment, the stratigraphic context of cesspit fill, and available biographical information about families associated with the deposits. But for a few updated stories, all biographical information about the residents and owners was researched by Laila Ellmoos (Ellmoos and Crook 2006) and draws heavily on the work of Grace Karskens (Karskens 1999a, b). More detailed information about the families, and stratigraphic record, can be found in *Keeping up with the McNamaras* (Crook et al. 2005, 43–123) and the original excavation reports (Godden Mackay 1999).

The 'Big Dig': The Cumberland and Gloucester Streets Site

The Cumberland and Gloucester Streets site is one of the best-known archaeological sites in Sydney. Nestled in the west slopes of Sydney Cove in the historic Rocks precinct, it is bounded by Cumberland and Gloucester Streets to the west and east, the Australian Hotel to the north and the Jobbins Terraces and 130 Cumberland Street to the south (Fig. 8.1). It is owned by Property NSW (formerly the Sydney Harbour Foreshore Authority) and is now preserved in situ beneath a youth hostel (Fig. 8.2). The 7-month excavation of the site in 1994, undertaken by local archaeologists Godden Mackay Logan, was known as the 'Big Dig'. It was a landmark for urban archaeology in Australia.

© Springer Nature Switzerland AG 2019
T. Murray, P. Crook, *Exploring the Archaeology of the Modern City in Nineteenth-century Australia*, Contributions To Global Historical Archaeology, https://doi.org/10.1007/978-3-030-27169-5_8

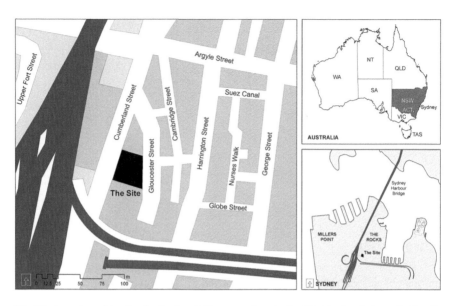

Fig. 8.1 Location of the Cumberland and Gloucester Streets site, The Rocks, Sydney. (P. Crook)

Fig. 8.2 The 'Big Dig' site, preserved in situ below a cantilevered building. (P. Crook 2010)

Used for various industrial purposes throughout the twentieth century, the site had been part of a densely populated residential and commercial block for much of the nineteenth century. The first wattle-and-daub huts appeared on the rocky ridges of the site in the 1790s, as evidenced by bedrock-cut postholes. This was shortly after British settlement in 1788 but prior to the land being officially granted to new settlers (Karskens 1999a, 27). More substantial stone and weatherboard dwellings were constructed on the site from the 1810s, and by 1822, there were 12 identifiable households living and working on the site (Karskens 1999a, 31–33). Many were convicts and emancipists who remained residents of the neighbourhood for many decades.

From the 1830s, freehold title was granted to owners of the previously unregulated allotments. Subdivision quickly followed and within a decade tenants outnumbered owner occupiers. New houses were quickly built, some replacing the old and others springing up in available spaces 'in the old yards and garden ground' (Karskens 1999b, 85). Purpose-built shops and a row of speculative terraces were built along Cumberland Street (Karskens 1999a, 45–46). (See Fig. 8.3 and discussion below). In the 1850s and 1860s, when the site was most densely populated, it is estimated that it comprised around 30 buildings accommodating approximately 165 people, not including lodgers and guests (Karskens 1999b, 93).

Fig. 8.3 Cumberland Street in the 1850s, showing the row of Nicholas's Rents, 120–126 Cumberland Street, and the detached shop at 128 Cumberland Street, south of the corner bakery. (W. Andrews, 'Cumberland Street, Sydney' after J. B. Henderson's 'Cumberland Street looking south' in his Sketches of New South Wales and Victoria 1855–1882, ML SVI/ST/CUMB/1, File no. FL3274062, courtesy of Mitchell Library)

Historian Grace Karskens has argued that, up to the 1870s, the population of the Cumberland and Gloucester Streets site, and The Rocks generally, was drawn from a range of socio-economic backgrounds, including 'almost all ranks—wealthy, middling and poor' (Karskens 1999a, 18). In the closing decades of the nineteenth century, after the middle and wealthier classes moved out to the burgeoning suburbs of Sydney, The Rocks became synonymous with the working classes. Men worked in shipping industry or on the wharves, while women tended to work in pubs, shops and boarding houses (Karskens 1999a, 18). This changing demographic, combined with an increasingly interventionist local government working to improve sanitation (see Chap. 7), and the growing slum narrative in the popular press (Mayne 1982, 1990, 1993), saw The Rocks become a target for reform as early as the 1891 when two homes (including 122 Cumberland Street) were demolished by the City of Sydney Improvement Board.

In response to the bubonic plague outbreak in 1900, the New South Wales Government resumed all buildings on the site, as part of a widespread campaign to 'cleanse' the wharfing district. Demolition was incremental as run-down houses were replaced with workshops, which were in turn replaced by a bus depot in 1934. At this point, the entire site was levelled and capped with bitumen and cement, which sealed 140 years of archaeological remains for a further 60 years.

The Excavation

The 'Big Dig' was conducted between April and October 1994 by a team of 20 archaeologists, planners, conservators and specialists assembled by Godden Mackay Heritage Consultants (now Godden Mackay Logan Pty Ltd, 'GML') and aided by some 500 volunteers (Godden Mackay 1999, 12, 13). The ambitious excavation was funded by the Sydney Cove Authority and guided by a research design prepared by GML and Grace Karskens (Godden Mackay and Karskens 1994).

The works exposed the remains of more than 40 separate buildings dating from 1810. Five-thousand cubic metres of deposit was removed, and over 425,000 artefacts were collected and analysed in 11 months (Godden Mackay 1999, vol. 3; Godden Mackay 1999, vol. 4i and 4ii; see also Crook et al. 2003; Crook et al. 2005 for details of the excavation and post-excavation projects).

Introduction to the Study Group

From the hundreds of artefact-rich assemblages across the CUGL site – some bearing more than 55,000 individual sherds[1] – 10 cesspit backfills were selected from 9 house lots (see Fig. 8.4 and Table 8.1). All but one of the fills was recovered in spits

---

[1] 118 context groups have more than 500 fragments, 310 had more than 100 fragments. MC B075, one of the many 'underfloor deposits' from 5 Carahers Lane, had 55,366 individual fragments.

Fig. 8.4 Location plan of cesspits in the study, as shown in 1880, within their house lot boundaries. (P. Crook after Percy Dove, ML FM4 7200, courtesy of Mitchell Library)

Table 8.1 Summary of house lots from the Cumberland and Gloucester Streets site, The Rocks, selected for analysis

Address	Built	Demolished	Master Context
1 Carahers Lane	c. 1848	1902	B197
3 Carahers Lane	c. 1848	1902	B077
5 Carahers Lane	c. 1856	1902	B294
122 Cumberland Street	c. 1833	1891	A138
124 Cumberland Street	c. 1833	c. 1907	A310
126 Cumberland Street	c. 1833	c. 1907	A140
93 Gloucester Street	c. 1822	1891	F044
97 Gloucester Street	c. 1817	c. 1907	C056 and C220
101 Gloucester Street	1822	c. 1907	C130

or layers, which have been grouped under a single Master Context (MC) for the purpose of this study. The MCs take the name of one of the largest individual contexts in each group. Each of these MCs is discussed in detail below.

The street addresses used below reflect the last known names and numbers allocated to these house lots. Like most modern cities, the names of streets and laneways and the numbers of houses change considerably. Carahers Lane, for example, was once known as Junction Lane and later Fraser Lane.

1 Carahers Lane (c. 1848–1902)

1 Carahers Lane, along with neighbouring 3 Carahers Lane, was a double-storey terrace located adjacent to the rear yard of the bakery (and later grocery store) at 118 Cumberland Street. Publican William Massey, who lived and worked across the laneway at 99 Gloucester Street, built 1–3 Carahers Lane between 1845 and 1848 as investment properties. Massey died in 1853, and in 1855 his widow, Mary Ann, married future parliamentarian William Henson and moved to the outer Sydney suburb of Ashfield. The Carahers Lane terraces, while now managed by absentee landlords, remained in family ownership until their demolition in 1902. A measured drawing and condition report of 1–3 Carahers Lane was made at this time (Fig. 8.5).

The terrace at 1 Carahers Lane was constructed of brick with a shingled roof (replaced with iron between 1882 and 1891, according to council rates records) and three and a half rooms. Figure 8.5 shows a 'parlour' and a kitchen on the ground floor, with fireplaces in each room, and stairs in the backroom leading to 'a lean-to half room probably intended for children' (Holmes 1999a, 106), and a main bedroom overlooking Carahers Lane. There were no fireplaces on the upper level. The enclosed yard was small, only 3.4 × 4.4 m, and the cesspit was built against the back rooms of the house, allowing direct seepage of liquid waste into the house foundations (Holmes 1999a, 107). With no laneway access to the yard, the refuse from the cesspit, when cleared, would have been tracked through the house to the street.

While they were noted in the rates records to be in 'good repair' in 1863, both 1 and 3 Carahers Lane were recorded as 'dilapidated' prior to their demolition in 1902 (Fig. 8.5). Figure 8.6 shows the frontage of 1–3 Carahers Lane in the right

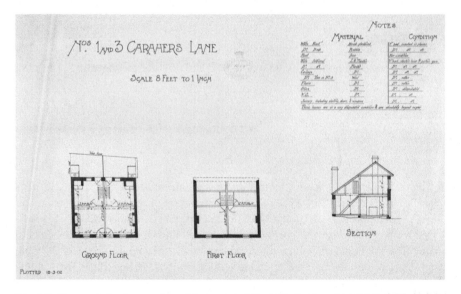

Fig. 8.5 Measured drawings and condition report of 1 and 3 Carahers Lane made prior to their demolition in 1902. (NSW Government Architect, 'Plans and Photographs of Buildings Demolished, 1902–07', courtesy of Mitchell Library)

Fig. 8.6 Carahers Lane, 1900, showing No. 1 and 3 in the front right, with 5–11 beyond. (SRNSW Digital ID: 4481_a026_000209, courtesy of State Records NSW)

foreground in 1900. The plasterwork is chipped and spalling in places and the windows in need of fresh coat of paint, but otherwise the façade of No. 1 appears sound considering its age.

The Cesspit Fill (MC B197)

The cesspit in the yard of 1 Carahers Lane (B196) was built adjacent to the back wall of the terraces, against the fireplaces, and was probably added after the building's initial construction in the late 1840s (Holmes 1999a, 107).[2] (See Fig. 8.8). This

---

[2] On the preliminary trigonometric survey of 1857 prepared for the planning of the sewer mains (Fig. 7.1), the cesspits were shown against the rear yard fence, but in 1865, these appear only as a faint outline, suggesting that they had been removed or had been incorrectly drawn (Fig. 7.2). At the time of demolition, the water closets are shown to be in the same location as the cesspits (Fig. 8.5). There was no evidence for a pit elsewhere in the yard of 1 Carahers Lane, but note the yard was only partly excavated (*The Cumberland/Gloucester Streets Site, The Rocks: Archaeological Investigation Report* 1996, vol. 6 Plan 199). If the survey is correct, it is possible that an earlier cesspit was constructed (perhaps in 1848?) and superseded in the late 1850s with the new pit adjacent to the house.

pit was then connected to sewerage mains in the mid- to late-1860s and filled with refuse before sealing.[3] The backfill was recovered in five separate fills (B197, B198, B207, B208 and B211) and has been grouped as MC B197. The uppermost layers of MC B197 were subject to some twentieth-century disturbance from the Engineering Works, and this is likely to be the source of the single conjoined artefact linking this fill with demolition rubble fill (B093) in the backyard of 3 Carahers Lane (and Holmes 1994 for further details of the excavation of this fill; Holmes 1999a; see Crook et al. 2005, 49).

None of the artefacts recovered from the fill has a first-manufacture date later than 1862 (Crook et al. 2005, 48–49 for details of the dated artefacts). While the ceramics may have been discarded 10 years or more after manufacture, the presence of a tobacco pipe, made by Glaswegian Charles Stewart who only operated from 1860 to 1861 (Wilson 1999a, 287), suggests an early 1860s date. In addition there is at least one vessel that was *last* manufactured in the 1860s: a blue 'Lozere' bowl (CUGL39292), with an Edward Challinor & Co. mark dating between 1842 and 1867.

The contents of the fill were typical of this kind of refuse discard: part clean-out and part week-to-week refuse (see Chap. 7 for discussion). The deposit contained some construction materials, perhaps the evidence of repairs undertaken at the time of the backfill. It also contained fragments of the sewerage pipe and toilet bowl of the water closet, consistent with the demolition fill that covered it. The remaining material comprised faunal refuse, domestic wares and utensils, food containers, personal items, toys, toiletries and pharmaceutical items.

The Occupants

The first known occupants of 1 Carahers Lane were the Wilsons: George, Agnes and their children. They lived at No. 1 from at least 1848 to 1856 during which time three children were born. (About a decade later, in c. 1867, George and some of his children returned to live at No. 1, after the death of Agnes). Family groups followed the Wilsons but stayed for shorter tenancies: James Agnew French and his family lived there in 1857, followed by the widow Hannah Watts with her three daughters in 1861 and Timothy McNamara and his family in 1863. In the closing decades of the century, two long-term tenants occupied No. 1: Thomas and Elizabeth Hines (1877–1887), followed by James Foy and his wife Margaret (1890–1900). See Table 8.2 for details of all owners and occupants.

While there are many gaps in the occupation history (1862, 1864–1866, 1868–1870, 1872–1876), there are at least three tenants that may be associated with the deposit: one-time labourer Timothy McNamara and his wife Ellen (listed once

---

[3] A similar sequence of events occurred at 97 Gloucester Street, across the laneway, and also owned by William Massey and family.

Table 8.2 Owners and occupants of 1 Carahers Lane from 1848 to 1902

Name	From	To	Yrs
Owners			
William Massey (Bird-in-Hand Hotel)	1848	1853	6
Mary Ann Massey [nee Benson, later Henson]	1853	1855	2
William and Mary Ann Henson	1855	1902	47
Occupants			
George Wilson (mariner, waterman and grocer)	1848	1856	9–10
James Agnew French (free mariner/labourer)	1857	1857	1–2
John McCraw (labourer/coxswain)	1858	1858	1–5
Hannah Adams [nee Watts, later Watts] (dressmaker)	1861	1861	1–6
Timothy McNamara/MacNamara (labourer, hotelkeeper)	1863	1863	1–4
George Wilson	1867	1867	1–9
James Warlow (mariner, engineer)	1871	1871	1–11
Thomas Hines (mariner/labourer)	1877	1887	11–17
James Day	1888	1889	2–4
James Foy (confectioner)	1890	1900	11–13
Thomas Moran (driver)	1901	1902	2–3

in 1863; resident for *maximum* of 5 years), mariner and labourer George Wilson (listed once in 1867; resident for *maximum* of 6 years) and mariner and engineer James Warlow (listed once in 1871; resident for *maximum* of 10 years).

All were immigrants occupying the same house in a neighbourhood of family and friends within the same decade, but their circumstances differed: the Irish-born McNamaras moved in 3 years after their marriage and cared for the first 2 of their 12 children at 1 Carahers Lane. George Wilson, who had lived in 1 Carahers Lane in similar circumstances with his young wife Agnes in 1848, returned to 1 Carahers Lane in 1867 a widow with 7 children to support. James and Mary Ann Warlow had been married for 9 years when they first appear in the records at 1 Carahers Lane and had at least one child, 2-year-old Margaret, when they moved in.

Of these known tenants, it is more likely that the McNamaras or the Wilsons were occupants during the time of the cesspit backfill, so the following biographical outlines focusses on these families.

George and Agnes Wilson (1848–1856 and 1867–1869)

Scottish and Irish immigrants George and Agnes Wilson lived at 1 Carahers Lane between 1848 and 1856, before moving to 118 Cumberland Street and later an unknown address on Gloucester Street. In 1867, 5 years after the death of Agnes (aged 41), George and six of his children returned to No. 1 Carahers Lane.

George was born in Inverkeithing, Scotland, in 1820 and came to Australia in 1842. He married a 21-year-old Belfast-born Agnes Hamilton a year later at Sydney's Scots Church. They had eight children born between 1844 and 1859, the youngest of whom died in infancy. George worked as a mariner, waterman and grocer to support his growing family. At the time of Agnes's death in 1862, he was in Moreton Bay, Queensland, working as a stevedore and has been away for over 3 months (*Empire*, 28 Feb. 1862: 4).

Not much is known of their time at 1 Carahers Lane, but the coronial inquest into Agnes's death reported that she 'had been known as an exemplary wife and mother, but latterly [had] indulged in intoxicating liquor' (*SMH* 28 Feb. 1862: 4), 'had been ailing and drank very hard' since her husband's departure and 'when drunk…would abuse her neighbours, one of whom last Thursday afternoon assaulted her' (*Empire*, 28 Feb. 1862: 4). She died of stomach inflammation while in the care of her 8- or 9-year-old daughter. This was perhaps the result of the family falling on harder times since their departure from 1 Carahers Lane.

It appears that George Wilson did not remarry after Agnes's death. As noted, George moved his family back to 1 Carahers Lane in 1867 before moving to 93 Gloucester Street and Cambridge Street in 1870 before relocating to Sydney's North Shore where George died in 1898.

Timothy and Ellen McNamara (1863)

Irish immigrants Timothy and Ellen (nee Hollingsworth) McNamara and their colonial-born daughter Ann were living at 1 Carahers Lane by 1863. Both were from the west coast (Timothy from Limerick and Ellen from Wexford) but appear to have met in the colony. Timothy likely migrated with his brothers John, Thomas and Patrick, all of whom lived near or on the Cumberland and Gloucester Streets site (Crook et al. 2005, 54). The McNamaras were married at St Mary's Cathedral, Sydney, in 1860 while Timothy was working as a labourer and Ellen as a housekeeper. Timothy was listed as a widower although details of his first wife are unknown.

Timothy and Ellen had 12 children born between 1861 and 1888, 3 of whom died in infancy. Their second child, a son named William, was born on 2 July 1863 at 1 Carahers Lane. In 1865, the family was living at 126 Cumberland Street, where Timothy's former sister-in-law Margaret – the widow of brother Thomas who had remarried Stephen Doyle in 1857 – was to live with her husband and two daughters for the next 14 years (see below). The McNamaras remained close to Margaret even after Thomas's death (she was present at Ann's birth in 1861); her sister Bridget had married Patrick McNamara and lived down the lane at 11 Carahers Lane from 1867 to 1896.

Timothy and Ellen lived in Redfern from 1870 to 1875 where they ran the Native Boy Hotel but retained freehold title of 213 Cumberland Street, near Charlotte Place, in The Rocks. They returned to No. 213 in 1875 and remained there—with at least two of their adult sons—until their deaths in 1896 (Timothy) and 1901 (Ellen). Timothy's death certificate described him as a 'retired hotelkeeper', but he had also been listed as a boatman in 1875 and as a proprietor of a general store (at 213 Cumberland Street) by 1877. (See Crook et al. 2005, 54–55, for further details.)

3 Carahers Lane (c. 1848–1902)

3 Carahers Lane was a double-storey terrace built by local publican William Massey in c. 1848 along with and mirroring 1 Carahers Lane (discussed above). As with No. 1, it remained in the Massey family after his death in the care of his wife Mary Ann who moved to the suburb of Ashfield following her marriage to William Henson.

It was constructed of double-skin brick on rubble-stone foundations with a shingled roof (replaced with iron between 1882 and 1891) and three and a half rooms apiece (Fig. 8.5). Like 1 Carahers Lane, the 'parlour' and kitchen, with fireplaces in each, were on the ground floor, with a lean-to at the back and a main bedroom overlooking Carahers Lane upstairs. Also like its neighbour No. 1, the cesspit was abutted the back of the house allowing seepage into the foundations (Holmes 1999a, 107), and with no laneway access to the yard, the waste would have been tracked through the house at clear-out time.

As noted, both 1 and 3 Carahers Lane were in 'good repair' in 1863 and 'dilapidated' prior to their demolition in 1902 (Fig. 8.5). No. 3 shows greater more evidence of chipped plasterwork than No. 3, and there is visible water damage under the eaves (Fig. 8.6) suggesting trouble with guttering (Fig. 8.7).

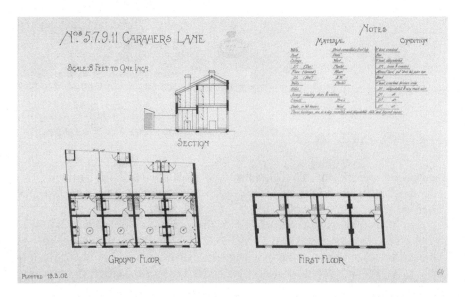

Fig. 8.7 Measured drawings of 5–11 Carahers Lane, prior to demolition in 1903. (NSW Government Architect, 'Plans and Photographs of Buildings Demolished, 1902–07', courtesy of Mitchell Library)

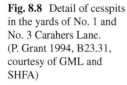

Fig. 8.8 Detail of cesspits in the yards of No. 1 and No. 3 Carahers Lane. (P. Grant 1994, B23.31, courtesy of GML and SHFA)

The Cesspit Fill (MC B077)

As with 1 Carahers Lane, the cesspit for No. 3 (B080; Fig. 8.8) was built some time after the construction of the main house and was connected to sewerage after 1866 when the sewer mains down Carahers Lane were completed.

The fill of B080 was recovered in four distinct units: B077, B102, B107 and B119. These have been grouped as MC B077. The top fill was noted to be dark brown, with some rubble, and above the top of extant stone wall of B080. The lowest fill, B119, had several whole bottles and a large fish skeleton in one corner (Holmes 1994, [Book 1] 54, 59, 61). The top of an oil or vinegar bottle recovered from the adjacent bakery at 118 Cumberland Street (B214) was found in the 3rd cesspit fill (B107; CUGL34470; CJ ID 30) and likely a result of sewerage pipe installation and is treated as an anomaly (Crook et al. 2005, 59).

Like 1 Carahers Lane, the contents of MC B077 are typical of cesspit backfilling, and also contained fragments of sewerage pipe and toilet bowl, indicative of the later demolition process and possible disturbance. The deposit contained some construction materials, perhaps the evidence of repairs undertaken at the time of the backfill: 39 nails, 4 fragments of roof slate and 55 of roof tile (note the main buildings were shingled), 10 fragments of brick, 10 fragments of window glass and a door hinge. There was also some evidence of metal working – foundry sand for metal casting and some slag – in the uppermost fills, and these are likely intrusive elements from the Engineering Works phase. The remaining material comprised faunal refuse, domestic wares and utensils, food containers, personal items, toys, toiletries and pharmaceutical items.

None of the catalogued artefacts in MC B077 has a TPQ later than 1863. The latest dating artefact was a stoneware ginger beer bottle (CUGL60090) made by Enoch Fowler in Camperdown between 1863 and 1878. A pharmaceutical bottle made for John Watson, Druggist, probably post-dates 1859 when Watson was first listed in 593 George Street, but it may be earlier or made any time until 1895 (Sands and Kenny 1858, 213; Sands 1895, 787). Several other items post-date the mid-1850s and 1860s (Crook et al. 2005, 59–60).

The short-term usage of these vessels supports the suggestion of a mid-1860s date and fortunately the absolute TPQ of 1863 and documentary minimum of 1866, coincide neatly with the long-term occupation of the Leggatts from 1863 to at least 1880 (see below).

The Occupants

Three tenants of 3 Carahers Lane in the period between 1848 and 1857 are known: John Phillips, a waterman (1848), Lock (1856) and Martin Keenan in (1857). (See Table 8.3). It is known how long Phillips and Lock lived there. Welsh-born Joseph Thomas, his Irish wife Catherine and five of their children lived at there from 1858 to at least 1861. The longest tenants of No. 3 were the Leggett family of Charles, his wife Catherine and their son Thomas, who resided there for 18 years, from 1863 to 1880.

Throughout the 1880s and until 1902, when the building was demolished, the property had a relatively high turnover of tenants, who stayed for an average of 3–5 years. Some of these tenants appear to have been related to each other, such as Thomas Quick who lived at 3 Carahers Lane in 1885, followed by John Quick (his brother?) between 1886 and 1888. F. Meadows occupied 3 Carahers Lane in 1890, while possible relative, William Meadows, lived there from 1891 to 1895.

As the cesspit backfill was deposited in 1866, we can confidently associate it with the Leggetts.

Table 8.3 Owners and occupants of 3 Carahers Lane from 1848 to 1902

Name	From	To	Yrs
Owners			
William Massey (Bird-in-Hand Hotel)	1848	1853	6
Mary Ann Massey [nee Benson, later Henson]	1853	1855	2
William and Mary Ann Henson	1855	1902	47
Occupants			
John Phillips (waterman)	1848	1848	1–9
Lock [no first name given]	1856	1856	1–2
Martin Keenan (labourer)	1857	1857	1–2
Joseph Thomas (boarding house)	1858	1861	4–7
James Thomas (general dealer)	1859	1859	1
Charles Leggett (mariner, wool jamber?)	1863	1880	18–21
William English (laundry)	1882	1882	1–3
William Webster Simpson (labourer, coal lumper)	1882	1884	3
George Halliday	1884	1884	1–2
Thomas Quick	1885	1885	1
George Allardice (lighterman)	1885	1887	3
Michael Morgan	1885	1887	3
John Quick	1886	1888	3
James Foy (confectioner)	1889	1889	1
John Sullivan	1889	1902	14
F. Meadows	1890	1890	1
William Meadows	1891	1895	5
Richard Headon/Eden	1896	1898	3
John Morgan (sailmaker)	1899	1899	1

Charles and Catherine Leggett (or Leggatt) (1863–1880)

The Leggetts were an Anglo–Irish couple who married in the colony in 1852, but their lives before migration have been difficult to tie down. According to his death certificate, Charles Leggett was born in London in c. 1827 and arrived in Australia in c. 1844, aged 17 years old, although no records of his birth or migration have been located. Catherine was born in Limerick, Ireland, in 1826 or 1830, the daughter of a farmer, Michael Hickey, and his wife Mary O'Keefe. It is not known when she migrated to Australia. They married at St Andrews Scots Church in Sydney in 1852.

They had a son, Thomas, born in Scotland in 1845 and who migrated to Australia c. 1872 and was living with them at No. 3 in 1874–1875. While it is possible that Thomas was the son of Charles only, perhaps from a prior marriage, both were named on his Thomas's death certificate, and both Charles and Catherine are stated to have had one deceased son, on their own death certificates (Crook et al. 2005, 62–63).

Thomas had died in September 1879, while Charles and Catherine were at No. 3, and he was boarding around the corner at the Hibernian Hotel, 116 Cumberland

Street. He was a seaman and fell through a hold in the ship *Fiona* as it pulled away from the wharf (*SMH* 6 Oct. 1879: 3). He was 34 years of age.

Charles died of cardiac failure 9 months later, in May 1880 at the age of 53. On his death certificate, his occupation was given as 'wool jammer' although in the postal directories for the same year, he was listed as a mariner, and the year prior, on Thomas's death certificate, he was 'a labourer'.

Charles's funeral was attended – and likely underwritten – by the brothers of the Royal Oak Court of the Ancient Order of Foresters (*SMH* 22 May 1880: 16). The AOF was a friendly society, and the Royal Oak order (Court No. 2222) met regularly in Millers Point, The Rocks, and the northern parts of the city.

The AOF may have provided support to Catherine after Charles's death, but we have no record of her living in the area after 1880. She was admitted to the Newington Asylum on 5 Feb 1889 and stayed for nearly 4 years before being discharged on 30 December 1892 (SRNSW NRS 4377 [7/3803 p.1098]; Reel 2848). She was readmitted 10 days later (SRNSW NRS 4377 [7/3803 p.1098]; Reel 2848) and appears to have lived out her remaining years in the Asylum. She died on 5 July 1899 from 'senile decay' and jaundice from an enlarged liver (Crook et al. 2005, 63).

5 Carahers Lane (c. 1856–1902)

5 Carahers Lane was the northern most of a row of four two-storey terraces (5–11 Carahers Lane[4]) built between c. 1854 and c. 1856. The row was either built by publican James Casey or by Owen Joseph Caraher and his brother-in-law Patrick Hogan, who lived and worked as tallow chandlers on nearby Gloucester Street and bought the block in 1856 (Crook et al. 2005, 64). All four terraces were retained by the Caraher family until c. 1880, at which time they were sold to John McDonald.

Like its neighbours in the terrace row, 5 Carahers Lane was a four-roomed terrace, built of brick with a slate roof. A condition report and measured drawing prepared in 1902 describe the row (Nos 5–11) as 'very insanitary', 'dilapidated' and 'beyond repair' (Fig. 8.7). Little can be seen of the row in the photograph taken in 1900 (Fig. 8.6), but like its neighbour at 1–3 Carahers Lane, 5–11 Carahers Lane show some evidence of patched plasterwork and water damage but otherwise appear sound.

The Cesspit Fill (MC B294)

Unlike 1 and 3 Carahers Lane, the cesspit of 5 Carahers Lane was positioned against the rear fence, not adjacent to the house. Its backfill was recovered in five stratigraphic units: B294, B360, B364, B374 and B386, which are grouped together as

---

[4] 7–11 Carahers Lane survived within the boundaries Cumberland and Gloucester Streets site, but were not excavated in 1994 (Holmes 1999a: 91).

MC B294. Few variations were noted amongst the fill (Holmes 1994, [Book 1] 100), and as the sewer pipe was retained in situ, the backfill deposit was not completely recovered (Holmes 1999a, 110).

Characteristically, the deposit contained numerous 'older' items: Chinese export porcelain, lead-glazed wares; shell-edged ware; a brushed stem clay pipe from the Netherlands (CUGL24196), probably imported before the 1860s (Wilson 1999a, 295, TS 270); and at least one blue transfer-printed bowl (CUGL40384) made by Copeland & Garrett and stamped 'Late Spode' – a mark used between 1833 and 1847. Of the registered and marked items post-dating 1845, most were stylistically dated or made by firms who operated for many decades. For example, a tobacco pipe (CUGL22776) marked 'McDOUGALL GLASGOW / T.MILO STRAND AGENT' was made by Duncan McDougall, Glasgow (1846–1967), for London tobacconist Thomas Milo c. 1852–1870.

There is a conjoin (CJ ID 20) of a Chinese porcelain bowl between the fourth fill (B374) and 'clean' sandy fill in the drain of the Bird in Hand (99 Gloucester Street) which was decommissioned c. 1850 (C195) – a few years before No. 5 was built.

Despite this, and the generally older character of MC B294, the deposit most likely dates to at least 1866 when the sewer lines were laid down Carahers Lane – a year before porter Patrick Guinan is first listed – and probably no later than the early 1870s, at which time Andrew and Anne Cummings were living at 5 Carahers Lane.

It may be that these older items were redeposited from an old rubbish dump by the new residents of 5 Carahers Lane, in c. 1867. The yard of 5 Carahers Lane was the subject of considerable disturbance, containing numerous rubbish pits filled with bone and horn, probably left by George Cribb or his successors, which were cut through and redeposited in the underfloor spaces (Crook 1999, Appendix 2). Certainly, none of the older-style ceramics survived in substantial fragments – in fact, overall, 5 Carahers Lane had the lowest number of intact items in the study group (see Chap. 10).

The fill itself comprised a range of domestic goods. In addition to fragments of sewerage pipe and cement bonding, there was at least 1 floor paver, 29 fragments of roof slate (255 g), 60 nails and 10 fragments of sandstock brick. 5 Carahers Lane had a large assemblage of faunal and shell waste. Some less common items in the deposit included a single feline humerus, coal and charcoal (not present in other cesspit backfills) and a cast-iron cooking pot, approximately 8″ in diameter (approximately 17.5 cm wide, by 13.5 cm high; CUGL52704).

The Occupants

5 Carahers Lane, built as an investment property, had a high turnover of tenants for much of its lifetime, with tenants staying a minimum of a year (or less) and a maximum of 6 years based on the data at hand from council rates records (from 1856) and post directories (from 1871).

The first documented occupant at 5 Carahers Lane in 1856 was a fellow named 'Andrew' (no other name given), followed by John Carmichael, a baker, in 1857;

Table 8.4 Owners and occupants of 5 Carahers Lane from 1856 to 1902

Name	From	To	Yrs
Owners			
Miss Casey (landlord; presumably daughter of James)	1854	1856	2
Hogan and Caraher (soap and candle factory, landlord)	1856	1858	1–5
Owen Joseph Caraher (landlord/soap and candle manufacturer)	1861	1880	20–25
John W. [or H.] McDonald (landlord)	1882	1902	21–23
Occupants			
Andrew [no first name given]	1856	1856	1–2
John Carmichael (baker)	1857	1857	1–2
William Webb	1858	1858	1–5
Phillis Boucher [nee Chester]	1861	1861	1–6
James Quinn	1863	1863	1–7
Patrick Guinan (porter)	1867	1867	1–5
Andrew Cummings (fireman) and Mary Anne Cummings [nee McKew]	1871	1871	1–11
Michael Byrnes	1877	1880	4–12
Michael Morgan	1882	1887	6–9
David Jenkins	1888	1888	1–3
Henry Moorehouse	1889	1894	6–9
Amy Walburn	1896	1898	3–6
William Leslie	1899	1902	4–5

William Webb in 1858; widow Phillis Boucher (and at least two of her children) in 1861; James Quinn in 1863 (who possibly lived at 166 Cumberland Street in 1858–1859); and bachelor Patrick Guinan in 1867 (Table 8.4). (See Crook et al. 2005, 67–68, for details of these residents). The Cummings family lived at the property for a year, or possibly less, in 1871. Towards the end of the nineteenth century, after John McDonald acquired the property from the Carahers, tenants stayed longer: Michael Morgan (1882–1887) and Henry Moorehouse (1889–1894).

Patrick Guinan (1867)

Irishman Patrick Guinan was living at 5 Carahers Lane in at least 1867. He had arrived in Australia as an assisted immigrant aboard the *Montmorency* in 1864 aged 22 years old (State Records Reel 2139, [4/4798]; Reel 2482, [4/4986]). He married Bridget Turner, also Irish, at Newtown in 1868, and they moved to regional New South Wales (Crook et al. 2005, 68). It is not known if Bridget lived at No. 5.

By the early 1870s, Patrick and Bridget Guinan were living in the town of Cowra where their two children were born: William Thomas in 1872 and John Bernard in 1879. Bridget died in c. 1900 and Patrick died in 1912 at West Wyalong, aged 70 years old. At the time Patrick was living at 5 Carahers Lane, he was working as a coachman.

122 Cumberland Street (c. 1833–1891)

In c. 1833 mariner Albert John Nicholas built four conjoined terraces and a free-standing shop at 120–128 Cumberland Street, replacing a row of tenements that had been built by convict butcher George Cribb 10 years previously (Karskens 1999a, 45–46). Known as 'Nicholas Rents', the buildings were auctioned in 1834 as 'four small cottages built of brick, each a frontage upon Cumberland Street of 13 feet 8 inches' (*The Australian*, 17 Jan. 1834: 3). (See Fig. 8.3 for a view of the terraces in 1850.)

At their sale, 122 Cumberland Street (the second from the northern end of the row) was purchased by Isaac Moore in 1839. By 1845, the property was in the ownership of Edward Brady (who owned other houses in the Rocks) and after his death in 1869, passed to his children who held it until the 1880s. In 1891, No. 122 was in the hands of William Henson who demolished the building and held onto the vacant lot until it was resumed by the Government in the early twentieth century (Figs. 8.8 and 8.10).

Similar to its neighbours, 122 Cumberland Street was a single-storey, two-roomed dwelling, built directly onto the footpath. The main structure was brick with a shingle roof and there was a timber kitchen and later a privy to the rear. The roof of No. 122 was replaced with iron between 1880 and 1882, while the roofs of 124–126 Cumberland Street were not repaired until 1891 – when No. 122 was demolished altogether.

The Cesspit Fill (MC A138)

The cesspit fill of A161 was recovered in one deposit: A138.[5] It was immediately below the general demolition rubble layer (A101) that occurred across 120–126 Cumberland Street 1904–1915 and was served as the base of the loam surface (A067) created for the Engineering Works (Wilson 1999b, 52, 56). This is curious given 122 Cumberland Street was demolished in 1891 and remained an open yard (Figs. 8.9 and 8.10) for 24 years. While the lack of intermediary deposits suggests some disturbance or cutting, A138 has no conjoins with other deposits, and it has been treated as a largely intact stratigraphic unit.

The deposit contained a range of artefacts dating from the 1850s to 1870s including an 1875 coin (CUGL10145), two spirit flasks first registered in 1872 (CUGL03248 and CUGL03249) and a glass marble probably from a Codd aerated water bottle, first patented in 1873 (CUGL03000). In addition, there were three banded plates or saucers (CUGL39505–6, CUGL 39484–5), which date generally from the mid-1870s onwards (Wilson 1999a, 219). (See Crook et al. 2005, 72, for additional discussion of dates in this deposit). These suggest that 122 Cumberland

---

[5] It is referred to as a Master Context (MC A138) for consistency.

Fig. 8.9 The yards of 120 and 124 Cumberland Street (with vacant lot of No. 122 in between) with 126–128 beyond (looking south), October 1901. The yard of 1 Carahers Lane is visible on the left. (SRNSW Digital ID: 4481_a026_000111, courtesy State Records of NSW)

Street may not have been connected to sewerage lines until the mid- to late 1870s. This may have been during the tenancy of a William Davis (1873), an unknown occupant in the years 1874–1875, or widowed-cum-newlywed laundress Margaret Hadden, who lived there from 1876 to 1878.

Forty-four vessels and objects from A138 were complete or near-complete (>90%) vessels. This represents 17.6% of the minimum vessel count and exceeds the relative count for all other cesspit fills, strongly suggesting this was a household (or other) clear-out.

The fill contained some construction materials, perhaps the evidence of repairs undertaken at the time of the backfill: 83 nails, 1 bolt, 11 fragments of roof slate, mortar and 212 fragments of window glass in at least 4 thicknesses. There were also 504 fragments of animal bone and shell. The remaining material comprised domestic wares and utensils, food containers, personal items, toys, toiletries, pharmaceutical items and one tool (a rasp). The only exceptional item in the deposit was a 6.25 kg lump of coral, probably a curio or decorative item.

Fig. 8.10 From left to right, 120–128 Cumberland Street, 1901. The vacant lot is No. 122. (SRNSW Digital ID: 4481_a026_000027, courtesy of State Records NSW)

The Occupants

Although constructed in c. 1833, the first reliable detail about the occupants of 122 Cumberland Street is from 1845 onwards, when the council rates began to be collected. The first recorded tenant at the property was Robert O'Neil, a labourer, who lived there from c. 1842 to 1845 and possibly until 1852. George Bond was a resident in 122 Cumberland Street in 1848 (possibly boarding with Robert O'Neil). (See Table 8.5.)

John and Sarah Lewis lived at 122 Cumberland Street from 1855 to 1859 with at least two of their daughters, Eliza and Sarah, who later married and lived locally. Charles Johnson lived at 122 Cumberland Street in 1856; he was probably a boarder with the Lewis's.

122 Cumberland Street had a high turnover of tenants from 1861 to 1880. Residents lived at this address for a minimum of 1 year (or less) and a maximum of 4 years. In this period, tenants at 122 Cumberland Street comprised a mix of families and single men (who probably lodged together, e.g. Patrick O'Connor and William Driscoll, in 1880). Jane and Thomas Conway were employed as a laundress and a

Table 8.5 Owners and occupants of 122 Cumberland Street from 1845 to 1891

Name	From	To	Yrs
Owners			
Isaac Moore (St Patricks Inn)	1839	1856	18
Edward and William Brady	1845	1867	23
William Henson	1871	1871	1
Mary Ann Smith [nee Brady]	1877	1882	6
William Henson	1891	1902	12
Occupants			
Robert O'Neill (labourer?)	1845	1845	1–
George Bond	1848	1848	1
Robert O'Neill (labourer)	1852	1852	1
John Lewis (cooper? waterman?)	1855	1859	5–10
Charles Johnson	1856	1856	1
Henry Williams (GPO)	1861	1861	1–5
Jane Conway (laundress)	1863	1863	1–4
Thomas Conway (drayman)	1864	1864	1–5
Joseph Duncan (labourer)	1867	1870	4–8
Michael Hogan	1871	1871	1–4
William Davis (stonemason/landlord?)*	1873	1873	1–5
Vacant	1875	1875	1–4
Margaret Hadden [nee Kirkman, later Yates and Clark] (laundress)	1876	1878	3–4
Alexander Clark	1877	1877	1–4
Ellen Kirkman	1878	1878	1–5
Vacant	1879	1879	1–2
Patrick Connor/O'Connor	1880	1880	1–3
William Driscoll (machine ruler)	1880	1880	1–3
Michael O'Brien	1882	1891	10–17

drayman, respectively, in 1863–1864 and Margaret Hadden, a widow, as a laundress, in 1876–1878. The longest-term tenant at the property was Michael O'Brien, who lived there from 1882 until 1891, prior to the building's demolition.

The earliest opportunity for the backfilling of the cesspit at 122 Cumberland Street is 1875 when the property was vacant (Sands 1875, 54). A William Davis had lived there in at least 1873. In 1876 the widow Margaret Hadden moved in and probably operated a laundry business from the property. She was there until at least 1877 and probably in 1878. Then in 1879, the property was vacant again.

There is a good probability that the 1875 and/or 1879 vacancies coincided with, or were caused by, necessary improvements and renovations to the property. So, while the backfill could have been deposited any time after 1875, perhaps well into the 1880s, there is a greater chance that it occurred in 1875 or 1879. It was likely that vacant properties tended to attract illegal dumping, although the closed yard of 122 Cumberland Street would have limited the access of immediate neighbours, probably reducing the likelihood of such activities, and the consequent possibility that the fill in the pit was deposited by anyone else other than the property's tenants or owner. Below we focus on those tenants.

Margaret Hadden and Alexander Clark (1876–1878)

Margaret Hadden (nee Kirkman, earlier Yates) was a widow who lived at 122 Cumberland Street from 1876 to 1877 with her young daughter also named Margaret and at least two of her sons from a previous marriage.

Margaret's family was from the Lancashire mill town of Bolton and took part in the assisted migration program to the colonies. They arrived in Australia aboard the *Agnes Ewing* in January 1842 when Margaret was 13 years old. Her father John Kirkman and brother James (21) were farm labourers, and her stepmother Alice and sister Ellen (18) were house servants. Another sister, Alice (11), also made the journey, and they travelled with the Morley family who were to live two doors down at 126 Cumberland Street from 1845 to 1848 and then again in 1859 (Crook et al. 2005, 75).

Also aboard was her future husband: Lancashire-born farm labourer John Yates who was 26 at the time. The pair married in 1847 and had several children born between 1849 and 1863, at least three of whom died in infancy. They lived at 100 Cumberland Street in 1857 (John was working as a greengrocer in this year) and appear to have moved around the state (and possibly interstate). John died in 1860 at Maitland Hospital; he was possibly working in the district as a gardener (see Crook et al. 2005, 75–76, for further details of the Yates family).

Margaret's extended family would have been well known in The Rocks. Margaret's sister Alice lived with her husband Thomas Gilson and their three daughters at 98 then 100 Cumberland Street from 1855 to 1880. Her eldest sister Ellen Smith lived on the corner of Cumberland Street and the Argyle Street Bridge from 1868 to at least 1871. Margaret's nieces, Jane Neal (nee Kirkman) and Sarah Diars (nee Kirkman), lived at various dwellings in The Rocks from 1871 to 1896 (Jane including 93 Gloucester Street in 1871; see below).

In 1867, at age 39 and while working as a laundress, Margaret Yates was married for the second time to Scottish seaman Arthur Hadden – 9 years her junior. The couple, and some of Margaret's children, lived at 98 Cumberland Street from 1867 to 1869 and then across the road at 105 Cumberland Street in 1870–1871. They had three children, all girls, born between 1868 and 1872, but only their eldest, Margaret (b. 1868), survived infancy.

Arthur died in 1871, aged 33 years. Widowed for the second time, Margaret moved with her surviving children to a house on the corner of Gloucester Street and the Argyle Street Bridge in 1873 (listed as 33 Gloucester Street). (See Crook et al. 2005, 75–76, for further details). In April 1877, at age 50, Margaret Hadden was married for the third time to another Scottish seafarer (a shipwright) about 10 years younger than her: Alexander Clark. Both were living at 122 Cumberland Street at the time of their marriage, which suggests that Alexander had been lodging there.

Margaret died in June 1878, just a year later, after a 3-week bout of enteritis. Her sister Ellen registered her death and gave her own address as 122 Cumberland Street.

William Driscoll and Patrick Connor (or O'Connor) (1880)

Two residents are listed as living in 122 Cumberland Street in 1880: William Driscoll, a machine ruler,[6] was recorded in the Sands' Directory for this year, and Patrick Connor (or O'Connor) was present when the property was assessed for annual rates. William was listed as a resident of 515 Kent Street in the 1878–1879 Electoral Roll for West Sydney and of 84 Gloucester Street in 1881–1882. Patrick had lived at 134 Cumberland Street from 1876 to 1877. There is no record of them marrying or fathering children in the birth, death and marriage registers. It is probable that 122 Cumberland Street was kept as a boarding house and that William and Connor were lodgers.

Michael O'Brien (1882–1891)

Irish immigrant Michael O'Brien lived at 122 Cumberland Street between 1882 and 1891. At age 19 he migrated with his family aboard the *Blundell* in 1853 arriving with six of his siblings. Unfortunately his mother, Elizabeth, was ill during the voyage and died soon after landing in Sydney. His father Cornelius married Mary Maloney in 1854.

Michael appears to have lived in The Rocks from the time of his family's arrival in 1853. He was a sponsor to Margaret Cox, the daughter of John and Mary Cox (120 Cumberland Street), in 1866. Before moving to 122 Cumberland Street in 1882, Michael lived at Queen Street (off Essex Street) in 1871 and at 136 Cumberland Street for 2 years from 1879. After moving away from 122 Cumberland Street, Michael O'Brien lived at 16 Little Essex Street for at least a decade from 1892.

124 Cumberland Street (c. 1833–c. 1907)

No. 124 Cumberland Street was one of Nicholas's Rents built by mariner Albert John Nicholas in c. 1833 (see discussion of No. 122, above). The house was purchased by John Winch at auctioned in 1834 and remained the Winch family home for nearly 30 years.

Like 122 Cumberland Street, No. 124 was a single-storey, two-room brick dwelling, with a shingle roof and dormer window, built directly on the footpath. (The roof was replaced with iron by 1891). It also had an attached kitchen, but it was built of brick and slightly larger than that of No. 126 Cumberland Street (Fig. 8.11). The cesspit was originally positioned along the northern fence, converted to sewerage in the 1860s and later rebuilt (as a water closet) adjacent to the kitchen (Figs. 8.9 and 8.11).

---

[6] A specialist of the book trades who ruled lines on a page aided by a machine.

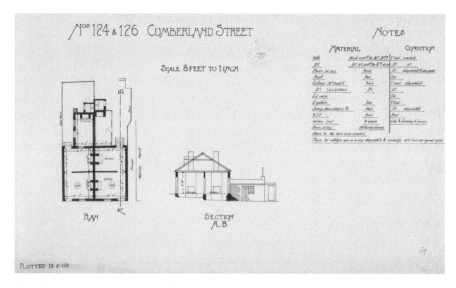

Fig. 8.11 Measured drawings of 124 and 126 Cumberland Street, prior to demolition in 1903. (NSW Government Architect, 'Plans and Photographs of Buildings Demolished, 1902–07', courtesy of Mitchell Library)

On 28 February 1861, 2 years prior to his death, John Winch sold 124 Cumberland Street to Louis Foucart. By 1863, it was owned by the shopkeeper Croft Hall, who in turn sold it to parliamentarian and Rocks property owner William Henson between 1871 and 1877. By 1880, 124 Cumberland Street had been purchased by local resident John Hoseman (probably as an investment), who retained the property until the early twentieth century.

In 1903, 124 Cumberland Street was deemed dilapidated, insanitary and 'beyond repair' (see Fig. 8.11). Photographs from 1901 show the façade of the building in a grimy state with minor chips in the render and a possible missing pane from the dormer window (Fig. 8.10). It was resumed by the state government and demolished by 1907.

The Cesspit Fill (MC A310)

Like its counterpart at 122 Cumberland Street, Cesspit A308, in the yard of 124 Cumberland Street, was built after 1845 and converted to sewerage in the mid- to late 1860s. The cesspit fill of A308 was unique in the study, owing to its complex relationship with a contemporaneous series of refuse pits in the yard. The pit back-fill was recovered in a single stratigraphic unit (A310) which was sealed by demolition rubble (A309) but is not a self-contained refuse deposit.

There are 13 conjoined vessels between the cesspit fill A310, adjacent refuse deposits (A322, A315) and yard surfaces A316, A319 and A307 (Table 8.6). These

Table 8.6 Sherds conjoining between MC A310 and associated deposits

| | | 124 Cumberland | | | | | | 126 Cumberland | | Eng Wks |
| | | A309 | A315 | A322 | A310 | A307 | A316 | A140 | A319 | A124 |
CJ #	Vessel	Cesspit demo	Refuse pit	Refuse pit	Cesspit fill	Rubble surface	Surface	Cesspit fill	Surface	Rubble base
143	Food preparation: pickle bottle			1	8					
166	Food storage: jar		1	1						
177	Food service: cup				1			1		1
179	Food service: muffin plate		2							
188	Food service: teacup		3	5						
215	Food service: bowl		3	5						
219	Food service: tea saucer			3	2					
220	Food service: plate			4	2					
222	Food service: dinner plate			4	1					
227	Food service: teacup		1	6						
228	Food service: teacup			1		2				
230	Food service: teacup		2	4						
231	Food service: teacup		1	9						
234	Food service: teacup or bowl		2	4						
235	Food service: teacup		2	8						
237	Food service: teacup or bowl			1	1					
243	Food service: plate, twiffler			10		3				
245	Food service: unidentified		1						1	
249	Food service: teacup		1	10						
252	Food service: unidentified			1			2			
331	Food service: plate, muffin			2		1				
346	Food service: glass, wine		2	3						

(continued)

Table 8.6 (continued)

		124 Cumberland				A307	A316	126 Cumberland		Eng Wks
		A309	A315	A322	A310	A307	A316	A140	A319	A124
346	Food service: glass, tumbler		8	6						
40	Hygiene: wash basin		1	16					2	
199	Food service: dish		1	6	3					
202	Food service: tea saucer		10	9	1					1
205	Hygiene: wash basin		5	29						
247	Food service: teapot			2	2					1
250	Food service: bowl		7	3	7					
422	Food service: tea saucer	2		9	1				1	
180	Food service: tea saucer		2	1	1				2	
201	Food service: teacup		5	12	2		1			
200	Hygiene: chamber pot		10	7	1		4		3	2
330	Food service: jug		6	21		3				1
	Total sherds	*2*	*76*	*203*	*32*	*9*	*7*	*1*	*9*	*6*
	Total vessels	*1*	*22*	*31*	*13*	*4*	*3*	*1*	*5*	*5*

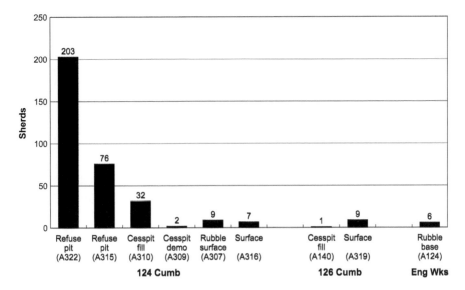

Fig. 8.12 Distribution of sherds conjoining between MC A310 and associated deposits

surface deposits in turn are linked with demolition material (A309) and a drain in the yard of 3 Carahers Lane (B059), as well as the rubble base for the Engineering Works (A124). Altogether, 85 fragment sets from 9 stratigraphic units form 34 vessels (Fig. 8.12). Interestingly, there are no conjoins between the demolition rubble (A309) and the A310 below, but the demolition rubble does conjoin with yard surfaces A319 (see Crook et al. 2005, 79–83, esp. Table 15 and Fig. 18).

We have argued previously that the refuse deposits adjacent to the cesspit were the source of disturbance or treadage in the later deposits but there was no disturbance of the main part of the fill (Crook et al. 2005, 80). The refuse deposits and cesspit fill are thus regarded as being the one fill, and the disturbance is considered negligible owing to the size of the assemblage. Even if numerous fragments have been lost to the Engineering Works (i.e. in addition to the known conjoins), 124 Cumberland Street still yields a greater number of vessels and matching sets than any other Rocks assemblage.

Artefacts from the assemblage are characteristically pre-1860s, and no artefact was known to have been first made after 1860. The latest-dating artefacts include a complete olive glass bottle (CUGL03526) marked 'C W & Co' and made by Cooper, Wood & Co, Edinburgh, probably between 1859 or 1860 and 1865 (Boow 1991, 177) and a perfume bottle (CUGL03612) dating from 1860, based on stylistic attributes. Several marked ceramic vessels ceased being produced in the 1850s and 1860s and several bottles, pipes, earthenwares and one halfpenny dating to the 1820s and 1830s were recovered from the fill (see Crook et al. 2005, 84, for a list of these items).

With a TPQ of 1859 or 1860, and given the sewer line was not present until 1866, the cesspit is most likely to have been backfilled in 1866; however, the early dates cannot be overlooked. While many of the ceramic vessels may be explained away by a time lag of 15–20 years, the presence of ready consumables such as clay pipes and ginger beer bottles *last* made three decades prior to their deposition suggests that *some* of this fill is derived from earlier rubbish dumps or a cache of goods. One could have been made in the 1840s and another in the late 1850s or early 1860s, suggesting that both of these dumps may have been made by the owner-occupiers: the Winches.

The Occupants

124 Cumberland Street was owned and occupied by John and Catherine Winch for around 27 years from c. 1834 to c. 1861. The Winches lived at this address with their two daughters Francis and Margaret, and it appears that their grandchildren were born and raised at this address in the early- to mid-1850s.

During the 1860s, 124 Cumberland Street was largely occupied by families, namely, the Puzeys in 1861–1864 and the Dibdens in 1867–1868 (Table 8.7). The longest ten-

Table 8.7 Owners and occupants of 124 Cumberland Street from 1834 to 1902

Name	From	To	Yrs
Owner–occupiers			
John George Winch (seaman/dealer)	1834	1861	27
Owners			
Charles Hall (landlord)	1863	1863	1–7
William Hall (landlord)	1867	1867	1–9
Croft Hall (landlord)	1871	1871	1–11
William Henson (landlord)	1877	1877	1–10
John Hoseman (labourer/mariner/landlord)	1880	1902	23–26
Occupants			
David Gourlay (captain, Governor-General steamer; son-in-law Winch)	1855	1855	1–
Hugh O'Neil (moulder – probably lodger)	1857	1857	1–?
George Puzey (mariner/labourer/gas worker)	1861	1863	3
Lucy Puzey (dealer)	1864	1864	1
Luckridge [John] Nichols	1865	1867	3–4
Frederick Dibden (waterman)	1867	1868	2–3
Donald Gray/Grey (shipwright/carpenter)	1869	1876	8–9
Edward Green	1877	1877	1–4
Charles Thomas Worth (dealer)	1879	1879	1–4
James Fuige	1880	1880	1–4
Edward Wright	1882	1887	6–10
John Monaghan (grocer)	1889	1889	1–4
Francis Gallagher	1890	1890	1–3
Vacant	1891	1891	1–2
John Anderson	1891	1894	4–5
Alfred Hoseman (hairdresser)	1895	1897	3–5
Eleanor Mason (greengrocer/newsagent)	1898	1899	2–4
Arthur Smith	1900	1902	3–4

ant at the property was Donald Gray (or Grey), a shipwright, who lived at this address for 8 years from 1869–1876. It is probable that Gray was unmarried as there are no records for him in birth, death or marriage registers. Subsequent tenants tended to be short term, staying for a minimum of 1 year (or less) and an average of 2–3 years. Alfred Hoseman, a hairdresser and the son of property-owner John Hoseman, lived with his family at 124 Cumberland Street for up to 3 years from 1895–1897.

John George and Catherine Winch (1834–1861)

John George and Catherine Winch (nee Byrne) owned and occupied 124 Cumberland Street from c. 1834 to 1861. John was the son of ex-convict, John Winch Snr, who arrived in Australia on the *Hillsborough* in 1799 (Garner 1997, 67 in Crook et al. 2005: 85). It is not clear if John George was born in the colony or came over with his convicted father. After a life at sea from the age of 9 or 10 years George was Chief Officer on the government schooner *Isabella* from 1830 to 1834 when he was 'appointed...as the fourth pilot of Port Jackson' (Garner 1997, 62; cited in Crook et al. 2005, 87).[7]

John married Catherine Byrne, the eldest daughter of Cumberland Street residents and ex-convicts Margaret Kelly and Richard Byrne, at St Phillips Church on 21 November 1827. She was 21 and he was either 27 or 29. John and Catherine had four children born between 1828 and 1835: Thomas James in 1828 (who died in infancy), Francis Jane in 1830, Margaret Elizabeth in 1833 and Eliza in 1835 (who died aged 6 months old). John had purchased the licence for the *Ship & Mermaid* from his father-in-law Richard Byrne on 7 July 1832, which he retained until 1833, but it is likely that Catherine was the publican at this hotel, as John was sailing the *Isabella* at this time.

In 1834 they purchased 124 Cumberland Street and moved in with their two daughters. In May 1837, their marriage was under some strain, as John cautioned the public not to give credit or purchase articles (or houses) from her (*Sydney Herald*, 1 May 1837: 1), but it is believed they continued to live under one roof. They were both listed as residents of Cumberland Street at various times. From 1851 to 1855, the Winches' youngest daughter Margaret and son-in-law David Gourlay lived at 124 Cumberland Street where their three children were born: Mary Catherine (1851), Elizabeth Jane (1852) and David (1854). They may also have taken in boarders as Hugh O'Neil – perhaps relative of neighbour Robert O'Neill – was listed as living at 124 Cumberland Street in 1857 (Cox and Co 1857, 27).

Catherine died in 1853, and John continued to live at 124 Cumberland Street until 1861 – just 2 years prior to his death – when he sold it to Louis Foucart on 28 February 1861; thereafter, the house was maintained as a rental property. John died at Liverpool Hospital on 22 December 1863 from the effects of jaundice.

---

[7] John was initially named as the member crew aboard the whaler the *Harmony* who committed mutiny against the captain but was not on the list of crew members found guilty and later pardoned (*Sydney Monitor*, 16 Jun. 1832: 2).

George and Lucy Puzey (1861–1864)

English immigrants George and Lucy Puzey and their children lived at 124 Cumberland Street for 2–3 years between 1861 and 1863. After George's death in 1863, Lucy and the children stayed at No. 124 until at least 1864.

Berkshire-born George and Londoner Lucy (nee Pearsall Leonard) married in 1852 in Aldgate, London, and migrated to Australia shortly after. They arrived as unassisted immigrants in c. 1853–1854, and their eldest son George was probably born in England or en route to Australia. The Puzeys had another five children born between 1855 and 1862, all in Sydney, but their third child, Lucy Emma, was born in 1856 in the Shoalhaven Region of NSW. The Puzeys had lived at several locations around The Rocks between 1858 and 1861 when they moved into 124 Cumberland Street (see Crook et al. 2005, 88, for details).

George worked as a mariner and labourer, and at the time of his death in 1863, he had been employed as a gas purifier at the Gas Works at Darling Harbour, on Sussex Street.

George was admitted to the Tarban Creek Lunatic Asylum on 21 April 1863. Three days later, it was reported that his wife Lucy had visited and had stated that:

> ...he was always a temperate and healthy man till a year ago he had a short attack of paralysis which [required?] little attention and soon passed away. Some time after that however [he] had another of a similar character which soon left him without leaving any manifest injurious effect. But about seven weeks since he was a third time seized with a severe paralytic affliction of his limbs which continued unabated in spite of every remedial means when on the 19 of March he was sent to the Infirmary in Sydney where he remained till the 21 April the day of his transferral hither. (Gladesville Hospital, formerly Tarban Creek Asylum, Medical Case Book No 16 30/3/1863–14/7/1864, State Records 4/8145, Folio 22)

These fits had left Puzey physically weakened and affected his memory, and his case notes suggest that his workplace – the Gas Works at Darling Harbour – was the cause of his illness. It is possible that he had suffered from epileptic seizures or some kind of aneurysm. Puzey remained at Tarban Creek Lunatic Asylum until his death on 5 June 1863, aged 36 years. Interestingly, the case notes also comment on his financial situation, stating: 'He is not [proposed?] of unbounded wealth but he has 500 in some bank to him unknown, and a gig and horse' (Medical Case Book No 16 30/3/1863–14/7/1864, State Records 4/8145, Folio 22).

It appears that Lucy continued to live at 124 Cumberland Street with her three children for at least a year after George's death. Between 1865 and 1868, she moved between The Rocks, Pyrmont and Darling Harbour before marrying Edinburgh-born Andrew Henderson in 1868. They had a son named Alfred born in the same year. Lucy Henderson died in 1900 at Petersham.

126 Cumberland Street (c. 1833–c. 1907)

Like 120 and 124 Cumberland Street, 126 Cumberland Street was part of Nicholas's Rents built by mariner Albert John Nicholas in c. 1833 (as discussed above). It was purchased initially by James Minton, who sold it to widow Mary Taylor for £125

Table 8.8 Owners and occupants of 126 Cumberland Street from 1845 to 1902

Name	From	To	Yrs
Owners			
William Massey (Bird-in-Hand Hotel)	1848	1853	6
Mary Ann Massey [nee Benson, later Henson]	1853	1855	2
William and Mary Ann Henson	1855	1891	47
John Hoseman (labourer/mariner/landlord)	1896	1902	7
Occupants			
Robert Morley (carpenter)	1845	1848	4–6
James Pennington	1852	1852	1–8
Patrick Colbert (labourer)	1855	1856	2–6
Martin Colbert	1857	1857	1–3
Alice Morley [nee Smith] (weaver)	1858	1859	2–5
Joseph and Lucy [nee McClelland] Donaldson (ships carpenter)	1861	1861	4–7
Timothy McNamara/MacNamara (labourer, hotelkeeper)	1865	1865	1–4
Stephen Doyle (painter and glazier)	1866	1879	14
Thomas Doyle	1878	1879	2–?
Henry Lapham (iron moulder) and Mary Jane Lapham [nee Young]*	1880	1902	23–24
John Keeffe (woodturner; probably a lodger)	1882	1882	1

1 month later. In 1840, it was conveyed to John Brown, brother-in-law of John Winch who lived next door at 124 Cumberland Street. Five years later, William Massey purchased 126 Cumberland Street, and when he died in 1853, it was transferred to his second wife, Mary Ann. Mary Ann and her second husband, William Henson, then held the property for over four decades, until 1896 when they sold it to John Hoseman (who had purchased No. 124 from them in 1880) (Table 8.8).

Like its neighbours 126 Cumberland Street was a single-storey, two-room brick dwelling with a shingle roof (replaced with iron by 1891), built directly on the footpath. It had an attached kitchen similar in size to 124 Cumberland Street but was weatherboard (Fig. 8.11) and, since at least 1868, had a cesspit alongside the kitchen (Fig. 7.2).

In 1903, along with its neighbour 124 Cumberland Street, No. 126 was deemed dilapidated, insanitary and 'beyond repair' (Fig. 8.11). The floorboards had already been pulled up, probably after its resumption by the state government, and it was demolished by 1907.

The Cesspit Fill (MC A140)

Like the cesspits at 122 and 124 Cumberland Street, Cesspit A139, in the yard of 126 Cumberland Street, was built after 1845 and converted to sewerage in the mid- to late 1860s.

The fill of A139 was recovered in two main deposits, A140 and A149, separated by a sandy lens (A147). There were three conjoins between the upper fill A140 and the lower fill A149: a green transfer-printed teacup (CJ ID 208) and two beer or wine bottles (CJ IDs 211 and 212) noted to have post-discard wear.

Other conjoins indicate links outside of the cesspit fill. Eight fragments from a brown transfer-printed plate in the 'Auld Lang Syne Pattern' (CUGL26691) were recovered from the lowest fill, yet the rest of the plate was found in a buried barrel in the neighbour's yard, dating from at least 1846 (CJ ID 195). The majority of the plate was from 128 Cumberland Street, and it remained as a single element in better condition than the fragments recovered from the 126 Cumberland Street cesspit, suggesting that the latter is the site of secondary deposition. Similarly, a small fragment of hand-painted earthenware plate (CUGL61211) (2.4g) was identified as conjoining (or being 'possibly the same as', CJ ID 179) with the refuse pit at 124 Cumberland Street (CUGL61209). These are anomalous cases of minor disturbance – probably resulting from pipeworks.

None of the catalogued artefacts in MC B077 have a TPQ later than 1860, but the deposit does offer some unique artefacts that may be attributed to one tenant. Kate Holmes (Holmes 1999b, 446) attributed the paint can fragments from the cesspit of 126 Cumberland Street to professional (house-)painter Stephen Doyle who lived from 1866 to 1879. The cans, along with two axe heads, were all recovered from the lowest fill, A149.

The Occupants

126 Cumberland Street was constructed in c. 1833; however, the first reliable detail about the people who lived at this address is from 1845 onwards, when the council rates began to be collected. Family groups tended to occupy 126 Cumberland Street from 1845 until the end of the nineteenth century.

Robert and Alice Morley and their children were the first recorded occupants; they lived there twice (1845–1848 and 1858–1859). James Pennington lived there in 1852 and Patrick and Martin Colbert from 1855 to 1857. Joseph and Lucy Donaldson and their only daughter Margaret lived at 126 Cumberland Street for up to 4 years (1861–1864). Soon thereafter, this address was home to two long-term tenants: Stephen and Margaret Doyle and their two daughters, for 14 years from 1866 to 1879, and the Lapham family from 1880 to 1902, a period of 22 years.

Stephen and Margaret Doyle (1866–1879)

Irish immigrants Stephen and Margaret Doyle (nee Galvin, later McNamara) lived at 126 Cumberland Street from 1866 to 1879.

Margaret was born in County Clare and migrated to Sydney at age 17, arriving aboard the *Pemberton* on 14 May 1849. She was recorded as a housekeeper and travelled alone. She was joined by her younger sister Bridget (23) and brother John (26) in c. 1853. Margaret married Thomas McNamara in 1852 at age 19. They had a daughter Ann, born in 1853, who probably died in infancy and a son, Thomas, born c. 1855.

In early 1854, Thomas (senior) took over the licence for the Clare Castle Inn, Parramatta Street (*SMH* 15 Apr 1854: 2). He died in January 1855 while resident at Clare Castle Inn, Parramatta Street. Later that year, Margaret moved back to The Rocks. She took over the licence of the Hand of Friendship on Cumberland Street (between Essex Street and Charlotte Place) from John Hourigan who stated that the raising of Cumberland Street had affected his trade (*SMH* 12 Sept. 1855, p. 4; *Empire*, 5 Dec 1855, p. 5). She ran the public house in March 1857 and had renewed the lease of the building from Thomas Glover in March 1857 for 3 years.

In September 1857, Margaret McNamara (nee Galvin) was married for the second time to fellow Irishman Stephen Doyle. Stephen had arrived in the colony from Dublin in 1856 (Karskens 1999a, 171) and was probably an unassisted immigrant. They had three daughters: Mary in 1858 (she died the same year), Charlotte in 1860 and Margaret in 1862.

Shortly after their marriage, Margaret's licence at the *Hand of Friendship* was transferred to Stephen (*Empire,* 17 Dec. 1857, p. 4). Stephen was listed as the publican here in 1858 and the following year Doyle was insolvent (see discussion in Chap. 10). In 1861, Stephen Doyle was listed at 176 Cumberland Street (Lilyvale) in the council rates records, either running a public house or boarding house at the premises. By at least 1866, and probably 1863, Doyle abandoned his career as a publican and resumed his work as a painter and decorator.

Margaret maintained strong links with the family of her first husband, the McNamaras. Margaret's sister Bridget Galvin was married to Thomas McNamara's brother Patrick in 1856, and they lived at 11 Carahers Lane from 1867 to 1896. Timothy McNamara was Margaret Doyle's brother-in-law from her first marriage, and he lived at 126 Cumberland Street in 1865, just 1 year before the Doyles moved in (Margaret also attended the birth of his first child Ann in 1861).

The Doyle family moved into 126 Cumberland Street in 1866 and lived there until 1880, at which time they moved next door to 128 Cumberland Street.

On 22 February 1881, shortly after they move, Stephen Doyle died from a stroke at the age of 52. Margaret continued to live at 128 Cumberland Street until her death c. 1908. Her youngest daughter, 'Miss Margaret', continued to live there until 1919 (Karskens 1999b, 206).

93 Gloucester Street (c. 1822–1891)

In c. 1795, convicts Ann Armsden and her husband, George Legg, built and lived in a shingle and weatherboard house on what would later be 93 Gloucester Street. After George drowned in 1807, Ann continued to live at the house and was remarried in 1810 to another George: baker George Talbot. Archaeological evidence indicates that the Armsden–Talbots replaced the earlier Armsden–Legg building with 'two semi-detached stone dwellings at some time before 1822' (Steele 1999, 253). The new stone building (later 91–93 Gloucester Street) was a two-storey terrace with five rooms apiece: 'three front rooms, one very small and oddly shaped…arranged along the street frontage in the old manner, with a wing of two rooms extending to the rear' (Steele 1999, 253–254). The entrances were reached from Gloucester Street by a set of stairs cut into the rock face.

Ann and George sold the southernmost house, 93 Gloucester Street (then known as 26 Cambridge Street), to Hugh Hector Innes Noble in c. 1822, and moved to Darling Harbour (Crook et al. 2005, 96). In April 1829, Noble sold 93 Gloucester Street to his brother-in-law William Henry Chapman who later sold it to William Massey for £170 in February 1844. Massey held onto the property until his death in 1853.

In the 1860s, 93 Gloucester Street was sold to shopkeeper Croft Hall and changed hands a number of times until it was demolished in 1891 (Karskens 1999a, 191). It had been a rental property since Massey's ownership and until its demolition in 1891. Most tenants stayed for an average of 1 to 2 years, and it is possible that 93 Gloucester Street was a boarding house.

The Cistern–Cesspit Fill (MC F044)

Sometime between 1810 and 1833, a water storage tank (F045) was built in the yard of 93 Gloucester Street, by George Talbot, or a later owner. It was rock-cut, 5 feet long, 3 feet wide and 6.5 feet deep (1.5 × 0.9 × 1.95 m) and positioned alongside the rear yard wall. It does not appear definitively as a cesspit or WC on any plans. There is a pencil outline on the 1865 trigonometric survey (Fig. 7.2), but this probably indicates the water closet installed after 1865 when the sewer lines came down Gloucester Street (Steele 1999, 258–266). Whether or not the pit was only ever used as a water cistern, or used at one time as a cesspool, it was backfilled when converted to a water closet.

The backfill was recovered as in two units (F042 and F044, grouped as MC F044). The fill contained two aerated water bottles with Dan Ryland's 'Safe Groove Patent' (CUGL59063 and CUGL73802) made between 1885 and 1888 (Jones 1979, 36) and two pennies dated to 1882 and 1884 (CUGL10155 and CUGL10157). In addition, there were two black transfer-printed tea saucers, marked 'Florence' with registration diamonds for October 1882 (CUGL40509–CUGL40510) and an 1874 threepence.

This establishes a TPQ of 1885 and suggests that the installation of the sewerage connections occurred within the last 6 years of the dwelling's life. It is possible that the installation was deferred owing to the fact that the house was built directly on a sandstone ledge (Steele 1999, 256–258). The sewer pipe laid in the 1880s was rock-cut (Fig. 8.13), and this would have been far more costly than laying pipes in a loam yard.

In the fill was also recovered the name stamp of a neighbour, C. G. Carlson, who lived at 83 Gloucester Street between 1868 and 1871. How this came to be in the fill deposited 15 years later is unknown.

Fig. 8.13 Rock-cut water cistern, later used as a cesspit then converted to a water closet in the 1880s. (Patrick Grant, 1994, Refs: B32.37, courtesy SHFA and GML)

Steele (1999, 266) noted that the water cistern was backfilled with 1.5 m of sandstone rubble and the upcast material from the installation of the sewerage pipe F055 and toilet F037. Above this, the humic cesspit fill (MC F044) was recovered in two stratigraphic units: the main fill F044 and the upper unit F042 which was an interface between the artefact-rich F044 and the demolition deposit (F025) above. There were three conjoins between the two deposits, and all nine vessels post-dating 1873 (noted above) were recovered from the lower fill, F044 – diminishing the likelihood that the later demolition fill had contaminated the earlier toilet-conversion fill.

The Occupants

The first recorded occupants at 93 Gloucester Street were the building's owners, Ann Armsden and George Talbot, who stayed until c. 1822 when they sold the home to Hugh Hector Innes Noble (Table 8.9). He lived there with his wife, Eliza Ann (nee Chapman), and their children until c. 1827. It is not known who occupied 93 Gloucester Street from 1828 to 1845.

Table 8.9 Owners and occupants of 93 Gloucester Street from 1845–1892

Name	From	To	Yrs
Owners			
William Massey	1845	1853	9
Mary Ann Massey [nee Benson, later Henson]	1853	1855	3
William and Mary Ann Henson	1856	1863	8
William Samuels	1861	1861	1
Croft Hall	1867	1871	5–17
Mary A. Hall [nee Chilcott]	1877	1877	1–10
H. Christison	1880	1880	1–5
William W. Pullyard	1882	1882	1–11
Catherine Fennelly [nee Brophy] (landlord/occupant)	1891	1902	11–21
John Kearney Estate (landlord)	1902	1902	1
Occupants			
Thomas Thompson (waterman)	1845	1845	1–4
Thomas O'Brien	1848	1848	1–8
Thomas King (butcher)	1852	1852	1–8
Robert Grace (seaman)	1855	1857	3–7
Emma Murphy	1858	1858	1–3
Robert Pascall	1859	1859	1–4
Agnes Ellars	1861	1861	1–5
Patrick Cassidy	1861	1861	1–5
John Buxton	1863	1863	1–4
James F. Binks (grocery store)	1864	1864	1–3
William Stokes (butcher)	1865	1865	1–3
John Murphy (dealer)	1866	1866	1–3
Vacant	1867	1867	<1
Thomas Brown (stonemason)	1867	1867	1–3
Vacant	1867	1867	<1
Donald Gray/Grey (shipwright/carpenter)	1868	1868	1–3
George Wilson (mariner, waterman and grocer)	1869	1869	1–2
Rosanna French [nee Boyd]	1869	1869	1–2
Jane and William Kitchen Neal (fruiterer/mariner)	1870	1871	2–4
Antoni Silver/Silva (lodger?)	1870	1871	2–?
James Wall (waterman, carpenter)	1873	1877	5–8
Alfred Henry Miller (boarding house)	1879	1879	1–4
William Byrnes/Bryant (van proprietor)	1880	1882	3–4
Vacant	1882	1882	<1
Peter Augustus Lett (nightwatchman/labourer)	1883	1888	6–8
Dennis Mitchell	1889	1889	1–2
John Funnell (sugar boiler)	1889	1889	1–2
Mary Ryan	1890	1890	1–2
David Munn	1891	1892	2–3

93 Gloucester Street had a high turnover of tenants from 1845, when council rates were first collected, until 1891 when the building was demolished. A different tenant appears in every rates record and surviving post-office directory until 1873, suggesting that 93 Gloucester Street was run as a boarding house in these years. It is known that Alfred Henry and Eliza Miller kept a boarding house at these premises in 1879.

The tenants who stayed the longest at 93 Gloucester Street were James and Eleanor Wall and eight of their children who lived there for 4–5 years in 1873–1877 and Peter and Honora Lett and their three children from 1883 to 1888 (for 5–6 years).

It is probable that the conversion to sewerage occurred within 6 years prior to the 1891 demolition of the Armsden–Talbot house. The conversion, and consequently the fill, probably occurred during the occupancy of Peter Augustus Lett and family.

Peter Augustus and Honora Lett (1883–1888)

Danish seaman Peter Augustus Lett and his Irish wife Honora lived at 93 Gloucester Street with their three children from 1883 to 1888.

Peter was born in Elsinore, Denmark, in c. 1842 and migrated to Australia in 1863 in the same year as his future wife, Honora Burns (or Byrnes) – a native of County Wicklow and a cook. Both were 21 at that time and they married in 1869, aged 27. They had four children born between 1871 and 1875, one of whom died in infancy: their surviving children were Augustus (1871), Margaret (1873) and Edward W. (1875).

Peter was known as a very strong man, 'able to carry a bale of wool from Millers Point to Pyrmont with very little effort' and worked variously as a nightwatchman, ship chandler and maritime dealer to support his family (Karskens 1999a, 152–3). The Lett family were living at 97 Gloucester Street in 1892 and 1893 then moved to Pyrmont. Peter died in September 1903 at which time his occupation was given as maritime dealer. His widow Honora died at Pyrmont in 1919.

97 Gloucester Street (c. 1817–c. 1907)

97 Gloucester Street was a single-storey stone building with four and a half rooms, a shingled roof and attic (Fig. 8.14). Three of the rooms were located on the ground floor, with the living room facing on to the street. The middle room of the house was the kitchen, which had a fireplace along the south wall and a staircase to the upper level on the northern wall. There was a room to the rear, possibly a bedroom, which led onto the yard, which was reached by steps. The upper rooms were located in a loft, and comprised an alcove to the rear, which accommodated the staircase, and a bedroom at the front with a skylight. 97 Gloucester Street was reached by a set of stairs leading from Gloucester Street (Fig. 8.15).

Convict George Cribb constructed 97 Gloucester Street in c. 1817 as a butcher shop adjoining his home at 95 Gloucester Street (on the corner of Gloucester Street

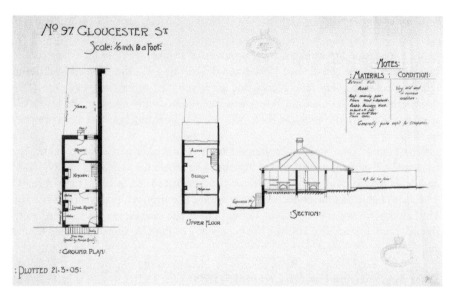

Fig. 8.14 Measured drawing of 97 Gloucester Street in 1905, prior to demolition. Drawn on 21 March 1905. Note no cesspit at all is shown in the yard. (NSW Government Architect, 'Plans and Photographs of Buildings Demolished, 1902–07'; courtesy of Mitchell Library)

Fig. 8.15 Gloucester Street in 1901, showing (from left to right) no. 101, 'The King House', recently white-washed; no. 99, once the 'Bird in Hand Hotel', now a boarding house; no. 97, once George Cribb's butcher shop; and no. 95, once the 'Whalers Arms' and now a boarding house. (SRNSW Digital ID: 4481_a026_000197, courtesy of State Records NSW)

and Cribbs Lane, later enlarged to become the *Whalers Arms*).[8] Cribb's slaughter yards were located to the rear of 95–97 Gloucester Street, bounded by what later became known as Carahers and Cribbs Lanes. Excavation revealed an earlier structure below the shop which Martin Carney argues explains the 'need for a "reopening" of the shop in 1817' (Carney 1999, 138).

In c. 1833, 97 Gloucester Street was sold to Albert John Nicholas and put it up for auction in January 1834 along with the neighbouring *Bird in Hand* public house at No. 99 (*The Australian* 17 Jan. 1834, p. 3). It was purchased by William Massey for £600. Between 1882 and 1891, the shingle roof of 97 Gloucester Street was replaced with iron. It was demolished c. 1905.

The Cesspit Fills (MCs C056 and C220)

97 Gloucester Street contained the most complex – and arguable best maintained – sanitary arrangements in The Rocks study group. Not only were there two separate cesspits, probably built within a decade of each other, but one was upgraded twice in its 40–45-year life. The earliest pit, C312, in the southwest corner was replaced in the 1860s, by cesspit C051 in the northwest corner, which within about a decade was connected to sewer lines, only to be reconnected or repaired in the 1880s.

First Cesspit: Southwest Yard (MC C220)

It is not certain when the brick cesspit C312 was installed, but it was built after the original house construction c. 1817, likely during or after William Massey's occupation from 1834 to 1853 (Carney 1999, 154). The Masseys owned and occupied both 97 and 99 Gloucester Streets (formerly the *Bird in Hand Hotel*) and may not have needed a cesspit on the shop allotment. Carney (1999, 154) speculated that the cesspit was built as recently as 1853–1854, after the death of William Massey, the marriage and relocation of his widow Mary Anne Massey and the separate leasing of 97 and 99 Gloucester Street.

The deposit is most likely to have been backfilled in the 1850s and contained a tobacco pipe marked 'UNCLE TOM'S CABIN / MURRAY, GLASGOW', made after 1852 (when *Uncle Tom's Cabin* was first published) but before 1861 when William Murray's factory closed. No other artefacts had a TPQ greater than 1852.

The deposit was recovered in three layers: C220, C225 and C240 (grouped for the purposes of this study as MC C220). A conjoining fragment of a crimson transfer-printed mug found in the fill of C240 was recovered from the occupation deposit in the west room of 5 Carahers Lane – one of the terraces facing the yard of 97

---

[8] He also built an adjacent building to the south of 97 Gloucester Street, known as the *Bird in Hand* (99 Gloucester Street), between 1817 and 1823.

Gloucester Street (CJ ID 65). The majority of the vessel was recovered from the cesspit fill (CUGL60596; 32.4 g), with a small 2 g fragment in the underfloor deposit (CUGL62912). The underfloor deposit of 5 Carahers Lane is unique, and was the subject of considerable disturbance, probably owing to the construction of a drain (Crook 1999 Appendix 2). It is possible that the discard of the mug occurred prior to the construction of 5 Carahers Lane. This single conjoin is considered an anomaly and probably the result of pipes being laid across fence lines at the same time.

Second Cesspit: Northwest Yard (MC C056)

The second cesspit in the yard of 97 Gloucester Street (C051) had a stone base and brick superstructure and was probably built in the mid- to late 1850s when the first cesspit (C312) was decommissioned and backfilled (Fig. 8.16). Within a decade, cesspit C051 was converted to sewerage and the pit backfilled; and piping was upgraded again in the 1880s (Carney 1999, 152–154) or possibly the 1890s as discussed below. This new piping was decommissioned and covered with two bricks and then covered with demolition fill (C039) associated with the final demolition, c. 1907. Carney (1994, 10) notes that WC does not appear on the 1905 detailed plan (Fig. 8.14) suggesting that the WC was demolished before the main building.

While the down pipe (C052) for the later modifications did disturb the backfill preceding the 1860s sewerage conversion, the fill deposit remained largely intact and enabled Carney to date the first conversion to at least 1861. Units C048 and C049 contain a mix of 1860s fill and '1880s material', and these were laid over the new piping and partially disturbed fill. These later deposits were excluded from the study group and MC C056 should be considered a *minimum*.

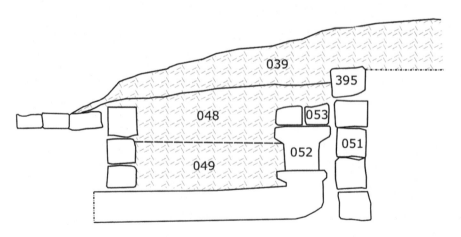

------Edge of sketch   NOT TO SCALE

Fig. 8.16 Cross-section of Cesspit C051 showing 'indicative' sketch of fills (Martin Carney, 1994, Trench Journal, p. 10, redrawn by P. Crook 2019)

The 1860s fill was removed in four stratigraphic units, and one 'clean-up' deposit (C066). The upper three layers (C056, C064 and C065) were artefact-rich fills, while the lowest layer (C067) was distinguished as anaerobic, cesspit residue. Parasite analysis found evidence of whipworm and roundworm eggs (Everett 1999, 303), but these were retrieved from C064, not C067. There were 19 vessels with conjoining elements recovered from C064 to C067 (note there were none with C056), the majority between C064 and C065. Allowing some shifting of deposits, particularly given the rising water in the cesspit (Carney 1994, 19), these deposits ought best be considered a minimum representation of the original quantity discarded.

None of the glass and ceramic vessels necessarily post-date the 1860s, with the exception of one near-complete, grey transfer-printed plate (CUGL40997) from C064[9] is marked 'J.F.W / FOLEY POTTERIES' and was made by James Wileman between 1869 and 1892. Other transfer-printed wares, glass bottles and tobacco pipes have a TPQ of 1862 (e.g. Challinor saucer CUGL61912, made 1862–1891; Davidson tobacco pipe CUGL23794, 1862–1911; and Crop tobacco pipe CUGL23070, 1856–1924).

Three coins for years 1895 (10170), 1889 (10164) and 1877 (10147) were recovered from the lower fills C065 and C064. These late dates are certainly out of character with the remainder of the fill. It is unlikely (but of course always possible) that these small items fell into the intact fills during demolition, largely because the down pipe C052 was left in situ and intact giving little reason to dig through the layers below the pipe. This disturbance is more likely to be the result of the laying of the new down pipe, which pushes back the date of sewer line repair to the late 1890s, not the 1880s as initially thought.

This disturbance may also account for the Wileman sherd dating from at least 1869. If this sherd and the coins are treated as anomalies, the deposit can be dated to the mid-1860s, at least 1862, and probably 1866 when the sewer pipe was laid down Carahers Lane.

The Occupants

97 Gloucester Street was first occupied by George Cribb who used it as a butcher shop from constructed in c. 1817 to 1827 (Table 8.10). The butchery firm of Murrell, Sandwell and Perks purchased the building in 1827 before becoming bankrupt in 1828. The occupants of 97 Gloucester Street from 1827 to 1845 are unknown. The building was converted to residential use sometime in this period. The first residential tenant recorded at this address was Patrick Howard, a labourer, in 1845. Thereafter, different tenants were recorded at 97 Gloucester Street every 2–5 years from 1845 (when the council rates were collected) until 1861.

Tenants tended to be a mix of families and single men (possibly boarding) and were short term (tending to stay an average of 2–3 years) with one exception. Joseph

---

[9] A small conjoining sherd (63230) was recovered from the clean-up deposit C066.

Table 8.10 Owners and occupants of 97 Gloucester Street from 1845 to 1902

Name	From	To	Yrs
Owners			
William Massey (Bird-in-Hand Hotel)	1845	1852	8
Mary Ann Massey [nee Benson, later Henson]	1853	1855	2
William and Mary Ann Henson	1856	1902	47
Occupants			
Patrick Howard (labourer)	1845	1845	1–4
Robert Heaney (bricklayer?)	1848	1848	1–8
Vacant	1852	1852	1–8?
Thomas Buckley (tailor) and Mrs Buckley	1855	1856	2–6
William Allen (confectioner)	1857	1857	1–3
Vacant	1858	1858	1–5
Alexander Dickinson	1861	1861	1–4
George Adams (mariner)	1861	1861	1–3
James Thomas (general dealer)	1863	1867	5–7
Thomas Swan	1868	1868	1–3
D. Maclaverty	1869	1869	1–3
John Stretton/Streeton	1870	1870	1–3
Joseph Thomas (boarding house)	1871	1887	17–19
Matthew McBride	1888	1889	2–4
Robert Gaffey (tip carter)	1890	1891	2–4
Peter Augustus Lett (nightwatchman/labourer)	1892	1893	2–4
Peter Johnson/Johnstone	1894	1900	7–10
James England	1902	1902	1

and Catherine Thomas lived at 97 Gloucester Street for up to 17 years from 1871 to 1887 (Joseph's brother James Thomas, a dealer, lived at the same address for 4–5 years in 1863–1867). Subsequent tenants included a bachelor, Robert Gaffey (1890–1891) and the Lett family (1892–1893) introduced above.

Owing to the complex nature of cesspit fills in this lot, it is necessary to outline several families although unfortunately we do not know detail of all of them.

Thomas and Mary Buckley (1855–1856)

Thomas Buckley was a tailor who lived at 97 Gloucester Street, with his wife Mary Buckley (nee Sweeney or Walsh) and family, for 1–2 years between 1855 and 1856. There appear to be two Thomas and Mary Buckleys living in the colonies at the time: Mary Sweeney and Thomas Buckley married in Melbourne in 1842 and appear to have remained their throughout their lives; the other Mary Walsh and Thomas Buckley had at least six children while living in the district of Bathurst. The eldest, James, would have been 13 when they lived at 97 Gloucester Street and the youngest, Mary, just 4 years old.

It is not known to where the Buckleys moved in 1856, but by 1858, Thomas was listed as a tailor at 216 Cumberland Street (Sands Sydney Commercial Directory 1858–1859). In 1860, 'an old man named Thomas Buckley, tailor' was charged with stealing from the Harbour View Hotel on Cumberland Street while intoxicated (*SMH* 25 Apr. 1860, p. 4). Nothing more is known of the Buckleys after this time.

William Allen (1857)

William Allen was a confectioner who lived at 97 Gloucester Street for at least 1 year in 1857. Unfortunately, we know nothing more about him than his name.

James Thomas (1862–1867)

James Thomas was a general dealer who lived at 97 Gloucester Street from 1862 to 1867. He was probably the brother of Joseph Thomas, who lived at 3 Carahers Lane in 1858–1861, 99 Gloucester Street in 1861–1870 and 97 Gloucester Street in 1871–1886. James was listed at each of these addresses, often while Joseph and Catherine Thomas were living there. He was also listed at 110 Cumberland Street in 1868. Unfortunately little more is known of the James.

Thomas Swan (1868)

Thomas Swan lived at 97 Gloucester Street in 1868. Ten years previously (1858), he had lived at one of the Smidmore buildings on Cumberland Street (6/164 Cumberland Street). Unfortunately, we have not been able to recover any additional information about his occupation, age or marital status.

Denis and Mary McClafferty (1869)

Denis and Mary (nee Sweeney) McClafferty (also spelt Maclaverty) lived at 97 Gloucester Street in 1869. They had arrived in Australia as assisted immigrants on the *Montrose* in 1864 with their infant son, Hugh. They had four more children in the colonies between 1863 and 1873, but only one (Sarah, born c. 1869) survived infancy (Crook et al. 2005, 115).

In 1866, an unemployed labourer D. McClafferty of Campbell Street sought assistance after being out of work for 3 months (SRNSW NRS 906 [4/581.2 p.161]). The individual was described as married, with two children, and had been in the colony for 2 years. It is likely to be this same Denis.

Mary died in 1874 and Denis married for the second time in 1875. His new wife was Sarah Macclafferly or McClafferly, and presumably a relative (possibly by marriage). Denis and Sarah had three more children between 1876 and 1885 and lived in a number of residences around The Rocks between 1877 and 1900 before moving to Granville (Crook et al. 2005, 115). Denis died of heart disease in 1905.

101 Gloucester Street (1822–c. 1907)

101 Gloucester Street, known as the *King House*, was most likely erected by its first recorded occupant: Daniel King, who there in 1822 with his wife Susan Tirely and their three young children and an assigned convict. An earlier building had been erected by c. 1812 and may have stood behind the King House in the 1820s (see Carney 1999, 140, for full discussion).

Council Rates records show that from 1845, 101 Gloucester Street was single-storey stone building with three rooms and a shingled roof, which was replaced with iron between 1880 and 1882. It is shown in a photograph from 1901 with a weathered façade showing cracks in the render, a loose gutter and well-worn threshold (Fig. 8.15).

Mrs Francis (or Frances) King of Erskine Street (likely a relative of Daniel King) was officially granted Lot 4, comprising 3.5 perches by Town Grant in 1839, and a year later she sold it to Mary Ann Wright of George Street. In 1847, Mary Ann and her husband James sold the property to William Massey for £100. On the death of Massey in 1853, 101 Gloucester Street passed into the ownership of Mary Ann, his second wife, who later married future parliamentarian William Henson in 1855. The Hensons retained ownership of 101 Gloucester Street until the early 1900s, at which time the building was resumed and demolished.

The Cesspit Fill (MC C130)

It is not known when the cesspit at 101 Gloucester Street was first installed, but it first appears on maps in 1857 (Fig. 7.1). Carney (1999, 144) argues that it was converted to sewerage some time after the 1850s and remained in use as a water closet until demolished c. 1907. The closet appears to have been repaired or renovated at some point, with a new dry-pressed brick wall (C132) and new above-ground piping (Carney 1994, 18–20). At this time, the fill below was sealed with a cement floor (C122).

The fill was excavated in four stratigraphic units: C127–C130, none of which have a TPQ later than 1861 – despite the structural evidence for modifications after the initial sewer conversion. Units C127 and C128 post-dated the dry-pressed brick wall but contained no artefacts post-dating 1845. The base sherd of a patterned plate, marked 'GEM' and made by George Jones from 1861 to 1873 (CUGL40965), was recovered from the third fill, C129. There was one conjoin identified between the 3rd and 4th fills (CJ ID 251), the majority of it being recovered from C129.

A fragment of a Chinese blue and white porcelain bowl (CJ ID 154) was identified as conjoining with sherds from three other layers in the yard of 101 Gloucester Street: a fill layer in the south yard dating from at least 1873 (C358), a refuse pit also in the south yard (C397) dating from at least 1837 and the retaining wall dating from at least 1846 (C250).

C397 and two other contemporaneous refuse pits in the yard (C239: 1861+; C387: 1845+; C397: 1837+) were briefly examined for comparability with the cesspit fill, supposing they were related to the same construction or renovation event. While another 'Gem' pattern sherd was identified in C239 and one unidentified but distinct scenic sherd from C397 was identified as matching 72997 from the fourth cesspit fill, there was no exceptional commonality, and connection between the three was ruled out.[10] It is likely that these pits were disturbed during installation of the sewer pipes through the yard, and small remnants found their way into the cesspit backfill.

Like 5 Carahers Lane, the assemblage contains some characteristically pre-1850 artefacts, including Chinese blue and white porcelain, and lead-glazed and unglazed utilitarian wares, alongside post-1840s tobacco pipes, transfer-printed and white earthenwares and light green condiment bottles as expected in c. 1860s deposits.

The Occupants

Daniel King, Susan Tirley and their three children were the first recorded occupants of 101 Gloucester Street from 1822 to 1823. It is not known who lived at 101 Gloucester Street between 1823 and 1845 (Table 8.11).

From 1845 to the 1860s, 101 Gloucester Street was mostly occupied by short-term tenants (single men and families) who stayed a minimum of 1 year (or less) and a maximum of 3–5 years.

Families, connected to each other through marriage, tended to occupy 101 Gloucester Street from the early 1870s until 1902. Elizabeth and Thomas Hines and their children lived at this address for 3 years from 1873, while Elizabeth's mother and brother (Caroline and James McCraw) lived there from 1879 to 1880. Thomas and Harriet Price and their children occupied 101 Gloucester Street from 1882 to 1893, followed by their daughter, the widowed Emily Layton, with at least four of her children from 1893 to 1902.[11] The cesspit backfill was most likely created during the occupation of George Beale.

---

[10] C239, C387 and C397 were determined 'Priority B' contexts, and ceramic and glass from these deposits were bulk bagged. These bulk bags (40948, 40950, 40926) were briefly examined in August 2003 but were not sorted and catalogued.

[11] One of Emily's daughters, Charlotte Ann, married John Hines – who was born at No. 101 – in 1898.

Table 8.11 Owners and occupants of 101 Gloucester Street from 1845 to 1902

Name	From	To	Yrs
Owners			
James Wright	1845	1845	1–4
William Massey (Bird-in-Hand Hotel)	1848	1852	5
Mary Ann Massey [nee Benson, later Henson]	1853	1855	2
William and Mary Ann Henson	1856	1902	47
Occupants			
Daniel King and Susan Tirley	1822	1823	>2
David Evans (cooper)	1845	1845	1–4
Charles Price	1848	1848	1–8
Vacant	1852	1852	1–8
Richard Donovan (boot and shoemaker)	1855	1856	2–6
Andrew Conway (cabinet maker)	1857	1857	1–3
William J. Foster	1858	1858	1–3
Richard Wild (grocer, Black Dog Inn)	1859	1859	1–2
James Agnew French (free mariner/labourer)	1859	1861	3–5
George Beale (waterman)	1863	1871	9–13
Thomas Hines (mariner)	1873	1875	3–6
Thomas Verrell (waterman)	1876	1882	7–8
James McCraw and Caroline McCraw [nee Saumons]	1879	1880	2?
Thomas and Harriet Price and family	1882	1902	21
Thomas Price (diver/waterman/pearl lugger)	1882	1884	3
Harriet Price (confectioner)	1885	1893	11
Emily Layton [nee Price] (confectioner/laundress)	1893	1902	10
William McLeod (lodger?)	1898	1898	1?

George and Mary Beale 1863–1871

George Beale was a waterman who lived at 101 Gloucester Street from 1863 to 1871. He had migrated from England in 1851 when he was 26 years old and worked as a boatman and possibly a labourer. He may have been the George Beale who married Mary Castigan (from County Armagh) at St Andrews Sydney on 25 August 1856. This couple had four children (one boy died in infancy). One of the couple's children, Margaret, was born at Kirribilli, Milsons Point on 1 January 1861, at which time George Beale's occupation was given as labourer and his place of birth as Canterbury, England.

George Beale the licenced watermen appears to have been involved in numerous disputes and minor criminal matters in the 1860s and 1870s. He appears to have lost his licence in 1867 for using the Governor's jetty in Farm Cove 'after being told it was illegal to do so' (*SMH* 23 Aug. 1867, p. 3). In 1871 he was charged with deserting his wife, and in 1873 he was charged with a more serious offence, maliciously stabbing fellow waterman John McLeod, and was sentenced to 6 months in Darlinghurst Gaol (*SMH* 6 Dec. 1873, p. 8 and *Evening News* 17 Feb. 1874, p. 3).

Fig. 8.17 Waterman
George Beale at the start of
his 6-month sentence in
Darlinghurst Gaol, 17
February 1874.
(Darlinghurst Gaol Photo
No. 960, SRNSW
NRS2138 [3/14031],
p. 93b)

On arrival his photograph was taken: the only image we have of a resident in our study (Fig. 8.17).

On 11 January 1877, George died at the age of 52, at the Sydney Infirmary from the effects of alcoholism and bronchitis.

References

Boow, James. 1991. *Early Australian Commercial Glass: Manufacturing Processes.* Sydney: Heritage Council of NSW.

Carney, Martin. 1994. Cumberland/Gloucester Streets Site Trench C Journal. *Excavation Journal.* Sydney. SHFA.

———. 1999. Trench C Report. In *The Cumberland/Gloucester Streets Site, The Rocks: Archaeological Investigation Report,* ed. Godden Mackay Heritage Consultants, vol. 3, 131–189. Sydney: Godden Mackay Logan Pty Ltd.

Cox, and Co. 1857. *Cox and Co.'s Sydney Post Office directory, 1857.*

Crook, Penny. 1999. The Meaningless Public Smile? Housing, Mass Consumption and Material Ambiguity in the Rocks, Sydney (c1833–c1931). BA honours thesis, Sydney: University of Sydney.

Crook, Penny. 2019. Approaching the archaeology of value: a view from the modern world, *Post-Medieval Archaeology* 53 (1): 1–20. https://doi.org/10.1080/00794236.2019.1601381.

Crook, Penny, Tim Murray, and Laila Ellmoos. 2003. *Assessment of Historical and Archaeological Resources of the Cumberland and Gloucester Streets site, The Rocks, Sydney*. 2nd rev. Archaeology of the Modern City 1788–1900. Sydney: Historic Houses Trust of New South Wales.

Crook, Penny, Laila Ellmoos, and Tim Murray. 2005. *Keeping up with the McNamaras: a Historical Archaeological Study of the Cumberland and Gloucester Streets site, The Rocks, Sydney*. Archaeology of the Modern City Series 8. Sydney: Historic Houses Trust of New South Wales.

Ellmoos, Laila, and Penny Crook. 2006. People+Place Database. In *EAMC Databases, Version 1.0*, ed. Penny Crook, Laila Ellmoos, and Tim Murray. Compact Disc. Sydney: Historic Houses Trust of NSW.

Everett, Claire. 1999. Parasite and Macrobotanical Specialist Report. In *The Cumberland/Gloucester Streets Site, The Rocks: Archaeological Investigation Report*, ed. Godden Mackay Heritage Consultants, vol. 4ii, 297–311. Sydney: Godden Mackay Logan Pty Ltd.

Garner, Val. 1997. *Irish on the Rocks: The Descendants of Richard Byrne & Margaret Kelly*. Jannali: Val Garner.

Godden Mackay. 1996. *The Cumberland/Gloucester Streets Site, The Rocks: Archaeological Investigation Report, Prepared for the Sydney Cove Authority*, Sydney.

———. 1999. *The Cumberland/Gloucester Streets Site, The Rocks: Archaeological Investigation Report, Prepared for the Sydney Cove Authority: Volume 1* . 1 vols. Sydney: Godden Mackay Logan Pty Ltd.

Godden Mackay, and Grace Karskens. 1994. *The Cumberland/Gloucester Streets Site, The Rocks: Archaeological Assessment and Research Design*. Godden Mackay Heritage Consultants for the Sydney Cove Authority and the Heritage Council of NSW.

Holmes, Kate. 1994. Trench B Journal. Sydney Harbour Foreshore Authority.

———. 1999a. Trench B Report. In *The Cumberland/Gloucester Streets Site, The Rocks: Archaeological Investigation Report*, ed. Godden Mackay Heritage Consultants, vol. 3, 87–129. Sydney: Godden Mackay Logan Pty Ltd.

———. 1999b. Metal Artefacts Report. In *The Cumberland/Gloucester Streets Site, The Rocks: Archaeological Investigation Report*, ed. Godden Mackay Heritage Consultants, vol. 4i, 367–456. Sydney: Godden Mackay Logan Pty Ltd.

Jones, David Vincent. 1979. *One Hundred Thirsty Years: Sydney's Aerated Water Manufacturers from 1830 to 1930*. Deniliquin: Reliance Press.

Karskens, Grace. 1999a. *Inside the Rocks: The Archaeology of a Neighbourhood*. Sydney: Hale & Iremonger.

———. 1999b. *Main Report—New Perspectives from the Rocks*. Edited by Godden Mackay. The Cumberland/Gloucester Streets Site, The Rocks: Archaeological Investigation Report 2. Sydney: Godden Mackay Logan Pty Ltd.

Mayne, Alan. 1982. *Fever, Squalor and Vice—Sanitation and Social Policy in Victorian Sydney*. St. Lucia: University of Queensland Press.

———. 1990. *Representing the Slum—Popular Journalism in a Late Nineteenth Century City*. Melbourne: The University of Melbourne.

———. 1993. *The Imagined Slum—Newspaper Representations in Three Cities 1870–1914*. London: Leicester University Press.

Penny Crook. 2019. Approaching the archaeology of value: a view from the modern world, *Post-Medieval Archaeology*, 53:1, 1–20, DOI: https://doi.org/10.1080/00794236.2019.1601381

Sands, John. 1875. *Sands Sydney Commercial Directory for 1875*. Sydney: John Sands.

———. 1895. *Sands' Sydney and Suburban Directory for 1895*. Sydney: John Sands.

Sands, John, and Thomas Kenny. 1858. *Sands and Kenny's Commercial and General Sydney Directory for 1858–9*. Sydney: Sands and Kenny.

Steele, Dominic. 1999. Trench H Report. In *The Cumberland/Gloucester Streets Site, The Rocks: Archaeological Investigation Report*, ed. Godden Mackay Heritage Consultants, vol. 3, 333–350. Sydney: Godden Mackay Logan Pty Ltd.

Wilson, Graham. 1999a. Ceramics and Tobacco Pipes Artefact Report. In *The Cumberland/ Gloucester Streets Site, The Rocks: Archaeological Investigation Report*, ed. Godden Mackay Heritage Consultants, vol. 4i, 205–366. Sydney: Godden Mackay Logan Pty Ltd.

———. 1999b. Trench A Report. In *The Cumberland/Gloucester Streets Site, The Rocks: Archaeological Investigation Report*, ed. Godden Mackay Heritage Consultants, vol. 3, 9–86. Sydney: Godden Mackay Logan Pty Ltd.

Chapter 9
The Commonwealth Block in Melbourne

This chapter presents a discussion of the historical background to cesspits from ten Lots on the Commonwealth Block, Melbourne (also called Little Lon and Casselden Place in the literature). It builds on previous publications by Murray and Mayne (Mayne and Murray 1999, 2001; Murray and Mayne 2001, 2003; Murray 2003, 2005, 2006, 2011, 2013), but the core of the specific documentation of the cesspits and associated structures draws heavily on the site reports created by Justin McCarthy for the Little Lon excavations (McCarthy 1989a, b) and by Godden Mackay Logan, Austral and La Trobe Universities for the second major phase (see Godden Mackay Logan et al. 2004a, b, c). It also reports some of the analysis of Lot 55A presented in the dissertation research by Paul Pepdjonovic (2012) and specific documentary research into the ownership and occupational histories of the houses and factories that comprised the Commonwealth Block precinct conducted by Barbara Minchinton for Murray's research there (see especially Minchinton 2014, 2017a, b).

Here our focus is on attempting to create credible links between the archaeological data derived from the excavation of places and the documentary data relating directly to those places. We will see that in some cases, those links can be established with reasonable certainty, but in others the archaeological record is too opaque to afford us a suitable level of confidence. In such cases the level of detail deriving from the documentary records is far more fine-grained than that flowing from the analysis of assemblages, raising important questions about the respective contributions to our overall understanding of the history of the precinct that can be made by archaeological and documentary evidence. At the end of this chapter, we will further characterise these questions by reporting stories about occupants (derived from Minchinton's research) that tell us much about life on the 'Commonwealth Block' but which cannot (at this point at least) be linked reliably to the archaeological record of its places.

© Springer Nature Switzerland AG 2019
T. Murray, P. Crook, *Exploring the Archaeology of the Modern City in Nineteenth-century Australia*, Contributions To Global Historical Archaeology, https://doi.org/10.1007/978-3-030-27169-5_9

A Brief History of Excavation

The archaeology of the Commonwealth Block (see Fig. 9.1) has been a cumulative exercise conducted first by private archaeological consultancies and in its penulti-mate stage by a collaboration between private consultancies and the La Trobe University Archaeology Department. The strong sense of continuity among the col-laborators was deliberate, with Justin McCarthy's Austral Archaeology having car-riage of the first major phase (that of Little Lon, sites A and C in Fig. 9.2) and a major stake in the excavation of site B (Fig. 9.2). This continuity was equally impor-tant in the development of the research questions and methodologies applied to the entire Block. Although Murray participated in the very early discussions convened by the then Victoria Archaeological Survey (now Heritage Victoria) prior to McCarthy's initial excavations, this input was largely peripheral to the perspectives of heritage architects and historians of Melbourne on the development of the initial research design. The balance of perspectives began to seriously change as a result of

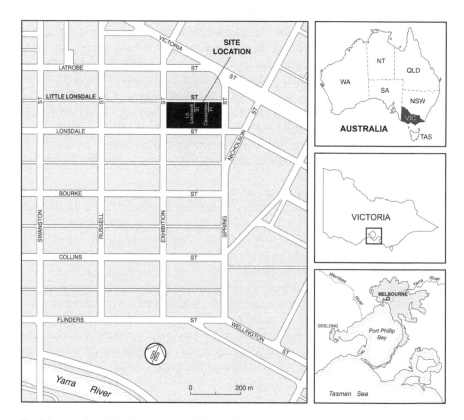

Fig. 9.1 Location of the Commonwealth Block. (Copyright owned by Murray)

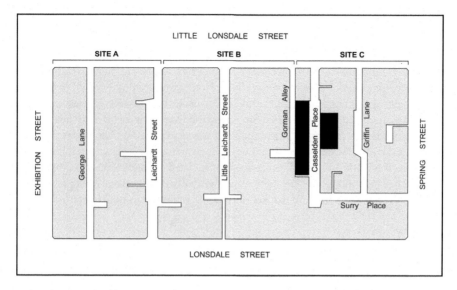

Fig. 9.2 Commonwealth Block, sites A, B and C. (Copyright owned by Murray)

a later collaboration between historian Alan Mayne and Tim Murray and bore fruit in the research design for the second major excavations at Casselden Place (site B). Subsequent research on the assemblages excavated from sites A, B and C conducted by Murray and Hayes (among others) further informed the creation of the research design for the final stage of excavation under the auspices of Godden Mackay Logan Heritage and La Trobe University.

Little Lon (1998)

From December 1987, Justin McCarthy undertook a 5-month excavation season. A tight development schedule meant that the work was conducted in a limited time and at short notice. The area excavated comprised sites A and C, approximately 6000 m^2 (Fig. 9.2). The excavation, conducted by four archaeologists with a team of volunteers over a 4-month period, revealed building foundations, hearths, cellars, cesspits and laneways. Due to multiple phases of occupation and concurrent demolition across the site, all deposits, with the exception of the 14 cesspits and some of the 11 rubbish dumps, were highly disturbed. A report of the excavation and finds was completed in 1988, and shortly thereafter the assemblage was transferred to Museum Victoria. At that time, the excavation at Little Lon was the largest urban archaeological investigation to have taken place in Australia (McCarthy 1989a, b). More than 200,000 artefacts were recovered.

Black Eagle and Oddfellows Hotels (1990)

McCarthy's 1989 report recommended that further investigation takes place on site B at the Commonwealth Block (Fig. 9.2). In 1990, archaeological investigation of the still extant Black Eagle and Oddfellows Hotels was conducted prior to the redevelopment of the buildings (McCarthy 1990). Both hotels were located on site B: the Black Eagle Hotel on Lonsdale Street and the Oddfellows Hotel on the corner of Little Lonsdale Street and Little Leichardt Street (Fig. 9.3). The excavation was conducted over a 5-week period and used the same recording and cataloguing processes as the Little Lon dig. The excavation focused on underfloor deposits within the hotels, and although the deposits were highly disturbed, a total of approximately 1710 artefact fragments were recovered. The assemblage was transferred to Museum Victoria in 1991.

17 Casselden Place (1995)

In 1995, a third season of archaeological investigation took place over 3 days at 17 Casselden Place within site B. The building on this site is one of the few remaining nineteenth-century cottages on the Commonwealth Block. The investigation monitored the removal of floors and recorded the underfloor deposits. A 1 × 1 metre test trench was also excavated within the cottage. A total of 1335 artefact fragments of the nineteenth- and twentieth-century provenance were recovered and deposited in Museum Victoria (Lane 1995).

Casselden Place Phase 3 Testing (2001)

The proposed development of the remainder of site B led to a test excavation to establish the archaeological potential of the area in 2001. A total of 4646 artefacts were recovered during this testing phase (Howell Muers et al. 2001). These were deposited at Museum Victoria.

Casselden Place (2002–2003)

A fifth season of excavation was conducted at Casselden Place in 2002–2003 by a team of archaeologists and volunteers from La Trobe University, Godden Mackay Logan and Austral Archaeology. The excavation was conducted in two phases: May to July 2002 and November to December 2002. It involved a more detailed exploration of site B prior to commercial development of the area. The excavation uncovered

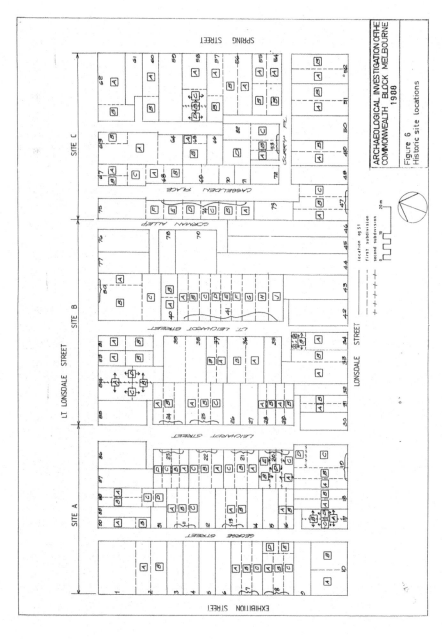

Fig. 9.3 Historic site locations on the Commonwealth Block. (Used with permission of Justin McCarthy and sourced from McCarthy 1989a)

similar features and deposits to the 1987 excavation including 25 cesspits and 9 rubbish pits. Approximately 296,000 artefact fragments were recovered, and an extensive program of cataloguing and analysis by a team of artefact specialists was undertaken. The report, electronic database, photographs and artefacts were deposited in Museum Victoria (Godden Mackay Logan et al. 2004a, b, c). More developed interpretations have been published in the *International Journal of Historical Archaeology* in 2006 (Volume 10/4) and Murray et al. (2019).

271 Spring Street (2017)

Excavation was conducted from mid-2017 by Godden Mackay Logan Heritage at the site of Industry Superannuation Property Trust (ISPT)'s redevelopment project known as 271 Spring Street and comprised much of the previously unexcavated sections of site C. Analysis of the excavated assemblage has yet to be completed, but preliminary studies indicate that its composition is broadly consistent with that found at the rest of the site. A total of 63,049 artefacts were recovered.

The most recent account of the archaeology of the 'Commonwealth Block' can be found in Murray et al. (2019), which focuses attention on the history and implications of our research there.

A Brief History of Analysis

Although archaeological and historical (primarily archival) research was first undertaken at Little Lon in 1988, and later in 1990 and 1995 (McCarthy 1989a, b, 1990; Lane 1995), comprehensive analysis of the site documents, artefact collections and documentary databases only really began in 1996 (Mayne and Murray 1999, 2001; Murray and Mayne 2001, 2003; Murray 2005). The goal of this later research, funded by the Australian Research Council, was to reconstruct life in a 'vanished community' and through this to critically assess the stereotypes of the slum and brothel district which had come to characterise the Commonwealth Block since the 1850s and which had influenced the research design of the Little Lon excavation. Those stereotypes of 'slumdom and brotheldom' were created during the nineteenth century and continued into the twentieth and twenty-first centuries (see Davison 1978; Davison et al. 1985; Leckey 2004). The Commonwealth Block was regarded, especially by social reformers of the time, as a sink of iniquity, a place of criminality, an area of vice and squalor, occupied by feckless itinerants.

Mayne and Murray considered that this was an unsatisfactory basis for understanding the social and cultural landscapes of the area. Mayne (1993) had already produced a historical critique of the nineteenth- and early twentieth-century slum stereotypes, and Murray and Mayne (2001) discussed an integrated approach, whereby historical archaeology could puncture slum stereotypes in order to piece together a more accurate picture of inner-city working-class neighbourhoods around the world. This approach has been applied to the analysis of the assemblage created through the excavation sites A and C by McCarthy (Fig. 9.2) (Mayne et al. 2000; Murray et al. 2019; Williamson 1998) and in Sydney (Crook et al. 2005; Crook and Murray 2004; Godden Mackay and Karskens 1994; Karskens 1997, 1999; Karskens and Thorp 1992; Murray and Crook 2005).

A renewed interest in urban historical archaeology focusing on the analysis of large and complex artefact assemblages and detailed research into relevant written documents had also born fruit in North America and South Africa (see the contributors to Mayne and Murray 2001; but see especially Praetzellis and Praetzellis 1992, 2005; Yamin 1998, 2000, 2001a, b) and built on fundamental research into artefacts and systems of interpretation that have guided urban historical archaeology since the late 1980s. We now know that inner-city communities during the nineteenth and early twentieth centuries were more socially and culturally diverse than the previous stereotypes have allowed, and new histories of cities are beginning to reflect this (e.g. Brown-May 1998; Cantwell and Wall 2001).

Melbourne's Commonwealth Block was a central city neighbourhood that existed for most of century (from roughly 1850 to 1950) as a place of working-class residence and employment. Intermeshed with these working-class networks was a complicated landscape of small-scale businesses and a cluster of large factories. Few traces now remain of this diverse community. Its people have long gone and, prior to excavation, the remains of the buildings and laneways were covered over by later structures and activities. Little Lon was a vanished community. Although constantly changing over its 'lifespan', change rapidly accelerated during the second half of the twentieth century and into the twenty-first century and introduced radically different forms and functions to the precinct.

Archaeological testing on previously unexcavated sections of Little Lon, listed as site B in Fig. 9.2 (Howell-Meurs et al. 2001; Long et al. 2001), confirmed the existence of deposits of similar complexity and importance to those originally revealed by McCarthy (1989a, b). McCarthy had identified three construction phases at Little Lon. The earliest phase of wood houses, followed by a phase of buildings with brick and bluestone; foundations, terminating in a phase of buildings with brick and concrete foundations. Excavation of sites A and C (the Little Lon site) revealed no unambiguous traces of the first phase, and McCarthy had emphasised the highly disturbed nature of the deposits as a result of taphonomic processes of horizontal and vertical displacement (through surface processes and building demolition) resulting in considerable mixing of deposits. A significant exception to this were cesspit deposits which were argued to have stratigraphic integrity on the basis of their being single-event abandonment phenomena.

The Little Lon sections of the Commonwealth Block exhibited a rich and highly varied assemblage spanning all of the major components expected on complex urban sites. Finds included figurines, fine china and quality wine and champagne vintages.

Our new perspective on the likely diverse nature of occupation in Little Lon, the work that had already been done in The Rocks in Sydney and in the initial analysis of assemblages from Little Lon, and the clear potential for a rich archaeological record at the Casselden Place site (site B), made it possible for us to frame several broad research themes that addressed the complex history of the site in a way that could recover the sense of a vanished community. These themes required us to do more than to simply rehearse a collection of stereotypes of the precinct as a slum, a place of poverty and deprivation and of brothels and criminality, an ethnic ghetto, the haunt of the socially and culturally marginalised and of course a place of commerce and industry.

Systematic excavation and analysis of site B were thought to have the potential to provide clear empirical information about places and the people who had lived there – what they ate and what things they used and threw away – that could be integrated with detailed documentary research about those places. It transpired that our expectations of the site and the assemblages we recovered from it were more than met after some 2 years of excavation and analysis (Godden Mackay Logan et al. 2004a, b, c).

Since 2003 the analysis of artefacts and contexts of site B has reached a level similar to that achieved for the assemblages derived from sites A and C. This assemblage-based research was also funded by the Australian Research Council and has allowed us to make significant strides towards developing an archaeology of the entire Commonwealth Block and to completely overhaul the site databases to the point where comparisons *within* the Commonwealth Block could be reliably undertaken. Perhaps the most important advances have been in defining the phasing of site B, describing the structural properties of that site and developing a firm basis on which to compare and contrast our existing analyses of sites A and C. These comparisons are the focus of this chapter and of ongoing research on the Block and a more complete publication of the archaeology of Melbourne, as well as underwriting potentially illuminating comparisons with sites in Sydney (see, for example, Crook and Murray 2004; Murray and Crook 2005; Murray et al. 2019).

The excavators recognised seven site phases for the whole Block. Phase I (pre-1837) covered the period of potential indigenous occupation of the site and ends with the official European settlement of the Port Phillip district. This phase includes the period of first contact and possible unofficial or ephemeral European occupation. Phase 2 (1837–1848) reflected the establishment of Melbourne and extends until the year in which the site was surveyed and subdivided making it available for development. Evidence of temporary or unofficial occupation of the place might well survive from this phase, but none has been unambiguously established. Phase 3 (1849–1890) covered the period of intensive (primarily domestic) occupation and subdivision until 1890, which marks the end of the economic boom that led to the depression in the following phase. Phase 4 (1891–1920) marked a change in the character of the site, with an increasing degree of mixed occupation by commercial and industrial enterprises as well as residences. This phase also covered the period of the First World War and includes the increasing presence of Chinese and other non-Anglo-Celtic occupants. Phase 5 (1921–1959) saw the Commonwealth Block being transformed into an almost exclusively light and heavy industrial zone. This was the period of 'slum clearance' following the Great Depression and the Second World War. Phase 6 (1960–1988) saw the closure of many of the industrial enterprises created during Phase 4 and the widespread demolition of standing structures as the Commonwealth of Australia prepared to redevelop the Block for government offices.

The Casselden Place site underwent a significant change as various sections of the block were acquired by the Commonwealth Government in preparation for redevelopment. During this phase the Commonwealth Block became part of Melbourne's expanding CBD fringe. Phase 7 (1989–2017) represented the period of redevelopment of the Block into three major office towers with a very small number of structures remaining from Phases 3–5. Development of the site has continued, with the final phase of archaeological excavation occurring in 2017.

These seven phases provide a chronological framework within which the deposits, structures and artefact assemblages exposed during the excavation of Little Lon and Casselden Place have been analysed. During the excavation of site B, a relative chronology for each excavation area was created, and these were arranged by Lot so that the storey of each occupation unit could be examined independently of its neighbours. The phasing system allowed separate Lots to be examined both individually and collectively (Fig. 9.3).

The conventional process of site phasing we have discussed represents the most fundamental integration of archaeological and documentary datasets, especially as it has established the units of analysis and comparison (both spatial and chronological) that support more the complex integrations presented here and elsewhere (Murray and Mayne 2001; Murray et al. 2019). This research is ongoing, but it is encouraging that the broad patterns of residence, the distribution of material culture and the complex mix of ethnicities and occupations that were noted by Mayne and myself for sites A and C seem broadly applicable to site B.

Commonwealth Block Stories

We have made it clear that a vital element of our original research agenda for the precinct had to do with seeking to provide a more accurate picture of life on the 'Commonwealth Block' between 1850 and 1950. Prior to McCarthy's initial excavations at Little Lon, the dominant image of the pace was one of slum dwellers experiencing dire poverty and attendant lawlessness. Indeed McCarthy's original research design could hardly avoid the image painted of the place by historians past and present (Annear 1996; Davison 1978; Davison et al. 1985). We have also outlined the origins and development of our own thinking about the historical archaeology of the place, which bore fruit in the extended research design for the second major phase of excavations at Casselden Place in 2002 (see also Murray et al. 2019).

The richness of the archaeological record of the Commonwealth Block has continued to be demonstrated through excavation and analysis. The documentary record of the precinct contains some evidence that can be readily aligned with the archaeological record, as we will discuss in the following account of the cesspits. Nonetheless it is also true that this absolutely does not exhaust the contribution that the documentary record can, and does, make to our exploration of a much more diverse and nuanced social history of the Commonwealth Block. In this sense the seemingly frequent absence of integrations between two such diverse datasets does not rule a meaningful contribution to reaching our overarching goal from *either* source on its own. We shall return to this point in the final paragraphs of this chapter.

Thus our overall impression of life on the Commonwealth Block derived from the documentary record is one of diversity of ethnicity and experience. While our original endeavour was to develop an account of the precinct that was fundamentally at odds with the tropes of 'slumdom' and 'brotheldom' using detailed analysis of the assemblages of artefacts and documents that recorded the lives of its inhabitants, we certainly do not shy away from the fact that crimes were committed in the precinct and that significant social and economic disadvantage existed there too. Our point has been that the Commonwealth Block was much more than this pretty lurid account, spanning important differences in the experiences of its inhabitants, not least of which were differences flowing from distinct ethnicities. Shaking the foundations of what have been long-running and highly popular accounts of prostitution, public drunkenness, robbery and street violence, deeply embedded in popular accounts of life in the nineteenth-century Melbourne, has been very difficult indeed and should be understood as being very much a work-in-progress (e.g. Murray 2005)!

In the next section, we outline the specifics of the Commonwealth Block study group, focusing on what we know of the occupants of each of these places at the times when the cesspit deposits were most likely to have been laid down. This is a highly particular account of those places. It does not include more detailed discussion of the lives of occupants from outside those target time periods nor does it focus on the lives of the people who owned those places and (most often) let them out to tenants. Our documentary research has uncovered a great many stories of people whose lives lie outside those pretty narrow confines, and it is our goal to publish more about them in the future. Our strong focus in this book is on limiting ourselves to discussions of documentary and archaeological assemblages that can be effectively integrated in ways that draws out the importance of empirical evidence in constructing new histories of the nineteenth-century city.

Introduction to the Study Group

The study group was composed of ten cesspits selected from all excavated cesspits located on the Commonwealth Block site, with the exception of the latest excavations at 271 Spring Street – which are still being analysed. Our goal was to create a viable cross-section of Lots and historical contexts across the site, which was based on an earlier estimation of potential analytical 'hot spots' on the 'Commonwealth Block' during the research design phase of the 'Casselden Place' project. What follows is a compilation of evidence about the archaeology of each place, a brief description of the assemblages recovered from each cesspit and a summary of the occupation histories of each place. Our focus is on linking the likely dates spanning the deposition of artefacts and ecofacts with the most likely occupants of the associated houses. For ease of reference, all artefact counts and descriptions of the components of the Commonwealth Block assemblage can be found in the relevant Tables in Chap. 10. The locations of all Lots listed below can be found on Fig. 9.3.

Lot 25C, Leichhardt Street (1851–1920)

From their earliest descriptions, the structures situated on Lot 25 were two-roomed brick houses. Peter Tucker's 1853 Will located one house on the northern section (27 × 51 feet) and two on the southern (20 feet 2 inches × 51 feet). The measurements of each dwelling vary over time with Lot 25A measuring 16 × 40 feet in 1865, 30 × 52 feet from 1867 to 1876 and then again from 1894 to 1899. During the intervening years (1877–1893), the measurements listed are 30 × 27 feet. Additionally, the property description included a coal shed in 1860. The two domiciles described on the southern section nearly always maintain the same dimensions. Between 1863 and 1865, they are listed as 18 × 40 feet, becoming 21 × 27 feet between 1870 and 1888 (25B lists 30 × 27 feet in 1883). From 1889 to 1893 the rate books list 30 × 27 feet followed by 24 × 27 feet (1894–99). The junior Peter Tucker's probate records describe the property as 'three small cottages composed of brick each containing two rooms. The records also note that the property was 'seldom let'. By the early decades of the twentieth century, the property was apparently in a state of disrepair. The Search Clerk Notes indicate that the southern portion (Lot 25B and 25C) had been abandoned by 1914, and probate records for Frederick John Tucker corroborate by describing the land as 'vacant and unimproved' with a value £300. In 1920 George Wharington's probate inventory records a two-roomed brick building on the northern portion of Lot 25 (25A) and claims that it, along with Lot 38, had been 'condemned by the Melbourne City Council and [was] unoccupied' (Godden Mackay Logan et al. 2004a, b, c, clxiv; MCC Rate Books; Citizens Rolls 1877–1882, 1888–1889; McCarthy 1989b, 168–169).

The Cesspit Fill (MC 1.010)

Lot 25C contained a complex of wall footings, concrete paving and drainage features and one cesspit. Cesspit 1.400 was rectangular in shape and lined with coursed, hammer-dressed bluestone rubble. The stonework was 30 cm wide on each side. The pit had a natural clay base, with internal dimensions of 1.80 m by 0.90 m in plan, and 1.35 m in depth. A deposit of clay fill (context 1.402) overlaid an artefact-rich deposit (1.010) at the base (Godden Mackay Logan et al. 2004b, 19). The cesspit was closed in April 1870 (Hayes 2011; Hayes and Minchinton 2016, 15).

Artefacts from the lower deposit 1.010 in stone-lined cesspit 1.400 were a mixed assemblage of glass, metal, bone and ceramic, largely recovered from the wet sieve. The glass and stoneware containers recovered from 1.010 included 153 beer/wine bottles and a range of other forms in smaller quantities, as well as fragments of a stoneware demijohn. One cherry stone and one plum stone were also recovered from 1.010 (see Tables 10.1, 10.2, 10.3, 10.4, 10.9 and 10.14). The cesspit was on site 25C, but there was only one cesspit for the three sites (25A, B and C) (Godden Mackay Logan et al. 2004b, 19).

Peter Tucker, and after his death his family, owned the property between 1853 and 1900. A variety of tenants occupied the property for between 1 and 2 years between 1851 and 1881. Chinese tenants were recorded in the late nineteenth and early twentieth centuries. The available directory and rate book information provides tantalising glimpses of these residents, but very little solid information has come to light thus far (Godden Mackay Logan et al. 2004c, clxiv-clxii; McCarthy 1989b, 168–169).

Overview of Occupants

William Smith (1868–1870)

Not much is known about Smith, save for the birth record of his son William Smith, born 15 August 1869 at the lying-in hospital. Smith was described as a labourer, aged 35, born in London, and William's mother was named Mary. Mary, aged 34, was born in Ballinasloe, Ireland. William and Mary were married in 1858. Mary was listed as having three children, Richard 8, John 6 and Catherine 4, from a previous marriage.

Jane O'Melia (1871–1872)

On 5 November 1873, Jane O'Melia married Andrew Thompson at the Registry Office Fitzroy. The records show that she was a widow in 1870. She was born in Down, Ireland, and had four living children and four dead. She is listed as a domestic, aged 41, living in Cardigan Street, Fitzroy. Her father was James McCulloch, a military man, and her mother was Jane McCushin. Andrew Thompson is recorded as a widower in 1871. He was born in Antrim Ireland, labourer, aged 40. He lived in Cardigan Street with Jane. Both were illiterate.

Table 9.1 Occupants of Lot
25C, Leichhardt Street

Years of occupation	Occupant name
1851–1852	John Murphy
1854	William Field
1857	Mrs Johnston
1858	Mrs Thompson
1859–1860	Alex Kinlock/Kimlock
1862	Peter Rimicke
1863	Mrs Robinson
1864	James Alley
1865–1867	Adolph Olingua
1868–1870	William Smith
1871–1872	James O'Melia
1873	Benson
1878	Mrs Parkins
1879	Charles Miles
	Hawker
1880	Alfred Draper
1881	Mrs Hurley
1897	Lue Tye

143 Lonsdale Street (1847–1918) (Lot 30)

The first building on the site 143 Lonsdale Street was a one-roomed wooden house
built in 1847–1848. By 1854, a brick house of four rooms and a kitchen was built,
and shortly after this a brick and stone extension was added (McCarthy 1989a, 128;
McCarthy 1989b, 182–185).

Cesspit M is located at the rear of Lot 30, a former residential house and shop site
on the corner of Leichhardt Street and Lonsdale Street. A square bluestone cesspit,
associated with a building on Lot 30 had been removed by demolition and development prior to the excavation (McCarthy 1989a, 20). However the backyard area was
intact and excavation revealed a wealth of information and artefacts. The pit was
sealed by the construction of the modern sewage system in 1899–1900. It is likely
that deposition occurred between 1875 and 1880. The bottles from this pit are of
later manufacture than from the other pits on site C. The main finds under the general demolition debris that covered this part of Lot 30 were three pits – a cesspit
(M), a bottle pit (N), and a small rubbish pit (O); Pit M was square in shape, constructed of bluestone and was about a metre in depth; it was filled with a wide variety of artefacts and was sealed by the modern type sewerage which had been
connected to this part of the site in 1899/1900 (McCarthy 1989a, 121–123).

The Cesspit Fill (Pit M)

Few of the recovered artefacts were datable by either maker's mark, pattern, decoration or technique of manufacture. Of this group artefacts were dated from reference
or local sources, with the bulk being ceramics or glass bottles. Five coins were also

found that had legible dates. These artefacts have an overall manufacture date range which extends from 1828. Most of the analysed ceramics were common domestic wares and included one toothpaste or bear grease pot (see Tables 10.1, 10.2, 10.3, 10.4, 10.9 and 10.14). There was a high percentage of bone material recovered from the pit, including both butchered and unbutchered examples from a range of animals. Other food residues were a large number of oyster shells and eight cherry seeds (McCarthy 1989a, 121–123). The cesspit was closed in January 1871 (Hayes and Minchinton 2016, 15).

Occupant History

The earliest records show that James Gamble owned the site, and a one-roomed wooden house situated there in 1847/1848; the house was then vacant. The next entry in 1854 and shows that in the intervening period a brick house of four rooms and a kitchen valued at £220 has been erected. In that year, the Council also received an Intention to Build Notice for 'an addition to the house (to be built of) brick and stone'. According to the records, no other changes were made to the house for the period that records were available (until 1918). Changes were apparently made in the yard and at the back of the house. In October 1857 an application to build a galvanised iron shed was received by the Council; in January 1858 an application to 'repair the fence and outbuildings at the back' was received. The final documented alteration to the site was an application of April 1871 'to build a wall with brick and stone including a fire place joining a right of way behind my premises'. At this time the premises are described variously as 'stone and brick house, five rooms and sheds' or 'brick and stone shop and four rooms'. The premises were used by various occupants as a residence as well as a place of business.Documents suggest that the property was a centre of prostitution between 1850 and 1900. Mrs Bond's store and Morris Cohen's furniture mart may have been cover for a brothel between 1876 and 1884. The different depositional patterns at the site may be a consequence of this (McCarthy 1989a, 127–129; McCarthy 1989b, 182–185).

The ownership of 143 Lonsdale Street changed regularly and the turnover of tenants was quite rapid. Between 1854 and 1856, it appears to have been used as a shop and residence. In 1857 Gamble let the place to Louis Amiet who named it the 'Swiss Boarding House' and managed it with others until 1861. Gamble sold the place that year (1861) and it was bought by George Gibbons who rented it out as a shop and residence. During Gibbons' period of ownership, 143 Lonsdale Street was used by a general dealer, a grocer and a pawn broker. In 1871 Gibbons sold to John F. Gunther a draper. Gunther made improvements such as building the back wall and used the premises himself as a shop until he sold it in 1876. In 1876 a Mrs Bond purchased the property and used it as a 'store' for 3 years. Between 1879 and 1885, two tenants used the premises as a furniture mart and a grocer's shop. There is a gap in the records between 1885 and 1889, but in the latter year, William Bond is given as the owner (presumably the husband of Mrs Bond), and he let the place to the first of the Chinese and 'Syrian' tenants who were to reside there. From 1889 to 1911 the shop had a variety of uses and was tenanted by predominately Chinese and 'Syrians' (most likely to have been Lebanese). Their occupations were listed as grocers, greengrocers, a bootmaker, importers of fancy goods, fruiterers and confectioners and a cabinet maker. In 1912 the premises were taken over by Annie and Joseph Kinnon who initially ran a drapers' shop and then became importers of fancy goods and drapery. They remained at the site at least until 1918 (McCarthy 1989a, 127–129; McCarthy 1989b, 182–185).

Overview of Occupants

Louis Amiet and others ran it as the 'Swiss Boarding House'. Thereafter George Gibbins, A. Bond, William Love, George Jameson and John Jamieson were the occupants. The longest occupant prior to Gunther was the Swiss Boarding House, but the most likely source of the artefacts is either George Jameson or John Jamieson, but most probably the latter.

John Jamieson (1870)

There are many 'John Jamiesons' in Melbourne at this time – at least four married in Victoria around 1869–1870. There is no entry in the Citizen rolls to tell us his occupation. It is possible that the entries in the rate book for 'Jamieson' and 'John Jamieson' are a continuation of the previous occupant 'George Jameson'.

John F. Gunther (1870–1875)

Johann Friederich Gunther was born in Germany about 1829 and came to Victoria about 1856. His future wife Theresa Heeb was born in Germany about 1837 and came to Victoria about 1857. Shipping records do not show her arrival. Theresa Heeb had an illegitimate daughter (Mary Ann Oatman) at Carisbrook in 1859 and married J F Gunther in 1861. He was a merchant and his father was a carpenter; she was described as a spinster and her father as a farmer.

J.F. Gunther bought 143 Lonsdale Street and set up a drapery there in September 1870. He and Theresa and Mary Ann lived there until he sold it in August 1875. From there they moved to Punt Road, South Yarra, where Theresa died in 1887. Mary Ann married another German emigrant in 1882 and had eight children by 1902, with only one dying young (aged 5) and the other seven living long lives in Victoria. When J F Gunther died in 1904, Mary Ann was living with him. His will, dated 14 November 1887, left everything to his daughter for her lifetime and there-after to her children, to be used for their maintenance until they reached 21 years. Gunther was a man some means. He left over £990 in the bank, about £300 in shares, a brick house of five rooms and a kitchen at 268 Punt Road South Yarra valued at £475 and two brick houses of five rooms and kitchens at 282 and 284 Punt Road South Yarra valued at £1000, which were let for 21/per week and 20/per week, respectively. Mary Ann died in 1909, leaving her children aged from 7 to 26, with the eldest son, aged 22. Gunther does not appear on any Victorian Electoral rolls, and there are no naturalisation papers for him. He was a Roman Catholic.

Table 9.2 Occupant list for
143 Lonsdale Street

Years of occupation	Occupant name
1854–1856	Charles Widman
1855	Charles Mercier
1856	Charles Gromann
1857–1861	Louis Amiet and others
1861–1863	George Gibbins
1863–1864	Vacant
1865	A. Bond
1866	William Love
1867–1868	George Jameson
1869	Vacant
1870	John Jamieson
1871–1876	John F. Gunther
1876–1879	Mrs Bond
1879	Morris Cohen
1880	James Maddigan
1882–1883	Morris Cohen
1884–1885	James Maddigan
1889–1911	Chinese and 'Syrian tenants

147 Lonsdale Street (1849–1950) (Lot 33B)

A brick house of two rooms was first recorded in 1849. The building at this Lot was
a shop and residence occupied by a number of tenants. Lot 33B was bounded on the
north by Eagle Alley, on the west by Lot 33A, on the south by Lonsdale Street and
on the east by Lot 34. Excavation exposed three rooms of a structure with stone
footings and a yard at the rear. A fourth room probably existed at the unexcavated
southern end of the structure. Lot 33B was created upon the subdivision of Nehemiah
Guthridge's original 1847 grant. The property measured 42 × 82 ft and was purchased in 1848 by Thomas Higginbotham who built a brick house on the Lot 33B
portion. An 1855 plan records a rectangular brick building fronting Lonsdale Street.
A small timber building is also shown apparently at the west end of Eagle Alley but
possibly at the rear of Lot 33B. The 1857 version shows a structure at the central
rear with its north wall in line with the Lot 34 boundary (Godden Mackay Logan
et al. 2004b, 96–110; McCarthy 1989b, 188–200).

The Cesspit Fill (MC 2.722)

A stone-lined cesspit (2.722), which appeared to have been cut into natural topsoil
(2.728), contained a residual fill (2.713/2.272) and was preserved in section at the
rear of the Lot. Artefacts recovered from Lot 33B are consistent with domestic
occupation although the assemblage may also have a nondomestic element. Tenants

Table 9.3 Owners list for
147 Lonsdale Street

Years of ownership	Owner's name
1848–1850	Thomas Higginbotham
1850–1879	William Brandt
1879–1888	Isabella Cornwall
1889–1913	George Ramsden and Executors
1913–1931	Peter Tucker Jr.
1931–1938	Leichardt Investment Proprietary Limited
1938–1950	Henry Edward Pett and Walter James Gorman

operating businesses at this Lot included a butcher, a bootmaker and Chinese cabinetmakers. Some of the deposits yielding numerous animal bones (e.g. 2.727 below the barrel cesspit) may relate to the butchery phase (1858–1872) (see Tables 10.1, 10.2, 10.3, 10.4, 10.9 and 10.14). No distinctive evidence of the Chinese occupation is evident in the assemblage. Few of the artefacts recovered from this Lot were useful for dating purposes (Godden Mackay Logan et al. 2004b, 96–110). The cesspit was voluntarily closed at some point before the installation of Cesspit 2.631 which was closed in October 1871 (Hayes and Minchinton 2016: 15).

Occupant History

The first tenants to occupy the site ran various businesses including a painter and a dress maker. From 1857 to 1872, butcher Henry Cornwell occupied the property. He had married Isabella Winter in 1856, and the births of eight of their children are recorded at this address. The family moved to adjoining Lot 33A in 1873. Some deposits appear to relate to the butcher phase of occupation. After this, cabinet makers rented the property, and then various other tenants before Chinese cabinet makers assumed tenancy in 1885 (Table 9.4).

All of the owners of Lot 33B also owned Lot 33A. These included William Brandt in 1850–1879, Isabella Cornwell in 1879–1888 and George Ramsden (later his estate) in 1888–1950. Tenancy records indicate two main businesses operated at the Lot during this period. First was Henry Cornwell's butchery in 1857–1872, followed by cabinet-making in 1874–1875, and from 1885 to at least 1918. In this later period, the occupants were Chinese. Brief tenancies included a carver and gilder (1876–1877) and a bootmaker (1879). Rate books describe the building variously as a shop, a house or as both. While the residential portion of the building may have been used at times for commercial purposes, it may be misleading to describe the premises as a 'shop' during these periods. For example, it is described as a shop during the tenancy of Henry Cornwell, but the family is also recorded as living there at that time (Godden Mackay Logan et al. 2004c, clxxvii; McCarthy 1989b, 188–200).

Table 9.4 Occupant list for 147 Lonsdale Street

Years of occupation	Occupant name
October 1848–June 1850	Thomas Higginbotham
1851–1852	Thomas Clapperton
1854–1855	Abraham Cohen
1856	Mrs Monk
1857	John Gee/Mrs Worrell
1857–1873	Henry Cornwell
1873	Vacant
1874	S. Smith
1875	A. Levi
1876–1877	Eleazer Mendoza
1878	Vacant
1879	Frederick Wolf
1880	Vacant
1881	Simeon Solomon
1881–1882	[Short-term tenancy]
1884	W. Watson/ Wing Loong
1885–1886	Ah An
1887–1892	Kong Goon
1894	Vacant
1895–1897	Chung Mow and/or Tung Shin
April 1897–1901	John Sing (Tung Shin)

Henry Cornwell or Cornwall (1857–1873)

Henry Cornwell was born at Tyssen Road, Stoke Newington, Surrey, to Edmund Cornwell and Ann Scott in 1834. His future wife Isabella Winter was born at Berwick-upon-Tweed, in 1836. In 1852 Henry Cornwell arrived in Australia, aged 18. In 1855 Isabella Winter arrived in Australia, aged 19. On 19 August 1856, they were married at St Peter's Church, Melbourne. At that time Cornwell described himself as an engineer (aged 23). Isabella (aged 21) had no occupation. On 31 October 1857, Henry and Isabella begin living at 147 Lonsdale Street, with Henry advertising himself as a butcher (Godden Mackay Logan et al. 2004c, clxxvii). Cornwell rented Lot 33B from 1857 to 1872. From August 1867 to November 1872, he also owned Lot 33A, which was leased to John Darbyshire and subsequently to Mrs Wallen.

In February 1879 the Cornwells bought the blocks on either side of Lot 33A – that is, Lot 32 and Lot 33B. Isabella bought Lot 33B for £930 with 'Henry Cornwell as consenting party only'; she also bought Lot 32. They appear to have occupied Lot 32 in 1884, and possibly also 1883 and 1885, but otherwise rented it to short-term tenants. Lot 33B had one longer-term (3 years) tenant, but was otherwise either vacant or had short-term tenants, suggesting that he bought the properties for their adjoining yards to his shop. In 1888 the Cornwells sold all three properties, but continued to rent Lot 33A [145 Lonsdale] until he sold the butcher business on 6 January 1890 to W.S. Arthur. In the 18980s the Cornwells lived in the nearby suburb of North Fitzroy and by 1899 at his home 'Corinella' in the adjacent suburb of Northcote. He died in 1915.

Lot 36A, Little Leichardt Street (1851–1898)

A brick house of three rooms was recorded on Lot 36A by 1852.

The Cesspit Fill (MC 1.230)

A large number of cultural features were exposed in Lot 36A. These included small brick structures, drains, postholes, earth-cut pits and cesspits.

In the extreme southwest corner of Lot 36A, preserved below the terracotta pipe 1.228 and the west end of wall footing 1.224 was a small, deep cesspit (1.230). Lined with hammer-dressed bluestone, the cesspit measured 1.05 m by 1.0 m across internally and 1.70 m deep above a flat clay base. Six metres to the east was a barrel-lined cesspit. With 26 staves forming the body of the barrel, preserved for up to 60 cm above the base, the cesspit was 80 cm deep. A number of circular postholes (including 1.299, 1.303, 1.304 and 1.305) were also exposed around the edge of the cesspit cut (1.275). The cesspit was voluntarily closed (Hayes and Minchinton 2016: 15) probably in the 1860s or early 1870s.

The fill deposit 1.231 in cesspit 1.230 yielded a significant quantity of glass and stoneware fragments (see Tables 10.1, 10.2, 10.3, 10.4, 10.9 and 10.14). Forty-five of these were whole bottles, often recovered in an upright position, suggesting they were placed, rather than thrown, into the pit. Large fragments of a near-complete stoneware demijohn were also found in fill 1.231. In addition, the fill deposit 1.231 yielded four fragments of a large iron spouted kettle and 160 fragments of wire-cut and wrought iron nails (Godden Mackay Logan et al. 2004b: 32–37).

Occupant History

Lot 36A had a complex history of ownership and construction in the second half of the nineteenth century. A brick house of three rooms was recorded in 1851–1852, owned by Mary Quinn. The ownership was passed to J Wareham in 1856, Thomas Geril in 1857 and back to Mary Quinn in 1861. The years 1860–1861 saw the property rated as having two brick houses, one of three rooms and one of two rooms. It is highly likely in this case that Lots 36A and 36B were assessed together. By 1868 the listed owner was James Henry Quinn, with a house of two brick rooms. The ownership was passed to George Howes in 1871, to John Howes in 1878 and to Mrs Annie Emma (Howes) Bates in 1879, who was still rated as owner in 1893. Between 1903 and 1932, the property was owned by the brothers James and Hugh Paterson [and their executors], who were painters and decorators. There were six different tenants of the property during the 1850s and another six during the 1860s. Charles Edward and Margaret Patzold leased the property between 1871 and 1893 (Godden Mackay Logan et al. 2004b, clxxvii; McCarthy 1989b, 209–213).

The property changed ownership regularly. There were 12 tenants during the 1850s and 1860s. From 1871 to 1893, Charles Edward and Margaret Patzold were long-term tenants. Margaret moved to Lot 38 when she was widowed (Godden Mackay Logan et al. 2004b, clxxvii; McCarthy 1989b, 209–213) (Table 9.5).

A succession of very short-term tenants occupied the dwelling in 1871. Note that the property is listed as being vacant in 1868–1870.

Charles Edward and Margaret Patzold (1871–1893)

The Patzold family arrived in Melbourne on the *LINDA* from Hamburg in November 1863. They were Prussians: mother Johanna, father Ferdinand (listed as 'farmer') and three children (Ernestine 24, Carl 18 and Johann 10). By the time Carl married Margaret Milley 6 years later (1869), he had changed his name to 'Charles Edward Patzold', but he seems to have more commonly used 'Edward'. He was a cabinetmaker; she was a 'domestic'. Margaret came from Kilkenny, Ireland, and was working as a 'domestic' when they married.

Charles Edward and Margaret started their married life living in Park Street, East Collingwood, but by the end of 1873, they were at Lot 36A and lived the rest of their lives in the area. Edward and Margaret Patzold had only one child; their daughter Catherine was born in 1872 and died after 5 days. Ferdinand Patzold (Edward and Joseph's father) died at the Northcote Convent (Little Sisters of the Poor) in 1895, and it is possible that Edward was also living there from this time until his death at the Convent in 1900. He does not seem to have been residing at Lot 36A, which is listed in Sands and McDougall as 'Mrs Margaret Patsol' alone. The condition of entry to the Little Sisters of the Poor convent was to have no other means of support,

Table 9.5 Occupant list for Location.36A	Years of occupation	Occupant name
	1849–1850	Thomas Sherwin
	1851–1852	W. Sutherland
	1853	Mrs Watson
	1854–1855	A. Altman
	1856	J. Warham
	1857–1858	Thomas Geril/Geirl
	1860	Thomas Bremer
	1862	Harris ? lich
	1863	George Twile
	1864	Hart/Mrs Turner
	1865–1867	Roger Ainsworth
	1868–1870	Vacant
	1871–1893	Charles Edward and Margaret Patzold
	1894–1898	Vacant

and in general the definition of 'aged' was 'over 60'. Edward was only 56 when he died of 'senile decay' (dementia), which presumably made living at home impossible (Godden Mackay Logan et al. 2004a, b, c Vol. 4, clxxvii; Minchinton 2014).

147 Spring Street (1849–1918) (Lot 55A)

A two-roomed house with a kitchen was built at 147 Spring Street by 1849–1850. It was owned by Samuel Morris from 1849 to 1855, and he lived in the property himself but also tenanted the premises. Morris was a plasterer and operated his business from the building. The property was sold to J. Haggerty in 1856 and was extended to four rooms. The place was leased to various tenants until 1872 when carpenter Thomas Judd purchased the property. It appears that Judd owned and occupied the house until 1892 after which time he let it to tenants. He also owned Lot 57B (McCarthy 1989a,76; McCarthy 1989b, 303). The size of the property was first recorded in 1866 measuring 24 × 40 feet (18 × 30 feet in 1874, 18 × 60 feet in 1876) and then 36 × 70 feet with six rooms by 1889, following additions and a recorded notice for a two-storey renovation by Thomas Judd in 1884 (McCarthy 1989b,304). The value of the site also fluctuated from £20 to £80 averaging around £60 pounds as recorded by probates (McCarthy 1989b, 303–304).

The Cesspit Fill (Cesspit B)

This was formed as a barrel cesspit over wooden planks. The cesspit was dug in Lot 55B section but was probably originally in the yard of the building on Lot 55A. The cesspit dates from 1849 to 1890. Cesspit B totalled nearly 6000 sherds, weighing 11.6 kilograms with a MNV of 153 ceramic and 40 glass vessels, and is highly fragmented (McCarthy 1989a, 117) (see Tables 10.1, 10.2, 10.3, 10.4, 10.9 and 10.14). The cesspit was closed in December 1871 (Hayes and Minchinton 2016, 15) (Tables 9.6 and 9.7).

255 Spring Street (1849–1918) (Lots 57A and B)

No. 255 Spring Street (Lot 57 on Fig. 9.3) was also known as 153 Spring Street in the Rate Records. Excavation of 255 Spring Street revealed bluestone and brick foundations of what the excavators thought to be related a quite a substantial house. The

Table 9.6 Owners list 147 Spring Street

Years of ownership	Owner's name
1849–1855	Samuel Morris
1856–1873	J. Haggerty (Hagerty)
1874–1898	Thomas Judd

Table 9.7 Occupant list 147
Spring Street

Years of occupation	Occupant name
1849–1850	George Brookes
1851–1852	Arthur Trevor Jones
1853	Samuel Morris
1854	Samuel Morris and Kirkam Stewart
1855	Samuel Morris and Ellen Usher
1856	Haggerty
1857	Mrs Thompson
1858	Mrs Pink/Pimm
1860	J. Haggerty/Mrs Nash
1861–1862	Mrs Nash
1863	Vacant
1866	Aaron Solomon
1868	William Wilmot
1869	Mrs Kennedy
1872–1880	Thomas Judd
1882–1884	Michael Vanstan
1887–1892	Thomas Judd
1893	Maria Stumpf
1894	Mrs Norris and Mrs Alice Lily
1897	Mrs Alice Lily
1898	Sarah Stanly
1899	Mrs Elizabeth Brown
1908	Mrs Mary Jones
1911–1913	Mrs Jane Ross
1915	Peter Hughes
1917	Robert Gilmour
1918	Vacant

foundations of all the walls appeared to be intact. The building was rectangular in shape with two equal size areas at the front that were probably divided into four rooms; behind this there was a single room, half the width of the front rooms; further behind this was a similar size brick extension. The bluestone foundation walls all appeared to be original, but the brick walls were post-1900 and had been built over the sewer line (McCarthy 1989a, 110). Records establish that Lot 57A had two owners between 1849 and 1915: Thomas Player until 1894 and Wallace and Railton thereafter.

The Cesspit Fill (Cesspit H)

Pit H was a cesspit which consisted of a wooden barrel or cask placed over a small square brick-lined pit. Pit H was built right on the boundary of 57A and 57B and may have served both properties. Pit J was also a cesspit and consisted of a barrel or cask with a clay outer lining sitting on horizontal lengths of timber. Under the timber beams supporting the barrel were the organic contents of an earlier cesspit. This sequence shows the evolution of the sanitary system most clearly (McCarthy 1989a, 110–111).

The Cesspit Fill (Cesspit J)

Pit J was associated with Lot 57B. The cesspit was voluntarily closed at an unknown date (Hayes and Minchinton 2016: 15), before a replacement barrel cesspit was installed. Pit J was a cesspit and consisted of a barrel or cask with a clay outer lining sitting on horizontal lengths of timber. This is a classic example of the type of cesspit advocated by the Central Board of Health, under the timber beams supporting the barrel were the organic contents of an earlier cesspit. This sequence most clearly shows the evolution of the sanitary system at Little Lon (McCarthy 1989a, 117–119). The cesspit was voluntarily closed at an unknown date (Hayes and Minchinton 2016, 15) (Table 9.8).

Ownership History

The original Crown Grant was made to Henry Boorn Foot, who then sold it to Thomas Cosier. Thomas Cosier left Lot 57 to his widow Mary Cosier, and after her death, she left it in trust to her two daughters, Ruth and Caroline. Mary married Thomas Player in 1848. On 12 October 1853, Mary Cosier registered the property signing the memorial 'Mary Player late Mary Cosier widow'. From 1853 to her death in 1892, Mary Cosier/Player collected rents and paid rates on Lot 57.

Lots 57A and 57B were owned by Thomas Player. According to the MCC valuation books and the directories, Thomas Player let the house to tenants for most of the period that it shows in the records (from 1851 to 1874). Player himself only lived in the house for a year or so in 1856 and again in 1870, although the records are scant from 1866 to 1874. In 1874 the rate books show that Player sold the house to Thomas Judd and that a person by the name of Hobson or Hodgson was the tenant (McCarthy 1989a, 110–119; 1989b, 312–316) (Table 9.9).

Lot 57B Cesspit appears to have been combined with Lot 57A, 255 Spring Street (also known as 155 Spring Street), from 1870 onwards, with the following occupants (Table 9.10):

Thomas and Mary Player (1856, 1870–1876)

Thomas Player was a Tasmanian convict. He was born in Bristol about 1818 and transported for 14 years at the age of about 15 for 'stealing from the person' – he said he stole a handkerchief from his master. He was convicted at Bristol on 2 July 1832 and arrived in Van Diemen's Land on 14 November 1833. His gaol report said his 'Connexions V. bad', but his report from the hulk was good. His only offence at Port Arthur was 'making use of insolent and contemptuous language to the schoolmaster' for which he suffered a 5-day solitary confinement on bread and water, but he gained his ticket of leave on 14 November 1838 (5 years after his arrival) and his conditional pardon on 14 December 1840. He was awarded his free certificate in 1846 (14 years after his conviction). He came to Victoria on the same year (Tasmanian convict number 56601 on the *Isabella*; Conduct report CON 31/1/35; Free Certificate No. 569).

Mary [Cosier] was born about 1810 and married Thomas Cosier in Oxfordshire. They had two children before arriving in Victoria about 1842 (England Census, Oxfordshire, Thame, piece 883, book 3, folio 9, page 12). Thomas was a carpenter, and died at the age of 43, leaving all his property (Lot 57, 153 Spring Street) to his wife for her use during her lifetime and thereafter to be held in trust for their daughters (PROV VPRS 460 PO 42928).

Thomas Cosier died in January 1848, and later that year, Mary married Thomas Player. Their first and only child was born the following year, but he died at the age of 1 in 1851, leaving Mary's two daughters as their only children. Thomas Player was a bootmaker, but he bought a property in Simpson's road (now Victoria Street, Richmond) and described himself as 'farmer' in 1856. It appears that Thomas and Mary may have had some years living apart about that time. Thomas published a notice in the *Argus* in January 1860 warning that 'ALL persons are hereby CAUTIONED against GIVING CREDIT to, or purchasing from, my wife, Mary Player, as I will not be responsible for any debts she may contract', and his bootmaking business moved to Collingwood and then to Fitzroy. However it was back at 153 Spring Street in 1864, and he and Mary were certainly together when she died in 1892. It is also possible that his notice was related to her dementia (evident at the inquest), but it would have been a very early onset if so (Minchinton 2014; SCN 42928).

Table 9.8 Occupant list 255 Spring Street	**Years of occupation**	**Occupant name**

Years of occupation	Occupant name
1849–1854	Thomas Player
1855	Thomas lee
1856	Miss Miriam Allcock/Edward Farmer
1857	Edward Dash
1858	James Cater and Edward Dash
1859	Thomas Player
1860	Mrs Hobart and Thomas Player
1861–1863	Vacant
1867–1876	Thomas Player
1877	Vacant
1878–1881	James Winter
1882–1891	James Morris
1891–1893	William Dunlop
1894–1896	F. Piercy/James Morris
1896	Frank O. Pearson
1898	Thomas Lilley
1899–1907	Mrs Alice Lily
1908–1910	Assid Hamaty
1911–1912	Florence Spry
1913–1924	Colonial Rubber Works
1915–1918	Richard Homsie

Table 9.9 Occupant list for Location 57A

Years of occupation	Occupant name
1851–1852	Patrick Purcell
1854	James Hayes
1855	Llewelyn Llewelyn
1856	Thomas Player
1857	J. Francis Collens
1858	Dupont
1860	Jonathan Harrison
1863	Mary Anne Hayes
1866	Mrs Caffray/Caffrey
1870	Thomas Player

Table 9.10 Occupant list for Location 57B

Years of occupation	Occupant name
1870–1876	Thomas Player
1876–1877	John Hennessy
1878	James Winter

7 Casselden Place (1851–1909) (Lot 69)

This house has been fully described by Murray and Mayne (Murray and Mayne 2002, 2003). What follows is a brief summary of the fill deposits and an outline history of the long-term occupants, the Maloney family.

The cesspit was located on a block of land that came to be designated Lots 69A and 69B. According to the Melbourne City Council valuation books, a wooden house of three rooms and valued at £8, owned by Lewis Hawkins, existed on the site in 1851–1852. The entry of 1854 shows the effect of the gold rush on property values as the wooden 'cottage' is now valued at £70. There was a new owner (Mrs Taylor) and a new tenant (Edward Thompson). In 1855 it was sold to a Mr Mulrooney, with one Patrick Ryan as tenant; the value had dropped to £30. In 1856 it was bought by J. Maloney with Patrick Ryan still the tenant and the value then was £15. During Maloney's period it is most often described as a 'wooden house', although in 1870 it is called a 'shanty' and in 1876 a 'wood shanty', and the value was a mere £6. From 1857 to 1863, it is described variously as also having a 'cow shed', 'cow yard' and a 'shed'. When Mrs Neylan acquired the property, the wooden house was demolished in 1891 and was replaced by a brick house of three rooms. Mrs Neylan and family continued to live there until at least 1898. (McCarthy 1989a, 107–108).

The Cesspit Fill (Cesspit A)

The cesspit was voluntarily closed at an unknown date (Hayes and Minchinton 2016: 15).

Some 2492 artefacts were recovered from this cesspit, and only about 10% were considered to be datable by either maker's mark, pattern, decoration or manufacture technique (see Tables 10.1, 10.2, 10.3, 10.4, 10.9 and 10.14). The ceramics almost all proved to be Staffordshire wares with their manufacture dates falling within the period 1802 to 1871. Most of the ceramics were common domestic wares. The glass artefacts from this pit indicate a date range from about 1840 to 1870. The range of functional types of bottles from this pit reflects the characteristics of the general bottle assemblage. The main functional categories represented include alcohol (black glass porter and 'wine' bottles, green glass wine and champagne bottles); aerated waters/ginger beer (Hamilton-type bottles and 'dump' sodas in glass and stoneware); pharmaceutical bottles; pickle, salad oil and vinegar bottles; and perfume bottles. The only type not represented are ink bottles in either stoneware or glass. Other glass artefacts found in this pit included fragments of a cut glass vase, drinking tumblers and chemists' vials. No absolute dates were obtained for this material, but the style and manufacture techniques indicate the 1860s (McCarthy 1989a, 106–109) (Table 9.11).

John Moloney arrived in South Australia in 1849 from County Clare, Ireland, with his sister Margaret and younger brother Edward. They sailed on the *Constance* with other 'government emigrants' who were mainly from the Shirley Estate in County Monaghan. Their sister Hannah arrived at Portland (again, from London) in July 1852 and went to work at Emu Creek (NW of Maryborough) for 6 months on £20 p.a. plus rations. The family was Roman Catholic, and Margaret and John, at least, were illiterate. John Moloney bought Lots 69A/B, Casselden Place, on 18 October 1854 for £345. John's will left a life interest in his house to his 'sister Hannah Moloney of Little Lonsdale Street' and thereafter to his 'sister Margaret Neylan of Little Lonsdale Street East'. By 1884 Margaret Neylan was living at 7 Casselden Street – John's house; Hannah died there in 1886. Thomas's wife Bridget had died in 1885. In 1887 Margaret moved to 5 Casselden Street while no 7 was rebuilt in brick (McCarthy 1989a, 107–108; Minchinton 2014).

Table 9.11 Occupant list for 7 Casselden Place	Years of occupation	Occupant name
	1854	Edward Thompson
	1855–1856	Patrick Ryan
	1856–1882	John Maloney

128 Little Lonsdale Street (1850–1910) (Lot 84A)

In 1847, Phillip Oakden purchased this land under the original crown grants. Historical records identify the earliest structure on Lot 84A as a two-roomed house built before 1849/1850, which in 1851/1852 was described as a six-roomed dwelling with coach house. Just 3 years later, Lot 84A was recorded as having two dwellings, one with six rooms and one with two rooms. However, by the time of Bibb's 1855 map, there was only one structure on this site, an L-shaped building with a front yard extending towards Little Lonsdale Street. Two houses are recorded in 1855 and

Table 9.12 Owners of 128 Little Lonsdale Street

Years	Name and building
1849–1850	William Raven *[house 2 rooms]*
1851–1853	Robert Scott *[house 6 rooms and coach house]*
1854	Thomas Banchell/William Merryfield *[brick house 6 rooms, stable and yard]*
1855–1867	William Hinds

again in 1880 and 1899. The 1899 plan shows a structure to the northwest of Lot 84A. Between 1855 and 1864, the six-roomed house was described as operating as a boarding house. By 1910, the L-shaped brick and bluestone structure was demolished and replaced by a two-storey factory (Godden Mackay Logan et al. 2004b, 23–25; Godden Mackay Logan et al. 2004c, ccxxix; McCarthy 1989b, 413–415).

The Cesspit Fill (MC 1.023)

The cesspit is lined with bluestone with a cement base. The fill comprised glass and stoneware items. A two-roomed house existed at this Lot in 1850, and by 1851 there were six rooms in a large brick building and a stable. The building was listed as a boarding house from 1855 to 1864. William Thomas continued as a boarding house keeper at this property from 1859 to 1870. Various short-term tenants occupied the property at other times. During Stage 1 of the Casselden Place excavations, a cesspit (1.023) was excavated. Subsequent analysis of historical plans has demonstrated that it actually fell within the boundaries of Lot 84A. Pit 1.023 was located at the south end of Lot 84A. Its walls were made of hammer-dressed bluestone up to 30 cm thick. The cesspit measured 1.10 m × 1.30 m (inside dimensions) and 80 cm deep. It featured a flat, 40 mm-thick cement base (1.258), laid over the underlying clay (1.259). The upper fill (1.024) of cesspit 1.023 was removed by backhoe and found to contain low levels of contaminants (Godden Mackay Logan et al. 2004b, 239–243). The cesspit was voluntarily closed at an unknown date (Hayes and Minchinton 2016, 15).

Tenants Occupancy

From 1874 there are two houses on the site. At the front there was a brick house of five rooms and a yard and at the rear a brick house of three rooms (Godden Mackay Logan et al. 2004a, 23–25; Godden Mackay Logan et al. 2004b, 239–243; Godden Mackay Logan et al. 2004c, ccxxix; McCarthy 1989b, 413–415).

Table 9.13 Occupants
of 128 Little Lonsdale Street

Years of occupation	Occupant name
1849–1850	William Raven
1851–1852	Robert Scott
1854	Thomas Blanchell
1855	Mrs Lloyd
1856	Mrs Simpson
1857–1859	William Hinds
1861–1867	William Thomas

Tenants of the Front Dwelling

Table 9.14 Occupant list for
the front dwelling of 128
Little Lonsdale Street

Years of occupation	Occupant name
1868–1871	William Thomas
1871	James Sheppard
1875	Vacant
1876	Mrs Mullins
1877	George Mullins
1878–1879	Henry Lighton
1880	Vacant

Tenants of the Rear Dwelling

The deposits have a TPQ of 1872 probably linked with Frederick Haberhauffe, but sadly we know little about him, beyond this notification in *The Argus* of 6 May 1880 which refers to the disposal of the property of the late William Kennon, who was the owner of Lot 41, Leichhardt Street, and Lot 43, Lonsdale Street:

> 'By order of Messrs Hugh Kennon and Harry Emmerton, Executors of the Will of William Kennon, Esq, Deceased have received instructions from the executors of the will of William Kennon, Esq., deceased to SELL by PUBLIC AUCTION, in their rooms, 45 Swanston street, on Thursday, 26th May, 1880, at twelve o'clock,
> LONSDALE STREET,
> All that piece of land, part of Allotment 5, Section 25, Melbourne, having a frontage of 29ft 4in to Lonsdale street by a depth of 72ft 6 in., on which are erected some brick sheds, occupied by Mr Haberhauffe as a cigar manufactory, at a nominal rent of 8s per week'.

Table 9.15 Occupant list for the rear dwelling 128 Little Lonsdale Street

Years of occupation	Occupant name
1874	Vacant
1875–1876	Frederick Haberhauffe
1877	Frederick Cooke
1878	Vacant
1879	John Williams
1880	Alfred Fletcher
31 July 1912	Lim Yen
17 July 1913	Lim Yow

Off 73 Little Lonsdale Street (1847–1918) (Lots 90A and B)

A one-roomed, brick house owned by James Merritt was present on the site in 1847–1848. Rooms had been added and it was being used as a residence and shop by 1849–1850. John Daly purchased the property in 1854 and leased it to many tenants. Many different businesses operated from the location over time. Lots 90A and 90B were originally separate but were amalgamated in 1858 (McCarthy 1989a, 129). From 1860 until 1898, the property changed ownership a number of times. From 1872 until 1880, bootmaker Theodore Oden was a long-term resident (McCarthy 1989a, 132–135; 1989b, 443–446).

The Cesspit Fill (Cesspit T)

Cesspit T was an early type of cesspit constructed as a hole in the ground without lining except for planks which may have been a cover. This pit appears to relate to the building at Lot 90. No above ground remains of the building at this Lot remained, and it was highly disturbed. Artefacts date from 1812 until about 1880, including two intrusive artefacts dating to 1879 and 1930 (Hayes and Minchinton 2016, 15). The cesspit was closed in December 1870 (Hayes and Minchinton 2016, 15).

Occupant History

The first entries in the rate books for this Lot indicate that a brick house of one room was extant in between 1846 and 1847 and that it was owned by James Merritt. The next entry for 1849/1850 describes the building as a house, with three rooms and shop, still owned by Merritt. The basic description of the house does not alter from this period (except for minor alterations such as the addition of a kitchen and sheds). John Daly bought the house from Merritt in 1854. He lived in the house himself in 1855, but from then on leased the property out to a large number of tenants. Daly owned the house until at least 1860. In 1866 the owner is given as A. O'Rourke. Different members of the O'Rourke family owned the place until about 1880 when a Miss Castle became the owner until about 1898.

Various activities were undertaken on the site. From 1849/1850 until 1855, it was used as a residence and (unspecified) shop. In 1856 it was a boarding house. In 1858 it was again a shop; in 1859 it was a grocers shop; in 1860 it was a residence and 'dealer's' shop. In 1861 it was to have its first use as a shoe and bootmakers shop by Luigi Nanuzzi, after which it was often used for this purpose. In 1862 John Bohn took it over as a bootmakers shop and residence and was in business there until 1872. Theodore Oden replaced him as a bootmaker until 1880 and in 1895 and 1908 by another bootmaker, Robert Harris. The coincidence of the sale of the property from the O'Rourkes to Miss Castle and the quitting of long-term resident Theodore Oden, both of which occurred in 1880, may have some significance for the artefacts recovered from the pit. Their deposition may have been related to a clean-up at this time (McCarthy 1989a, 132–135l; 1989b, 443–446) Table 9.16 lists the occupants of Lots 90A and 90B.

John C. Bohn (1862–1872)

John Christian Bohn was born in Germany in 1803, where his father was a farmer. He married there at age 20 and had at least two daughters (Caroline and Louise) before he emigrated to the Australian Colonies in 1848. His wife and family (including Caroline's husband and daughter) followed in 1853. Caroline had married in Hamburg and had at least two children in Melbourne before her husband died in 1865; he was a restaurant keeper at 153 Great Collins Street, Melbourne. She remarried in 1867 and moved to Forbes NSW. John Bohn, or John C Bohn, set up business as a shoemaker at 110 Little Lonsdale St in 1862 when he was nearly 60 years of age. He worked there for about 10 years before moving to Forbes in NSW to be with his daughter. He died there at the age of 80 in 1883 and was listed as 'shoemaker' on his death certificate (Minchinton 2014; NSW death records NSW 1883/7677).

	Years of occupation	Occupant name
Table 9.16 Occupant of 110 Little Lonsdale Street	1847–1848	James Merrit
	1849–1850	George Sefton
	1851–1852	Benjamin Brothwell
	1854	Richard Wilson/Alexander Chard
	1855	John Daly
	1856	Harrn Weitmann/Patrick Joyce
	1857	J. Leary/P. Meyer
	1858	Woodman/Mrs Ward
	1859	Charles Cuff
	1860	Owner J. Daly or tenant Walter Lavette
	1861	Luigi Nanuzzi
	1862–1872	John C Bohn
	1873	Anton Fox
	1873/1874–1880	Theodore Oden
	1882–1887	Edward Tipper
	1888	Vacant
	1889	E. Tipper/Mrs Brown
	1891	E. Tipper/Miss Brown/Scott
	1892	Miss Brown/David Green
	1894	Moukpat Shekrey
	1895–1908	Robert Harris
	1910–1913	A.H. Jack
	1915–1918	Charlie Hing Lee

Concluding Remarks

We have made it clear that a vital element of the original research agenda for the precinct had to do with seeking to provide a more accurate picture of life on the Commonwealth Block between 1850 and 1950. Prior to McCarthy's initial excavations at Little Lon, the dominant image of the place was one of the slum dwellers experiencing dire poverty and attendant lawlessness. Indeed McCarthy's original research design was much influenced by accounts of the place by historians past and present. We have also outlined the origins and development of our own thinking about the historical archaeology of the Block, which bore fruit in the extended research design for the second major phase of excavations at Casselden Place in 2002 (see Murray et al. 2019). Significantly a more intense engagement with a wider corpus of documentary data has been the main driver of this reassessment of 'life on the Commonwealth Block'. However, having said this, it is vital to remember that the impetus for this reanalysis came from the archaeologists working on the site. The requirements of intense site documentation, particularly information about occupants and owners and the evolution of structures on the site, supported a very profitable reassessment of the history of the Block. Archaeological data have played an important role in this reassessment, but we need to be clear that there is still much work to be done in revealing the nature and depth of that importance.

We now very briefly report three narratives that exemplify a related point about history-making in the nineteenth-century city. Here we return to an earlier discussion about the limits of integrating evidence drawn from the archaeological and documentary records about specific places (such as house lots). What follows are document-based narratives of occupants who left no clearly identifiable traces in the archaeological record of the Commonwealth Block, because they were *owners, not occupiers*. These narratives offer perspectives on the sheer diversity of the human experience of the area and mark the importance of inquiries into the owners of the house lots as well as their occupants. They are drawn from a wide variety of documentary sources used to create lot histories and additional sources such as shipping records, newspapers, police records and probates to flesh out information about specific occupants of those places. As such their relevance to our present inquiry has to do with contextual matters. Often owners and occupiers were not one and the same, but there can be little doubt that each shaped the histories of each of our target places. We shall return to this discussion in Chap. 11.

Madam Diana De Beaumont aka Madame Diane de Beaumont-Beaumbac: Owner of Lots 26 and 27, Leichardt Street

Diane De Beaumont-Beaumbac first came notice in 1863, when she was reported as running a licensed brothel at the Old Ship Inn, Clarence Street, Sydney. Unfortunately for her (at least), she had to leave Sydney in a hurry when a street prostitute died in her premises after an attack of *delirium tremens*. Although no conviction was recorded against her, it must have been clear that getting out of town was a good idea. We next hear of her a few months later when she fetched up in Melbourne in connection with a licence for the Mistletoe Hotel in Mackenzie Street (near Victoria Street, not far from the 'Commonwealth Block'). A few months later again, she appears to have had the licence for the All Nations Hotel at South Melbourne. However in the following year she was insolvent, describing herself as a 'widow'. Despite this setback, Madame de Beaumont was back in business by the end of 1864 at the Café Français at 223 Great Bourke, where she had a 'private room for ladies'. The courts heard later that the 'private room' was more likely to be used for sly-grog consumption than for genteel coffee-drinking, although she does appear to have spoken French (her first advertisements in Sydney were in both French and English). By 1871 she had moved to 144 Russell Street, where she ran a 'fruit shop' selling fruit, confectionery and refreshments. It must have been a very lucrative business, since a thief managed to steal 'five diamond rings, three diamond brooches, two diamond bracelets and other jewellery to the value of £300' from her safe.

Her next brush with the police was not nearly so positive. In December that year, she was charged with procuring young girls for her brothel. Running a house of ill-fame was one thing, and sly-grog selling could be forgiven, but decoying and ruining innocent girls was something else. She left Melbourne, again with no conviction recorded, and disappeared from history. Given her previous activities, it is at least likely that she took up business somewhere else – under an assumed name.

Diana De Beaumont owned two properties in Leichardt Street, and while she was a 'spinster' when she bought them in 1870 and 1871, she made a statutory declaration in 1873 when she sold them to Mrs Bond saying that she was a widow 'and had been for over 20 years' indeed.

Mary and George Williams: Tenants of Lot 26, Leichhardt Street (1871–1876)

The Williams were husband and wife career criminals who were also tenants of Madame de Beaumont for part of their time on the Commonwealth Block and nearby areas. In 1855 Mary Anne Copley (as she was then) arrived in South Australia from Ireland as an assisted immigrant. In 1864 George Williams arrived in Adelaide on *Lord Raglan* from London. They were married, and in 1870 George and Mary Williams travelled from Adelaide, South Australia, to Melbourne on *Coorong*. Between 1871 and 1872, Mary Williams rented Lot 41A, Little Leichardt Street; from 1871 to 1873, Mary Williams rented Lot 26, Leichardt Street (Madam de Beaumont's); and between 1874 and 1876, George Williams rented the same address. Theirs (and Madame de Beaumont's) stories align closely with the powerful slum narrative of the Commonwealth Block.

William Hinds: Owner of Lot 84A, Little Lonsdale (1853–1895)

William Hinds and his wife were both born in Ireland but married and had their first child (son James) in Scotland. They emigrated as assisted passengers on the *Thomas Arbuthnot* to Port Phillip in 1841. They were described as 'farm servants', but they do not appear to have lived outside Melbourne after their arrival in Port Phillip. By 1851 they had a grocer shop in Queen Street, and by 1854 they had moved to Spring Street where they ran the Ulster Family Hotel. Four more children were born in Melbourne, but only two survived to adulthood. Son James married and had three children before dying in 1867 at the hotel, aged 27. The two daughters both married and had numerous children.

From 1854 onwards William Hinds was a publican, owning and running what became the New Treasury Hotel in Spring Street. He accumulated a substantial property portfolio, including a house in Camberwell named after his birthplace ('Coleraine-villa'), another in Hawthorn, and houses in Leichardt Street and Lonsdale Street and in Bennett's Lane. His estate was valued at approximately £15,000 when he died in 1895.

References

Unpublished Sources

Application – Applications for Certificate of Title: Supporting Documents Relating to the Issue of Torrens Titles Under the *Transfer of Land Act* are Held at PROV in VPRS 460 Applications for Certificate of Title.

Directory – Data Extracted from Post Office Directories Held by SLV [Microfiche at PROV]: PP=Port Phillip Directories, B=Bailliere's, SK=Sands & Kenny, SM=Sands & McDougall.

Cesspool closures: PROV VPRS 3103 MCC Health Committee Reports.

Godden Mackay Logan, Austral Archaeology and La Trobe University. 2004a. Casselden Place, 50 Lonsdale Street, Melbourne, Archaeological Excavations Research Archive Report, Volume 1: Introduction and Background. Melbourne: ISPT and Heritage Victoria.

———. 2004b. Casselden Place, 50 Lonsdale Street, Melbourne, Archaeological Excavations Research Archive Report, Volume 2: Trench Reports. Melbourne: ISPT and Heritage Victoria.

———. 2004c. Casselden Place, 50 Lonsdale Street, Melbourne, Archaeological Excavations Research Archive Report, Volume 4(i): Appendices. Melbourne: ISPT and Heritage Victoria.

Howell-Meurs, J., C. Williamson and P. Davies. 2001. Casselden Place Development Phase 3. Testing Results, 2 vols. Unpublished Report to Industry Superannuation Property Trust. Melbourne: Andrew Long and Associates.

Lane, S. 1995. Archaeological Investigation of the Cottage at 17 Casselden Place, Melbourne. Unpublished report to the Heritage and Environment Group, Australian Construction Services.

Leckey, J.A. 2004. Low, Degraded Broots? Industry and Entrepreneurialism in Melbourne's Little Lon, 1860–1950, unpublished Ph.D. dissertation, Department of History, University of Melbourne, Melbourne.

Long, A., C. Williamson, M. Goulding and J. Howell-Meurs. 2001. Casselden Place Development Phase 3. Archaeological Planning Report. Unpublished report to Industry Superannuation Property Trustees. Melbourne: Andrew Long and associates.

McCarthy, J. 1989a. *Archaeological Investigation of the Commonwealth Offices and Telecom Corporate Building Sites. The Commonwealth Block, Melbourne*, Volume 1. Report to Department of Administrative Services and Telecom Australia, Melbourne, VIC.

———. 1989b. *Archaeological Investigation of the Commonwealth Offices and Telecom Corporate Building Sites. The Commonwealth Block, Melbourne*, Volume 5: Appendices. Report to Department of Administrative Services and Telecom Australia, Melbourne, VIC.

———. 1990. *Archaeological Investigation. Site B, the Black Eagle and Oddfellows Hotels, the Commonwealth Block, Melbourne Victoria*, 2 vols. Unpublished report to the Department of Administrative Services.

MCC Val Bk — Melbourne City Council Valuation Field Books [VPRS 8915].

MCC Rate Bk — Melbourne City Council Rate Books [PROV VPRS 5708 P/9 online or Microfiche].

Intention to Build – Melbourne City Council Notices of Intention to Build [PROV VPRS 9288].

OLM — Old Law Memorial, 'Old Law Library', LandVic at Laverton.
SCN — Search Clerk Notes, 'Old Law Library', LandVic at Laverton.
CT – Certificate of Title, LandVic [database available at Laverton].
Minchinton, B. 2014. 2014 Research – Report 4, 29 September 2014. In Murray's possession.
Williamson, C. 1998. Slums and Sluts: Lonsdale Street Project Report. Unpublished report for the La Trobe University, Melbourne.

Published Sources

Annear, R. 1996. *Bearbrass: Imagining Early Melbourne*. Melbourne: Reed Books.
Brown-May, A. 1998. *Melbourne Street Life; The Itinerary of Our Days*. Melbourne: Australian Scholarly Publishing.
Cantwell, A., and D.D. Wall. 2001. *Unearthing Gotham: The Archaeology of New York City*. New Haven: Yale University Press.
Crook, P., and T. Murray. 2004. The Analysis of Cesspit Deposits from The Rocks, Sydney. *Australasian Journal of Historical Archaeology* 22: 44–56.
Crook, P., L. Ellmoos, and T. Murray. 2005. *Keeping up with the McNamaras: A Historical Archaeological Study of the Cumberland and Gloucester Streets Site, The Rocks, Sydney*. Sydney: Historic Houses Trust of NSW.
Davison, G. 1978. *The Rise and Fall of Marvellous Melbourne*. Melbourne: Melbourne University Press.
Davison, G., D. Dunstan, and C. McConville. 1985. *The Outcasts of Melbourne: Essays in Social History*. Sydney: Allen & Unwin.
Godden Mackay, L., and G. Karskens. 1994. The Cumberland/Gloucester Streets Site, The Rocks: Archaeological Assessment and Research Design. Godden Mackay Heritage Consultants for the Sydney Cove Authority and the Heritage Council of NSW.
Hayes, S. 2011. Amalgamation of Archaeological Assemblages: Experiences from the Commonwealth Block Project Melbourne. *Australian Archaeology* 73: 13–24.
Hayes, S., and B. Minchinton. 2016. Melbourne's Waste Management History and Cesspit Formation Processes: Evidence from Little Lon. *Australian Archaeology* 82 (1): 12–24.
Karskens, G. 1997. *The Rocks. Life in Early Sydney*. Melbourne: Melbourne University Press.
———. 1999. *Inside the Rocks, The Archaeology of a Neighbourhood*. Alexandria: Hale and Iremonger.
Karskens, G., and W. Thorp. 1992. History and archaeology in Sydney: Towards Integration and Interpretation. *Royal Australian Historical Society Journal* 78: 52–75.
Mayne, A. 1993. *The Imagined Slum: Newspaper Representation in Three Cities, 1870–1914*. Leicester: Leicester University Press.
Mayne, A., and T. Murray. 1999. 'In Little Lon … Wiv Ginger Mick': Telling the Forgotten History of a Vanished Community. *Journal of Popular Culture* 33 (1): 49–60.
———, eds. 2001. *The Archaeology of Urban Landscapes: Explorations in Slumland*. Cambridge: Cambridge University Press.
Mayne, A., T. Murray, and S. Lawrence. 2000. Historic Sites: Melbourne's 'Little Lon. *Australian Historical Studies* 31 (114): 131–151.
Minchinton, B. 2017a. Prostitutes' and 'Lodgers' in Little Lon: Constructing a List of Occupiers in Nineteenth-Century Melbourne. *Australasian Historical Archaeology* 35: 64–70.
———. 2017b. Women as Landowners in Victoria: Questions from Little Lon. *History Australia* 14 (1): 67–81.
Murray, T. 2003. *Exploring the Modern City: Recent Approaches to Urban History and Archaeology*. Sydney: Historic Houses Trust of NSW.F.
———. 2005. Images of 'Little Lon': Making History, Changing Perceptions. In *Object Lessons: Archaeology and Heritage in Australia*, ed. J. Lydon and T. Ireland, 167–185. Melbourne: Australian Scholarly Press.

————. 2006. Integrating Archaeology and History at the 'Commonwealth Block': 'Little Lon' and Casselden Place. *International Journal of Historical Archaeology* 10 (4): 395–413.

————. 2011. Research Using Museum Collections Need Not be a 'Vale of Tears', Though It Often Is. In *Caring for Our Collections. Papers from the Symposium 'Developing Sustainable, Strategic Collection Management Approaches for Archaeological Assemblages'*, ed. C.H.F. Smith and T. Murray, 79–88. Melbourne: Museum Victoria.

————. 2013. Expanding Horizons in the Archaeology of the Modern City: A Tale in Six Projects. *Journal of Urban History* . first published on March 6, 2013 as. https://doi. org/10.1177/0096144213479308.

Murray, T., K. Buckley, S. Hayes, G. Hewitt, J. McCarthy, R. Mackay, B. Minchinton, C. Smith, J. Smith, and B. Woff. 2019. *The Commonwealth Block, Melbourne: A Historical Archaeology*. Sydney: Australasian Society for Historical Archaeology.

Murray, T., and P. Crook. 2005. Exploring the Archaeology of the Modern City: Issues of Scale, Integration and Complexity. *International Journal of Historical Archaeology* 9 (2): 89–109.

Murray, T., and A. Mayne. 2001. Imaginary Landscapes: Reading Melbourne's 'Little Lon. In *The Archaeology of Urban Landscapes: Explorations in Slumland*, ed. A. Mayne and T. Murray, 89–105. Cambridge: Cambridge University Press.

————. 2002. *Vanished Communities: Investigating History at 'Little Lon', An ARC Funded CDROM*. Melbourne: La Trobe University and Swish Group.

————. 2003. (Re)Constructing a Lost Community: Little Lon: Melbourne, Australia. *Historical Archaeology* 37 (1): 87–101.

Pepdjonovic, P. 2012. 'One man's trash': A Historical Archaeological Insight into 19th Century Working Class Domestic Practice, at 'Little Lon', Melbourne. Unpublished BA (Hons.) dissertation, Archaeology Department, La Trobe University.

Praetzellis, A., and M. Praetzellis. 1992. Faces and Facades: Victorian Ideology in Early Sacramento. In *The Art and Mystery of Historical Archaeology: Essays in Honor of James Deetz*, ed. A.E. Yentsch and M.C. Beaudry, 75–99. Florida: CRC Press.

Praetzellis, M., and A. Praetzellis, eds. 2005. *Putting the 'There' There: Historical Archaeologies of West Oakland, 1-880 Cypress Freeway Replacement Project*. California: Anthropological Studies Center, Sonoma State University.

Yamin, R. 1998. Lurid Tales and Homely Stories of New York's Notorious Five Points. *Historical Archaeology* 31 (1): 74–85.

————. (ed.) 2000. Tales of Five Points: Working-Class Life in Nineteenth-Century New York. Reports prepared for Edwards and Kelcey Engineers, Inc. and General Services Administration (Region 2), 6 vols. John Milner Associates, West Chester, Pennsylvania.

————. 2001a. Becoming New York: The Five Points Neighbourhood. *Historical Archaeology* 35 (3): 1–5.

————. 2001b. Alternative Narratives: Respectability at New York's Five Points. In *The Archaeology of Urban Landscapes: Explorations in Slumland*, ed. A. Mayne and T. Murray, 154–170. Cambridge: Cambridge University Press.

Chapter 10
Domestic Consumption: Patterns and Comparisons

Overview of the Selected Deposits: A Basis for Comparison

Roughly contemporaneous cesspit backfills present an excellent basis for the numerical comparison of material culture. Numerous studies built on cross-comparative analysis have provided fascinating insights into life in the modern city (see Chap. 7). As we have demonstrated in the previous two chapters, there is great variability in cesspit construction, and not all cesspits were filled equally. It is unwise to suppose that all cesspit backfills are equally representative assemblages of household contents. For this reason, it is important to draw out the similarities and differences between the nature of the deposits selected for study, so that similarities and differences between their contents may be more confidently interpreted.

The first factor to consider is the size of each assemblage. Across the study sample, the total sherd count varies from 804 to 10,409 sherds with an average of 3778. The recorded weight varies from 5.3 to 136.8 kg with an average of 36.8 kg (see Table 10.1). This is a considerable range. When considering both sherd count (Fig. 10.1) and weight (Fig. 10.2), it is clear that the Melbourne assemblages are larger in total, and mostly on average, than the Sydney deposits. This requires some contextualization when interpreting patterns observed in household deposits throughout this chapter. Within each group, the range is reduced but still significant. The largest Sydney assemblage, 124 Cumberland Street, with nearly 6400 artefacts is eight times the size of the smallest assemblage, 1 Carahers Lane (804 items) and 2000 sherds more than the second largest assemblage, 3 Carahers Lane. The largest Melbourne assemblage, 128 Little Lonsdale Street, with 10,409 sherds is nearly five times the size of the smallest assemblage, 147 Lonsdale Street, with 2172 sherds.

© Springer Nature Switzerland AG 2019
T. Murray, P. Crook, *Exploring the Archaeology of the Modern City in Nineteenth-century Australia*, Contributions To Global Historical Archaeology, https://doi.org/10.1007/978-3-030-27169-5_10

Table 10.1 Quantity and weight of sherds from all classes in each assemblage

City	Building code (MC)	No. of sherds	%	Weight[a] (kg)	%
Sydney	Cara 001 (B197)	804	3.4%	13.1	6.2%
	Cara 003 (B077)	4331	18.3%	20.0	9.5%
	Cara 005 (B294)	1190	5.0%	6.9	3.3%
	Cumb 122 (A138)	1695	7.2%	20.9	9.9%
	Cumb 124 (A310)	6385	27.0%	41.2	19.5%
	Cumb 126 (A140)	2170	9.2%	37.9	17.9%
	Glou 097 (C056)	2786	11.8%	40.0	18.9%
	Glou 097 (C220)	1113	4.7%	8.9	4.2%
	Glou 101 (C130)	1071	4.5%	5.3	2.5%
	Glouc 093 (F044)	2115	8.9%	17.4	8.2%
	Subtotal	23,660	100.0%	211	100.0%
Melbourne	Cass 007 (Cesspit A)	2492	4.8%	31.7	6.0%
	Leic L25C (1.010)	7446	14.4%	136.8	26.0%
	Lons 143 (Cesspit M)	4074	7.9%	30.5	5.8%
	Lons 147 (2.722)	2172	4.2%	24.6	4.7%
	LtLei L36A (1.230)	7431	14.4%	112.3	21.4%
	LtLon 073 (Cesspit T)	3118	6.0%	64.9	12.4%
	LtLon 128 (1.023)	10,409	20.2%	39.7	7.6%
	Spri 147 (Cesspit B)	5899	11.4%	11.6	2.2%
	Spri 255 (Cesspit H)	6107	11.8%	50.2	9.5%
	Spri 255 (Cesspit J)	2448	4.7%	23.3	4.4%
	Subtotal	51,596	100.0%	525	100.0%
Total		**75,256**		**736.9**	

[a] Weights were only recorded for artefacts physically inspected during re-analysis projects, excluding certain items on display or missing

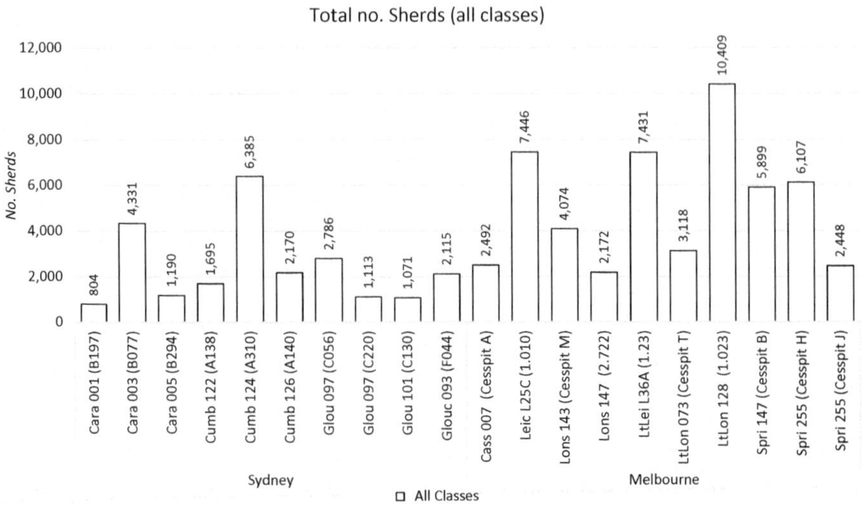

Fig. 10.1 Total number of sherds (all classes) in each assemblage

Fig. 10.2 Total weight of sherds (all classes) in each assemblage

These variances are reduced further when we consider the minimum number of vessels (Table 10.2, Fig. 10.3). Six assemblages contain a minimum of approximately 300–430 vessels and the rest are below 250. There is a clear dominance of ceramic to glass vessels which in part reflects the high breakage rate of glass and the smaller proportion of diagnostic features. This is reflected clearly in the ratio of sherds to MNV (Fig. 10.4) with more glass sherds per MVC than ceramic. Overall, there was a range of 3.7–15.7 sherds per minimum value allocation – with the notable exception of 147 Spring Street which has 26.5 fragments per minimum count. This demonstrates the importance of using MVCs (Schiffer 1987, 19–20; Sussman 2000; Crook et al. 2005, 31–32); analysis based on sherd count alone would significantly exaggerate the size of these three assemblages.

Given the exclusion of building materials, bone and shell from the study, it is necessary to briefly examine the frequency of sherds to characterize the composition of each assemblage (see Figs. 10.5 and 10.6, Tables 10.1 and 10.2) as there is no available weight and MVC data to compare with the other classes.[1]

All deposits are dominated by ceramic, glass and bone and share a relatively regular distribution with regard to material class (Fig. 10.5 and Table 10.3). The relatively small proportions of building materials[2] (under 10%) can be misleading, as, for example, the 1.5-m-deep rubble fill in cistern–cesspit of 93 Gloucester Street was recovered separately (see Chap. 8).

---

[1] As noted in Chaps. 7 and 8, weights were not recorded, nor MVCs calculated in the original phases of cataloguing for either CUGL or CB.

[2] The artefact class 'building materials' include bricks, roof tiles, sewerage pipes, plaster samples and the like. Nonstructural items, such as nails, door handles and brackets, appear under 'metal'.

Table 10.2 Minimum number of vessels, sherd counts and average number of sherds per MVC for ceramic and glass

City	Bldg code (MC)	Sherds			Minimum number of vessels			Average sherds per MVC		
		Ceramic	Glass	Total sherds	Ceramic	Glass	Total MNV	Ceramic	Glass	Cer. and glass Avg.
Sydney	Cara 001 (B197)	332	173	505	107	31	138	3.1	5.6	3.7
	Cara 003 (B077)	477	1340	1817	144	75	219	3.3	17.9	8.3
	Cara 005 (B294)	502	237	739	176	31	207	2.9	7.6	3.6
	Cumb 122 (A138)	452	546	998	119	62	181	3.8	8.8	5.5
	Cumb 124 (A310)	2365	1695	4060	337	79	416	7.0	21.5	9.8
	Cumb 126 (A140)	602	649	1251	159	46	205	3.8	14.1	6.1
	Glou 097 (C056)	624	896	1520	162	83	245	3.9	10.8	6.2
	Glou 097 (C220)	345	209	554	118	21	139	2.9	10.0	4.0
	Glou 101 (C130)	221	222	443	86	28	114	2.6	7.9	3.9
	Glouc 093 (F044)	438	353	791	103	53	156	4.3	6.7	5.1
	Subtotal	6358	6320	12,678	1511	509	2020	4.2	12.4	6.3
Melbourne	Cass 007 (Cesspit A)	1000	659	1659	113	50	163	8.8	13.2	10.2
	Leic L25C (1.010)	1223	5470	6699	206	222	428	5.9	24.6	15.7
	Lons 143 (Cesspit M)	888	1227	2115	123	61	184	7.2	20.1	11.5
	Lons 147 (2.722)	591	536	1184	107	36	143	5.5	14.9	8.3
	LtLei L36A (1.230)	686	4080	4974	125	219	344	5.5	18.6	14.5
	LtLon 073 (Cesspit T)	1709	916	2633	303	112	415	5.6	8.2	6.3
	LtLon 128 (1.023)	1832	2507	4339	228	122	350	8.0	20.5	12.4
	Spri 147 (Cesspit B)	870	4217	5112	153	40	193	5.7	105.4	26.5
	Spri 255 (Cesspit H)	1923	2125	4048	293	91	384	6.6	23.4	10.5
	Spri 255 (Cesspit J)	549	800	1349	113	34	147	4.9	23.5	9.2
	Subtotal	11,271	22,537	34,112	1764	987	2751	6.4	22.8	12.4
Total		**17,629**	**28,857**	**46,790**	**3275**	**1496**	**4771**	**5.0**	**17.5**	**8.8**

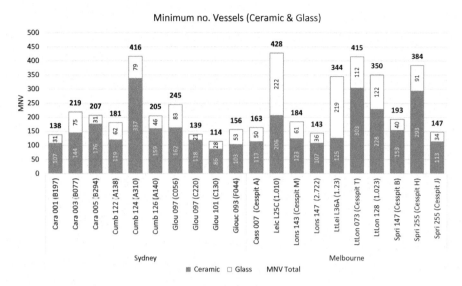

Fig. 10.3 Minimum number of ceramic and glass vessels in each assemblage

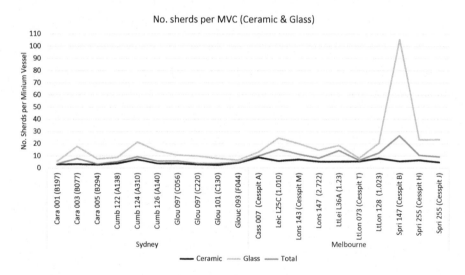

Fig. 10.4 Average number of sherds per MVC

Looking at the relative composition shown in the percentage chart (Fig. 10.6), 3 Carahers Lane is the most striking, being nearly half comprised of bone and shell refuse (most of this is fragmentary), with a greater proportion of glass vessels and a relatively small ceramic assemblage. It is clear that 3 Carahers Lane and Lot 36a Little Leichardt Street have a disproportionately small ceramic assemblage. The high proportion of organic material at 255 Spring Street suggests the discard of more short-term refuse than hard rubbish.

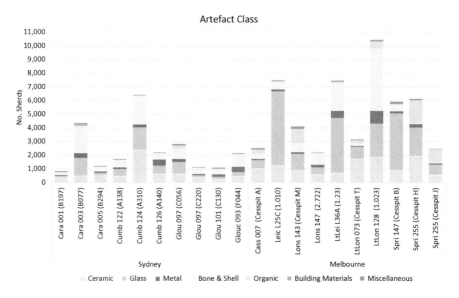

Fig. 10.5 Total number of sherds from each artefact class in each assemblage

Table 10.3 Quantity of sherds from each artefact class in each assemblage

City	Bldg code (MC)	Ceramic	Glass	Metal	Bone and shell	Organic	Building mat.	Misc.	Total
Sydney	Cara 001 (B197)	332	173	63	148	2	81	5	804
	Cara 003 (B077)	477	1340	338	1950	31	177	18	4331
	Cara 005 (B294)	502	237	94	303	4	43	7	1190
	Cumb 122 (A138)	452	546	124	524	–	11	38	1695
	Cumb 124 (A310)	2365	1695	202	2081	4	22	16	6385
	Cumb 126 (A140)	602	649	445	438	8	15	13	2170
	Glou 097 (C056)	624	896	210	737	198	49	72	2786
	Glou 097 (C220)	345	209	84	420	7	42	6	1113
	Glou 101 (C130)	221	222	178	352	–	93	5	1071
	Glouc 093 (F044)	438	353	373	890	3	30	28	2115
	Subtotal	6358	6320	2111	7843	257	563	208	23,660

(continued)

Table 10.3 (continued)

City	Bldg code (MC)	Ceramic	Glass	Metal	Bone and shell	Organic	Building mat.	Misc.	Total
Melbourne	Leic L25C (1.010)	1223	5470	130	477	102		44	7446
	Lons 143 (Cesspit M)	888	1227	114	650	1017	6	172	4074
	Lons 147 (2.722)	591	536	190	828	4		23	2172
	LtLei L36A (1.230)	686	4080	504	1999	80		82	7431
	Spri 147 (Cesspit B)	870	4217	149	463	26	1	173	5899
	Spri 255 (Cesspit H)	1923	2125	257	69	1639	15	79	6107
	Spri 255 (Cesspit J)	549	800	80	–	995	4	20	2448
	Cass 007 (Cesspit A)	1000	659	88	346	280	63	56	2492
	LtLon 128 (1.023)	1832	2507	920	4532	515		103	10,409
	LtLon 073 (Cesspit T)	1709	916	62	169	224	1	37	3118
	Subtotal	11,271	22,537	2494	9533	4882	90	789	51,596
Total		**17,629**	**28,857**	**4605**	**17,376**	**5139**	**653**	**997**	**75,256**

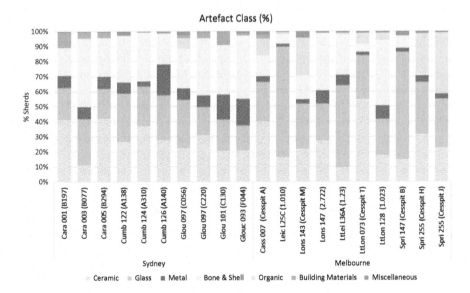

Fig. 10.6 Percentage of sherds from each artefact class in each assemblage

Integrity

The integrity of vessels is another important consideration. Overall, the Melbourne assemblages have a higher number and proportion of complete, near-complete (>90%) and substantially complete (>75%) glass and ceramic vessels (Table 10.4, Figs. 10.7 and 10.8). No. 7 Casselden Place (Cesspit A) and (off) 73 Little Lonsdale Street have the most intact assemblages. Of the Sydney assemblages, 122 Cumberland Street, 1 Carahers Lane and 97 Gloucester Street have the greatest number and percentage of intact fragile items, followed by 3 Carahers Lane and 124 Cumberland Street, but 'substantially intact' vessels comprise no more than one quarter of the assemblage. In contrast, McCarthy and Ward (2000: 122) reported one cesspit fill from a privy pit fill in Minneapolis for which more than half the vessels were over 75% complete.

Three Sydney deposits were significantly disturbed. 1 Carahers Lane was partly destroyed by a machine base for the Engineering Works. 101 Gloucester Street and the second cesspit fill at 97 Gloucester Street were disturbed by later repairs to the water closets. The refuse pits of MC A310 in 124 Cumberland Street were disturbed, but the cesspit fill itself appeared to remain intact. In Melbourne off 73 Little Lonsdale Street (Cesspit T) also has intrusive element: an 1879 Ridgway's plate in a pit known through MCC records to have been closed in December 1870. This sherd is presumed to have been introduced during later sanitation works. All other deposits were intact.

Dating

The establishment and revision of *terminus post quem* (TPQ) dates was a significant component of the assemblage analysis for both study groups (see Chaps. 8 and 9 and Table 10.5). For the Melbourne assemblages, we were guided by the detailed historical research of cesspit closures prepared by Barbara Minchinton and dating determined by Sarah Hayes (Hayes and Minchinton 2016). A small number of revisions were made to the TPQs on closer examination of the catalogue records. For cesspits with no record of closure, the assemblages are based on their TPQ alone. Dates were discussed in Chaps. 8 and 9 and have been summarized in Table 10.5.

In Sydney, Karskens's historical research established the date of the introduction of the sewerage line in 1866 (Sewerage and Water Supply, 10th report, 1866 1867; Karskens 1999a, 89), but records of individual connections to and from, and supersession of pits from one type to another, were not readily available.

Five of the nine Sydney cesspits converted to sewerage had TPQs predating the introduction of sewer lines in 1866 – an unsurprising result of deposition lag. Altogether seven of the deposits were backfilled in the late 1860s, probably during the same installation episode. That is, when the sewer came down the street, nearly all houses took the opportunity to connect. While the backfills do share temporal

Table 10.4 Intactness of glass and ceramic vessels and containers in each assemblage

City	Bldg code (MC)	Complete/near complete	Substantially complete	10–50%	<10%	Unidentified	Total
Sydney	Cara 001 (B197)	29	91	37	105	243	505
	Cara 003 (B077)	71	75	193	206	1272	1817
	Cara 005 (B294)	4	–	51	218	466	739
	Cumb 122 (A138)	127	142	132	74	523	998
	Cumb 124 (A310)	157	318	515	337	2733	4060
	Cumb 126 (A140)	6	16	112	117	1000	1251
	Glou 097 (C056)	177	84	149	83	1027	1520
	Glou 097 (C220)	16	8	67	40	423	554
	Glou 101 (C130)	12	–	11	39	381	443
	Glouc 093 (F044)	44	22	59	48	618	791
	Subtotal	643	756	1326	1267	8686	12,678
Melbourne	Cass 007 (Cesspit A)	308	426	421	444	60	1659
	Leic L25C (1.010)	214	185	2971	1182	2147	6699
	Lons 143 (Cesspit M)	330	158	285	58	1284	2115
	Lons 147 (2.722)	148	149	251	237	399	1184
	LtLei L36A (1.230)	203	137	621	1062	2951	4974
	LtLon 073 (Cesspit T)	536	408	930	262	495	2631
	LtLon 128 (1.023)	70	88	430	427	3324	4339
	Spri 147 (Cesspit B)	3	1	1443	682	2983	5112
	Spri 255 (Cesspit H)	237	140	580	600	2491	4048
	Spri 255 (Cesspit J)	205	126	191	53	774	1349
	Subtotal	2254	1818	8123	5007	16,908	34,110
Total		2897	2574	9449	6274	25,594	46,788

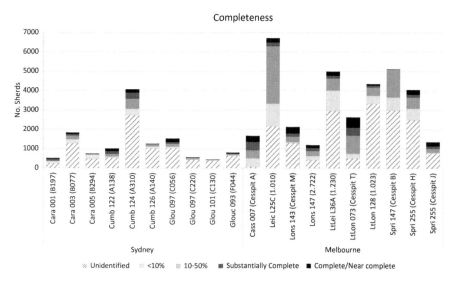

Fig. 10.7 Intactness of glass and ceramic sherds in each assemblage

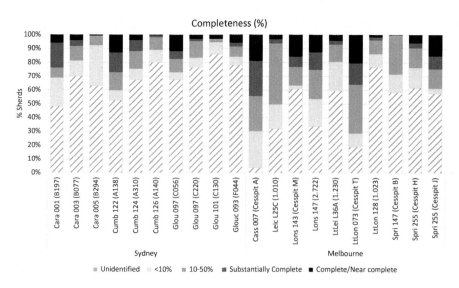

Fig. 10.8 Percentage of intact glass and ceramic sherds in each assemblage

comparability from a depositional point of view, 5 Carahers Lane and 124 Cumberland Street stand out as being 'older' deposits, probably the goods of residents occupying these places prior to the sewerage conversion. The remaining three fills were formed in the 1850s, 1870s and 1880s, respectively, and variation should be expected in their contrast to the 1860s material.

Table 10.5 Summary of features of each assemblage in the study group

City	Bldg code (MC)	Sherds	MNV[a]	TPQ	Likely date of deposition	Owner at the time of deposition	MNV >50%	Sherds >50%	Nature of deposition	Post-deposition disturbance
Sydney	Cara 001 (B197)	505	138	1862	1866	Henson (Massey)	22.4%	23.8%	Primary backfill	Yes: eng. works
	Cara 003 (B077)	1817	219	1863	1866	Henson (Massey)	27.2%	8.0%	Primary backfill	Minor: eng. works
	Cara 005 (B294)	739	207	1867	1866	Caraher	1.7%	0.5%	Secondary backfill: 'stockpiled' yard refuse	None
	Cumb 122 (A138)	998	181	1875	Mid to late 1870s	Mary Ann Smith, late Henson (Massey)	37.3%	27%	Primary backfill	Anomalous: yard drainage works
	Cumb 124 (A310)	4060	416	1860	1866	Croft Hall (late Winch)	19.7%	11.7%	Secondary backfill and primary refuse pit	Some: yard drainage works
	Cumb 126 (A140)	1251	205	1860	1866	Henson (Massey)	4.8%	1.8%	Primary backfill	Minimal
	Glou 097 (C056)	1520	245	1862 (1866)	Late 1860s	Henson (Massey)	35.0%	17.2%	Primary backfill	Yes: WC repairs, 1890s
	Glou 097 (C220)	554	139	1852	> c. 1854	Henson (Massey)	23.8%	4.3%	Primary backfill	Anomalous: yard drainage works
	Glou 101 (C130)	443	114	1861	1866	Henson (Massey)	14.3%	2.7%	Secondary backfill: 'stockpiled' yard refuse	Yes: WC repairs, post-1870s
	Glou 093 (F044)	791	156	1885	Late 1880s	Will Pullyard or Catherine Fennelly	16.4%	8.3%	Primary backfill	None
Melbourne	Cass 007 (Cesspit A)	1659	163	1854	Late 1860s/ early 1870s	Maloney	52.1%	44.2%	Primary backfill	None reported

(continued)

Table 10.5 (continued)

City	Bldg code (MC)	Sherds	MNV[a]	TPQ	Likely date of deposition	Owner at the time of deposition	MNV >50%	Sherds >50%	Nature of deposition	Post-deposition disturbance
	Leic L25C (1.010)	6699	428	1870	Apr. 1870	Tucker	21.8%	6.0%	Primary backfill	None reported
	Lons 143 (Cesspit M)	2115	184	1870	Jan. 1871	Gunther	33.7%	23.1%	Primary backfill	None reported
	Lons 147 (2.722)	1184	143	1847	Before c. 1861 (no later than Oct. 1871)	Brandt	47.6%	25.1%	Primary backfill	None reported
	LtLei L36A (1.230)	4974	344	1852	Likely Jul. 1871[b]	Quinn/Howes	23.4%	6.8%	Primary backfill	None reported
	LtLon 073 (Cesspit T)	2633	415	1879[c]	Dec. 1870	O'Rourke	32.9%	35.9%	Primary backfill	Yes: post-1879
	LtLon 128 (1.023)	4339	350	1872	Not known (likely by mid 1870s)[d]	Hinds	13.1%	3.6%	Secondary backfill	None reported
	Spri 147 (Cesspit B)	5112	193	1862	Dec. 1871	Haggerty	2.1%	0.1%	Secondary backfill	None reported
	Spri 255 (Cesspit H)	4048	384	1849	Likely by Jul. 1876[e]	Player/Cosier	20.3%	9.3%	Primary backfill	None reported
	Spri 255 (Cesspit J)	1349	147	1863	By Jul. 1876[e]	Player/Cosier	34.7%	24.5%	Primary backfill	None reported

[a] Glass and ceramic only

[b] Hayes and Minchinton (2016, 17) argue that 1.230 was mostly closed when contemporaneous barrel cesspit 1.279, on the same lot, was closed by council order. They note also that bluestone cesspit 1.230 was a close match to the 1861 Council circular specifying the construction of bluestone-lined pits, suggesting this was built c.1861 (Hayes and Minchinton 2016: 15). It is curious that the pit has a TPQ of 1852

[c] Fragments of a Ridgway plate (LL81011) made after 1879 are considered intrusive

[d] Hayes and Minchinton (2016, 20) argue that most bluestone cesspits were closed in the early to mid-1870s voluntarily or by MCC order and replaced by nightpans

[e] The cesspit was installed in 1862. The pit on the neighbouring property was closed by July 1876, so this may have been too

Altogether the cesspits may be grouped into four categories:

1. Cesspits abandoned pre-1866 (the first cesspit in 97 Gloucester Street)
2. Cesspits converted to sewerage in or after 1866 and probably before 1870 (1–5 Carahers Lane, 124–126 Cumberland Street)
3. Cesspits converted to sewerage c. 1866–1870, and upgraded or repaired in the late 1880s or 1890s (97 and 101 Gloucester Street)
4. Cesspits converted 10–20 years after the availability of sewer lines (93 Gloucester, 122 Cumberland Street)

For further discussion of the implications of these dates for understanding the connection of houses to sewerage services in The Rocks, see Crook et al. (2005, 139–143), and for Melbourne, see Hayes and Minchinton (2016).

Deposition Events

For their detailed study of the depositional processes of 11 privy pits and cisterns in Minneapolis, John McCarthy and Jeanne Ward (2000, 113) identified six processes that could give rise to fills found in privies:

1. Direct deposition of human and other wastes
2. Accidental loss of objects
3. Deliberate placement of artefacts and/or other materials into the feature to serve as percolation fill
4. Gradual, long-term accumulation of direct household refuse
5. Rapid deposition of household refuse, and possibly other materials, such as might occur as part of a major cleaning or site abandonment event
6. Redeposition of household refuse originally deposited or 'stockpiled' in yards.

The picture that is building from the study sample is that these nineteenth-century antipodean backfills derived in part from household refuse originally deposited or 'stockpiled' in yards – there simply are not enough complete vessels to argue for clear-out deposits. These include 7 Casselden Place, (off) 73 Little Lonsdale Street, 124 Cumberland Street, 5 Carahers Lane and 101 Gloucester Street.

At least three deposits contained some evidence of direct privy deposition: B386 (5 Carahers Lane), A138 (122 Cumberland Street) and C064 (97 Gloucester Street, second cesspit). This was recovered from the lowest level of the 5 Carahers Lane pit, and A138 was recovered as a single-unit fill; but the parasite remains from the second cesspit fill at 97 Gloucester Street were recovered from one of the middle, artefact-rich deposits. This is considered a result of the disturbance of the lowest, anaerobic layer (C067), caused by the installation of the pipe C052, not evidence that the pit was not cleaned out prior to connection.

At least part of the 126 Cumberland Street deposit – namely, the paint cans and work tools – appears to represent a clearance event. However the remaining deposits appear to be the result of opportunistic refuse, probably short-term stock piles of week-to-week refuse collection, with significant proportions of food scraps (animal bone) and disposable containers.

With the exception of Cesspits A and T, these assemblages are not outstanding examples of clearance deposits – well-preserved dumps of useable but otherwise unwanted household vessels – a point worth bearing in mind when the matching sets are examined.

Overview of the Residents

In the previous chapters, we outlined brief biographies of all residents occupying the selected 19 houses within a decade or so of the deposition dates of the 20 cesspit backfills. We have reduced this number to 54 individuals most likely to be responsible for discarding these fills (see Table 10.6), and we summarize some demographic characteristics of these families below. It is important to note once again that we do not have data on all residents, most notably for properties with a high occupancy turnover or those run as boarding houses. In addition, the dated records of cesspit closures in Melbourne – often to the day – have revealed a peculiar problem when compared and contrasted to detailed occupancy records (where available). The timing of sewerage repairs coincides with temporary vacancies in some properties and seems to represent renovations made by incoming tenants or owners, prior to moving in. In these cases, even though the cesspits may have been filled during the new residents' *occupancy*, the items used as fill are less likely to be their own, unless those residents brought old unwanted items from their former residence for the express purpose of discarding them. Unfortunately, even when precise dates of discard and tenancy are known, we cannot always tie individuals to assemblages with the high degree of accuracy we would like.

Of the residents we do know, much of the information we have about their occupations has been derived from post-office directories and rate records and where available, birth, death and marriage certificates (see Chaps. 8 and 9). We have more aggregated information about The Rocks residents courtesy of Laila Ellmoos's database of over 2000 individuals prepared between 2001 and 2004 (Ellmoos and Crook 2006), but even then we noted that the 'occupations pursued by Rocks people is incomplete' (Crook et al. 2005, 135). Occupations were given for just 46.9% of these Rocks listings in post-office directories in the defined study area between 1855 and 1900, and these provide only the occupation of the heads of households, not their spouses, adult children or lodgers, except on rare occasions. With the occupations identified from birth, death and marriage certificates and other research, we know the occupations of 983 of our 2061 individuals, that is, 47.6%.

Table 10.6 Selected list of occupants most likely to be responsible for the backfill deposits

Building	MC	TPQ	Closure date	Residents	Place of birth/ethnic grouping	Known occupations	Married: ages	Children/boarders living at this address	Religion
1 Cara	B197	1862	1866	Timothy and Ellen McNamara (1863)	Ireland: Limerick, labourer's son (T); Wexford, farmer's daughter (E)	Labourer/boatman/storekeeper/hotelkeeper (T); housekeeper (E)	1860: 32 (T; widower); 21 (E)	Ann b. 1861; William b.1863, d. 1865	RC
				George Wilson (1867) (Widower: Agnes died 1862)	Scotland: Inverkeithing (G) Ireland: Belfast (A)	Mariner/labourer/grocer (G)	1843: 22 (G); 21 (A)	Christina (b. 1844), William (b. 1845), George (b. 1847, d. 1887), Agnes (b. c1849), Alexander (b. 1851), Malcolm (b. 1854), James (b. 1858)	Pres./CoE (G); RC (A)[a]
3 Cara	B077	1863	1866	Charles and Catherine Leggatt (or Leggett) 1863–1880	England: London (Ch) Ireland: Limerick, farmer's daughter (Ca)	Mariner/wool jammer/labourer	1852: 25 (Ch)	None (Thomas d. 1879, aged 34)	CoE
5 Cara	B294	1852	1866	Patrick Guinan (1867)	Unknown: probably Ireland	Coachman	Bachelor	None	RC
				Other tenants: unknown					
122 Cumb	A138	1875	Mid-1870s	William Davis (1873)	Unknown	Unknown	Unknown	Unknown	Unknown

(continued)

Table 10.6 (continued)

Building	MC	TPQ	Closure date	Residents	Place of birth/ethnic grouping	Known occupations	Married: ages	Children/boarders living at this address	Religion
				Vacant (1875)	–	–	–	–	–
				Margaret Hadden, Alexander Clark and family (1876–78) (widow, Arthur Hadden d. 1871)	England: Bolton, Lancashire (MH) Scotland: Aberdeen (AC)	Laundress (MH); shipwright (AC)	1877: 50 (MH), b 40 (AC)	1st mrg (Yates): John T. (1849); maybe Martha A. (1853); Barbara (1859); George A. (1862)c 2nd mrg (Hadden): Margaret (b. 1868) Other: Margaret's sister, Ellen	Pres.
				Boarding House? Michael Driscoll, Peter Connor/O'Connor 1880	Unknown	Machine-ruler (book-binder, MD); unknown (PC)	Bachelors	NA	Unknown
				Michael O'Brien	Ireland	Unknown	Unknown	Unknown	Unknown
124 Cumb	A310	1860	1866	John George and Catherine Winch (owner-occupiers 1834–1861; C d. 1853), and family, incl. son-in-law David Gourlay (1850–c. 1854)	Sydney, English parents (J); Sydney, The Rocks – Irish parents (C)	Seaman, pilot, dealer, publican (J); publican (C); seaman (DG)	1827: c.27 (J), 21 (C)	Francis Jane (1830), Margaret Elizabeth (1833). Son-in-law: David Gourlay (m. Margaret 1850, and their children: Mary Catherine (1851), Elizabeth Jane (1852) and David (1854)	CoE (J), RC (C)

					England: Berkshire (G) England: London (L)	Mariner, labourer, gas worker (G); dealer (L)	1852: both c. 26	Charles Valentine, (1855); Lucy Emma (1856); and Harriet (1862)	CoE (G & ?L)
				George and Lucy Puzey, and family (1861–1864; G. d. 1863)					
				Luckridge (or John) Nichols (1865–1867)	Unknown	Unknown	Unknown	Unknown	Unknown
126 Cumb	A140	1860	1866	Stephen and Margaret Doyle, and family (1866–1880)	Ireland: Dublin (S) Ireland: Clare (M)	Painter and glazier, publican (S): publican (M)	1857: c. 27 (S), c. 32 (M)	Charlotte (1860), Margaret (1862)	RC
93 Glouc	F044	1885	Mid to late 1880s	Peter Augustus and Honora Lett (1883–1888)	Denmark: Elsinore (P) Ireland: Wicklow (H)	Ship chandler/maritime dealer, nightwatchman, labourer; cook (H)	1869: 28 (P), 27 (H)	Augustus (1871), Margaret (1873) and Edward W (1875)	CoE
97 Glouc	C220	1852	Mid to late 1850s	Thomas Buckley (tailor) and Mary Buckley (1855–1856)	Unknown	Tailor (T)	Unknown	James (1842), Ellen (1847), Richard (1848), Mary (1851)	Unknown
				William Allen (1857)	Unknown	Confectioner	Unknown	Unknown	Unknown
	C056	1862	1866	James Thomas (1863–1867)	Unknown	general dealer	Unknown	Unknown	Unknown
				Thomas Swan (1868)	Unknown	Unknown	Unknown	Unknown	Unknown
				D. Maclaverty (1869)	Unknown	Unknown	Unknown	Unknown	Unknown

(continued)

Table 10.6 (continued)

Building	MC	TPQ	Closure date	Residents	Place of birth/ ethnic grouping	Known occupations	Married: ages	Children/boarders living at this address	Religion
101 Glouc	C130	1861	1866	John Stretton/ Streeton (1870)	Unknown	Unknown	Unknown	Unknown	Unknown
				George (and Mary?) Beale 1853–1871[d]	England: Canterbury (G) Ireland: Armagh (M)	Waterman; labourer	1856 (ages unknown)	Margaret (1861); others?	Unknown
7 Casselden Place	Cesspit A	1854	Not known (voluntary)	Edward Thompson (1854)	England	Draper and General Agent	Unknown	Unknown	Unknown
				Patrick Ryan (1855–1856)	Unknown	Unknown	Unknown	Unknown	Unknown
				John Maloney (1856–1882)	*Ireland*	*Labourer*	*Never married*	*None*	*RC*
25c, Leichhardt Street	1.010	1870	Apr. 1870	William and Mary (nee Manning) Smith (1868–1870)	England (W), Ireland (M)	Labourer (W)	1858: 24	William (1869)	RC
143 Lonsdale Street	Cesspit M	1870	Jan. 1871	John Jamieson (1870)	Unknown	Unknown	Unknown	Unknown	Unknown
				John F. and Theresa (nee Heeb) Gunther (1871–1876)	Germany	Draper (J)	1861:30 (J), 24 (T)	Unknown	RC

147 Lonsdale Street	2.722	1847	Before c. 1861 (no later than Oct. 1871)	Henry and Isabella (nee Winter) Cornwell (1858–1873)	England (H), Scotland (I)	Butcher (H), Domestic (I)	1856: 23 (H), 24 (I)	Edmund, (1858), John (1860), Annie (1862), Isabella (1864), Henry (1866), Edith (1868), Alice (1870), Frank (1872), Bessie (1875), Alexander (1878)	C of E
Lot 36a, Little Leichhardt Street	1.230	1852	Not known (voluntary) but likely in Jul. 1871e	Vacant (1868–1870)					
				Charles and Margaret Patzold (1871–1893)	Prussia (C) and Ireland (M)	Cabinet maker (C), laundress (M)	1869: 24	Daughter Catherine, born in 1872 and died after 5 days	RC
Off 73 Little Lonsdale Street	Cesspit T	1879f	Dec. 1870	John C Bohn (1862–1872)	Germany	Bootmaker	1823: 20 (in Germany)	2 children Caroline and Louise born in Germany	Unknown
128 Little Lonsdale Street	1.023	1872	Not known (likely by the mid-1870s)g	*Tenants of the front dwelling::* Unknown (1872–1873)					
147 Spring Street	Cesspit B	1862	Dec. 1871	William Wilmot (1868)	Unknown	Ironmonger	Unknown	Unknown	Unknown
				Mrs. Kennedy (1869)	Unknown	Unknown	Unknown	Unknown	Unknown

(continued)

Table 10.6 (continued)

Building	MC	TPQ	Closure date	Residents	Place of birth/ ethnic grouping	Known occupations	Married: ages	Children/boarders living at this address	Religion
255 Spring Street (57A)	Cesspit H	1849	Not known (no data) but likely to have been closed by Jul. 1876[b]	Unknown (1870–1871)					
				Thomas and Mary Player (1864–1876)	England: Bristol (T), Oxfordshire (M)	Labourer (T), domestic (M)	1848: 30 (T), 32 (M)	None	Congregational/ Wesleyan
255 Spring Street (57B)	Cesspit J	1863	Closed before Jul. 1876	Mary Anne Hayes (1863)	Unknown	Unknown	Unknown	Unknown	Unknown
				Unknown					
				Mrs Mary Caffray/ Caffrey (1866)	Ireland	Sex worker	Prior to 1851	Joseph (1853), John (1855)	RC
				Vacant (1867–1869)					
				Thomas Player (1870)[i]	England: Bristol	Labourer, bootmaker	1848: 30	None	Congregational/ Wesleyan
				Jones (1871)	Unknown	Unknown	Unknown	Unknown	Unknown
				Vacant (1872–1876)					
				John Hennessy (1876–1877)	England	Tailor	Unknown	Unknown	Unknown
				James Sheppard (1874)	Unknown	Carpenter	Unknown	Unknown	Unknown
				[Unknown] (1875)					
				Mrs Mullins (1876)	Ireland	Unknown	Unknown	Unknown	RC
				George Mullins (1877)	Unknown	Unknown	Unknown	Unknown	Unknown

	Tenants of the rear dwelling: [Unknown] (1874)	Frederick Haberhauffe (1875–1876)	Germany	Cigar box manufacturer	Unknown	Unknown	Unknown

a The Wilsons were married at the (Presbyterian) Scots Church, but Agnes was buried in a Roman Catholic cemetery and George a Church of England one

b Margaret was about 18 when she was first married, to John Yates, in 1847 (they had 10 children in their 12 year marriage; Yates died in 1859). Margaret was 39 when she married a 30-year-old bachelor Arthur Hadden in 1867 and had been a widow for 8 years (they had 3 children in their 4 year marriage; Arthur died in 1871, aged 33)

c John and George appear in the Electoral Roll for 1878 as living at 122 Cumberland Street. Their brothers Charles (b. 1851), William H. (b. 1856) and Elijah (b. 1860) – all of eligible voting age – were not listed, suggesting that they lived and/or worked away from their mother. Barbara did not marry until 1880, to a John William Baldwin, in Sydney (456/1880), so it is reasonable to deduce that, at the age of 17, she was still living with her mother at 122 Cumberland Street, helping with the laundry work. It is not certain when Martha A. married, but it was probably in 1885, to an Edward E. Gibbons, in Sydney (304/1885), in which case she was probably also at 122 Cumberland Street. Alternatively, she may have married Edward Smith in Grafton in 1872 (2273/1872), in which case she probably was not living in Sydney

d It is not certain that the English-born George Beale and one-time labourer married to Mary Castigan is the same George Beale living at 101 Gloucester Street from 1863–1871. The speculated family data is shown in italics

e Hayes and Minchinton (2016, 17) argue that 1.230 was mostly closed when contemporaneous barrel cesspit 1.279, on the same lot, was closed by council order. They note also that bluestone cesspit 1.230 was a close match to the 1861 Council circular specifying the construction of bluestone-lined pits, suggesting this was built c.1861 (Hayes and Minchinton 2016, 15). It is curious that the pit has a TPQ of 1852

f Fragments of a Ridgway plate (LL81011) made after 1879 is considered intrusive

g Hayes and Minchinton (2016, 20) argue that most bluestone cesspits were closed in the early to mid-1870s voluntarily or by MCC order and replaced by nightpans

h The cesspit was installed in 1862. The pit on the neighbouring property was closed by July 1876, so this may have been too

i In 1870, MCC rate records list Mary Player as the owner and Thomas Player as the occupant of 57B

Sydney

Of the 21 selected Rocks families, we know the occupations of only 14, and of these we know that few remained constant. At least nine were mariners or involved with the sea trades at some time being mariners, pilots, ship chandlers or shipwrights. At least six of these nine took odd jobs as labourers at some time; and four of these mariner–labourers, plus one other seaman (George Winch), were listed as dealers at one time or another. It may seem a curious mix of trades, seafaring, labouring and retailing, but the links are not too difficult to suppose. Seafaring is a largely physical pursuit and can be irregular. If not out on a voyage, picking up work as a labourer may have been a good alternative for short-term work. Ships carried goods, and mariners often spent time in other colonial or international ports, being familiar with supply and demand. It appears from directory records and a few remaining photographs that setting up a shop in the front parlour of a small terrace house was not uncommon (Crook et al. 2005, fig. 13).

Overall, the Sydney occupations may be best described as *predominantly* skilled and semi-skilled, including some specialized trades such as book-binding. Others, such as storekeeping and hotelkeeping, may be considered entrepreneurial as well as requiring small business management and administrative skills.

As for religion, 6 of the heads of Sydney households were protestant, 5 were Catholic, and the remaining 11 were of unknown faith. Interestingly, the Winches and Wilsons appear to have been of mixed denomination; wives Catherine Winch and Agnes Wilson were both Roman Catholic, while their husbands were either Presbyterian or Anglican.

Eight of the heads of household were born in Ireland, 5 in England, 3 in Scotland, 2 in Australia (of Irish and English parentage), 1 from Denmark and the remaining 11 unknown. Five of the couples were of mixed ethnic backgrounds: both Charles Leggatt and George Beale were from England and their wives from Ireland; English-born Margaret Hadden was twice married to Scotsmen; Scotsman George Wilson's wife was Irish, as was the wife of Dane, Peter Augustus Lett. Only four of the nineteen individuals for whom a birthplace is known, came from major cities (i.e. London, Dublin and Belfast). The remainder were born in rural communities, or smaller industrial towns (such as Bolton, Lancashire).

Melbourne

Of the Melbourne group, we know at least 1 occupation of 17 of the 24 residents. The occupations present a more diverse group than those from The Rocks. There were three labourers (Smith, Maloney and Player, who was also listed as a boot-maker), a carpenter (Sheppard) and cabinet maker (Patzold). Henry Cornwall was a butcher by trade. There were also retail traders: drapers Gunther and Thompson, ironmonger Wilmot. Hennessy was a tailor and Bohn a bootmaker (as was Thomas

Player) and Haberhauffe as a cigar box manufacturer. The women served as domestics (Isabella Cornwall and Mary Player), a laundress (Margaret Patzold) and a sex worker (Mary Caffray). The religious affiliations of the residents of the Commonwealth Block were mostly similar to those in The Rocks, reflecting the significant numbers of migrants from Ireland and the rest of the United Kingdom, with smaller numbers from Germany, France and Switzerland. Not represented in our sample but identified in the ownership and occupancy records of the Block were Jewish migrants (Melbourne's fist synagogue was close by the Block), Chinese and people from the Middle East (variously described as Syrians or Afghans).

Comparative Analysis

In this section, we describe and establish patterns that derive from the relationship of classes of material culture and house lots in our study group. We examine the function and homogeneity of tablewares and teawares, glass bottles, drinking vessels and pharmaceutical containers in each assemblage. We seek to interpret these patterns through narratives of the individuals and families described above. Integrating historical and archaeological information at this scale raises several significant issues concerning the constraints on interpretation and the reliability of interpretations that we offer. These will be more fully discussed in the Chap. 11.

Tablewares

Ceramic and glass tablewares have long been the subject of historical archaeological interest. Much of this is, of course, motivated by the nature of the resource: that ceramic vessels were both fragile enough to break frequently and become rubbish and yet are robust enough to survive in abundance, while other traces of material life such as furnishings, household linens and clothing do not.

Tablewares have the added currency of being important elements in the practice of 'genteel dining' (Fitts 1999; Richards 1999; Wall 1999; see also Young 2003, 161; A. Praetzellis and Praetzellis 2004). Much of the discourse about 'genteel dining' habits is rightly associated with middle-class assemblages, but some researchers have seen the marks of 'respectability' in working-class assemblages (Lydon 1995; Karskens 1999a, 140–144, 154–166; Yamin 2001a), and others have argued that China cups are clear evidence of the middle-class aspirations of working peoples (e.g. Beaudry et al. 1991).

Middle-class dining habits did change significantly in the nineteenth century, evolving from communal, pot-served stews to stove-cooked meals to be served on a plate and becoming more elaborate and structured. This was a result of developments in both the material and social worlds of nineteenth-century middle-class people. First, technological changes such as the development of enclosed stoves, rather than open fires, sped up cooking times to allow for more dishes to be prepared. Second, the development of fine earthenware in the late eighteenth century brought the dinner services of aristocrats into the reach of middle-class incomes. Changes in the production and promotion of these wares led to increased variety in the shape of vessels, allowing great functional diversity. Third, cities began to segregate living and working neighbourhoods, and middle-class men found themselves travelling to work and remaining there all day. Rather than partaking in the more traditional luncheon meal with the family (and probably employees), the dinner meal became an important ritual that gave the family the opportunity to come together (Cantwell and Wall 2001, 211).

Most archaeological studies of these 'rituals' examine the broad material and decorative types represented and the ratio of tea to tablewares (e.g. Wall 1991, 1999). Other studies (e.g. Fitts 1999; Walker 2004, 23–26) consider the range of functions present in an assemblage and the extent to which these may be considered matching sets (see also Lydon 1995). The motivating interests behind these inquiries are the extent to which consumers were able to purchase the entire dinner services and to what extent they may have conformed to the middle-class standard for structured, and well-mannered, meal-taking. It must be noted that owning the equipage for individual place meals and abundant serving vessels is not necessarily proof of the enactment of middle-class rituals, nor of a shared belief in the values that govern them.

The selected cesspits from Sydney and Melbourne give us the opportunity to compare and contrast the table and teawares discarded by the mariners, labourers, bootmakers and small-scale merchants of 19 houses in the second half of the nineteenth century.

There are limitations on using archaeological relics, as robust they are, to examine functional variation. The strict division of plate function by size (as per Miller 1980, 27), for example, is complicated by the fact that manufacturers undermeasured their wares to get around the industry's price-fixing agreements (Miller 2003). Further, the diameter of vessels reduced to small rim sherds (i.e. <3 cm) cannot be estimated with confidence and is effectively invisible in the archaeological record. Some specialized wares, such as meat or fish drainers, are not readily identified by their perforations on an otherwise flat surface, but vegetable dishes are readily distinguished from platters if all we have is a fragment from the slighter thicker, footless base of the vessel. Substantially complete serving vessels are certainly less common in archaeological assemblages than individual service wares, and this may reflect greater care taken in their treatment, rather than a reduction of use. This compounds the difficulty of identifying specialized wares from small fragments but has not rendered it impossible, as many specialized vessels have been identified in our study group.

When we first analysed tablewares from Sydney in 2005, we noted that 'some interesting patterns [had] emerged from the comparisons' (Crook et al. 2005, 145). We found that the majority of Sydney houses were dominated by large plates with

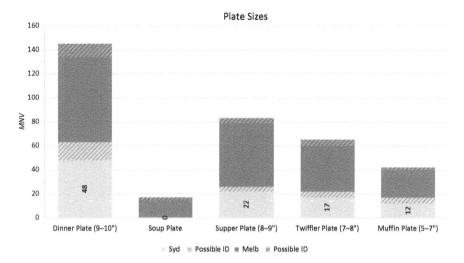

Fig. 10.9 Minimum number of plates of different sizes in all assemblages

far fewer muffin plates of the kind associated with tea service. This pattern continues across the Melbourne assemblages (Fig. 10.9) with 70% of all 352 *identifiable* plates across all both groups coming from supper, soup[3] or dinner plates.

All but 5 of the 20 assemblages had at least 3 plate sizes and 12 had one or more muffin, twiffler, supper *and* dinner or soup plate (Table 10.7, Figs. 10.10 and 10.11). Of the five assemblages with one or two sizes (A138, A140, C220, C130, Cesspit B), all but A138 (122 Cumberland Street) were from the most fragmented assemblages (Fig. 10.7) suggesting that diversity in plate sizes, or lack thereof, is the result of the intactness of the assemblage.

Interestingly, 1 Carahers Lane had only one tentatively identified dinner plate, two suppers and three tentatively identified supper plates, alongside seven muffins and twifflers (three tentatively identified). A similar pattern occurs at 93 Gloucester and Lot 36A Little Leichardt Street, with equal numbers of larger and smaller plates. This *may* suggest a deliberate selection of smaller, rather than the full-sized dinner plates perhaps for savings of cost or serving preferences.

There is a similar level of differentiation in the range and quantity of specialized serving vessels such as vegetable dishes, soup and the smaller sauce tureens, among other serving dishes (Table 10.8). All of these vessels would have been part of a basic dinner service – with the exception of the possible meat drainer at 124 Cumberland Street and the pressed glass berry bowl, both of which were common.

---

[3] Soup plates were not identified in The Rocks assemblages. They require the full profile of the plate to determine the wide marly and deep well. Some dinner plates in The Rocks assemblages may be soup plates.

Table 10.7 Minimum number of individual tablewares and cutlery in selected cesspit deposits

	CARA 001 (B197)	CARA 003 (B077)	CARA 005 (B294)	CUMB 122 (A138)	CUMB 124 (A310)	CUMB 126 (A140)	GLOUC 093 (F044)	GLOU 097 (C056)	GLOU 097 (C220)	GLOU 101 (C130)	CASS 007 (CESSPIT A)	LEIC L25C (1.010)	LONS 143 (CESSPIT M)	LONS 147 (2.722)	LTLEI L36A (1.230)	LTLON 073 (CESSPIT T)	LTLON 128 (1.023)	SPRI 147 (CESSPIT B)	SPRI 255 (CESSPIT H)	SPRI 255 (CESSPIT J)	Total MNV
Plates																					
Dinner plate (9–10″)	1[1]	5[1]	7[5]	7[1]	9	9[3]	1[1]	7[2]	2[1]		8[5]	8[1]	11	8	2[1]	11[2]	7	3	9[2]	4	119[26]
Soup plate^	5[2]										2	2	2			2	2				15[2]
Supper plate (8–9″)	4[2]	3	1[1]	4[1]	4	3	2[1]	2		1	2	9	11	5	4	9[1]	6[1]	1	6	4	75[8]
Twiffler plate (7–8″)	3[1]	4[1]	2[1]		3		1[1]	2			2	8[1]	3[1]	3[1]	3	6[1]	5[1]		8[1]	4[1]	55[10]
Muffin plate (5–7″)			3[3]		2		1	1			2	3[1]	2		1	4	2[2]		4[1]	2	35[7]
Unidentified plate	4	6	16	9	15	15	4	4	2	11	9	11	9	6	11	35	24	35	22	15	263
Minimum no. plates	17[6]	18[2]	29[10]	20[2]	33	27[3]	9[3]	16[2]	4[1]	12	25[5]	41[3]	38[1]	22[1]	21[1]	67[4]	46[4]	39	49[4]	29[1]	562[53]
Minimum no. sizes represented	4	3	4	2	4	2	4	4	1	1	5	5	5	3	4	5	5	2	4	4	
Other individual tablewares																					
Egg cup	3	2	1	2	1	2	1[1]	1	2			1	1[1]		1	1[1]					19[3]
Cutlery																					
Knife					1		2				1	1[1]		2[2]	2[1]		1[1]	1[1]			11[6]
Fork							1			1											2
Fork/spoon								1								1					2
Spoon	1		2[1]				1														4[1]
Spoon, tea				1																	1
Unidentified		2		1	3				2								2			1	15
Minimum no. cutlery	1	2	2[1]	2	4		4	1	2	1	1	1[1]		2[2]	2[1]	1	3[1]	1[1]		1	35[7]

Children's vessels																				
Child's mug						1									3[1]					6[2]
Child's Cutlery		1[1]									1[1]									1[1]
Minimum no. children's vessels		1[1]				1				1					3[1]					7[3]
Minimum no. individual vessels	21[6]	20[2]	33[11]	27[2]	37	29[3]	15[4]	21[2]	8[1]	13	26[5]	44[5]	39[2]	26[3]	23[2]	72[6]	49[5]	41[1]	49[4]	31[1]	624[66]

# Indicates the number of items speculatively attributed to this category, i.e., '7[2]' indicates that of the 7 dinner plates identified in this assemblage, two were tentatively identified as dinner plates.

A classification for soup plates was not available when the Sydney assemblages were classified. Some dinner plates may meet the Melbourne definition of a soup plates.

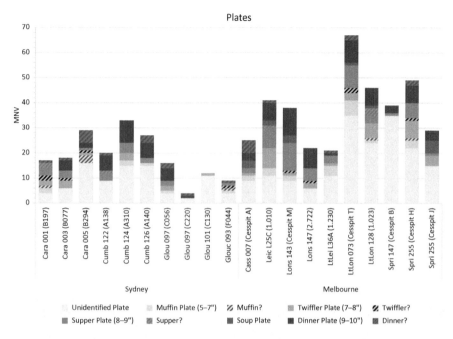

Fig. 10.10 Minimum number of plates of various sizes in each assemblage

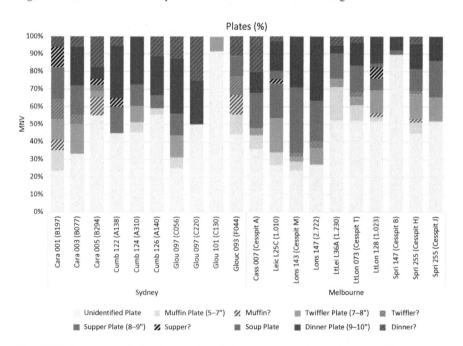

Fig. 10.11 Percentage of minimum number of plates of various sizes in each assemblage

Table 10.8 Minimum number of table serving vessels in selected cesspit deposits

	CARA 001 (B197)	CARA 003 (B077)	CARA 005 (B294)	CUMB 122 (A138)	CUMB 124 (A310)	CUMB 126 (A140)	GLOUC 093 (F044)	GLOU 097 (C056)	GLOU 097 (C220)	GLOU 101 (C130)	CASS 007 (CESSPIT A)	LEIC L25C (1.010)	LONS 143 (CESSPIT M)	LONS 147 (2.722)	LTLEI L36A (1.230)	LTLON 073 (CESSPIT T)	LTLON 128 (1.023)	SPRI 147 (CESSPIT B)	SPRI 255 (CESSPIT H)	SPRI 255 (CESSPIT J)	Total MNV
Table serving vessels																					
Vegetable dish			3[3]		1	1[1]				1[1]		1[1]									7[6]
Dish covers		3[3]			2[2]	2	2[1]	1		1		1				2[1]	1		3		18[7]
Covered dish											1						1				2
Dish stand			1[1]																		1[1]
Soup tureen				1																	1
Sauce tureen		1																			1
Unidentified tureen	1[1]	1[1]	2[2]					3[3]													6[6]
Platter dish						1					1						4[1]		4		11[2]
Dish drainer/openwork plate					1																1
Berry bowl dish	1[1]																				1[1]
Dessert comport stand																1[1]					1[1]
Various serving dishes	5	3	6	6	9	5	1	6	1	4	2	15	6	4	4	12	4	5	17	1	116
Various serving bowls	2	2	3	3	8	2		5		2	2		1	1		3	1	1	2		38
Unidentified serving vessels											3		1	2	12	1	7	5			31
Minimum no. of table serving vessels	9[2]	10[4]	15[6]	10	21[2]	11[1]	3[1]	15[3]	1	8[1]	9	17[1]	8	7	16	19[2]	18[1]	11	26	1	235[24]
Minimum no. of types	*3*	*4*	*4*	*2*	*4*	*4*	*2*	*3*	*1*	*3*	*3*	*3*	*1*	*1*	*1*	*3*	*4*	*1*	*3*	*1*	

(continued)

Table 10.8 (continued)

	CARA 001 (B197)	CARA 003 (B077)	CARA 005 (B294)	CUMB 122 (A138)	CUMB 124 (A310)	CUMB 126 (A140)	GLOUC 093 (F044)	GLOU 097 (C056)	GLOU 097 (C220)	GLOU 101 (C130)	CASS 007 (CESSPIT A)	LEIC L25C (1.010)	LONS 143 (CESSPIT M)	LONS 147 (2.722)	LTLEI L36A (1.230)	LTLON 073 (CESSPIT T)	LTLON 128 (1.023)	SPRI 147 (CESSPIT B)	SPRI 255 (CESSPIT H)	SPRI 255 (CESSPIT J)	Total MNV
Cruets																					
Butter dish/tub					1							1			1¹						3¹
Salt dish					1			1¹													2¹
Sugar bowl/mustard pot					2¹																2¹
Unidentified cruet				2				2											1		5
Minimum no. of cruets				2	4¹			3¹				1			1¹				1		12³
Total serving vessels	9	10	15	12	25	11	3	18	1	8	9	18	8	7	17	19	18	11	27	1	247
Total individual vessels	21	20	33	27	37	29	15	21	8	13	26	44	39	26	23	72	49	41	49	31	624
Ratio individual to serving vessels	2.3	2.0	2.2	2.3	1.5	2.6	5.0	1.2	8.0	1.6	2.9	2.4	4.9	3.7	1.4	3.8	2.7	3.7	1.8	31.0	

# Indicates the number of items speculatively attributed to this category

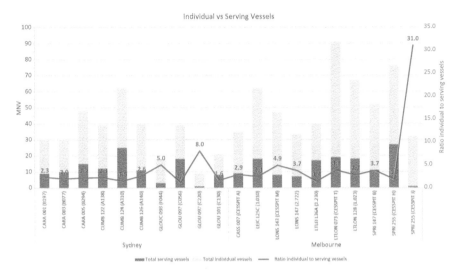

Fig. 10.12 Ratio of individual to serving vessels in each assemblage

All assemblages have at least one serving vessel, but in the cases of 97 Gloucester Street (second fill, C220) and 255 Spring Street (Cesspit J), there was only one serving dish of unidentified form in each assemblage. This is despite C220 having four plates, two egg cups and an unidentified piece of cutlery and Cesspit J having 29 plates and egg cup and an unidentified item of cutlery. There is a marked lack of serving vessels in this household, and it does not appear to be a result of the assemblage size. While Cesspit J is one of the smaller assemblages of the Melbourne group, the smallest assemblage 147 Lonsdale Street (2.722) had an average ratio of 3.7 individual vessels for each serving vessel (Fig. 10.12). Overall the average ratio was 4.4 and 2.7 if we exclude the outliers, C220 and Cesspit J.

Conversely, the earlier pit at 97 Gloucester Street (C056) and assemblages Lot 36a Little Leichhardt Street (1.230) and 124 Cumberland Street (A310) each have one serving vessel for every 1.2, 1.4 and 1.5 individual vessels. This is a significantly high proportion of serving vessels, given that a typical dinner service had only a dozen or so service vessels, even for a set totalling 112 pieces (e.g. the 'Daisy Gold Band', Montgomery Ward and Co. 1895, 531). Thus you might expect a ratio of six plates to every service dish.

Matching Sets

Over two thirds of ceramic food service vessels (69.9%, n = 934) were transfer-printed including flow transfer print. This is slightly higher than the overall ratio of transfer prints to other forms of decoration (see Figs. 10.13 and 10.14 and

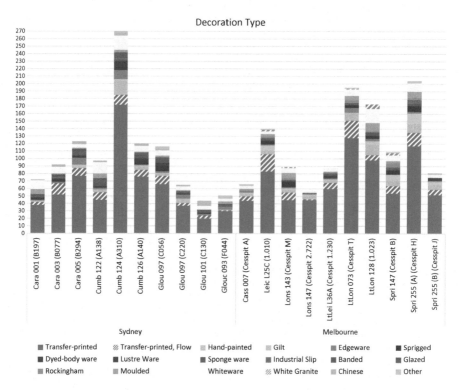

Fig. 10.13 Minimum number of food service, tea and beverage vessels in all assemblages, by primary decoration type

Table 10.9). The food service transfer prints were dominated by blue designs which made up 70% of transfer-printed ($n = 660$) and 38.5% of the 1353 tablewares across all deposits. The dominance of this type suggests a degree of homogeneity that is not visible when looking at the assemblages themselves. A variety of transfer-printed designs, and variation for well-known patterns such as 'Willow' (Copeland 1980), were a staple of the pottery trade as individual manufacturers sought to distinguish themselves from their competitors. A total of 90 named patterns were identified across food, tea and beverage vessels from both the Sydney and Melbourne groups (see Table 10.10). Aside from the common patterns ('Willow', 'Asiatic Pheasants', 'Rhine', etc.), most appear only in one city (Table 10.10).

Looking more closely at transfer-printed and other distinct patterns, there is evidence for matching sets among tablewares in the study group although more tea rather than tableware sets were identified. All but three assemblages (B294, F044 and C200) had at least one set of matching vessels inclusive of tablewares, most with a mix of tea and tablewares (Fig. 10.15, Table 10.11). The majority (79%) were from 'complementary' sets: groups with matching pattern but with small variations in the pattern design (Crook et al. 2005, 32). Many 'complementary' sets comprised common patterns such as 'Willow', 'Fibre' and 'Rhine', and while they may well

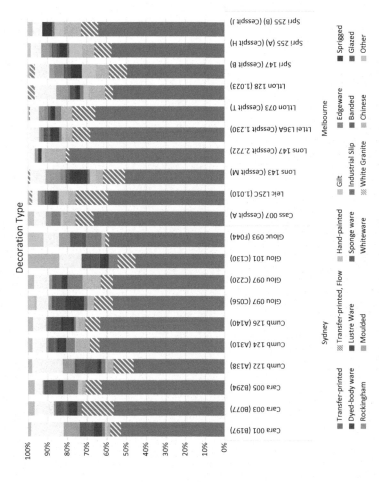

Fig. 10.14 Percentage of food service, tea and beverage vessels in all assemblages, by primary decoration type

Table 10.9 Minimum number of food service, tea and beverage vessels in each assemblage, by primary decoration type

Primary decoration	Cara 001 (B197)	Cara 003 (B077)	Cara 005 (B294)	Cumb 122 (A138)	Cumb 124 (A310)	Cumb 126 (A140)	Glou 097 (C056)	Glou 097 (C220)	Glou 101 (C130)	Glou 093 (F044)	MNV Sydney	MNV Sydney %	Cass 007 (Cesspit A)	Léic L25C (1.010)	Lons 143 (Cesspit M)	Lons 147 (2.722)	LiLéi L36A (1.230)	LiLon 073 (Cesspit T)	LiLon 128 (1.023)	Spri 147 (Cesspit B)	Spri 255 (A) (Cesspit H)	Spri 255 (B) (Cesspit J)	MNV Melbourne	MNV Melbourne %	MNV Total	MNV Total %
Transfer-printed	38	52	77	45	172	76	66	37	20	30	613	58.4%	44	83	45	45	60	128	98	54	117	52	726	60.4%	1339	59.5%
Transfer-printed, flow	4	15	10	10	13	9	11	4	4	1	81	7.7%	6	23	10	1	8	23	7	10	18	7	113	9.4%	194	8.6%
Hand-painted	1	2	2	3	19	4	3	6		1	39	3.7%	4	5	3	6	3	10	14	7	12	7	71	5.9%	110	4.9%
Gilt	1	3		1	2	2	1		2		10	1.0%	1	7	3	1	2	1	5	8	14	4	46	3.8%	56	2.5%
Edgeware	1	2	9	2	12	1	2	5	2	4	40	3.8%	3	1	1	1	1	6	3		2	1	18	1.5%	58	2.6%
Sprigged	2	2	1	1	4	2	7	1	1		21	2.0%		4	7	1		3	3	5	7	4	34	2.8%	55	2.4%
Dyed-body ware		2	2		6	5	1				16	1.5%	1	1	1		3	1	1	1	1		9	0.7%	25	1.1%
Lustre ware	1			1	2	1	3	1	1		10	1.0%					1						1	0.1%	10	0.4%
Sponge ware	1	1	1	6	2	6	6	1		1	24	2.3%	2	2				1	5	2	3		13	1.1%	37	1.6%
Industrial slip		1			2						3	0.3%	1	1			1	1		1	4		8	0.7%	11	0.5%
Banded	2	2	6	4	7	2	1	2	2	2	30	2.9%			2		2								30	1.3%
Glazed	2	2					1	2	2	2	13	1.2%	2	1	2			1	1	1			8	0.7%	21	0.9%
Rockingham														2	7		1	3	11	3	2		16	1.3%	16	0.7%
Moulded	6	1	1	6	3	1	2	1		3	24	2.3%	2	3	7		1	6	19	3	9		43	3.6%	67	3.0%
Whiteware	12	9	5	15	19	8	7	5	5	4	89	8.5%	4	4	1	2	5	9		8	11	4	73	6.1%	162	7.2%
White granite											0	0.0%		2				1	6	3			13	1.1%	13	0.6%
Chinese	1	3	4	2	4	3	1	2	7	4	27	2.6%	2							1			10	0.8%	27	1.2%
Others			4	2	2		4			4	10	1.0%		1				1			3	2	10	0.8%	20	0.9%
Total	72	92	123	97	270	120	116	65	44	51	1050	100%	66	140	89	57	88	195	173	109	204	81	1202	100%	2251	100%

Table 10.10 Minimum
number of food service, tea
and beverage vessels in
named patterns in Sydney
and Melbourne

Pattern	Sydney	Melbourne
Albion	10	6
Asiatic Pheasants	5	20
Auld Lang Syne	1	0
Australia	0	3
Bavarian girl	1	0
Birds and flowers	0	1
Bridge of Lucano	1	0
British flowers	0	1
British rivers	1	0
British star	0	1
Broseley	1	3
Cable	5	0
Camilla	0	1
Castle	0	8
Chantilly	11	1
Chensi	0	1
Claremont house	1	0
Continental views	0	1
Coral	0	2
Corinthian	0	1
Corsina	3	0
Countries of Russia	1	0
Crimean War	0	1
Crystal	0	1
Dresden views	0	2
Eton College	0	0
Fairy Villas	0	1
Favourite	0	1
Fibre	19	39
Filigree	0	2
Florence	2	0
Forest	2	0
Formosa	0	0
Gem	8	0
Giraffe	1	0
Gothic	0	1
Hyacinth	2	0
Hyacinth	1	0
Ionic	0	1
Irish scenery	3	0
Italian	1	3
Italian lakes	0	1
Jar and fisherman	1	0
Jessamine	3	0
Juvenile sport	1	0

(continued)

Table 10.10 (continued)

Pattern	Sydney	Melbourne
Lace	7	0
Lake scenery	0	1
Lange Lijsen	1	0
Lily	0	1
Lily of the valley	1	0
Lozere	1	0
Lucerne	0	2
Macaw	0	1
Medici	3	0
Montezuma	1	2
Nankin	0	1
Oriental	0	3
Oriental scenery	0	1
Pagoda	1	0
Palestine	16	0
Peacock	7	0
Pear	0	1
Pekin	0	1
Pelew	0	2
Persian rose	0	2
Rhine	18	16
Rhone	0	2
Rhone scenery	0	2
Rural scenery	0	4
Seaweed	10	1
Seine	0	7
Swiss cottage	0	1
Sydney	2	0
Temple	0	6
The Philosopher	0	1
The Rhine	0	1
The Season	0	2
Tuscan	0	1
Two temples	19	13
Tyrol	0	5
Venus	0	4
Vermicelli	1	0
Versailles	0	1
Victoria fibre	1	0
Vine	1	0
Virginia water	3	0
Watteau	0	0
Whampoa	0	1
Wild rose	1	9
Willow	82	175
Total	**261**	**373**

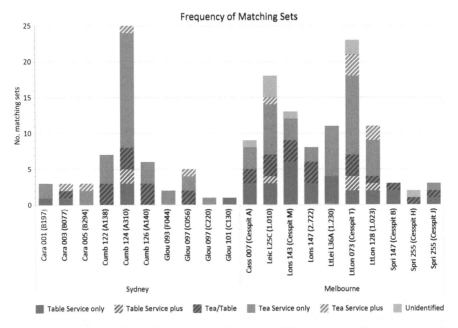

Fig. 10.15 Frequency of matching sets, by functional type. 'Table service plus' is a set comprised entirely of table service vessels but for one other tea service or other items. A 'tea/table' set has a mix of table and tea vessels

have been used as a set, they bear no direct evidence of having been manufactured, and thereby purchased, as a set. Some have matching patterns, in different colours ('complementary colour' or 'CC'). Thirty-four sets were 'matching', that is, identical patterns in the same colour and often with makers' marks. (For a complete list of all matching sets, see the appendix in Chap. 12.)

The majority of matching vessels were recovered from the Melbourne assemblages (Figs 10.15, 10.16, and 10.17; see also Appendix in Chap. 12). This is not a factor of the cataloguing process; in fact, additional groups were identified during the assemblage analysis. Setting aside teawares which are discussed below, 147 Lonsdale Street (2.722), 124 Cumberland Street (A310), Lot 25C on Leichhardt Street (1.010) and 143 Lonsdale Street (Cesspit M) have the most matching sets with at least seven each. The largest sets in all cases were 'Willow' vessels (Figs. 10.16 and 10.17). 124 Cumberland Street had at least 15 identifiable serving vessels in the 'Willow' pattern, and 73 Little Lonsdale Street (Cesspit T) had at least 34 individual 'Willow' vessels. These are all considered 'complementary' sets and were likely accumulated piecemeal.

Setting aside 'Willow', overall the sets identified have few vessels – often only a pair of items. Returning to the typical dining service discussed above, the average 'matching set' identified in these assemblages (with 3.5 vessels) would be just over 3% of a standard of 112-piece service. Such smatterings of homogeneity in ceramics hardly represent cohesive, complete dinner services gracing the tables of these working-class families, but they do indicate a preference for, and curation of, certain patterns.

Table 10.11 Matching sets that include table service vessels

City	Location	Table service only	Table service plus	Tea service only	Tea service plus	Tea/table	Unidentified	Total no. of sets
Sydney	Cara 001 (B197)	1		2				3
	Cara 003 (B077)	1			1	1		3
	Cara 005 (B294)			2	1			3
	Cumb 122 (A138)			4		3		7
	Cumb 124 (A310)	3	2	16	1	3		25
	Cumb 126 (A140)			3		3		6
	Glou 093 (F044)			2				2
	Glou 097 (C056)			2	1	2		5
	Glou 097 (C220)			1				1
	Glou 101 (C130)	1						1
Melbourne	Cass 007 (Cesspit A)	3		3		2	1	9
	Leic L25C (1.010)	3	1	7		3	3	18
	Lons 143 (Cesspit M)	6		3		3	1	13
	Lons 147 (2.722)	3		2		3		8
	LtLei L36A (1.230)	4		7				11
	LtLon 073 (Cesspit T)	2	2	11	3	3	2	23
	LtLon 128 (1.023)	2	1	5	2	1		11
	Spri 147 (Cesspit B)	2				1		3
	Spri 255 (Cesspit H)					1	1	2
	Spri 255 (Cesspit J)	1		1		1		3
Total		32	6	71	10	30	8	157

'Table Service plus' is a set comprised entirely of table service vessels but for one other tea service or other item. A 'Tea/Table' set has a mix of table and tea vessels

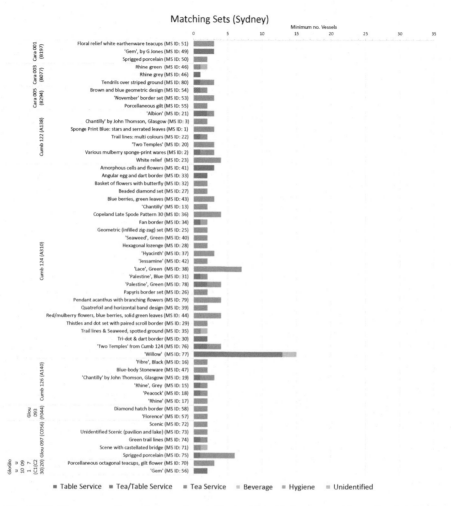

Fig. 10.16 Frequency of vessels in each matching set from Sydney assemblages, by functional type

Teawares

Like dining, the rituals of drinking tea are a subject of interest for historical archaeologists. While the more formal settings of an 'afternoon tea' are best associated with studies of middle-class consumption (Wall 1991, 1994; see also Cook et al. 1996, 57–58; Cantwell and Wall 2001; Yamin 2001b; Hayes 2011), there has been some discussion of it in the context of working-class cultures (Lampard 2009; Crook 2011). While we shy away from the term 'respectability' (see above), it is clear that working-class people drank tea and owned tea drinking equipage, and like any other practice of domestic consumption, tea drinking was an important medium for social interaction. It likely occurred with its own cultural associations and rules, regardless

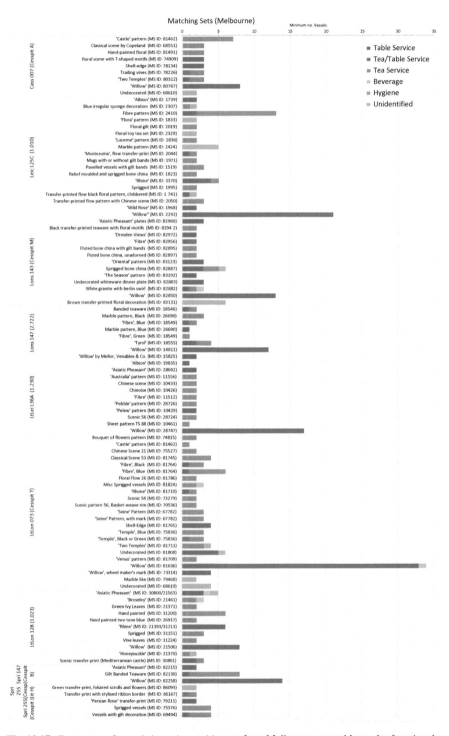

Fig. 10.17 Frequency of vessels in each matching set from Melbourne assemblages, by functional type

of the intended purpose of tea sets offered for sale in the market place (L. Cohen 1982). So when we look for high-quality, special purpose and homogenous tea services in the archaeological record of working-class families and do not find vessels aspiring to meet the middle-class norm, we should not be disappointed.

At least 897 vessels were identified as teawares in the study group, inclusive of teacups and saucers, teapots, slop bowls, sugar bowls and creamers and coffee cans and mugs. Given the difficulty of distinguishing slop and sugar bowls, teapot lids and creamers from sauce tureens and other covered vessels, it is likely that this number of tea-related vessels is higher. Nevertheless, the teawares in the study group are vast and diverse and, as noted above, are overrepresented with respect to matching sets (Fig. 10.15, Tables 10.11 and 10.12). This is partly due to the nature of teawares and the fact that cups and saucer sets were sold as a set.

As with tablewares, we see Location 25c Leichardt Street (1.010) containing a large number of matching teawares among 8 sets but less than (off) 73 Little Lonsdale Street (Cesspit T) with 14 sets and the 17 sets at 124 Cumberland Street in The Rocks (Table 10.11).

124 Cumberland Street had no less than 98 tea serving vessels, including a minimum of 45 cups, 44 saucers and 4 teapots, which were recovered from the cesspit backfill and adjacent refuse deposits. In addition, there were at least 21 other vessels that may be teawares but were too small to identify with confidence: 18 teacups/bowls, 2 tureens/teapots and 1 plate/saucer. This is three times the size of the teaware assemblages from its neighbours 122 and 126 Cumberland Street and still larger the 73 Little Lonsdale Street and Location 25c Leichardt Street. This is not a reflection of the overall assemblage at 124 Cumberland Street which was only 17% larger than the second largest Rocks assemblage (see Fig. 10.3).

As we discussed in Chap. 8, while the date of cesspit backfilling is certainly post-1866, much of the fill derives from rubbish pits probably dating to the departure of widower John Winch, who had owned and lived at the property for 30 years. While the presence of *some* material of the Puzey family or later occupants is most likely, the deposit is considered to represent a range of goods accumulated by the Winch family over a 10–15-year period. This represents 3–5 teacup and saucer sets purchased each year and a new teapot every 3–4 years.

It is clear that at least some of these were not purchased piecemeal, for approximately 40% of the teawares came from 16 varieties of 'matching sets' (Figs. 10.15 and 10.16, Table 10.11). In addition to the eight individual teacup and saucer sets (MS# 26–27, 29, 32, 39–40, 42–43) and multiple cups or saucers with no corresponding saucer or cup (MS# 13, 78), at least four patterns were purchased in multiple cup-and-saucer sets (MS# 36–38, 44).

The most frequent of these was the green transfer-printed design, marked 'LACE' (but without a maker's name), for which four teacups and three saucers, varying from 25% to 90% intact (MS# 38; Figs. 10.18 and 10.19). All the teacups were 4.75″ in diameter (121 mm) with scalloped rims and Q-ring-style handles. Two of the saucers were 7″ diameter and the third 6.5″. The other matching cup and saucer sets with additional cups or saucers included Pinder, Bourne and Hope's dark-blue 'Hyacinth' (MS# 37; Fig. 10.20), a Copeland flow blue pattern depicting flowers and birds (MS# 36; Fig. 10.21).

Table 10.12 Minimum number of teawares in selected cesspit deposits

Tea serving vessels	CARA 001 (B197)	CARA 003 (B077)	CARA 005 (B294)	CUMB 122 (A138)	CUMB 124 (A310)	CUMB 126 (A140)	GLOU 097 (C056)	GLOU 097 (C220)	GLOU 101 (C130)	GLOUC 093 (F044)	CASS 007 (CESSPIT A)	LEIC L25C (1.010)	LONS 143 (CESSPIT M)	LONS 147 (2.722)	LTLEI L36A (1.230)	LTLON 073 (CESSPIT T)	LTLON 128 (1.023)	SPRI 147 (CESSPIT B)	SPRI 255 (CESSPIT H)	SPRI 255 (CESSPIT J)	Total MNV
Teacup	13^{3}	17^{1}	23^{6}	22^{4}	65^{5}	33^{3}	22^{9}	21^{11}	10^{5}	7	10^{2}	26^{8}	11	8	8^{4}	42^{13}	41	17^{12}	48^{3}	14^{7}	458^{96}
Tea bowl	1										1										3^{1}
Tea saucer	7^{2}	7^{2}	14^{10}	17^{7}	44^{13}	14^{7}	16^{5}	3^{3}	3^{2}	10^{5}	12	32^{2}	11^{6}	6^{2}	9^{3}	33^{2}	40	9^{4}	40	10^{7}	337^{82}
Coffee can			1^{1}		1^{1}		2^{2}	1^{1}													5^{5}
Tea mug	2		1^{1}		2^{2}		1^{1}	2^{1}		2^{2}	1^{1}	3^{3}	1		2^{1}		2^{1}	1^{1}	1^{1}	4^{1}	24^{16}
Teapot		1		1	5^{2}	1	1			2^{1}						2^{1}			2		17^{4}
Teapot lid												2			2^{2}						2
Small/slop bowl			1	1	4^{2}					1			3^{3}	4^{4}	4^{4}	4^{4}	1	6^{6}	3^{3}	1^{1}	18^{12}
Unidentified tea vessels	4	3	5							5	4	2^{1}	3	4	4	4^{4}	1	4	8	1^{1}	33^{23}
Minimum no. of tea serving vessels	23^{5}	25^{3}	40^{18}	41^{11}	121^{25}	48^{10}	42^{17}	27^{16}	13^{7}	22^{8}	24^{3}	65^{14}	26^{9}	18^{6}	25^{14}	86^{25}	85^{1}	34^{23}	102^{7}	30^{17}	897^{239}
Minimum no. of types represented	4	3	5	4	6	3	5	4	2	5	4	4	3	2	4	5	4	4	5	4	

# Indicates the number of items speculatively attributed to this category

Fig. 10.18 One of the green transfer-printed 'LACE' teacups from 124 Cumberland Street (CUGL39203)

Fig. 10.19 Remains of two 'LACE' tea saucers from 124 Cumberland Street (CUGL39201 and CUGL39202)

Fig. 10.20 The Hyacinth teacups from 124 Cumberland Street (CUGL 26283 and CUGL26284)

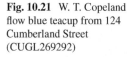

Fig. 10.21 W. T. Copeland
flow blue teacup from 124
Cumberland Street
(CUGL269292)

There were two examples of cups and/or saucers matching a teapot: a 'Two Temples' teapot corresponding to a single cup and a sprigged earthenware cup-and-saucer set with a corresponding oval teapot with sprig bouquets along the rim and waist.

No more than three sets of matching vessels were recovered from any other houses in The Rocks. While 3 Carahers Lane and 122 and 126 Cumberland Street all had sets of common patterns such as 'Rhine', 'Chantilly' and blue sponge-print wares that may well have purchased piecemeal, 1 Carahers Lane and 93 and 97 Gloucester Street (first cesspit fill, C056) each had at least two distinct or marked pieces that were probably bought as a set. These were two 'Florence' saucers registered in 1882 (93 Gloucester Street), three hand-painted porcelain teacups (97 Gloucester Street, first cesspit fill, C056) and an Ironstone teacup and saucer made by Edward Challinor (1 Carahers Lane).

Moralizing and Educational China

Only two of the deposits in the study group contained 'moralizing' or educational China – plates, mugs and other food service vessels with 'improving' mottos and/or depictions from religious or children's literature (Kevill-Davies 1991, 66–73). As a class of archaeological relics and household goods, they sit between food and tea service vessels and possibly home décor as it is likely some 'gifts' were retained for display rather than use. While intended for use in the nursery and strongly associated with middle-class cultures of moral improvement, these wares are frequently found in archaeological deposits of working-class households (e.g. Karskens 1999a, 141; Brighton 2001, 25–28).

Among the 100,800 ceramic sherds recovered from the Cumberland and Gloucester Streets site as a whole, approximately 30 vessels of 'moralizing' China were identified. These included children's mugs and plates with mottos such as 'Present for a Good Girl' and 'Lessons on Temperance and Frugality', as well reli-

gious vessels depicting verses of the Lord's Prayer or one bowl commemorating the life of John Wesley. At Little Lon with just under 146,000 ceramic sherds, only one item was identified as a child's gift: a small mug with the name 'William' printed on it (LL81339). Other sherds bore script that may form part of moralizing slogans such as '[b]e honest' (LL80635) and 'not think… but try & do…' (LL11101) but none were present in the assemblages under study.

We do have two items from Sydney. The cesspit fill of 124 Cumberland Street (A322) yielded a small green transfer-printed sherd, probably from a cup or small bowl, with a book and the words 'HOLY/[BIBLE]' (CUGL73437). No. 93 Gloucester Street had a small, red transfer-printed mug with 'LESSONS FOR YOUTH/ON/ INDUSTRY/TEMPERANCE/FRUGALITY' (CUGL60586 and CUGL73716; Fig. 10.22). Two sherds from the same red transfer-printed mug with the script of an unidentified story were found in the fills of the second cesspit fill at 97 Gloucester Street (CUGL60596, conjoining with a fragment from 5 Carahers Lane underfloor deposit, CUGL62912; Fig. 10.23).

Home Décor

The decoration of the home with figurines, vases, ornaments and bric-a-brac is a well-known phenomenon of the Victorian age (D. Cohen 2006; Mullins and Jeffries 2012; Kingstone and Lister 2018). Whilst most strongly associated with middle-

Fig. 10.23 Remains of red transfer-printed mug from 97 Gloucester Street and 5 Carahers Lane cesspits (CUGL60596 and CUGL62912)

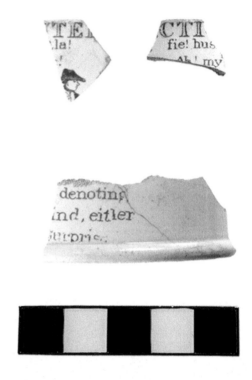

class consumption and the cult of domesticity that saw a rise in embellishment of the home in the most tasteful styles, working-class urban families decorated their homes with objects and images that suited their tastes and interests (L. Cohen 1982). Their capacity to furnish was tempered by the size and insecurity of their accommodation, moving frequently from rented dwellings with multipurpose rooms with limited opportunity for display. Decorative items needed to be portable, and some served the dual purpose of pleasing objects and tradeable assets of sufficient value to be loaned at the pawn shop – as was speculated at Five Points (Yamin 2001a, 166).

The archaeological record of decoration and collectibles comprises a diverse class ranging from exotic shells that may have formed part of natural history collection (Steele 1999) and decorative tacks and tassel holders: the enduring remnants of plush furnishings (Iacono 1999). Here we focus on the durable class of goods from ceramics.

Staffordshire ornaments were mass-produced in a variety of styles including well-known figures and scenes as well as arrangements of cottages, animals and other scenes pleasing to the eye. Their popularity was spurred by the changes in production in the 1830s and 1840s with a three-piece mould and a flat-back design for ornaments to be positioned against a wall (Harding et al. 2000, 6–7). This innovative design allowed for the creation of thousands of works depicting famous historical, political and royal figures such as Queen Victoria, Prince Albert and Lord

Fig. 10.24 Fragments of a figurine titled 'Death of Nelson' (LL75936)

Horatio Nelson – one of which was recovered from 7 Casselden Place (LL75936; Fig. 10.24).[4]

Across the study group, a minimum of 38 figurines were identified, 26 of them from Little Lonsdale (Table 10.13). Aside from the Nelson figurine and a fragment of a zebra's hind leg from 255 Spring Street (LL83069), the majority of figures from Melbourne and Sydney appear to be generic groups of female figures, children and rural scenes. A fragment from a figurine of Napoleon was identified in association with 5 Carahers Lane, from the underfloor deposit, not the cesspit backfill which is the subject of this study (CUGL67936).

Overall, 255 Spring Street (Cesspit H) had the most decorative items with a minimum of nine, followed by Lot 36A Little Leichardt Street (1.230), 7 Casselden Place, 128 Little Lonsdale and Lot 25C Leichardt Street.

What to make of these decorative embellishments? While we resist drawing strong conclusions about nationalist pride with respect to the selection of figurines, it is clear that efforts were made to decorate and improve these small homes. It is interesting that significantly more Melbourne assemblages had decorative items but no moralizing China.

---

[4] There is a possibility that two figures are represented among the sherds, but this is unlikely.

Table 10.13 Minimum number of decorative and collectible items from all assemblages

Function	Subfunction	Cara 001 (B197)	Cara 003 (B077)	Cara 005 (B294)	Cumb 122 (A138)	Cumb 124 (A310)	Cumb 126 (A140)	Glou 097 (C056)	Glou 097 (C220)	Glou 101 (C130)	Glou 093 (F044)	TOTAL SYDNEY	Cass 007 (Cesspit A)	Leic L25C (1.010)	Lons 143 (Cesspit M)	Lons 147 (2.722)	LtLei L36A (1.230)	LtLon 073 (Cesspit T)	LtLon 128 (1.023)	Spri 147 (Cesspit B)	Spri 255 (Cesspit H)	Spri 255 (Cesspit J)	TOTAL MELBOURNE	TOTAL MNV
Figurine	Animal/bird						1					1	1				2					1[1]	4	5
Figurine	Human											0		1		1		2	1		2		7	7
Figurine	Human/animal							1				1											0	1
Figurine	Scene											0	3										3	3
Figurine	Unidentified	2		2[2]	1	2	1			1	1	10	1[1]	3[1]	2		1	1[1]	2	1		1	12	22
Vase	Flower							1[1]				1	2[2]	2[2]			1[1]	2[2]	2[1]	1[1]	4[1]		14	15
Vase	Hanging						1					1											0	1
Unidentified	vessel											0					2[1]		2[1]		3[1]		7	7
Unidentified	Unidentified		1									1					2[2]						2	3
Total		2	1	2[2]	1	2	3	2[1]	0	1	1	15[3]	7[5]	6[3]	2	1	8[4]	5[3]	7[2]	2[1]	9[2]	2[1]	49	64

Drinking, Alcohol and Soda Bottles

There were very strong opinions about the consumption of alcohol. While many middle-class observers, particularly those from Calvinist traditions, abstained from drinking alcohol and condemned the 'demon drink', others were more pragmatic. In the New South Wales Select Committee on the Condition of the Working Classes, Edward Wise, MLC, argued that intemperance is the result, not the cause, of poor living conditions (*Votes & Proceedings* 1859–60: 96); that is, poverty will drive you to drink. Wise concluded that improving domestic circumstances through aid and education would prevent (or at least limit) alcohol abuse among the working classes.

The presence of alcohol containers in archaeological deposits in working-class households is no more surprising than the mere *presence* of such containers on middle-class sites, but interpreting the significance of their quantities is far more difficult. While some glass bottle forms are certainly associated with beer, wine or gin, they were not used exclusively for storing alcohol, because unlike today's disposable containers, they were frequently reused for other liquids (Carney 1999, 18–19; Reckner and Brighton 1999, 71; see also Ellis and Woff 2018).

When we first examined the container assemblage from the Cumberland and Gloucester Streets site, we were surprised by the small number of bottles per household: 3–15 for all houses except 97 Gloucester Street (second cesspit) which had 25. In the case of 124 Cumberland Street, that is more than three tea-and-saucer sets for every bottle of beer, wine or gin (Crook et al. 2005: 158). The Melbourne assemblages were considerably higher: with at least 18 beverage bottles in the smallest assemblage and 178 and 185 in 1.230 and 1.010, respectively (Table 10.14 and Fig. 10.25). In the case of 1.230 that is over two dozen bottles for every tea-and-saucer set. Is this evidence for tea totalling in Sydney but less so in Melbourne? Not necessarily. It is a matter of context and timing and whether we are looking at last week's table liquor or a year's accumulation of reusable bottles.

Bottles comprised over 50% of minimum vessel counts in context 1.230 and at least 37 bottles were complete, and many were said to have been placed upright (see Chap. 9). This is a large quantity of bottles to stockpile in an ordinary household. Similarly, over one third of 1.010 were comprised of bottles. Neither deposit had a large number of beverage service vessels (Tables 10.14 and 10.15, Figs. 10.26 and 10.27).

Reckner and Brighton (1999, 66) note that drinking small serves of beer, wine and porter was acceptable in American temperance circles, but gin, rum and whiskey were intrinsically intemperate. While most working-class people probably judged their own tolerance limits of alcohol consumption irrespective of middle-class campaigns (Karskens 1999b, 180; Reckner and Brighton 1999, 76–78), it is interesting to note that beer and wine bottles made up the majority of containers in all houses (Table 10.14 and Fig. 10.25). Gin and spirit bottles made up about 10% of all bottles.

We believe that an alcoholic, George Beale, was living at 101 Gloucester Street. While the state of his health while at No. 101 cannot be confirm, he died in the

Table 10.14 Minimum number of beverage bottles, by type

Bottle type	Cara 001 (B197)	Cara 003 (B077)	Cara 005 (B294)	Cumb 122 (A138)	Cumb 124 (A310)	Cumb 126 (A140)	Glou 097 (C056)	Glou 097 (C220)	Glou 101 (C130)	Glou 093 (F044)	MNV Sydney	Cass 007 (Cesspit A)	Léic L25C (1.010)	Lons 143 (Cesspit M)	Lons 147 (2.722)	LtLéi L36A (1.230)	LtLon 073 (Cesspit T)	LtLon 128 (1.023)	Spri 147 (Cesspit B)	Spri 255 (Cesspit H)	Spri 255 (Cesspit J)	MNV Melbourne	MNV Total
	Sydney											Melbourne											
Beer/wine/stout	4	7	5	4	11	13	21	1	4	10	80	19	153	12	12	156	33	38	11	45	14	493	573
Gin/schnapps/spirits	2	1	3	10	2	3	4	2	1	1	29	6	3	5	2	9	5	13	3	6	1	53	82
Ginger beer		2	1		5	2		5		2	17			1	1	1	6	3	1	1		14	31
Aerated water	1	1	1	1	1					2	7		5	2	1	2	6		1	1	1	19	26
Unidentified bottle	8	5	6	0	6	5	5	1	4	3	43	1	16	2	7	16	6	1	2	5	7	63	106
Total bottles	**15**	**16**	**16**	**15**	**25**	**23**	**30**	**9**	**9**	**18**	**176**	**26**	**177**	**22**	**23**	**184**	**56**	**55**	**18**	**58**	**23**	**642**	**818**
Total MNV	*138*	*219*	*207*	*181*	*416*	*205*	*245*	*139*	*114*	*156*	*2020*	*163*	*428*	*184*	*143*	*344*	*415*	*350*	*193*	*384*	*147*	*2751*	*4771*
Bottles % of total MNV	*11%*	*7%*	*8%*	*8%*	*6%*	*11%*	*12%*	*6%*	*8%*	*12%*	*9%*	*16%*	*41%*	*12%*	*16%*	*53%*	*13%*	*16%*	*9%*	*15%*	*16%*	*23%*	*17%*

# Indicates the number of items speculatively attributed to this category

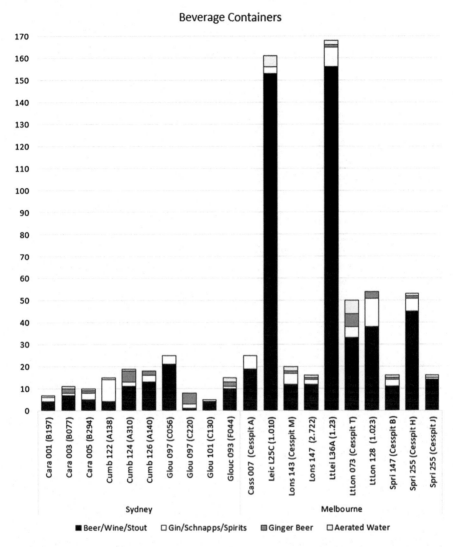

Fig. 10.25 Minimum number of glass and ceramic containers intended for storing and shipping alcoholic beverages (beer/wine/stout and gin/schnapps/spirits) and non-alcoholic beverage bottles (ginger beer and aerated waters)

Sydney Infirmary in January 1877. Intriguingly, this deposit had the second lowest number of alcoholic beverage containers – just four beer/wine and one spirit bottle – and the smallest group of beverage serving vessels (Tables 10.14 and 10.15, Figs. 10.26 and 10.27).

Overall, the Sydney assemblages, despite having fewer beverage containers, had a proportionately higher number, and arguably greater diversity, of service vessels. These may suggest a greater investment in presentation and serving of beverages, although they were not necessarily just for alcoholic drinks.

Table 10.15 Minimum number of beverage serving vessels from all assemblages

Type	Cara 001 (B197)	Cara 003 (B077)	Cara 005 (B294)	Cumb 122 (A138)	Cumb 124 (A310)	Cumb 126 (A140)	Glou 097 (C056)	Glou 097 (C220)	Glou 101 (C130)	Glou 093 (F044)	Cass 007 (Cesspit A)	Leic L25C (1.010)	Lons 143 (Cesspit M)	Lons 147 (2.722)	LtLei L36A (1.230)	LtLon 073 (Cesspit T)	LtLon 128 (1.023)	Spri 147 (Cesspit B)	Spri 255 (Cesspit H)	Spri 255 (Cesspit J)	MNV TOTAL
Glass tumbler	3	8	2[1]	8	10	4	7	7	1	2[2]	8[1]	10[2]	15	10	7	15[1]	13[1]		5	8	143
Wine glass	3	3	1	2	6	2	1	2	1	1	3	1			1	7	3	2			39
Spirit glass				6																	6
Sherry glass					2																2
Rummer													1	1[1]							2
Glass mug				1								1									2
Tumbler/scotch			1[1]																		1
Unidentified glass		2									1	1[1]		1[1]					1		6
Decanter		1	1		6[1]				1	1						1					11
Unidentified glass vessel																			4	1[1]	5
Total	**6**	**14**	**5[2]**	**17**	**24[1]**	**6**	**8**	**9**	**3**	**4**	**12[1]**	**13[3]**	**16**	**12[2]**	**8**	**23[1]**	**16[1]**	**2**	**10**	**9[1]**	**217**

Superscript numerals indicate the number of items speculatively attributed to this category

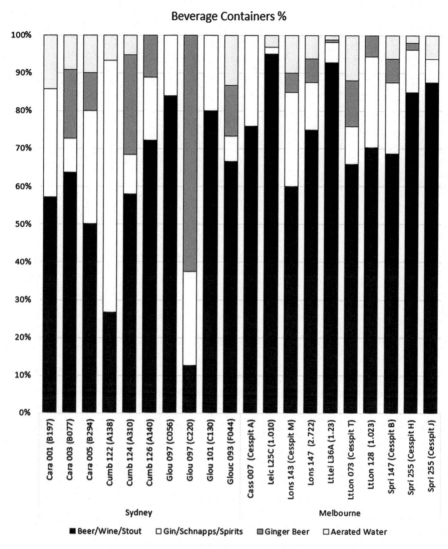

Fig. 10.26 Percentage of glass and ceramic containers intended for storing and serving beverages. Minimum number of beverage serving vessels from all assemblages

Life After Bankruptcy: The Doyle Family – A Case Study

Here we move away from comparative analysis of households to focus on one household assemblage and the story of those responsible for its creation: the Doyles who lived at 126 and later 128 Cumberland Street. As outlined in Chap. 8, Stephen and Margaret (nee Galvin, later McNamara) Doyle were Irish immigrants and publicans. Stephen also worked as a painter.

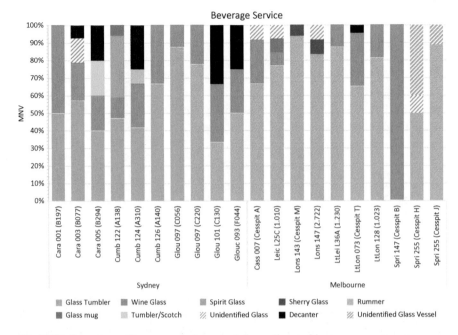

Fig. 10.27 Percentage of beverage serving vessels from all assemblages

They had married in September 1857, 1 year after Stephen's arrival in the colony. He was 28 and working as a painter; Margaret was 25. Margaret had arrived in the late 1840s, had married Thomas McNamara and had two children (Ann and Thomas) and had been widowed at the age of 23, in 1855. Thomas and Margaret were publicans of the Clare Castle Inn, Parramatta Street (now Broadway), at the time of his death, and Margaret was awarded the license of the 'Hand of Friendship' in Cumberland Street, later that year. It was transferred to Stephen in December 1857 (*Empire* 17 Dec. 1857, p. 4) shortly after their marriage.

Over the next few years, Stephen is listed as a publican at various addresses on George and Cumberland Streets: the 'Hand of Friendship' on Cumberland Street, 1858–1859; 'George Street' and 'Lower George Street' in 1859–1860, the Clare Tavern, 543 George Street in Sands of 1861 and a public house at 176 Cumberland Street (originally Lilyvale Cottage and named the Clare Tavern in 1859 by Thomas Lynch) in the rates Assessment Books of the same year. It is not known whether these duplicate addresses indicate the transfer of his license from one establishment to another or that he in fact ran both at some stage.

He advertised his damp-proofing and painting services in 1858 (*SMH* 21 Apr. 1858, p. 1) while at 206 Cumberland Street and licensee of the Hand of Friendship. In March the following year, he was looking to sublet rooms in Prince of Wales Hotel on George Street to 'respectable families on reasonable terms' (*SMH* 5 Mar.

1859, p. 10). One month later, he transferred the license for the Hand of Friendship to Margaret's brother-in-law Patrick McNamara (*SMH* 19 Apr. 1859, p. 3).

In May 1859 and June and September 1860, he also appears on the city council's books as a contractor, performing various 'odd jobs', alongside his sister-in-law's husband, Patrick McNamara, Michael McNamara (who appears not to be related) and Margaret's brother John Galvin (City of Sydney Archives, NSCA-ITM-84663 [65/0157]). He is listed as 'Stephen Doyle, Publican of George Street', and the contracts included road works, building a brick wall and extending the sewer line.

On 2 September 1859, in the midst of these 'odd jobs', and shortly after being fined 20s. (plus court costs) for permitting music and dancing at the Prince of Wales 'without having first obtained written permission from a magistrate' (*SMH* 16 Aug 1859: 5), Stephen Doyle became insolvent. He was apparently running two public houses at the time, the Prince of Wales Hotel (probably Lower George Street) and the Hand of Friendship on Cumberland Street (Ins No. 4591), even though Patrick McNamara had acquired the license 6 months earlier. His debts amounted to £410, and he owned furniture to the value of £20 and apparel to the value of £10. He claimed to have no landed property, although just a year before, he claimed freehold title to a house at Athlone Place in the Electoral Roll of 1859–1860. He owed two sums of rent, one to Julia Johnstone for the Prince of Wales Hotel (£43 6 s. 8d.) and another to Thomas Glover for the Hand of Friendship (£19 10s.). He also owed £17 19 s. for groceries to R & S Watson's Family and Retail Grocery Warehouse, on the corner of Cumberland and Essex Streets, and £32 to butcher Andrew McCrath.

An 'account of receipts and disbursements' from March to September 1859 listed the following items:

License	40.0.0
Overcharge in Porters Ale	18.0.0
Loss of Rental of Glovers Premises for 4 months at 15% per week	12.0.0
Household Expenditure	180.0.0
Sundry payments as for receipts	20.0.0

Elsewhere, the 'amount of daily takings in the Prince of Wales Hotel' was shown to average £1 10s. per day – that is, £237 15 s. per half year – and a mere £3 15 s. more than the expenses.

When the insolvency file was first lodged in September 1859, the Doyles were living on George Street (probably at the Prince of Wales), but by October Doyle stated that he lived on Cumberland Street.

There is an inventory of marketable furnishings from one of the hotels, taken room by room:

Bar	Cellar
License – a few full bottles of Ale and Porter; a small quantity of gin, rum and brandy – several glasses and decanters, fixtures, parlour behind bar, 1 Table	1 large cask of ale
	Front parlour
	Sofa and mattress, table and cover, chimney
	glass, 8 pictures, 7 chairs, chest of drawers
Bedroom 1	containing apparel and sundries
Bedstead, bed and bedding, wash stand, service	*Kitchen*
glass and clothes	Kitchen table and cooking utensils, a small
Bedroom 2	quantity of earthenware – Russell's stove.
Bedstead bed, bedding, wash stand and service	*Underneath cellar*
Bedroom 3	Large room formerly billiard room. One
2 bedsteads	large table
	[SRNSW Insolvency 4591]

The Doyle's primary assets were four bedsteads and accompanying bed-linen, a sofa, three tables, seven chairs, eight pictures, a chest of drawers and various liquor, glasses, decanters and fittings from the bar. A 'small quantity of earthenware' is mentioned in the kitchen, along with cooking utensils. These were sold at public auction on 21 September 1859, and advertisement noted the stove: 'A first-rate Russell's patent oven, nearly new; also, a small quantity of household furniture, &c., &c.' (*SMH* 21 Sep 1859, p. 6).[5]

The Doyles continued operating as publicans for 2 years after the insolvency (the debts were still standing in December 1862), until Stephen returned to his original trade as painter and decorator – by at least 1863, when he is listed as living on Kent Street (Sands 1863, 66). By this stage he and Margaret had two daughters: Charlotte, born in 1860, and Margaret, born in 1862.

It was likely a difficult time for the Doyles as they tried to get back on their feet. This may have played a role in a court action that was taken against Doyle by a Mary Coffee to recover £5 10s. in unpaid wages (*Empire* 9 Jul. 1861, p. 5). He was also fined 5 s. assaulting one Robert Marrow – who was in turn fined 20s. for 'obscene language' (*SMH* 7 Feb. 1862, p. 5).

By 1866, they were listed at 126 Cumberland Street, just 1 year after Timothy and Ellen McNamara (Margaret's brother-in-law from her first marriage) had lived there. It is possible that they lodged there together, briefly, or perhaps the McNamaras were able to recommend the Doyles to their landlords, the Hensons, when they were ready to move in.

The cesspit which would have been converted to sewerage at the time of the Doyles's move or shortly after it was backfilled with a range of items, including some items we can directly associate with Stephen's work. Almost 20 kg of heavily rusted paint cans or kettles were recovered from the lowest level of the fill (A149). Of the few substantially intact fragments, one was 180 mm in diameter and the other 200 mm tall. While the fragmented nature of tin posed a significant challenge to the

---

[5] The Doyles appear to have moved to Brickfield Hill, on the southern side of Sydney town, and ran the Clare Tavern on the corner of George and Liverpool Streets from August 1860.

calculation of a minimum vessel count for the cans, we speculate that there were at least eight kettles tossed into the disused pit.

Other nondomestic items in the lowest fill included two axe heads and a heavily abraded salt-glazed, ginger-beer bottle (CUGL39337), which Graham Wilson argued may have been used by Doyle as a pestle to grind pigments to mix in with his paints. The wear marks run the length of the bottle and are 'consistent with the vessel, in its whole state, being used as a pestle for grinding abrasive materials' (Wilson 1999, 325). The bottle was impressed with the mark of local potter Thomas Field: '[F]IELD/[P]OTTER/[SY]DNEY', which dates from 1848 to 1854, at least 11 or 12 years before the Doyles arrived on site. No painter's or glazier's tools are listed in the insolvency inventory, but it is likely that Doyle had retained at least some tools, perhaps stored at his home and/or not of sufficient value to itemize. Whether or not it was Doyle himself who first bought the bottle for its ginger beer, he may have used it to store the linseed oil or turpentine necessary for paint-mixing and may later have used it for grinding. Perhaps, as he was re-establishing himself in the trade, and repaying his debts, such make-do equipment was a necessary measure. Perhaps, too, by c. 1866, business was good and his prospects improving, so these makeshift tools were no longer required.

Other elements of the assemblage also suggest that the family's prospects were on the mend. They were settling into long-term residency at 126 Cumberland Street, where they stayed until 1880, before moving into next door in the larger, and free-standing, 128 Cumberland Street, where the Doyle girls continued to live until 1919.

The material snapshot we have of their life in the mid-1860s, from the cesspit backfill, unfortunately does not encompass the furniture as did the insolvency inventory, but it does provide a postscript to the 'small quantity of earthenware' documented in 1859. As the comparison above has shown, 126 Cumberland Street had as many domestic comforts as its neighbours and had matching tea-and-saucer sets and the most diverse range of serving vessels, after 124 Cumberland Street.

The Doyles remained at 126 Cumberland Street until 1880 when they moved next door into the four-roomed home at 128 Cumberland. Stephen died at home on 22 February 1881, aged 52, leaving behind his wife, two daughters and stepson. He died of *apoplexy endocarditis* a form of heart attack and from which he suffered for just 3 hours. His death must have come as a shock to Margaret – we presume – now a widow for the second time.

Margaret and at least one of her daughters continued on at No. 128 until her death c. 1908, when Miss Margaret, and possibly her sister Charlotte took over the leasehold until 1919. Spanning 39 years, the Doyles were the longest-term tenants of 128 Cumberland Street, and many of the fine artefacts recovered from under the floorboards have a greater possibility of being associated with this family than any other. One notable example is a gold filigree earring with faceted beryl stones (CUGL50990), described by specialist Nadia Iacono as displaying 'highly skilled craftsmanship', an accessory that 'stands alone as a piece of considerable value, even today' (Iacono 1999, 69).

While the earring is typically associated with the Doyles, it is important to remember that it may have been lost by any one of the tenants, and boarders, who

lived at 128 Cumberland Street from 1833 to 1931. Further, the only datable artefacts recovered from below the floorboards that necessarily post-date 1880 are
amber beer bottles first manufactured in the 1920s and are likely to have been
deposited at the time of demolition – certainly after the Doyle girls moved on in
1919. It is also hard to reconcile such fine objects with the limited income the
women must have survived on after the death of Stephen Doyle, but again, the item
may have been purchased in better times.

This somewhat counterintuitive occurrence of fine jewellery in the home of
bankrupted individual raises questions about data quality as well as the limits of
interpretation. In other words, we are currently unable to distinguish between an
interpretation that emphasizes their recovery from bankruptcy and whether it is an
artefact of deposition. We can however confirm that ceramic and glass tablewares
had been restored to a respectable standing just a few years after bankruptcy, even
though the painter's tools suggest a good measure of economy.

This detailed case story, embellished by an impressive but limited suite of historical records, is a counterpoint to the more abstract comparative analysis presented above. The success of these strategies will be discussed further in Chap. 11.

References

Beaudry, Mary, Lauren J. Cook, and Stephen A. Mrozowski. 1991. Artifacts and Active Voices:
    Material Culture as Social Discourse. In *The Archaeology of Inequality*, ed. Randall H. McGuire
    and Robert Paynter, 150–191. Oxford: Blackwell.
Brighton, Stephen A. 2001. Prices That Suit the Times: Shopping for Ceramics at the Five Points.
    Historical Archaeology 35: 16–30.
Cantwell, Anne-Marie E., and Diana diZerega Wall. 2001. *Unearthing Gotham: The Archaeology
    of New York City*. New Haven & London: Yale University Press.
Carney, Martin. 1999. Glass and Bottle Stoppers Artefact Report. In *The Cumberland/Gloucester
    Streets Site, The Rocks: Archaeological Investigation Report*, ed. Godden Mackay Heritage
    Consultants, 4i, 15–121. Sydney: Godden Mackay Logan Pty Ltd.
Cohen, Deborah. 2006. *Household Gods: The British and Their Possessions*. New Haven: Yale
    University Press.
Cohen, Lizabeth. 1982. Embellishing a Life of Labor: An Interpretation of the Material Culture
    of American Working Class Homes, 1885–1915. In *Material Culture Studies in America*, ed.
    Thomas J. Schlereth, 289–305. Nashville, Tenn: American Association for State and Local
    History.
Cook, Lauren J., Rebecca Yamin, and John P. McCarthy. 1996. Shopping as Meaningful Action:
    Towards a Redefinition of Consumption in Historical Archaeology. *Historical Archaeology*
    30: 50–65.
Copeland, Robert. 1980. *Spode's Willow Pattern and Other Designs After the Chinese*. London:
    Cassell Ltd.
Crook, Penny. 2011. Rethinking Assemblage Analysis: New Approaches to the Archaeology of
    Working-Class Neighborhoods. *International Journal of Historical Archaeology* 15: 582–593.
    https://doi.org/10.1007/s10761-011-0158-6.
Crook, Penny, Laila Ellmoos, and Tim Murray. 2005. Keeping up with the McNamaras: a Historical
    Archaeological Study of the Cumberland and Gloucester Streets Site, The Rocks, Sydney. In
    Archaeology of the Modern City Series 8. Sydney: Historic Houses Trust of New South Wales.

Ellis, Adrienne, and Bronwyn Woff. 2018. Bottle Merchants at A'Beckett Street, Melbourne (1875–1914): New Evidence for the Light Industrial Trade of Bottle Washing. *International Journal of Historical Archaeology* 22: 6–26. https://doi.org/10.1007/s10761-017-0412-7.

Ellmoos, Laila, and Penny Crook. 2006. People+Place Database. In *EAMC Databases, Version 1.0*, ed. Penny Crook, Laila Ellmoos, Tim Murray, and Compact Disc. Sydney: Historic Houses Trust of NSW.

Fitts, Robert K. 1999. The Archaeology of Middle-class Domesticity and Gentility in Victorian Brooklyn. *Historical Archaeology* 33: 39–62. https://doi.org/10.1007/BF03374279.

Harding, Kit, Adrian Harding, and Nicholas Harding. 2000. *Miller's Staffordshire Figures of the 19th and 20th Centuries: A Collector's Guide*. London: Octapus Publishing Group Ltd.

Hayes, Sarah. 2011. Gentility in the Dining and Tea Service Practices of Early Colonial Melbourne's "Established Middle Class". *Australasian Historical Archaeology* 29: 33–44.

Hayes, Sarah, and Barbara Minchinton. 2016. Cesspit Formation Processes and Waste Management History in Melbourne: Evidence from Little Lon. *Australian Archaeology* 82: 12–24.

Iacono, Nadia. 1999. Miscellaneous Artefacts Report. In *The Cumberland/Gloucester Streets Site, The Rocks: Archaeological Investigation Report*, ed. Godden Mackay Heritage Consultants, vol. 4ii, 13–118. Sydney: Godden Mackay Logan Pty Ltd.

Karskens, Grace. 1999a. *Inside the Rocks: The Archaeology of a Neighbourhood*. Sydney: Hale & Iremonger.

———. 1999b. Main Report—New Perspectives from the Rocks. In *The Cumberland/Gloucester Streets Site, The Rocks: Archaeological Investigation Report 2*, ed. Godden Mackay. Sydney: Godden Mackay Logan Pty Ltd.

Kevill-Davies, Sally. 1991. *Yesterday's Children: The Antiques and History of Childcare*. Antique Collectors' Club.

Kingstone, Helen, and Kate Lister, eds. 2018. *Paraphernalia! Victorian Objects*. Nineteenth Century. New York, NY; London, UK: Routledge.

Lampard, Susan. 2009. The Ideology of Domesticity and the Working-Class Women and Children of Port Adelaide, 1840-1890. *Historical Archaeology* 43: 50–64.

Lydon, Jane. 1995. Boarding Houses in The Rocks: Mrs Ann Lewis' Privy, 1865. *Public History Review* 4: 73–88.

McCarthy, John P., and Jeanne A. Ward. 2000. Sanitation Practices, Depositional Processes, and Interpretive Contexts of Minneapolis Privies. *Historical Archaeology* 34: 111–129.

Miller, George L. 1980. Classification and Economic Scaling of 19th Century Ceramics. *Historical Archaeology* 14: 1–40.

———. 2003. *Potters' Dozens and Evolving Vessel Sizes*. Formerly Delivered at SHA Conference.

Montgomery Ward & Co. 1895. *Catalogue and Buyers Guide No 57, Spring and Summer, 1895*. Dover Publications.

Mullins, Paul R., and Nigel Jeffries. 2012. The Banality of Gilding: Innocuous Materiality and Transatlantic Consumption in the Gilded Age. *International Journal of Historical Archaeology* 16: 745–760. JSTOR.

Praetzellis, Adrian, and Mary Praetzellis. 2004. More than "Just a Place to Start From": Historical archaeologies of West Oakland. In *Putting the 'There' There: Historical Archaeologies of West Oakland, 1–880 Cypress Freeway Replacement Project*, ed. Mary Praetzellis and Adrian Praetzellis, 305–328. California: Anthropological Studies Center, Sonoma State University.

Reckner, Paul E., and Stephen A. Brighton. 1999. Free From All Vicious Habits: Archaeological Perspectives on Class Conflict and the Rhetoric of Temperance. *Historical Archaeology* 33: 63–86.

Richards, Sarah. 1999. *Eighteenth-Century Ceramics: Products for a Civilised Society*. Manchester & New York: Manchester University Press.

Sands, John. 1863. *Sands's Commercial and General Sydney Directory for 1863*. Sydney: John Sands.

Schiffer, Michael B. 1987. *Formation Processes of the Archaeological Record*. Albuquerque, NM: University of New Mexico Press.

Sewerage and Water Supply, 10th report, 1866. 1867. In *Votes and Proceedings of Legislative Assembly of New South Wales 1866*, 4–5:30–31.

Steele, Dominic. 1999. Animal Bone and Shell Artefacts Report. In *The Cumberland/Gloucester Streets Site, The Rocks: Archaeological Investigation Report*, ed. Godden Mackay Heritage Consultants, vol. 4ii, 139–237. Sydney: Godden Mackay Logan Pty Ltd.

Sussman, Lynne. 2000. Objects vs Sherds: A Statistical Evaluation. In *Studies in Material Culture Research*, ed. Karlis Karklins, 96–103. Pennsylvania: The Society for Historical Archaeology.

Walker, Mark. 2004. Aristocracies of Labor: Craft Unionism, Immigration, and Working-Class Households. In *Putting the "There" There: Historical Archaeologies of West Oakland, 1–880 Cypress Freeway Replacement Project*, ed. Mary Praetzellis and Adrian Praetzellis, 207–236. California: Report Prepared by Anthropological Studies Center, Sonoma State University.

Wall, Diana diZerega. 1991. Sacred Dinners and Secular Teas: Constructing Domesticity in Mid–19th-Century New York. *Historical Archaeology* 25: 69–81.

———. 1994. *The Archaeology of Gender: Separating the Spheres in Urban America*. New York: Plenum Press.

———. 1999. Examining Gender, Class, and Ethnicity in Nineteenth-Century New York City, Historical Archaeology. *Historical Archaeology* 33: 102–117.

Wilson, Graham. 1999. Ceramics and Tobacco Pipes Artefact Report. In *The Cumberland/Gloucester Streets Site, The Rocks: Archaeological Investigation Report*, ed. Godden Mackay Heritage Consultants, vol. 4i, 205–366. Sydney: Godden Mackay Logan Pty Ltd.

Yamin, Rebecca. 2001a. Alternative Narratives: Respectability at New York's Five Points. In *The Archaeology of Urban Landscapes: Explorations In Slumland*, ed. Alan Mayne and Tim Murray, 154–170. Cambridge: Cambridge University Press.

———. 2001b. From Tanning to Tea: The Evolution of a Neighborhood. *Historical Archaeology* 35: 6–15. https://doi.org/10.1007/BF03374389.

Young, Linda. 2003. *Middle-class Culture in the Nineteenth-Century: America, Australia and Britain*. Hampshire, UK; New York: Palgrave Macmillan.

Chapter 11
Local and Global Lessons from 20 Cesspits from Australia

We began this book with two fundamental aims. The first was to chart the evolution of our thinking about the historical archaeology of the modern city through the histories of two related long-term research projects in Sydney and Melbourne. Doing this required us to explore our research into different aspects of this pretty broad agendum, which ranged from the detailed reanalysis of iconic sites such as First Government House and the Hyde Park Barracks in Sydney; descriptions of overarching analytical perspectives such as the principles of transnational archaeologies, migration, consumption and sanitary reform in the nineteenth century; and the creation of new relational databases that would support inter-site research (see Crook et al. 2006a, b) through to detailed analyses of target sites in Sydney and Melbourne.

The second aim was to describe our take on a comparative approach to urban archaeology through the vehicle of a single comprehensive methodology linked to the analysis of two large assemblages in two major colonial cities in Australia. One important element of this second aim was an understanding that this approach would allow us to identify similarities as well as differences and to ponder what *both* might mean. Significantly this 'open' attitude to whatever patterns might emerge through these comparisons has led us to accept ambiguity and uncertainty and not to try to suppress these in favour of conventional readings of class and ethnicity in the archaeology of the modern city.

Consequently this book reports work that has evolved over the past 20 years and indicates issues and problems that will drive further research at both places and which might possibly be regarded as having perspectives that might prove useful elsewhere. Thus our book really is about things which are unresolved and continuing, rather than resolved and complete. Indeed one fundamental outcome is the sense that the evolving agendum of comparing assemblages between different cities in Australia still has some way to go, and that future developments might well help us deal with contemporary ambiguities and datasets that currently do not readily integrate beyond creating archaeological 'backstories' to narratives of lives and the histories of places that are founded on documents (be they written, oral or photographic).

© Springer Nature Switzerland AG 2019
T. Murray, P. Crook, *Exploring the Archaeology of the Modern City
in Nineteenth-century Australia*, Contributions To Global Historical
Archaeology, https://doi.org/10.1007/978-3-030-27169-5_11

Our book and other publications about the history and archaeology of both precincts (see especially Crook et al. 2005; Karskens 1997, 1999, 2001, 2006; Lydon
1999; Mayne and Murray 1999, 2001; Murray 2006a, b; Murray and Crook 2005;
Murray and Mayne 2001, 2003; Murray et al. 2019) contain many stories about
people and places that shed a great deal of light about the experience of migration
and the process of making lives in new lands. These stories join many others, particularly those from the United States (see e.g. Beaudry and Parno 2013; Brighton
2009; Dawdy 2000; Franklin and Fesler 1999; Praetzellis and Praetzellis 2004a;
Praetzellis and Praetzellis eds. 2004b, 2009; Ross 2012; Rothschild and Wall 2014;
Silliman 2005; Singleton 1999; Voss 2015; Yamin 1998, 2001a, b; but see also
Young 2003), that have illuminated our understanding of migration as one of the
most fundamental forces in shaping the modern world.

Nonetheless it would be wrong to assume that the construction of such narratives
is the only (or even the most important) goal of the historical archaeology of the
modern city. In Chap. 10 we closed discussion with a detailed case study of the
Doyle family from The Rocks in Sydney. We know a great deal about them from
both archaeological and written documentary data. However, the discussion of the
provenance of the beryl earring found in the subfloor deposits at 128 Cumberland
Street demonstrates that there are limits to our capacity to explore its meaning with
any degree of certainty. This is a highly specific example of the issues of the integration of diverse datasets that are common enough in historical archaeology. How
should we respond to them?

Some years ago Adrian Praetzellis considered the importance of storytelling in
historical archaeology:

> But this is not to say that some specific story lurks within the soil and artifacts waiting to be
> freed by the archaeologist. On the contrary. The site contains many potential stories, but
> every one is the product of the archaeological imagination that pulls together historical and
> archaeological facts into an interpretation that is more than the sum of the parts of which it
> is made and more than its excavator can document in the usual way. (1998:1)

This makes a lot of sense, especially when we consider that not all stories are the
same and that not all are the outcomes of a rich integration of the many distinct
datasets that urban historical archaeologists routinely articulate in analysis. For
example, some stories might be more narrative identifying methodological challenges and the many ambiguities that exist within those datasets. Other stories might
be more about the presence or absence of items of material culture – telling stories
of manufacture, import replacement, trade and consumption. Still others might dif-
ferentiate between assemblages that can be securely linked to individuals or families and those that are accretions of deposits made at places where there was a high
turnover of individuals who cannot be so securely connected with specific elements
of target assemblages. Finally there are stories that reflect the differences between
assemblages linked to family dwellings and those more clearly associated with business, industry or in the case of the Commonwealth Block, prostitution (see also
Murray 2006b). Our research has not yet advanced to the point where the outcomes
of the comparison of intercity assemblages have developed, and to the point where

the rich integrations occasionally achieved at the level of the site or the household (as previous publications such as Crook et al. 2005 presented for The Rocks or Murray and Mayne 2001 did at Casselden Place) could be reported here.

In this book we have presented examples of a number of these stories and focused hard on seeking to enhance the stock of reliable empirical information about the contents of the 20 cesspits and the people and places that are linked to them. In Chap. 10 we reported the empirical outcomes of a comprehensive assemblage analysis and in Chaps. 8 and 9 presented detailed discussions of individuals and families directly related to those places (but see also Crook et al. 2005 and Murray and Mayne 2001). In every case we have paid particular attention to the contexts of deposition, the vectors of assemblage accumulation (see especially Chap. 7) and issues of integrity and dating, to provide a clearer picture of the events that most likely created the deposits we have reviewed.

This has been a complex and labour-intensive process that sought to ensure that the 20 cesspits from two Australian cities that became the capitals of two distinct Australian colonies could be meaningfully compared – notwithstanding the fact that they were excavated at different times, by different teams and recorded differently. Given the histories of the analysis of both cesspit groups, we also needed to ensure that the comparison of the various assemblages was meaningful as well. Thus at the core of this comparative investigation into the 20 assemblages lies a clear methodology for ensuring that they can be meaningfully, consistently and reliably compared. For this reason a significant element of the methodology of comparison is the construction of databases which operate across different scales, be they the site, the neighbourhood, the city or still more broadly across nations and the globe. Ensuring the comparability of such a diversity of databases (which will be vital for the pursuit of the comparative agendum in urban historical archaeology) exists as a major challenge for the future of such intercity or international comparisons. There are others.

Comparison and Comparability: Some Challenges for Further Research

In the previous chapter, we began a process of integrating archaeological and documentary evidence, so that we could describe and establish patterns occurring within material culture derived from house lots in our study areas. We were careful to emphasise that difficulties in interpretation existed, insofar as issues of data quality constrained our capacity to support an interpretation focusing on the lives of individuals.

We now take these matters further by refining our analysis of assemblages from 20 backfilled cesspits from the Sydney and Melbourne sites in conjunction with occupancy data from the surrounding city blocks by considering other contextual issues such as residential mobility.

In this discussion we have not focused on matters of class, gender, ethnicity or religious affiliation, although as we have discussed in Chaps. 8 and 9, there is documentary evidence to allow us some access to these issues. In Chap. 10 we discussed elements of the assemblages from both cities (such as tablewares, teawares, décor and 'moralising china') that have in the literature been interpreted as providing useful evidence about class aspiration. The current state of our analysis of these assemblages does not support clear linkages between the distributions of material culture and the occupants of our target sites. In fact we are still some way from securing such linkages between material culture and changing ethnicities in both precincts. Little seems to have changed since the assessment made by Murray of the outcomes of the second major phase of excavation on the Commonwealth Block:

> One of the most striking aspects of the archaeological analysis thus far is the relative lack of direct and unambiguous evidence of ethnic or cultural differences among residents. While the historical records make much of the developing ethnic diversity at Casselden Place, the archaeological record is either silent or equivocal. (Murray 2006b: 404)

At that time Murray observed that the disjunction between the rich detail of the written documentary records about ethnicity and other matters, such as class and gender, and the equivocal archaeological records of the site raised important issues for future research. One of the most important of these has to do with the mechanics of consumption. What material culture was available for consumption at this time? Was the outcome of homogeneity in the material culture of these places a function of availability rather than choice? To go further – as ethnic communities solidified their occupation of places like The Rocks and the Commonwealth Block over the course of the nineteenth century, were trading links with the home countries forged that could provide an alternative supply of material culture to the residents? Of course there are items of Chinese material culture ranging from ceramics to coins, but these are not particularly numerous given what we know about the extent of Chinese activity in Casselden Place. It is also the case that such material culture is not a reliable indicator of ethnicity as it is commonly found on sites of this period.

Our data are more responsive to inquiries about the nature (and archaeological consequences) of residential mobility. Once again the documentary record, while far from complete in every particular, contains valuable data about occupants and occupancy. Allowing for inevitable *lacunae* in the datasets, we have been able to establish the difference between places that were occupied by the same families for extended periods and others that had a swifter turnover. We shall return to this discussion later in the chapter.

At this point we can observe that the broad patterns identified at both sites (The Rocks and the Commonwealth Block) in Chap. 10 are not the same and that identifying plausible responses to difference remain a key challenge for future research. In Chap. 10 we described broad differences within and between the two precincts. Difference (like similarity) invites explanation and the exploration of whether that outcome is either counterintuitive, expected, or both. Earlier in this book, we canvassed core issues related to generalisations about class, consumption, the consequences of migration, the potential presence of ethnogenesis, the plasticity of cultural norms or more mundane matters related to the discard of material culture or the management of waste in nineteenth century cities. Our data indicate that within some broad boundaries, the *composition* of the 20 cesspit assemblages is both similar and different within and between the two precincts. The most obvious differences appear to lie in the relative frequencies of functional types. So is this difference the outcome of a difference in functions or some other factors which are skewing the distributions such as the types of places being investigated: boarding houses, brothels or other places with a high turnover of tenants? It is also important to recall that we are observing cesspit assemblages composed of both discarded and curated items. So a continuing task is to account for the patterns in terms of their *local* contexts, so that we might identify the key historical drivers that are behind these patterns in each of the Sydney and Melbourne sites. This might be expressed as engaging in a process of operationalising stages 1 and 2 of the schematic of global material culture represented in Fig. 11.1.

Doing this allows us to proceed to stage 3 and eventually later stages in that schematic, as we seek to comprehend the nature of both similarity and difference between target assemblages in both cities. Thus our second task to build on existing comparative data to get a clearer idea of the nature of variability observed at a scale beyond the household, the site or indeed the city. Of course this process of changing the scale of comparison rests on the assumption that as one moves back and forth

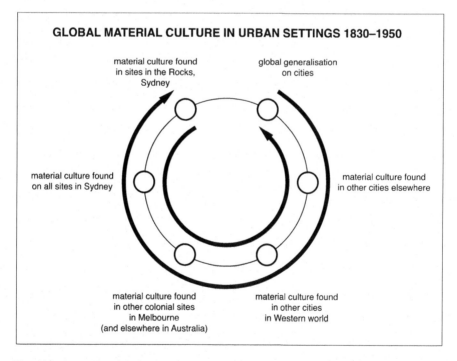

GLOBAL MATERIAL CULTURE IN URBAN SETTINGS 1830–1950

material culture found in sites in the Rocks, Sydney

global generalisation on cities

material culture found on all sites in Sydney

material culture found in other cities elsewhere

material culture found in other colonial sites in Melbourne (and elsewhere in Australia)

material culture found in other cities in Western world

Fig. 11.1 Schematic of global material culture in urban settings 1830–959. (First published in Mayne and Murray (2001), p. 104)

through the different stages represented in the schematic, that new data (using a form of recursive reasoning), issues and possibilities come into focus and spur new lines of inquiry that might more effectively integrate the different datasets we have created or might simply provide new challenges for both theory *and* method.

In Search of Integration: Sorting Signals from Noise

Operationalising the above schematic requires a tacking back and forth between the datasets of urban historical archaeology and the different scales of observation and analysis. In our case the comparison of sites from The Rocks and the Commonwealth Block helped us to overturn the conclusions Murray and Mayne had reached in an earlier discussion of the assemblage from Casselden Place on the Block. At this time we confidently observed:

> The *archaeological record* of Casselden Place is very difficult to integrate into this fine-grained documentary analysis. The key point to emerge from its detailed analysis is the remarkably low level of variability in assemblage structure and composition between houses occupied by the same people (such as the Moloneys at Location 69), and those (such as the Harts, the Cummings, and the Taylors at Location 74B) which experienced a more rapid turnover of occupants. (Murray and Mayne 2001: 102)

Eighteen years later the observations about the difficulties we encountered when seeking to integrate the documentary and archaeological records of the site remain true, but the data presented in Chap. 10 (particularly Tables 10.7, 10.8, 10.9, 10.10, 10.11, 10.12, 10.13, 10.14, and 10.15) demonstrate that there is significant variability within the assemblages. But what is the significance of this variability beyond reinforcing our original interpretation that duration of occupation by known individuals and their families is a significant factor in our analysis? At one level this might simply be seen as describing noisy variation or, at another, allowing the identification of a clear signal about the importance of the duration of occupancy. It also sets us the challenge of engaging more effectively with 'noisy' historical and archaeological to tell different kinds of stories of the kind we discussed earlier in this chapter.

The discussion of ambiguities and uncertainties with respect to the integration of archaeological and written documentary records at Casselden Place prompted the development of the comparative schematic illustrated above. Murray and Mayne understood that they had embarked on voyage of discovery – finding plausible strategies for integrating the diverse data related to people, material culture and archaeological contexts at specific sites and within vanished communities. They were confident that the documentary record would figure centrally in all of this, and the research we present in this book clearly affirms that expectation. However Mayne, Crook and Murray have also had to grapple with an archaeological record that has been and continues to be far more equivocal. Selecting the appropriate scale of comparison and generalisation between and among archaeological records in order to operationalise the schematic beyond the first two stages has proved to be the most significant challenge for us. In this reading, at its most inclusive, the archaeology of the modern city is the archaeology of the modern world. It therefore seems self-evident that through the process of recursive reasoning moving back and forth between the various stages of the schematic (and the varieties of scale that these represent), new patterns will emerge to engage us.

Murray and Mayne observed that this is not without risk as archaeologists will have to move beyond the safe harbours of conventional social and cultural theory and contemporary historical understanding to confront new problems. They will also have to move from the conventions of archaeological practice to incorporate global perspectives in the construction of global relational databases that are built with the goal of comparison in mind. Then there is the equally thorny issue of the curation of databases to facilitate comparison. We (Murray and Crook) do not minimise the difficulty of this challenge. So, there is much more than just theory to grapple with!

It is equally true that not all archaeologists will want to embrace the virtues of larger-scale comparative data analysis and generalisation. The attractions of a focus on the particular and the richness of archaeologies of the household or the single sites in the modern city are real enough, especially if one aspires to achieving a level of integration that goes beyond site phasing and the establishment of chronology or indeed beyond describing the contents of assemblages. This is the historical archaeology of flesh and blood people that has great power in communicating the value of historic sites to our various audiences and which connects directly to conventional historical and anthropological discourse about the genesis of the modern city around the globe. However we stress that adopting the process of recursive reasoning also makes it possible to move from large-scale generalisation back to specific places and people, with new perspectives drawn from the wider world. It is also important to stress that we are aware that these important specificities of place, people and time are themselves the products of concepts, categories and units of analysis which are built from acts of comparison and generalisation. To argue otherwise would be to accept that at all levels of discussion every historical or archaeological observable must be unique. This is an argument that would effectively spell the end of our search for a broader understanding of life in the modern city.

These are the dual challenges of pixilation and scale which we discussed in Chap. 2. Both challenges are of prime importance as we seek to establish the tolerance limits of theory and method and to understand that the complexities of the archaeology of the modern city require us to be ready to subject our theoretical and methodological armoury to rigorous assessment (see also Murray and Crook 2005; Orser 2010). So, rather than being an end, the comparative approach holds out the prospect of a new beginning.

Concluding Remarks

Throughout this book we have stressed that the research we present here is very much a work in progress. We have outlined the trajectory of the evolution of our approach over the last few decades, but we have also stressed that further developments, particularly through an engagement with understanding the archaeology of transnational forces related to the movement of people, goods, technology and systems of government, administration, manufacturing and agriculture, are clearly in prospect. This is especially the case in exploring the archaeology of ethnogenesis in colonial and postcolonial societies.

That clear prospect of developments resulting from an engagement with multiple frames of reference from the household right up to the global archaeology of the modern city supports an expectation that more sophisticated and deeper integrations of archaeological and historical evidence in places like the Commonwealth Block and The Rocks will occur. In our present circumstance, we have tried to be transparent about our doubts and reservations that might flow from the integrations we have offered in this book. We have also stressed that such doubts should not wholly constrain the kinds of stories we think should be told in order to reach some verisimilitude about our accounts of life in both precincts. Naturally we would be delighted if all of our stories could be based on readily demonstrated integrations of diverse historical and archaeological data, but in its place, we have opted for transparency about the limits and shortcomings of what we have presented here and have identified challenges for future research.

There is still much for us to learn from the abundant archaeological and written and photographic records from The Rocks in Sydney and the Commonwealth Block in Melbourne and from comparisons between these places and other city sites around the world, most recently the city of Buenos Aires (see e.g. Riccardi 2015). We have seen that our target sites in Sydney and Melbourne were both working class districts characterised by housing, cottage industries and small businesses in the second half of the nineteenth century. Nonetheless they were far from being identical. The Commonwealth Block was regarded as an area of crime, brothels and poverty; the area received a lot of attention from moral reformers (and from historians of Melbourne) from the 1850s onwards. While it has been important for historical archaeologists to demonstrate that this precinct was diverse in its population (and their occupations), it is also counterproductive to pretend as if there was no prostitution, gambling, drug-taking and associated criminality occurring there.

The first of the critical points of the original research for the precinct was the need to redress perceived historical imbalances and to comprehend a community that changed dramatically over the course of its existence and which was much more than a foul slum full of feckless itinerants living at the margins of society. While the 'image' of The Rocks in Sydney was somewhat more subdued, there is no doubt that it, too, was understood by citizens of Sydney as being occupied by people at the bottom of the social ladder. Our goal of redressing historical imbalances applies equally here too, and to that extent, we have been greatly assisted by the work of historians such as Grace Karskens and Alan Mayne.

Our archaeological investigations suggest more complex histories for both precincts, where the homogeneity of the slum stereotype can be challenged by evidence for a sense of community among residents and many young families striving for respectability. Towards the end of the nineteenth century, many ethnic minority groups, particularly the Chinese, moved into both areas and operated businesses,

before changing again in the early twentieth century with the appearance of factories (particularly in the Commonwealth Block). Of course they are not represented
in the assemblage analyses we present here, but they are a critical part of the 'total'
histories of both precincts, once again underscoring the need to use our different
types of evidence in ways that enhance our understanding of the places and
their people.

In the late 1940s, the Commonwealth Government of Australia acquired the
Melbourne land and subsequently demolished the majority of the buildings in the
area, thereby erasing many of the structures that were either the homeplaces or the
work sites of its residents. This erasure was accelerated by high-rise redevelopment
initiated in the late 1980s. The historical archaeology of the entire Commonwealth
Block is wholly a consequence of the development process. The history of development in The Rocks has been just as intense, but it occurred earlier than in Melbourne,
in response to development pressures that were first most strongly felt in Sydney.
Nonetheless the historical archaeology of that locale was again primarily the outcome of the development process and a growing recognition among the citizens of
Sydney of its highly significant heritage values.

Which brings us to the second of the critical points of our research. Notwithstanding
the production of high-quality reports by the two major heritage consultancies
involved in the excavation of The Rocks and the Commonwealth Block (GML and
Austral Archaeology), it was the post-excavation analysis of both precincts that has
underwritten research into the historical archaeology of the modern city in both
Sydney and Melbourne. In The Rocks, the Sydney Harbour Foreshores Authority,
the Historic Houses Trust of New South Wales and the Youth Hostels Association
were intimately involved in supporting and managing that process, but major invest-
ments by the Australian Research Council in a long series of linked projects in both
cities provided key financial input that made a sustained engagement with the
archaeology of both precincts possible. In Chap. 2 we discussed out objective of
'going back to the boxes' which allowed us to seek an enhanced understanding of
the archaeology of the early modern city in Australia. That search has led to a re-
evaluation of sites such as First Government House and the Hyde Park Barracks in
Sydney, as well as underpinning new baseline studies of previously excavated sites
in The Rocks and on the Commonwealth Block. Perhaps the most direct impact has
been on the evolution of research design in the archaeology of the second and third
phases of excavation at the Commonwealth Block.

However there has been a more fundamental (and possibly more important)
impact on our perception of value of the archaeology of the modern city. A particularly powerful outcome is that the cultural capital of the cities of Sydney and
Melbourne has been significantly enhanced, and the potential to make a meaningful Australian contribution to a global comparative archaeology of the modern city
has been demonstrated. Thus the value of a financial investment in revealing the
heritage value of inner-city places has been further justified by showing what we
can learn from a close engagement with the archaeological outcomes of the development process. Yet it needs to be understood that an important element of the
transformation of the contents of archived boxes into an information that would

slowly build to a significant contribution towards creating a coherent historical archaeology of both cities, has been funded by governments local, state and federal. Of course in Melbourne private developers (particularly the Industry Superannuation Property Trust) of the Commonwealth Block met the upfront costs of preparing reports and artefact catalogues, but this was (and remains) only the first step in a long journey to create histories of both cities that result from the integration of data drawn from archaeological sites as well as documents and other historical data. It seems self-evident that archaeologists and historians of the modern city need to support heritage agencies in backing continuing research on archived collections as a basis for ensuring the ongoing social and cultural significance of these places.

Importantly when we contemplate the evolution of changing communities we embrace the realities of the growth of the modern city in the nineteenth century. At The Rocks and the Commonwealth Block, we confront the reality of mass migration to Australia from Europe, Asia and the Americas with the introduction of a wide diversity of cultures and religions (as well as the chequered histories of the migrants). For many of our occupants during this time, both precincts provided their first experience of life in a city at the end of the world. They also became their base to find a way of living in a new land that might repay the very high emotional (and economic) costs of leaving home to recreate the substance of their lives elsewhere.

This large-scale movement of people had distinct consequences for the older city of Sydney and the young Melbourne (at the beginning of our story barely two decades old). Rapidly expanding populations placed particular strains on infrastructure, for example, forcing the Melbourne City Council to address issues related to the management of garbage and human waste, the maintenance of law and order and the pressing need to respond to clear evidence of the consequences of poverty through the creation of schools and non-government provision of social services. For better or worse responses to all of these pressures occurred throughout the post-contact histories of both precincts, continuing into the twentieth and twenty-first centuries, when the above-ground physical remains of those pasts were erased and sites redeveloped. Importantly although these remains in many cases (with the notable exception of the Big Dig Centre in Sydney – https://thebigdig.com.au) have vanished from public view, the historical archaeology of The Rocks and the Commonwealth Block has begun to restore truer histories of both precincts and their constituent communities.

References

Beaudry, M.C., and T.G. Parno. 2013. Introduction: Mobilities in Contemporary Historical Archaeology. In *Archaeologies of Mobility and Movement*, ed. M.C. Beaudry and T.G. Parno, 1–16. New York: Springer.

Brighton, S.A. 2009. *Historical Archaeology of the Irish Diaspora: A Transnational Approach*. Knoxville: University of Tennessee Press.

Crook, P., L. Ellmoos, and T. Murray. 2005. *Keeping up with the McNamaras: A historical Archaeological Study of the Cumberland and Gloucester Streets site, The Rocks, Sydney*. Archaeology of the Modern City Series 8. Sydney: Historic Houses Trust of New South Wales.

————. 2006a. *People+Place: A guide to using the database. Archaeology of the Modern City Series*, 9. Sydney: Historic Houses Trust of New South Wales.

————. 2006b. EAMC Databases, Version 1.0. In *Exploring the Archaeology of the Modern City Project Databases*, ed. P. Crook, L. Ellmoos, and T. Murray. Sydney: Historic Houses Trust of NSW.

Dawdy, S.L., ed. 2000. Creolization. *Historical Archaeology* 34 (3): 1–133.

Franklin, M., and G. Fesler, eds. 1999. *Historical Archaeology, Identity Formation, and the Interpretation of Ethnicity*. Williamsburg: Colonial Williamsburg Foundation.

Karskens, G. 1997. *The Rocks: Life in Early Sydney*. Melbourne: Melbourne University Press.

————. 1999. *Inside The Rocks: The Archaeology of a Neighbourhood*. Sydney: Hale and Iremonger.

————. 2001. Small Things, Big Pictures: New Perspectives from the Archaeological of Sydney's Rocks Neighbourhood. In *The Archaeology of Urban Landscapes: Explorations in Slumland*, ed. A. Mayne and T. Murray. Melbourne: Cambridge University Press.

————. 2006. Making City Lives: Urban Archaeology and Australian Social, Cultural and Urban History. In *Cities in the World, 1500–2000*, ed. A. Green and R. Leech. Leeds: Maney Publishing.

Lydon, J. 1999. *Many inventions': The Chinese in the Rocks, Sydney 1890–1930*. Clayton: Monash University.

Mayne, A., and T. Murray. 1999. In-Little-Lon-Wiv-Ginger-Mick': Telling the Forgotten History of a Vanished Community. *Journal of Popular Culture* 33 (1): 49–60.

————. 2001. The Archaeology of Urban Landscapes: Explorations in Slumland. In *The Archaeology of Urban Landscapes: Explorations in Slumland*, ed. A. Mayne and T. Murray. Cambridge: Cambridge University Press.

Murray, T. 2006a. Introduction. *International Journal of Historical Archaeology* 10 (4): 291–298.

————. 2006b. Integrating Archaeology and History at the Commonwealth Block: 'Little Lon' and Casselden Place. *International Journal of Historical Archaeology* 10 (4): 385–403.

Murray, T., and P. Crook. 2005. Exploring the Archaeology of the Modern City: Issues of Scale, Integration and Complexity. *International Journal of Historical Archaeology* 9 (2): 89–109.

Murray, T., and A. Mayne. 2001. Imaginary Landscapes: Reading Melbourne's 'Little Lon. In *The Archaeology of Urban Landscapes: Explorations in Slumland*, ed. A. Mayne and T. Murray. Cambridge: Cambridge University Press.

————. 2003. (Re) Constructing a Lost Community: 'Little Lon', Melbourne, Australia. *Historical Archaeology* 37 (1): 87–101.

Murray, T., K. Buckley, S. Hayes, G. Hewitt, J. McCarthy, R. Mackay, B. Minchinton, C. Smith, J. Smith, and Bronwyn Woff. 2019. *The Commowealth Block, Melbourne: A Historical Archaeology*. Sydney: Australasian Society for Historical Archaeology.

Orser, C. 2010. Twenty-First Century Historical Archaeology. *Journal of Archaeological Research* 18: 111–150.

Praetzellis, A. 1998. Introduction: Why Every Archaeologist Should Tell Stories Once in a While. *Historical Archaeology* 32 (1): 1–3.

Praetzellis, A., and M. Praetzellis. 2004a. Becoming Jewish Americans. In *Putting the "There" there: Historical Archaeologies of West Oakland*, ed. A. Prezellis and M. Praetzellis, 68–71. Rohnert Park: Anthropological Studies Centre, Sonoma State University.

Praetzellis, M., and A. Praetzellis, eds. 2004b. *Putting the 'There' There: Historical Archaeologies of West Oakland, 1–880 Cypress Freeway Replacement Project*. Report Prepared by Anthropological Studies Center. Rohnert Park: Sonoma State University.

————, eds. 2009. *South of Market: Historical Archaeology of 3 San Francisco Neighborhoods*. The San Francisco – Oakland Bay Bridge West Approach Project. Report Prepared by Anthropological Studies Center. Rohnert Park: Sonoma State University.

Riccardi, P. 2015. A Tale of Two Cities: Nineteenth Century Consumer Behaviour in Melbourne and Buenos Aires. Unpublished PhD dissertation, La Trobe University.

Ross, D.E. 2012. Transnational artefacts: Grappling with fluid material origins and identities in archaeological interpretations of culture change. *Journal of Anthropological Archaeology* 31 (1): 38–48.

Rothschild, N., and D. Wall. 2014. *The Archaeology of American Cities*. Gainesville: University of Florida Press.

Silliman, S. 2005. Culture contact or colonialism? Changes in the archaeology of native North America. *American Antiquity* 70 (1): 55–74.

Singleton, T.A., ed. 1999. *"I, Too, Am America": Archaeological Studies of African-American Life*. Charlottesville: Univ. Virginia Press.

Voss, B. 2015. What's new? Rethinking Ethnogenesis in the Archaeology of Colonialism. *American Antiquity* 40: 655.

Yamin, R. 1998. Lurid Tales and Homely Stories of New York's Notorious Five Points. *Historical Archaeology* 31 (1): 74–85.

Yamin, Rebecca. 2001a. Alternative narratives: Respectability at New York's Five Points. In *The Archaeology of Urban Landscapes: Explorations in Slumland*, ed. A. Mayne and T. Murray, 154–170. Cambridge: Cambridge University Press.

———. 2001b. Becoming New York: The Five Points Neighbourhood. *Historical Archaeology* 35 (3): 1–5.

Young, L. 2003. *Middle Class Culture in the Nineteenth Century: America, Australia and Britain*. New York: Palgrave Macmillan.

Appendix 1: List of Matching Sets

© Springer Nature Switzerland AG 2019   269
T. Murray, P. Crook, *Exploring the Archaeology of the Modern City
in Nineteenth-century Australia*, Contributions To Global Historical
Archaeology, https://doi.org/10.1007/978-3-030-27169-5

City	Location	MC	MS ID	Type	Description	Table service				Tea service				Table/tea	Beverage service		Hygi.	Unid.	Total MNV
						IND	SHD	UNID	Total	IND	SHD	UNID	Total	UNID	IND	SHD			
MEL	Cass 007	Cesspit A	81462	M	'Castle' pattern				0	7			7						7
MEL	Cass 007	Cesspit A	68551	M	Classical scene by Copeland				0	3			3						3
MEL	Cass 007	Cesspit A	81491	M	Hand-painted floral				0	3			3						3
MEL	Cass 007	Cesspit A	74909	C	Rural scene with T-shaped motifs	3			3				0						3
MEL	Cass 007	Cesspit A	78134	C	Shell-edge	3			3				0						3
MEL	Cass 007	Cesspit A	78226	C	Trailing vines				0	2			2	1					3
MEL	Cass 007	Cesspit A	80312	C	'Two Temples'	1			1	2			2						3
MEL	Cass 007	Cesspit A	80767	C	'Willow'	7	1		8				0						8
MEL	Cass 007	Cesspit A	68610	C	Undecorated				0				0					2	2
MEL	Cass 007	Cesspit A	81453	C	Tumblers: panelled				0				0		2				2
MEL	Leic L25C	1.010	1739	C	'Albion'	1	1		2				0						2
MEL	Leic L25C	1.010	2307	C	Blue irregular sponge decoration				0	1			1					1	2

MEL	Leic L25C	1.010				1	1	2	11	11	13
MEL	Leic L25C	1.010	2410	C	Fibre pattern			13			13
MEL	Leic L25C	1.010	1833	M	'Flora' pattern	0		2		0	2
MEL	Leic L25C	1.010	2019	C	Floral gilt	0				2	2
MEL	Leic L25C	1.010	2329	C	Floral toy tea set	0		2		0	2
MEL	Leic L25C	1.010	1836	C	'Lucerne' pattern	0				2	2
MEL	Leic L25C	1.010	2424	C	Marble pattern	0		5		0	5
MEL	Leic L25C	1.010	2044	C	'Montezuma', flow transfer-print	1				1	2
MEL	Leic L25C	1.010	1971	C	Mugs with or without gilt bands	0				2	2
MEL	Leic L25C	1.010	1519	C	Panelled vessels with gilt bands	0				3	3
MEL	Leic L25C	1.010	1823	C	Relief moulded and sprigged bone China	0				2	2
MEL	Leic L25C	1.010	3370	C	'Rhine'	4				1	5
MEL	Leic L25C	1.010	1995	C	Sprigged	0				2	2

(continued)

City	Location	MC	MS ID	Type	Description	Table service			Tea service		Table/ tea	Beverage service	Hygi.	Unid.	Total MNV
MEL	Leic L25C	1.010	1741	C	Transfer-printed flow black floral pattern, clobbered	1		*1*		*0*				1	2
MEL	Leic L25C	1.010	2050	C	Transfer-printed flow pattern with Chinese scene			*0*	3	*3*	*3*				3
MEL	Leic L25C	1.010	1968	C	'Wild rose'	2		*2*		*0*					2
MEL	Leic L25C	1.010	2292	C	'Willow'	12	9	*21*		*0*					21
MEL	Leic L25C	1.010	2098	C	Panelled tumblers			*0*		*0*		3			3
MEL	Leic L25C	1.010	2243	C	Fluted tumblers			*0*		*0*		4			4
MEL	Lons 143	Cesspit M	82960	C	'Asiatic Pheasant' plates	3		*3*		*0*					3
MEL	Lons 143	Cesspit M	82942	C	Black transfer-printed teaware with floral motifs			*0*	2	*2*	*2*				2
MEL	Lons 143	Cesspit M	82972	M	'Dresden views'	1	1	*2*		*0*					2
MEL	Lons 143	Cesspit M	82956	C	"Fibre"	1		*1*		*0*	1				2

Site	Location	Context	Cat. No.	C/M	Description									Total
MEL	Lons 143	Cesspit M	82895	C	Fluted bone China with gilt bands			*0*		2	*2*			**2**
MEL	Lons 143	Cesspit M	82897	C	Fluted bone China, unadorned			*0*		2	*2*			**2**
MEL	Lons 143	Cesspit M	83123	M	'Oriental' pattern	3		*3*			*0*		1	**3**
MEL	Lons 143	Cesspit M	82887	C	Sprigged bone china	3		*3*	2	2	*2*			**3**
MEL	Lons 143	Cesspit M	83192	M	'The Season' pattern	2		*2*			*0*			**2**
MEL	Lons 143	Cesspit M	82883	M	Undecorated whiteware dinner plate	3		*3*			*0*			**3**
MEL	Lons 143	Cesspit M	82882	C	White granite with berlin swirl	1		*1*	1	1	*1*	1		**3**
MEL	Lons 143	Cesspit M	82850	C	'Willow'	9	3 1	*13*			*0*			**13**
MEL	Lons 143	Cesspit M	83131	C	Brown transfer-printed floral decoration			*0*			*0*		6	**6**
MEL	Lons 143	Cesspit M	82522	C	Mitred drinking glass			*0*			*0*	5		**5**
MEL	Lons 147	2.722	18546	C	Banded teaware	1		*1*	1	1	*1*			**2**

(continued)

City	Location	MC	MS ID	Type	Description	Table service			Tea service			Table/ tea	Beverage service	Hygi.	Unid.	Total MNV
MEL	Lons 147	2.722	26690	C	Marble pattern, black	1		0	2	1	3					3
MEL	Lons 147	2.722	18549	C	'Fibre', blue			1	1		1					2
MEL	Lons 147	2.722	26690	CC	Marble pattern, blue	1		1			0					1
MEL	Lons 147	2.722	18549	CC	'Fibre', green			0		1	1					1
MEL	Lons 147	2.722	18555	C	'Tyrol'	2		2	2		2					4
MEL	Lons 147	2.722	14811	C	'Willow'	8	4	12			0					12
MEL	Lons 147	2.722	15825	M	'Willow' by Mellor, Venables & Co.	2		2			0					2
MEL	Lons 147	2.722	17572	M	Tumblers with ovoid facets			0			0		3			3
MEL	LtLei L36A	1.230	19835	C	'Albion'		1	1			0					1
MEL	LtLei L36A	1.230	28692	C	'Asiatic Pheasant'	1	1	2			0					2
MEL	LtLei L36A	1.230	11556	C	'Australia' pattern			0	2		2					2
MEL	LtLei L36A	1.230	10433	C	Chinese scene			0	2		2					2
MEL	LtLei L36A	1.230	10426	C	Chinoise			0	1	1	2					2

MEL	LtLei L36A	1.230	11512	C	'Fibre'				0	2		2		2
MEL	LtLei L36A	1.230	28726	C	'Pebble' pattern				0	1	1	2		2
MEL	LtLei L36A	1.230	10429	M	'Pelew' pattern	2			2			0		2
MEL	LtLei L36A	1.230	28724	C	Scenic 56				0	1	1	2		2
MEL	LtLei L36A	1.230	10461	C	Sheet pattern TS 88				0	1		1		1
MEL	LtLei L36A	1.230	28747	C	'Willow'	11	4	2	17			0		17
MEL	LtLon 073	Cesspit T	74815	C	Bouquet of flowers pattern				0	2		2		2
MEL	LtLon 073	Cesspit T	81462	C	'Castle' pattern				0	1		1		1
MEL	LtLon 073	Cesspit T	75527	C	Chinese Scene 21				0	2		2		2
MEL	LtLon 073	Cesspit T	81745	C	Classical Scene 53				0	4		4		4
MEL	LtLon 073	Cesspit T	81764	CC	'Fibre', black	1			1	2		2		3
MEL	LtLon 073	Cesspit T	81764	C	'Fibre', blue		1		1	5		5		6
MEL	LtLon 073	Cesspit T	81786	C	Floral flow 26				0	2		2		2
MEL	LtLon 073	Cesspit T	81824	C	Misc sprigged vessels				0	2		2	1	3

(continued)

City	Location	MC	MS ID	Type	Description	Table service			Tea service			Table/ tea	Beverage service	Hygi.	Unid.	Total MNV
MEL	LtLon 073	Cesspit T	81710	C	'Rhone'	1		*1*	1		*1*					2
MEL	LtLon 073	Cesspit T	73279	C	Scenic 54			*0*	2		*2*					2
MEL	LtLon 073	Cesspit T	70536	C	Scenic pattern 56, basket-weave rim			*0*	2		*2*					2
MEL	LtLon 073	Cesspit T	67782	C	'Seine' pattern			*0*	3		*3*					3
MEL	LtLon 073	Cesspit T	67782	M	'Seine' pattern, with mark			*0*	3		*3*					3
MEL	LtLon 073	Cesspit T	81765	C	Shell-edge	3	1	*4*			*0*					4
MEL	LtLon 073	Cesspit T	75836	C	'Temple', blue			*0*	2	1	*3*					4
MEL	LtLon 073	Cesspit T	75836	CC	'Temple', black or green			*0*	2		*2*	1				2
MEL	LtLon 073	Cesspit T	81711	C	'Two temples'			*0*	2	1	*3*				1	4
MEL	LtLon 073	Cesspit T	81808	C	Undecorated	5		*5*			*0*				1	6
MEL	LtLon 073	Cesspit T	81709	C	'Venus' pattern			*0*	2		*2*					2
MEL	LtLon 073	Cesspit T	81636	C	'Willow'	24	8	*33*			*0*		1			34
MEL	LtLon 073	Cesspit T	73314	M	'Willow', wheel maker's mark	4		*4*			*0*					4

MEL	Site	Context	No.	Fabric	Description								Total
MEL	LtLon 073	Cesspit T	79468	CC	Marble like (blue/grey)		0	0				2	2
MEL	LtLon 073	Cesspit T	68610	C	Undecorated		0	0				4	4
MEL	LtLon 073	Cesspit T	68368	C	Wine glass: TS 9		0	0		2			2
MEL	LtLon 073	Cesspit T	81626	C	Tumblers: panelled		0	0		7			7
MEL	LtLon 073	Cesspit T	68368	C	Wine glass: TS 9		0	0		2			2
MEL	LtLon 073	Cesspit T	81626	C	Tumblers: panelled		0	0		7			7
MEL	LtLon 128	1.023	30800/21563	C	'Asiatic Pheasant'	3	3	0			1	1	5
MEL	LtLon 128	1.023	21461	C	'Broseley'	3	0	2	2		1		3
MEL	LtLon 128	1.023	21371	M	Green Ivy leaves		0	2	2				2
MEL	LtLon 128	1.023	31200	M	Hand-painted		0	6	6				6
MEL	LtLon 128	1.023	26917	M	Hand-painted two-tone blue		0	2	2				2
MEL	LtLon 128	1.023	21393/31213	M	'Rhine'	5	6	0			1		6
MEL	LtLon 128	1.023	31151	C	Sprigged		0	3	3				3
MEL	LtLon 128	1.023	31224	M	Vine leaves		0	2	2				2

(continued)

City	Location	MC	MS ID	Type	Description	Table service				Tea service		Table/ tea	Beverage service	Hygi.	Unid.	Total MNV
						3	3	2								
MEL	LtLon 128	1.023	21506	C	'Willow'	3	3	2	8		0					8
MEL	LtLon 128	1.023	21370	C	'Honeysuckle'				0	1	1				1	2
MEL	LtLon 128	1.023	30801	M	Scenic transfer-printed (Mediterranean castle)	2			2	1	1					3
MEL	Spri 147	Cesspit B	82215	C	'Asiatic Pheasant'	1	1		2		0					2
MEL	Spri 147	Cesspit B	82130	CC	Gilt banded teaware	1			1	7	7					8
MEL	Spri 147	Cesspit B	82258	CC	'Willow'	11	3		14		0					14
MEL	Spri 255	Cesspit H	86093	M	Green transfer-printed, foliated scrolls and flowers				0		0				2	2
MEL	Spri 255	Cesspit H	86167	C	Transfer-printed with stylised ribbon border				0	1	1	1				2
MEL	Spri 255	Cesspit J	79211	C	Persian Rose' transfer-printed	2			2		0					2
MEL	Spri 255	Cesspit J	75376	C	Sprigged vessels				0	4	4					4
MEL	Spri 255	Cesspit J	69494	C	Vessels with gilt decoration	1			1	3	3					4

City	Site	Context	No.	Ware	Description									Total
MEL	Spri 255	Cesspit J	76541	C	Tumblers with ovoid facets			0			0		2	2
SYD	Cara 001	B197	51	C	Floral relief white earthenware teacups			0	3		3			3
SYD	Cara 001	B197	49	C	'Gem', by G Jones	2	1	3			0			3
SYD	Cara 001	B197	50	C	Sprigged porcelain			0	2		2			2
SYD	Cara 001	B197	52	C	Wine glasses: baluster knop	1		0			0		2	2
SYD	Cara 003	B077	46	M	Rhine green			0	1		1	1		2
SYD	Cara 003	B077	46	CC	Rhine grey	1		1			0			1
SYD	Cara 003	B077	80	C	Tendrils over striped ground		1	1	2		2			3
SYD	Cara 005	B294	54	CC	Brown and blue geometric design			0	1	1	1			2
SYD	Cara 005	B294	53	C	'November' border set			0	3		3			3
SYD	Cara 005	B294	55	C	Porcellaneous gilt			0	2		2			2
SYD	Cumb 122	A138	21	C	'Albion'	1		2	1		1			3

(continued)

City	Location	MC	MS ID	Type	Description	Table service	Tea service	Table/ tea	Beverage service	Hygi.	Unid.	Total MNV
SYD	Cumb 122	A138	3	M	Chantilly' by John Thomson, Glasgow	0	2					2
SYD	Cumb 122	A138	1	M	Sponge print blue: stars and serrated leaves	0	3					3
SYD	Cumb 122	A138	22	CC	Trail lines: multicolours (blue/brown)	1	1					2
SYD	Cumb 122	A138	20	C	'Two Temples'	0	3					3
SYD	Cumb 122	A138	2	C	Various mulberry sponge-print wares	1	2					3
SYD	Cumb 122	A138	23	M/C	White relief	0	4					4
SYD	Cumb 122	A138	24	C	Tumblers/large shot glasses	0	0		2			2
SYD	Cumb 124	A310	41	C	Amorphous cells and flowers	3	0					3
SYD	Cumb 124	A310	33	C	Angular egg and dart border	2	0					2
SYD	Cumb 124	A310	32	M	Basket of flowers with butterfly	0	2					2

SYD	Cumb 124	A310	27	M	Beaded diamond set					0	2	2	2
SYD	Cumb 124	A310	43	M	Blue berries, green leaves					0	3	3	3
SYD	Cumb 124	A310	13	C	'Chantilly'					0	2	2	2
SYD	Cumb 124	A310	36	M	Copeland late spode pattern 30			1		0	4	4	4
SYD	Cumb 124	A310	34	C	Fan border		1			1			2
SYD	Cumb 124	A310	25	C	Geometric (infilled zig-zag) set					0	2	2	2
SYD	Cumb 124	A310	40	M	'Seaweed', green					0	2	2	2
SYD	Cumb 124	A310	28	C	Hexagonal lozenge					0	2	2	2
SYD	Cumb 124	A310	37	M	'Hyacinth'					0	3	3	3
SYD	Cumb 124	A310	42	C	'Jessamine'					0	2	2	2
SYD	Cumb 124	A310	38	M	'Lace', green					0	7	7	7
SYD	Cumb 124	A310	31	C	'Palestine', blue	1				1	1	1	2
SYD	Cumb 124	A310	78	CC	'Palestine', green	1		1		2	2	2	4

(continued)

City	Location	MC	MS ID	Type	Description	Table service				Tea service			Table/ tea	Beverage service	Hygi.	Unid.	Total MNV
SYD	Cumb 124	A310	26	M	Papyrus border set				*0*	2		*2*					2
SYD	Cumb 124	A310	79	CC	Pendant acanthus with branching flowers				*0*	2	2	*4*					4
SYD	Cumb 124	A310	39	C	Quatrefoil and horizontal band design				*0*	2		*2*					2
SYD	Cumb 124	A310	44	C	Red/mulberry flowers, blue berries, solid green leaves				*0*	4		*4*					4
SYD	Cumb 124	A310	29	C	Thistles and dot set with paired scroll border				*0*	2		*2*					2
SYD	Cumb 124	A310	35	C	Trail lines and Seaweed, spotted ground				*0*	1		*1*				1	2
SYD	Cumb 124	A310	30	C	Tri-dot and dart border	2			*2*			*0*					2
SYD	Cumb 124	A310	76	C	'Two temples'	2			*2*	1	1	*2*					4
SYD	Cumb 124	A310	77	CC	'Willow'	9	2	2	*13*			*0*				2	15

													1
SYD	Cumb 124	A310	45	C	Wine/sherry glass, cut, arched panels on bowl; 'bladed' knop					0		0	1
SYD	Cumb 124	A310	45	M	Wine/sherry glass, cut, arched panels on bowl; 'bladed' knop					0		0	2
											2		
SYD	Cumb 126	A140	16	C	'Fibre', black			0	2	0	2		2
SYD	Cumb 126	A140	47	C	Blue-body Stoneware			0	2	0	2		2
SYD	Cumb 126	A140	19	C	'Chantilly' by John Thomson, Glasgow	1		1	2	1	2		3
SYD	Cumb 126	A140	15	C	'Rhine', grey	1		1	1	1	1		2
SYD	Cumb 126	A140	18	C	'Peacock'	1		1	1	1	1		2
SYD	Cumb 126	A140	17	C	'Rhine'			0	2	0	2		2
SYD	Glou 093	F044	58	C	Diamond hatch border			0	2	0	2		2
SYD	Glou 093	F044	57	M	'Florence'			0	2	0	2		2
SYD	Glou 097	C056	72	C	Scenic			0	2	0	2		2

(continued)

City	Location	MC	MS ID	Type	Description	Table service				Tea service				Table/ tea	Beverage service		Hygi.	Unid.	Total MNV
SYD	Glou 097	C056	73	C	Unidentified scenic (pavilion and lake)				*0*	2			*2*						2
SYD	Glou 097	C056	74	C	Green trail lines	1			*1*	1			*1*						2
SYD	Glou 097	C056	71	C	Scene with castellated bridge				*0*	1			*1*					1	2
SYD	Glou 097	C056	75	M/C	Sprigged porcelain	1			*1*	5			*5*						6
SYD	Glou 097	C220	70	C	Porcellaneous octagonal teacups, gilt flower				*0*	3			*3*						3
SYD	Glou 101	C130	56	C	'Gem'	2			*2*				*0*						2
Total						179	50	21	*250*	249	5	5	*261*	5	44	5	1	37	600

Index

A

Alcohol, 245
Antipodean cities, 16
Archaeological data, 104
    archaeologically reliable datasets, 105
    archaeological records, 260, 262
Archaeological heritage, 77
Archaeological records, 262
Archaeological research projects
    single-site research, 23
    See also Australian Research Council
Assemblages, 1, 3, 10, 15
Australia
    ambiguity, 257
    Anglo–Celtic populations, 32
    Anglo–Saxon civilization, 34
    assemblages, 257
    British government policy, 32
    capital investment, 33
    cohesion *vs.* diversity, 32
    colonial cities, 257
    colonial governments, 34, 38
    Colonial Land and Emigration
        Commission, 38, 39
    colonial legislation, 38
    discovery of gold, 37
    ecological sustainability, 37
    economic refugees, 33
    ethnicities, 31
    eviction, 34
    generalisation, 31, 37
    global market, 35
    global mobility, 33

Hyde Park Barracks
    archaeology, 43
    assemblage-based analyses, 43
    British family reunion scheme, 41
    Depot and Destitute asylum, 43
    engagements, 43
    Georgian design, 39
    mobile workforce, 39
    moral and religious instruction, 40
    securing migrant labour, 41
    starvation, 41
    transportation, 40
    unprotected females, 41
    Waters of Harbour, 40
    workhouses, 41
immigration, 31, 32, 38
indigenous peoples, 32
indigenous societies, 35
local/British private philanthropy, 38
mass movements, 31
middle-class groups, 37
migration, 36, 37, 266
modern city, 265
multicultural *vs.* monocultural society, 32
nationalities, 31
nation-building, 33
pastoral economies, 35, 37
political and cultural connectedness, 34
political context, 32, 33
'push' and 'pull' factors, 36
racial and cultural destiny, 34
sectarian enmities, 36
settler societies, 35

© Springer Nature Switzerland AG 2019
T. Murray, P. Crook, *Exploring the Archaeology of the Modern City
in Nineteenth-century Australia*, Contributions To Global Historical
Archaeology, https://doi.org/10.1007/978-3-030-27169-5

Australia (*cont.*)
   social dislocation, 33
   social historians, 36
   starvation, 34
   sweepings of England, 38
   transoceanic migrations, 31
   transportation, 37
   trauma of dispossession, 35
   uncertainty, 257
Australian economy, 22
Australian historical archaeology, 8, 15
Australian Research Council (ARC), 1, 10,
     166, 168
   Linkage Scheme, 1

B
Big Dig, 111, 113, 114
   See also Cumberland and Gloucester
     Streets site (CUGL)
Brickmaking, 54

C
Casselden Place, *see* Little Lon
Cesspits, 95, 96, 101–103, 166, 204, 210
   archaeological sites, 102
   Australian cities, 259
   backfill assemblages, 102
   carbolic acid, 97
   categories, 209
   cesspit fills, 106
   clearing, 102
   composition, 261
   construction, 97, 100, 197
   definition, 96
   discrete layers, 100
   documentation, 161
   empirical information, 259
   exploration, 95
   installation/repair, 100
   intra-site analysis, 105
   key problem, 97
   leakage/seepage, 101
   problematic, 101
   quality, 101
   sanitary malfunction, 97
   Sydney
      sewerage, 204
Chronological resolution, 10
Cisterns, 100
City sanitation, 96
Class aspiration, 260

Colonial city
   Sydney
     municipal provisions, 97
     water supply, 97
Colonial customers, 86
Colonial merchants, 87
Colonisation, 24
Commonwealth Block, 1, 3, 7, 8, 260,
     264, 265
   See also Little Lon
Commonwealth Block, Melbourne
   7 Casselden Place (1851–1909)
     cesspit, 185
     the Cesspit Fill (Cesspit A),
       185, 186
     occupants, 185
     wooden house, 185
   128 Little Lonsdale Street (1850–1910)
     Bibb's 1855 map, 186
     the Cesspit Fill (MC 1.023), 187
     historical records, 186
     L-shaped building, 186
     tenants, 187–189
   143 Lonsdale Street (1847–1918)
     excavation, 173
     occupants, 174, 175
     sewage system, 173
   147 Lonsdale Street (1849–1950)
     the Cesspit Fill (MC 2.722), 176
     excavation, 176
     occupant history, 177–179
     tenants, 176
   147 Spring Street (1849–1918)
     the Cesspit Fill (Cesspit B), 181
     tenants, 181
     two-storey renovation, 181
   255 Spring Street (1849–1918)
     153 Spring Street, 181
     bluestone foundation walls, 182
     the Cesspit Fill (Cesspit H), 182
     the Cesspit Fill (Cesspit J), 183
     excavation, 181
     ownership history, 183, 184
   archaeology, 162, 169
   cesspits, 170
   delirium tremens, 192
   documentary research, 168
   document-based narratives, 192
   ease of reference, 171
   ethnicities, 170
   excavation
      17 Casselden Place (1995), 164
      271 Spring Street (2017), 166

Black Eagle and Oddfellows Hotels
   (1990), 164
Casselden Place (2002–2003), 164, 166
Casselden Place Phase 3 Testing
   (2001), 164 (*see* Excavation)
   heritage architects, 162
   historians, 162
   Little Lon (1998), 163
farm servants, 193
historical archaeology, 191
intense site documentation, 192
life impression, 170
life reassessment, 191
Little Lonsdale Street (1847– 1918)
   the Cesspit Fill (Cesspit T), 189
   occupant history, 189, 190
   residence, 189
Lot 25C, Leichhardt Street (1851–1920)
   the Cesspit Fill (MC 1.010), 171, 172
   measurements, 171
   occupants, 172
   vacant and unimproved, 171
Lot 36A, Little Leichardt Street
   (1851–1898)
   the Cesspit Fill (MC 1.230), 179
   occupant history, 179, 180
occupants, 161, 170
owners and occupiers, 192
ownership and occupational histories, 161
phases, 168, 169
research themes, 168
slum clearance, 169
stereotypes, 166
stratigraphic integrity, 167
structural properties, 168
substantial property portfolio, 194
taphonomic processes, 167
tenants, 193
urban historical archaeology, 167
working-class networks, 167
Commonwealth Government, 169
Comparative archaeology, 265
Comparative Assemblage Analysis, 10,
   104–105, 197–254
Comprehensive analyses
   households
      archaeological research projects, 105
      culture of conformity, 104
      daily life dimension, 104
      limitations of archaeology, 105
Consumer revolution, 84
Contemporary historical archaeology, 22
Creamware, 63–65

Crook's approach, 14
Cultural theory, 263
Culture of conformity, 104
Cumberland and Gloucester Streets site
   (CUGL)
   1 Carahers Lane (c. 1848–1902)
      artefacts, 118
      double-storey terrace, 116
      house foundations, 116
      occupants, 118–120
      plasterwork, 117
      sewerage, 118
      tenants, 119
      week-to-week refuse, 118
   3 Carahers Lane (c. 1848–1902)
      anomaly, 122
      artefacts, 123
      demolition process, 123
      distinct units, 122
      double-storey terrace, 121
      metal working, 123
      occupants, 123–125
      seepage, 121
      sewerage, 122
   5 Carahers Lane (c. 1856–1902)
      occupants, 126, 127
      plasterwork, 125
      sewerage, 126
      stratigraphic units, 125
      substantial fragments, 126
      tobacco pipe, 126
      two-storey terraces, 125
   93 Gloucester Street (c. 1822–1891)
      archaeological evidence, 143
      occupants, 145, 147
      sewerage, 144
      shingle and weatherboard house, 143
      stratigraphic units, 145
      tenants, 144
      trigonometric survey, 144
   97 Gloucester Street (c. 1817–1907)
      Carahers and Cribbs Lanes, 149
      demolition, 151
      excavation, 149
      First Cesspit (MC C220), 149, 150
      occupants, 151, 152, 154
      parasite analysis, 151
      sanitary arrangements, 149
      Second Cesspit (MC 056), 150
      sewerage, 150
      structure, 147
   101 Gloucester Street (1822–c. 1907)
      construction/renovation event, 155

Cumberland and Gloucester Streets site
        (CUGL) (cont.)
    council rates records, 154
    King House, 154
    occupants, 155, 156
    stratigraphic units, 154
    122 Cumberland Street (c. 1833–1891)
        construction materials, 129
        Engineering Works, 128
        lack of intermediary
            deposits, 128
        Nicholas Rents, 128
        occupants, 130–133
        structure, 128
        tenancy, 129
    124 Cumberland Street (c. 1833–1907)
        assemblage, 137
        Engineering Works, 137
        Nicholas's Rents, 133
        occupants, 138–140
        refuse deposits, 137
        sewer line, 137
        stratigraphic unit, 134
        structure, 133
    126 Cumberland Street (c. 1833–1907)
        conjoins, 142
        floorboards, 141
        minor disturbance, 142
        Nicholas's Rents, 140
        occupants, 142, 143
    artefact-rich assemblages, 114
    assemblages, 111
    the 'Big Dig', 111, 113, 114
    biographical information, 111
    excavation, 114

D
Database management system, 11
Deductive strategies, 8
Demolition rubble, 60
Deposition events
    cesspit, 252
    comparative analysis
        drinking, alcohol and soda bottles,
            245, 247
        home décor, 241–243
        households, 249
        moralizing/educational China,
            240, 241
        tablewares, 219–221, 227,
            228, 233
        teawares, 235, 237, 240
    damp-proofing, 250
    demolition, 254
    earthenware, 252, 253
    highly skilled craftsmanship, 253
    impressive, 254
    insolvency inventory, 253
    interpretation, 254
    marketable furnishings, 251
    minimum vessel count, 253
    nondomestic items, 253
    opportunistic refuse, 209
    painting services, 250
    privy, 209
    processes, 209
    residents
        cesspit, 210
        Melbourne, 218
        occupancy, 210
        occupations, 210
        sewerage repairs, 210
        Sydney, 218
    stockpiled, 209
Deposits
    building materials, 199
    cross-comparative analysis, 197
    dating, 204, 209
    factor, 197
    integrity, 204
    Melbourne
        assemblages, 197
    minimum value allocation, 199
    percentage chart, 201
    Sydney
        assemblages, 197
Digital humanities, 9
Domestic goods, cheapening, 82

E
EAMC Archaeology Database,
        12, 13
Economic refugees, 23
Educational China, 240, 241
English potteries, 63
E-research, 9
Ethnogenesis, 264
Europe, 31, 35, 38
Exploring the Archaeology of the Modern City
        (EAMC), 1, 10, 16, 91
    archaeological data (see also
        archaeological data)
    ceramic/glass vessels, 106
    documentary research, 106

F
Farm Cove, 69
Financial investment, 265
First Government House
        (FGH), 2
    accommodation, 52
    administrative centre, 51
    archaeological investigation,
        48, 49
    archaeological record, 53
    architectural features, 50
    brickmaking, 54
    building, 54
    cove, 55
    cultural significance, 77
    demolition, 57, 59
        rubble, 60
        stages, 59
        stock piles, 59
    drainage system, 53
    EAMC approach, 47, 49–51
    historical–archaeological
        investigations, 47
    historical event, 53
    history, 51
    location, 48
    masonry structure, 54
    privacy, 52
    public works department, 52
    roads/drainage channels, 53
    stages of excavation, 48
    stone foundations, 55

G
Globalisation, 81
Global Material Culture, 11
Global trade, 81, 83
Gold rushes, 37
Goods/chattels, 60
Governor king's spode, 61, 62
Governor's guard house, 68
    broken tiles, 75
    clothing, 72
    corridor, 72
    drawings, 73
    eastern/middle rooms, 72
    establishment, 69
    Farm Cove, 69
    floor plan, 75
    front room, 72
    internal wall, 75
    measurement, 73

official residences, 71
passage, 73
primary documents, 70
public buildings, 70
public works, 69
rear rooms, 72
roof, 76
semi-demolition, 75
structure, 73
verandah, 75

H
Heritage protection
        movement, 77
Historical archaeology
    assemblages, 258
    challenges, 263
    chronology, 263
    comparative data analysis, 263
    datasets, 258
    engagement, 264
    ethnic minority groups, 264
    generalisation, 263
    heritage consultancies, 265
    imbalances, 264
    integration, 258, 264
    intercity/international
        comparisons, 259
    inter-site research, 257
    Melbourne, 257
        cultural capital, 265
        heritage agencies, 266
        high-rise redevelopment, 265
    modern city, 258
    scales, 259
    storytelling, 258
    Sydney, 257
        cultural capital, 265
        development process, 265
        re-evaluation sites, 265
        sustained engagement, 265
Home décor, 241–243
Household links
    ceramic manufacture, 104
    free garbage disposal, 103
    historical documentation, 103
    organic refuse/garbage, 103
    rubbish disposal, 103
Human waste
    efforts to remove, 96
    minimisation, 95
Hyde Park Barracks, 2

I
Industrial revolution, 82
Industry Superannuation Property Trust
    (ISPT), 166
Integrated analytical framework, 7
International trade, 81
Interpretation, 259

L
Little Lon, 7–9
Living ruins
    designs, 57
    repairs, 56
    shingle roof, 56
Local enterprises, 86

M
Masonry structure, 54
Master Context (MC), 115
Matching sets, 269–284
Material culture, 2, 7, 14, 15, 22, 24, 25, 35,
        43, 81, 104, 105, 107, 219
    analysis, 90
    archaeological, 84, 262
    cesspit, 197
    consumption, 82, 260
    distribution of goods, 83
    documentary evidence, 259
    ethnicity, 260
    fashions/gadgets, 90
    focus, 82
    generalisations, 261
    global distribution, 82
    items of, 258
    linkages, 260
    movements, 81
    operationalising stages, 261
    retail institutions, 86
    rich social life, 84
    social interaction, 84
Mechanisation, 83
Melbourne, 204, 209, 243
Migration, 2, 22, 24–26, 81, 82
    archaeological record, 90
    convictism, 21
    emigrants, 87–89
        written accounts, 89
    experience of, 258
    urban centres
        Melbourne, 21
        Sydney, 21
Modern economic system, 85
Moralizing China, 240, 241

O
Occupancy, 260, 262, 266
Occupants, 260
Olive–brown-banded creamware, 64, 66
Overcrowding *vs.* disease, 96

P
Pastoralism, 22
People + Place database, 12, 13
Public works department, 52

Q
Queensware, 62, 63

R
Recursive reasoning, 263
Reflexive approach, 8
Research design, 8
Residential mobility, 259, 260

S
Sea chests, 88
Sewerage scheme, 96
    Melbourne
        cesspit, 101
        discovery of gold, 101
        sanitary reforms, 101
        sewers and water supply, 101
    Sydney
        cesspit, 100
        flushing mechanism, 100
        harbour outlets, 98
        infrastructure, 99
        sewer lines, 98
Sherds, 66
Slum, 9, 15
Social theory, 263
Storehouses, 54
Strategic Partnerships Industry – Research and
        Training (SPIRT) Scheme, 1, 10
Swiss Boarding House, 174, 175
Sydney *vs.* Melbourne, 10, 14, 15

T
Tablewares, 60, 67
    archaeological relics, 220
    assemblages, 221
    cesspits, 220
    earthenware, 220
    genteel dining, 219

matching sets, 220, 227, 228, 233
middle-class dining habits, 219
segregate living and working
    neighbourhoods, 220
serving vessels, 221, 227
specialized wares, 220
technological changes, 220
Tank Stream, 96
Teawares
    assemblages, 237
    LACE, 237
    matching sets, 237
    matching vessels, 240
    middle-class consumption, 235
    Q-ring-style handles, 237
    respectability, 235
    social interaction, 235
Technological change, 81
Tendril pattern
    fragments, 66
    plate, 67
    tablewares, 67
    teacup, 68
Terminus post quem (TPQ), 204
Thematic research goals, 105
The Rocks, 111
Trade, 81–83
    tariffs, 86
Transnational archaeologies
    colonialism, 24
    development contexts, 23
    global mobility, 24
    historical archaeology, 24
    historical documentation, 22
    imperialism, 24
    indigenous–settler interactions, 22, 23
    interdisciplinary collaboration, 22
    material culture, 22
    migration, 21
    modern city
        artefact assemblages, 26
        colonialism, 26
        cultural homogeneity and
            heterogeneity, 26
        ethnicities, 26
        evolution of, 25
        goal, 25
        identities, 26
        imperialism, 26
        inner-city communities, 26

        interpretation, 26
        mass production and consumption, 26
        migration, 25, 27
        reflexive process, 25
        social and cultural change, 25, 26
        urban communities, 25
    modern world system, 23
    movements of people, 23
    multiscalar approach, 21, 24
    nation-building, 24
    nineteenth century
        industrialisation, 22
        slum life, 21
        urban poverty, 21
    pace and intensity, 23
    political context, 25
    social and cultural change, 21
    social and cultural uniformity, 23
    social reform, 21
    urban archaeological assemblages, 22
Transnational archaeology, 7
Transnational comparisons
    assemblages, 14, 15
    deductive and inductive reasoning, 16
    material culture, 14
    middle-class consumption, 14
    movement of goods, 15
    movements of people, 15
    museum basements, 15
Travelling light, 87

U
Urban archaeology, 2, 11, 84, 105, 163, 257
    Urban historical archaeology, 9, 26, 262
Urban communities, 10
Urban historians, 21
Urban historical archaeology, 9, 167
Urbanism, 7

V
Victoria Archaeological Survey, 162

W
Waste management, 95
    domestic waste, 95
    human management, 96
Willow-pattern prints, 83

Printed by Printforce, the Netherlands